REPORTS FROM BEYOND

REPORTS FROM
BEYOND

A JOURNEY THROUGH LIFE
TO REMOTE PLACES

PATRICK RICHARDSON

REPORTS FROM
BEYOND

A JOURNEY THROUGH LIFE
TO REMOTE PLACES

PATRICK RICHARDSON

ULTIMA
THULE
PRESS

ULTIMA
THULE
PRESS

First published in 2008 by
Ultima Thule Press
65 St Stephen Street, Edinburgh EH3 5AH

www.reportsfrombeyond.com

Versions of most of the articles originally appeared in *The Herald*, the *Sunday Herald*, *The Scotsman*, *The Daily Telegraph* and *The Sunday Telegraph*. Maps redrawn from maps © Collins Bartholomew Ltd 1986 and 2003. Reproduced by kind permission of HarperCollins Publishers www.collinsbartholomew.com

ISBN: 978-0-9558448-0-5

British Library Cataloguing-in-Publication Data
A catalogue record for this book is available from the British Library

Designed and typeset by Tom Gorham
Set in Sabon 10pt after a template by James Hutcheson

Printed and bound by Gutenberg Press, Malta

All photographs by Patrick Richardson, the author.

Author's Note:
To protect their privacy, the identities of certain people in this book have been changed, along with a few place names.

FSC

Mixed Sources
Product group from well-managed forests, and other controlled sources
www.fsc.org Cert no. TT-CoC-002424
© 1996 Forest Stewardship Council

The paper used for this book is FSC-certified and totally chlorine-free. FSC (the Forest Stewardship Council) is an international network to promote responsible management of the world's forests.

Journey's end –
still alive, this
autumn evening.

BASHO

My jeep waiting for me on the road to Mt Tavanbodg (4,373 m.), western Mongolia

CONTENTS

I
GLIMPSES INTO THE FORMATIVE YEARS

My first experience of travelling abroad was almost disastrous. When I was thirteen I went on a school trip to Lake Thun in Switzerland. At the time I believed that foreign countries, like school, existed for my personal entertainment, and visiting one was an opportunity to behave as badly as possible. I was heavily influenced by my roommates, the school's notorious Nichol twins, and the three of us were caught stealing an expensive Swiss cuckoo clock in a jeweller's shop. We were sent home in disgrace, and the headmaster threatened my distraught mother, Rosemary, that if it happened again I would be expelled on the spot.

It was an inauspicious beginning to my travelling career, but it didn't end there. The next July my parents took the family for our first summer holiday abroad. Not surprisingly, my sister, Minka, and I were excited as we set off by car to drive from Scotland to the Basque country in northern Spain. On the way we stopped to see my father's mother, Ethel, an eccentric Communist who lived in a large rambling house in Staines in Middlesex. While everyone was having afternoon tea in the library, I went for a dip in the swimming pool. It obviously hadn't been used for years, as it was murky and half-covered with water lilies. Unfortunately, my grandmother omitted to tell me it was only a metre deep at the sides. When I plunged off the springboard I didn't dive out far enough, so I hit my head on the bottom of the pool, and the nearest doctor had to be summoned to put six stitches in my forehead.

The following day we broke the journey in Sussex, where I was born, to see old friends of my parents. Trying to bond with my father, Timothy, I drank two pints of the local potent cider and, within half an hour, vomited over our friends' carpet. A few days later, we stopped at a hospital in Bordeaux to have the stitches removed. The doctor who attended me was a young trainee, and he was so nervous during the procedure that I had to talk to him non-stop to give him confidence, rather than the other way round.

That second holiday on the Continent had consequences that my mother, sister and I should have guessed. The fact is that my father loved Spain so much he didn't want to go anywhere else. For three years we returned to the Basque country or drove down to El Rompido, a blindingly white village in south-west Andalusia. Each time, my mother, who was a large and powerful woman, drove the entire way while my father, who couldn't drive, sat in the front smoking a cigar.

These trips were also marked by small, but memorable, incidents. Once, near the town of Zarauz in the Basque country, we camped on a hill overlooking the bay. At midnight my father was awakened by suspicious noises and, armed with a hammer, had to chase away a prowler circling our tent.

The following year, when I was seventeen, I passed my driving test. Just outside San

Sebastián in Spain, I pestered my mother to allow me to drive the car so much that in the end, against her better judgement, she agreed. Twenty minutes later I knocked a cyclist off his bike and, after she ascertained that he wasn't hurt, she took over and we fled the scene without delay.

My mother herself, who was a larger-than-life character, was an intrepid traveller. In 1920, when she was only five, her father took her on a flight with Sir Alan Cobham, the long-distance aviation pioneer, in his open-air Tiger Moth bi-plane. In the mid-1930s, a grateful patient of her recently deceased father, William, who was a much-loved doctor, left her a legacy of £1,000. The moment she received it she packed her typewriter, cashed the cheque and said to her horrified mother, 'I'm off to Europe to write some articles!' She spent the next six months travelling alone in Italy and Sicily, which was an exceptional thing for any woman to do in those days, far less one of only twenty. In the 1960s, after my sister and I stopped going on family holidays, my mother talked my father into going to the Greek Islands, which were still unknown at the time. Again, he liked the new destination so much he refused to go anywhere else, except back to Spain. But my mother was unusually resolute, so she travelled by herself to Russia, Poland and dozens more Greek islands until she persuaded him to go with her to France, Germany and Italy.

The summer before I went to university I sailed from Venice to Israel, where I had volunteered to work on a kibbutz. The journey down the rugged Adriatic coast and through

My mother (aged five) about to fly with Sir Alan Cobham, the long-distance aviation pioneer

My mother in Piazza San Marco, Venice, in the 1930s

the sparkling Mediterranean was unforgettable. The top deck of the ship was awash with youthful volunteers who were going to work on kibbutzim as well, as it was a fashionable thing to do at that time. During the day a lot of them played guitars and flirted with each other, and at night we slept outside in our sleeping bags under the moonlight. It was a magical beginning to my first independent trip abroad. It was also the first time I realized how much I was drawn to boats, water and the sea – a passion that was reflected later in my river journeys up or down the Amazon, Congo, Irrawaddy, Niger and Yangtze rivers, and in my voyages around the Pacific.

The kibbutz, Kfar Hannasi, was in upper Galilee, which was near the Golan Heights. It was just prior to the Six Day War, and the Golan Heights still belonged to Syria. Once, they shelled us, and everyone had to take shelter in the bunker under the dining hall, but their aim was so inaccurate that some Arabs in a settlement twenty kilometres into Israel were killed instead. Most of the time I had to get up at dawn to shift irrigation pipes in the orange orchards. It was very wet work, as I had to wade around for long periods in flooded fields. As ill luck would have it, the wellington boots I was given were far too loose, but my request for better- fitting ones, like most of the volunteers' requests, was ignored. It wasn't my only cause for complaint. The volunteers were housed in the most basic wooden huts, and several times I woke up to find scorpions in my shoes. Yet although we were expected to work up to ten hours a day without being paid a penny, we weren't allowed the same small privileges as the native kibbutzniks, and we even had to pay for stamps for our letters home.

Soon I noticed a nasty-looking red streak running up my leg from an infected blister on my heel. I went to see the kibbutz doctor, who suggested that I take time off. However, the kibbutz secretary, who was the person in charge of the volunteers, insisted that I continue working. I was still worried, so one weekend I went to see a private doctor in Tel Aviv. He told me that if I had delayed any longer I would have had serious blood poisoning. Furious, I went back to Kfar Hannasi, collected my belongings and stormed out of the kibbutz.

Afterwards, I met two students from Birmingham with whom I travelled round Lake Tiberius and down through the Negev Desert to Eilat on the Red Sea. One of them was Mike, a well-built, smooth-talking twenty-year-old with a goatee beard. Usually the three of us slept outside, and many evenings I watched jealously as he coaxed a seemingly inexhaustible stream of young women into his sleeping bag. At the time, Eilat was just a collection of shacks overlooking a beach. One night we were invited to a party on the third floor of a half-completed block of flats. For some reason – probably burst water-mains – the floor was flooded. It was there, on brand new armchairs and sofas knee-deep in water, that for the first and only time I saw an orgy take place.

I have other lingering memories of Israel. After I left Mike I met up with my sister, who had also been working on a kibbutz, and we travelled up the coast. One evening we slept on a beach near a hamlet forty kilometres north of Jaffa. It was a very dark, moonless night, so I stripped off and went for a swim in the sea. Thinking I was swimming parallel to the beach, I swam backstroke for twenty minutes before turning to do breaststroke. It was only then that, to my horror, I realized I had swum so far out I couldn't see the shore. For a few seconds I panicked until, to my intense relief, I was able to make out the hamlet's faint glow in the inky blackness.

A week later we took the train from Athens to Munich. As we were passing through Yugoslavia, peasants came round the compartments selling *slivowitz* (plum brandy). I didn't know what it was, so I bought a bottle and started drinking it as the train entered Germany. By the time the train pulled into Munich I was completely drunk. When we left the station we went straight to the Hofbräuhaus, as many people do. This was the city's largest beer hall, where a lederhosen-clad Bavarian brass band was playing. To everyone's amusement, I clambered onto a table and attempted to conduct the band until I fell off, hit my head on the ground and passed out.

Although Israel was a highly formative experience for a naïve nineteen-year-old, it was nothing compared with what was to come. In my second year at university I was selected, along with my sister, to be one of thirty Edinburgh students on an overland bus expedition to India during the summer holidays. In retrospect, it was probably the turning point in my life. The expedition was called Comex (short for Commonwealth Expedition). The patron was the Duke of Edinburgh and the trip was organized by a former Indian Army officer whose dream was to 'break down the barriers that divide people in the Commonwealth'. Eleven self-sufficient, self-financed buses departed from eleven British universities. Each student was selected for the specific skills he or she could contribute to the bus. For example, a mechanical engineering student became the bus mechanic, a medical student became the doctor and a domestic science student became the cook. I was studying politics, but I was chosen to be one of the three drivers as I had five years' driving experience, longer than any other applicant.

It took five weeks for us to reach New Delhi as, after the Turkish border with Persia, as Iran was called at the time, the road to India consisted of rutted tracks for thousands of kilometres. To keep to our schedule we regularly had to drive for twelve hours a day. It was travelling through the barren deserts of Central Asia towards seemingly endless mountain ranges that I realized for the first time how eager I was to see what lay beyond. It was a trait that has lasted my entire life: wherever I go I invariably want to go further.

After the expedition disembarked in the Indian capital, we all shook hands with Indira Gandhi, the prime minister of India, prior to everyone separating to travel through different parts of the subcontinent for a month. I took the train south to Madras, Madurai and Cochin. Tragically, the expedition's journey back from India was marred by disaster. In Yugoslavia the bus from Durham University was involved in a horrendous accident with a crane. The

Me (in the middle), meeting Indira Gandhi, the prime minister of India, in New Delhi

cause was hotly disputed, but the student driver maintained that, as he was approaching the crane, its jib swung loose without warning. The Yugoslav authorities claimed that he fell asleep at the wheel. Whatever the reason, as the crane passed by, all fifteen students sitting on the left-hand side of the bus were decapitated before the bus overturned in a field. Our bus was the first from the expedition to arrive on the scene, only an hour after the crash. The sight of the black plastic body-bags, which the emergency services had laid out along the road, will haunt me forever.

If the crash was bad enough for my sister and I, it was worse for my parents. Each bus had the words 'Comex Expedition to India, Patron HRH the Duke of Edinburgh' painted prominently on both sides. When the rescue services arrived at the scene, all that could be made out on the side of the overturned bus was the word 'Edinburgh'. In addition all the buses, which were brand new, had been registered simultaneously and the twisted number plates of the Durham bus were identical to those of Edinburgh apart from one letter. In the resulting confusion, Reuters reported that it was the bus from Edinburgh, and not Durham, that had crashed.

That weekend my parents were in the holiday cottage they rented in the Pentland Hills outside Edinburgh. Two kilometres up a track that led off a usually deserted minor road, it was very isolated and had no electricity or telephone. My father was up a ladder, painting the walls and listening to his portable radio when the programme was interrupted by a BBC newsflash. It reported that fifteen students from the Edinburgh contingent of the Comex Expedition to India had been killed in a bus crash in Yugoslavia. Distraught at the possibility that both of their children might have been killed, my parents jumped into their red Mini in order to rush back to Edinburgh. It had been raining heavily, and as the car crossed a swollen stream it got stuck. They spent thirty minutes trying to get it out until they gave up and ran up the muddy track to the road.

There, an hour later, they managed to flag down a passing car being driven by two nuns. They took my parents to the head office of *The Scotsman*, one of the country's two broadsheet newspapers, where my mother and father spent the night awaiting further news. When they heard nothing, my mother contacted one of her female friends, who was the secretary to an influential MP. He started pulling strings at the Foreign Office in order to ascertain the names of the dead. Even so, eight hours passed in total until my parents learned that it was the bus from Durham, and not from Edinburgh, that had been involved in the accident. Later, my mother told me that her hair started to go grey from that night onwards, after which she felt life would never be the same again.

Obviously, there was a massive media outcry about why students, who had had only two weeks' tuition prior to sitting the obligatory Public Service Vehicle Test, had been allowed to drive buses with thirty passengers over 20,000 kilometres to India and back. Despite the crash, India was a revelation to me, and its sights, sounds and smells gave me a taste for travelling that has remained with me all my life.

The following April, along with Mike, my flatmate and would-be radical editor of the student newspaper, I went to Czechoslovakia on a student exchange that Edinburgh University's politics department had arranged with Charles University, Prague. It was the height of the 'Prague Spring', when Alexander Dubček, the head of the Communist party, was trying to establish 'Socialism with a Human Face' in Czechoslovakia. The Soviet Union was extremely alarmed, and every day animated crowds gathered on Prague's street corners, eagerly awaiting the newspapers or discussing political developments. In back alleys at night, tiny theatres, such as the Theatre on the Balustrade, mounted daring, experimental plays. One evening, I went with Mike to hear a lecture in the economics faculty that was being given by Rudi Dutschke. He was Europe's most notorious revolutionary student, so afterwards Mike and I approached him to see if he would give us an interview. He agreed, and at eleven o'clock that same night we met him in the basement of a smoky bar. There Mike and I interviewed him for two hours, during which I took copious notes.

After Prague, I took the train to Berlin. While I was in my compartment I heard a passenger say that Dutschke had just been shot in the head and was critically ill in hospital. When I got to Berlin, though, I didn't have much time to think about him. The Shah of Persia was on a state visit, and tear gas drifted across the streets surrounding the Free University, where I was staying, as riot police fought pitched battles with students demonstrating against his autocratic regime.

As soon as I got back to Edinburgh, Mike casually asked to see my notes. Naturally, I handed them over without thinking. A few days later I opened Britain's most prestigious liberal broadsheet and was amazed to see the banner headline 'WORLD EXCLUSIVE – LAST INTERVIEW WITH DUTSCHKE' on a centre, double-page spread. It was written by Mike, of course, and he introduced his article by describing how he had spent two hours interviewing Dutschke alone in the basement of a smoke-filled bar in Prague. Four months later, the Soviet Union invaded Czechoslovakia and Russian tanks rolled through the streets of Prague.

Meanwhile, spurred on by our experience of India, my sister and I went to North America for the summer. She was going to work as an au pair for a wealthy family in Hyannisport on Cape Cod. I planned to travel around the USA before going to work on a tobacco farm in Canada on a scheme organized for me by BUNAC (British Universities North America Club). As usual, my journey was marked by incidents, some of them shockingly violent. We'd no sooner arrived at the youth hostel where we were staying when a deranged youth plunged a knife into the chest of the man standing next to my sister in the lift. From New York I went to Washington DC on my ninety-nine-dollars-for-ninety-nine-days Greyhound Bus ticket, and found the city still literally smouldering because of rioting in the black ghettoes. Next, I travelled down to New Orleans and San Antonio. But I already hated the States so much – it was the height of the Vietnam War, and Martin Luther King and Robert Kennedy had just been assassinated – that I decided to spend the rest of my time in Mexico instead.

While I was in the queue for visas in Laredo in Texas I found myself behind a German engineer who worked for Volkswagen in Mexico City. His visa had expired and he had been obliged to go to the nearest border to get an extension. When I met him he was returning to Mexico City and he offered me a lift, which I gladly accepted. At over a thousand kilometres, it was the longest ride I've ever had. As soon as we parked outside his house in the capital he invited me to stay with him, which I also accepted. But I didn't stay for long. Mexico City was in uproar, as twenty-five students protesting about the Olympic Games, which it was due to host, had just been killed in a vicious gun battle. Shocked, I was in the Plaza Mayor when I saw a bus with the destination 'Guatemala City' written above the driver's cab. The words sounded so exotic that I immediately went to the bus station and bought a ticket.

Twenty-eight hours after arriving in Mexico City, I arrived in Guatemala City. It was night, and I felt as if I was going from the fat into the fire. Marxist guerrillas had just assassinated the United States ambassador and the right-wing military government had dispatched tanks into the darkened streets. For the second time in as many days, I didn't hang around. The next morning I travelled to the colonial town of Antigua, which lay in the shadow of Volcán de Agua, a 3,766-metre-high volcano. Three days later I hitched a lift to Lake

Atitlán. The driver was a doctor from Guatemala City who was going to see his mistress in his secluded weekend retreat. As we drew up by the stunning lakeside, he invited me to come and see his house. Positioned halfway up a forested hillside, it had panoramic views over the tranquil lake to the surrounding volcanoes. He introduced me to his mistress, who was a gorgeous, dark-skinned young woman with gleaming, waist-length black hair, and that afternoon he took me out in his speedboat. As it curved gracefully across the water, I remember being green with envy of him and his lifestyle.

A month later I returned to the United States, where I travelled up the west coast to Los Angeles. With the exception of Tokyo, it was the shortest visit to a city I've ever made. I arrived at 6 a.m., took one look at the concrete canyons, flyovers, six-lane highways and skyscrapers, and departed at 8 a.m. Los Angeles was everything I hated in cities, and have hated ever since. Afterwards I headed for San Francisco, which, with its intimate, colourfully painted wooden houses, I liked as much as I loathed Los Angeles. Despite being moderately well-travelled by now, in many ways I was still surprisingly inexperienced. It was the year after the summer of love and flower power, and on Haight-Ashbury, where the hippies hung out, I remember seeing advertisements for the Grateful Dead and Jefferson Airplane and wondering who they were. Then, on my way north, I passed through Chicago. Along with Washington DC, it too was in uproar, as the Democrats were holding their annual convention and Mayor Daley's police had just tear-gassed and brutally beaten up thousands of students demonstrating against the Vietnam War.

When I got to Canada, the contrast between the rioting cities in the United States and the tobacco farm couldn't have been starker. Situated in peaceful, flat southern Ontario, it consisted of a group of wooden barns surrounded by virgin forest. The farm was owned by Roy, a small, lean man who had fled from East Germany at the end of the Second World War.

Every morning we commenced work at 5 a.m., while it was still dark. First, we emptied the kiln of the previous day's cured tobacco. It was an extremely dangerous activity as we had to balance precariously on twenty-metre-high rafters under the roof before we worked our way down. After breakfast, at 7 a.m. we started going along the tall tobacco rows and picking the still-moist, ripe, yellow leaves. These we put into what looked like a long, coffin-like wooden box, which was pulled by a loveable chestnut nag called Giovanni. By the time our team finished at 3 p.m., our hands were covered with such thick black tar that we could scrape it off with a knife.

Although picking tobacco was backbreaking work, I loved the experience of being on the farm. By British standards the job was well-paid and I saved a lot, as we lived for free in the dark, cramped bunkhouse and could have unlimited helpings of the huge plates of beef, green beans and roast potatoes which were plonked in front of us at every meal. As well as that, the hobos and migrant workers that the harvest attracted were like characters from a John Steinbeck novel. At the end of the season, they were so rowdy that the Riot Act had to be read out in neighbouring Tillsonburg, where many of them flocked to get drunk or pick up prostitutes.

When I returned from the States, I told my mother I had been to Guatemala. She had worked as a journalist in London prior to the Second World War, and without ado she disappeared and fished out a timeworn article she had written. It was entitled 'Colourful Guatemala' and described local festivals where 'skyrockets shoot up into the starlit sky, and dancing throngs in their best costumes jostle in sixteenth-century churches to light candles and place corn, slices of orange and blossoms at the foot of the altar'. It even described the wind, which had 'a hothouse smell, warm, damp and scented'.

'I didn't know you'd been there!' I exclaimed.

'I haven't!' she countered without blushing. 'I just went to the local library, read some travel guides and made it up.' It was partly from her that I caught my desire to write. After she had a family she stopped writing for publication, but whenever she went abroad she inundated her friends with innumerable postcards crammed with vivid descriptions of

My grandfather, Henry Marriot Richardson, with my grandmother, Ethel, and their family (my father front row, left) at their large, six-bedroom house in Dulwich, London

tumbledown villages, hunched women in black on donkeys and gnarled men sitting around smoking pipes. If her friends were going to places she had visited, she supplied them with detailed instructions on how to get there, how long it would take, where to stay, where to eat, what to do during the day, what to do at night, and where to go next after they left.

I must have also inherited an interest in writing from my father's side of the family. His father, Henry Marriot Richardson, was a playwright and writer, but he was better known as the first salaried general secretary of the National Union of Journalists from 1918 until 1936, and the president of the International Federation of Journalists from 1930 until 1932. As part of his work, he knew H.G. Wells, George Bernard Shaw and G.K. Chesterton, as well as the press barons Lord Beaverbrook, Lord Northcliffe and Lord Rothermere. My father was also a journalist until, after 1945, the stigma of being a conscientious objector during the Second World War, when he had to work on a farm in Sussex, put paid to his career and he became the publicity director for a large agricultural company instead.

For two successive years I went back to Canada to pick tobacco during the university summer holidays. As I was going through Customs at Niagara Falls on the second occasion, a friendly immigration officer asked me what I planned to do in Canada. As soon as I told him I was going to pick tobacco, he requested proof of my right to work there. I showed him the social security card that had been issued to me of the end of my first harvest. 'You don't wanna work on tobacco,' he commented as he handed it back, after examining it carefully. 'That's for losers.'

'But it's good money!' I protested.

'Nope, it's not. It's peanuts,' he replied dismissively. 'You wanna get a job on a pipeline.'

I made enquires in Toronto and discovered that a large pipeline bringing oil from Alaska was just about to reach Ontario. So I changed my plans and decided to see if I could find get a job on it. While I was waiting, I went to the leafy town of Oshawa. I soon found a room in a two-storey clapboard house overflowing with obese, unemployed residents and teary, likeable alcoholics. I also got a job drilling holes with a jackhammer in the concrete floors of the town's large Ford factory. Not surprisingly, after two days I couldn't stand the noise or the bone-shaking vibrations. So I handed in my notice, and successfully answered a newspaper advertisement for guinea pigs in a project run by McMaster University. They were carrying out research into the effect of pornography, and my 'job' – embarrassing to recall – consisted of sitting in a room where I was shown photographs of nude women in order to measure the speed of my erection.

For the time being, I made friends with Gary, a burly, blond-haired young Canadian who lived close by. In a while the pipeline reached Ontario, and we started driving at 5 a.m. in his Chevrolet to the yard of Majestic Oil Company. Sited forty kilometres outside Oshawa in the countryside, it was lit by giant arc lights and was overflowing with gargantuan yellow

My father in Sussex in the 1930s

machinery and rough, unshaven men desperately competing for the extraordinarily well-paid, unskilled jobs. For a month we hung around every morning in the dark, trying to convince one of the crews to take us on. At length, overjoyed, we succeeded. Gary was told to report to a man called Bill and I was told to report to a Yugoslavian supervisor called Josip. I searched for him up and down the pipeline until I found him stuffing what looked like thick brown candlesticks into holes in the ground. He had a brusque manner and, after I introduced myself, he thrust a pole into my hands. 'Here,' he instructed, 'your job is to plunge this up and down in the holes.'

'Why?' I asked, unsuspectingly. 'What are we doing?'

'Laying dynamite,' came the laconic answer. It was only then I realized that we were powder monkeys on a dynamite crew.

The work itself wasn't hazardous, as the dynamite sticks couldn't explode unless they were wired up. When they were, everyone was evacuated, naturally. Even so, passing cars could detonate sections of the pipeline if drivers turned their radios on and tuned into the wrong frequency. To prevent this happening, large parts of the countryside were cordoned off. In spite of that, some cars unknowingly slipped through the net and workers did in fact get blown up.

The work on the pipeline was gruelling, as we worked like slaves from 5 a.m. until 9 p.m., seven days a week. But it was worth it. With overtime and danger money, I saved over $600 a week, which was a fortune in those days. There weren't many who saved as much as that, though. As soon as most workers finished their two-week shift, they either donned their black leather jackets and roared off on their gleaming Harley-Davidsons, or flew for the weekend to Las Vegas to gamble away their hard-earned money.

When the dynamite job was over, we quickly found work with Olympic Pipelines, as by now we had experience. This time we worked on the skid truck, which was a gigantic lorry and trailer almost as high as a house. The job was the toughest I've had in my life. After other crews had finished clearing fences from farms and dug the pipeline trench, Gary and I had to load the trailer every morning with heavy railway sleepers. This had to be done very accurately, because if the sleepers weren't aligned properly the load could shift and tip over. Once they were correctly loaded, the skid truck slowly drove along the trench as Gary and I hurled eight sleepers every ten metres onto the ground. These were to support the pipes before they were welded together and the completed section was lowered into the trench.

As ill luck would have it, Roy, the driver of the skid truck, was a mean, bigoted racist, who resented my being at university as well as our liberal ideas. Soon our relationship with him deteriorated badly and he set out to break us. This he tried to do by driving faster and faster. For three weeks we managed to keep up until, one day, he changed from first to second gear. That was unheard of, so we considered taking him to the union. Nonetheless, we concluded that it was useless, as our working relationship with him had irrevocably broken down. In the end, driven to the edge of human endurance, we handed in our notice although it meant losing thousands of dollars.

Working on tobacco harvests and oil pipelines during my student days gave me a glimpse into the rough underbelly of life. It was also perhaps the first unconscious step in my growing rejection of society. If so, it was shortly followed by a second, even more significant one. At university I had been very political and, along with would-be revolutionary Mike, I had shared a flat with Robin Cook, the future foreign secretary in Tony Blair's Labour government. But, like many others of my generation, I was beginning to doubt that conventional politics was the best way to provide radical change. As soon as I finished my studies I went to Sicily, where I had arranged to meet my girlfriend. To my dismay, I received a telegram from her, regretting that she couldn't make it, as her brother was unexpectedly getting married. I was sitting in a cheap café in Palermo reading *The Times* – in some ways I was still remarkably conventional – and wondering what to do, when two young hippies walked in.

One was a burly, bearded, prematurely balding Jew called Jacob. Although he was only nineteen he already spoke seven languages and, after winning a scholarship from Eton, had just finished his first year at Christ Church College, Oxford. The other was a tall, long-haired Belgian drifter called Michel. He had a prominent nose and didn't say much, although later I discovered that amongst Jacob's friends in London he had a cult status as a Zen-like figure on account of his placid nature and enigmatic utterances. I wasn't aware of it at the time, but meeting him was a seminal moment in my life.

'We're hitching across North Africa to Marbella in Spain, where my parents have got a place. Fancy coming?' Jacob asked.

'Why not?' I replied. My plans had gone haywire and I had nothing better to do. I also liked the way Jacob continually challenged my rapidly changing, conventional ideas. Two days later the three of us started hitchhiking across Tunisia, Algeria and Morocco. Jacob, one of the most compelling characters I've ever met, wore dirty, ragged jeans and went barefoot. When we stopped in towns on the way, Michel, to whom I paid little attention, strummed an old guitar that he couldn't play before hopefully holding out a hat. Two weeks later, after going down to Fez, Meknes and Marrakesh, we crossed the Strait of Gibraltar and headed up to the 'place' of Jacob's parents in Marbella. It was vast. Built of white marble, it had countless rooms surrounded by immaculate lawns on which gardeners worked all year round in order to have them ready for the two-week-long summer visit of his parents. The remaining time they divided between their Mayfair flat, where they had live-in Spanish servants, and their four-bedroom thatched 'cottage' in a picture-postcard village outside Windsor.

They clearly weren't happily married. His father, Elias, was a bald, thickset man who was one of Europe's top executives; because he was always so busy, I rarely saw him. Jacob's mother, Yvonne, was a petite, charming, sophisticated Parisian, with whom, right from the start, I got on famously. Despite her husband's wealth, she loved to discuss, in a fashionable, Left Bank sort of way, my fading Marxist ideas. I was flattered by her interest in me and found her generous and hospitable. She probably thought that I was a good influence on her rebellious, immature son, as I was three years older and I appeared to be relatively sensible. On the other hand, she didn't have much time for Michel. He was the same age as myself, but she undoubtedly felt that his aimless drifting set a bad example to Jacob. Not that Michel cared. Once, while we were sitting around the table in the garden having breakfast, she turned to me, 'So, Patrick, what do you want to do in life?'

'I don't know. Go into politics or become a trade unionist?' I answered uncertainly. She turned to Michel, who, as usual, had hardly spoken all morning.

'And what about you, Michel? What do you want to become?'

'A Coca Cola bottle,' he smiled, mysteriously.

Jacob and Michel had known each other since they were children, as Michel's parents owned the adjacent villa in Marbella. They too were extremely wealthy. His father was a successful businessman who had made a fortune exporting coal to South America. When they weren't in southern Spain, they lived in an elegant, French-style mansion in woods outside Antwerp. In the town itself, Michel had a ramshackle attic so close to the cathedral that he could almost lean out the window and touch the clock. He was the family's black sheep, as he never seemed to have any money or a job, although now and again he claimed to 'sell pullovers'. The rest of the time he spent in London. There, regardless – or maybe because – of the fact that he never said anything meaningful, he enjoyed considerable success sleeping with attractive Chelsea debutantes.

When I returned to Britain from Spain I moved from Edinburgh to London. I had no idea what to do, as by now I was disillusioned with the idea of going into politics. Staying in a flat in fashionable South Kensington, in the meantime I got work as a supply teacher of English in a deprived school in Kennington. It was a riotous place, and if the teachers finished a lesson without unruly pupils setting fire to newspapers at the back of the classroom and breaking windows, the class was regarded as a success. I was quickly sick of it. Not that it didn't have its moments. Once, a recalcitrant pupil ran out the classroom and, to everyone's amazement, I chased him through the school and across the playground, before I finally caught him in the street.

Casting around for something to do, for a while I toyed with the unimaginative idea of going to the Inns of Court, which, to my mother's annoyance, Jacob's mother offered to finance. She had become very supportive of me and intermittently, while her husband was away on business and Jacob was studying in Oxford, she took me out in the family's chauffeur-driven Rolls Royce to eat in London's best fish restaurants. Years later, I wasn't surprised to learn that she and her husband were divorced and she was now living by herself in Paris. Once, I even visited her in her small, but beautifully furnished, flat which was right in the shadow of Notre Dame Cathedral. However, I left feeling saddened as, to me, she seemed lonely, with the days when she had presided so graciously over the family breakfast table in the garden in Marbella now merely a distant memory.

I had been teaching for some months when, out of the blue, I got a phone call from Michel. 'Hi, Patrick. You want to go to Sweden?' he asked in his heavily accented English.

'OK!' I replied, without hesitation. Owing to my increasing rejection of society – after all, it was the end of the 1960s – I had abandoned the idea of becoming a barrister, but I still didn't know what to do. That December we hitchhiked through freezing northern Germany and took a ferry from Hamburg to Gothenburg in Sweden. Twenty-four hours later we got a lift to the town of Örebro, where I wanted to see Debby, a ravishing blonde Swede I had had a brief affair with in Marbella. The address she had given me was in a block of flats. Her father, who she had warned us was a grumpy general, opened the door. He took one look at our stubbly, dishevelled appearance and shouted, 'She's not here!' and slammed the door in our faces.

Once in Stockholm, we took the ferry to Turku in Finland, where Michel wanted to see a young Finnish woman whom he had also met in Marbella. The ship, which was swarming with drunks, threaded through wooded archipelagos. After it docked in Turku, we walked to the end of the main street. However, it was –34°C and Michel feared his nose was going to freeze off, so we promptly turned round and caught the same boat back. From Stockholm we hitchhiked back down through southern Sweden. The countryside was covered in deep snowdrifts and, outside red wooden houses, Christmas trees were laden with twinkling white lights. One of our lifts was with some Sicilians. They had a touring puppet theatre and Michel and I sat squashed in the back of their van along with outsize wooden figures of men with painted moustaches and women with sensuous red lips.

As soon as I returned to Britain from Sweden, I decided, for want of anything better to do, to return to Edinburgh to study for a two-year postgraduate law degree at university. It didn't last long. After a year I couldn't stand the sight of any more, to me, boring law cases. Heavily under the influence of the rebellious Jacob, who had dropped out of Oxford to become a guard on the London Underground, I also decided to leave university. Now, for the first time in my life, apart from having a few violin lessons at school and writing poems in my teens, I wanted to do something creative. So I decided to become a classical guitarist, despite the fact that, at the age of twenty-three, I had never played the guitar before. In retrospect, I can see that, as well as having loved classical guitar music for some time, I was probably influenced by Eva, my mother's mother. She was a highly musical woman who, since the age of five, had played with her four sisters, all under the age of ten, in their own quintet. By their early twenties they had become professional musicians and were, as the Mather Quintet, very well known. They even gave a benefit concert in London's Albert Hall

The Mather Quintet: my maternal grandmother (left) with her four sisters c. 1917

for the families of the victims of the *Lusitania*, which had been torpedoed, with huge loss of life, by a German submarine in the First World War.

I was a very diligent student. Living off the money I had saved in Canada, I found myself a teacher and, convinced that if I worked hard enough I could make up for lost time and still reach concert standard, started practising scales for six hours a day. In fact, I took it so seriously that, a year later, I moved back to London in order to have private lessons with a retired ex-professor of the Royal Academy of Music. A hunched, authoritarian old Austrian, she was, like all excellent teachers, extremely demanding. Supporting myself financially by doing supply teaching, this time in a school in Dulwich, I moved in with friends of Jacob's who had squatted a spacious, two-storey Victorian villa in nearby Crystal Palace. There I practised for four hours every day, and every Wednesday evening took the 2B bus from Brixton across London to her house in Swiss Cottage. Although I quickly progressed because of the number of hours I was practising, playing the classical guitar didn't come easily. The end came one evening, a year later. Frustrated at my lack of natural ability, she ripped my fingers from the fret-board and shouted 'Mr Richardson, you are, and always vill be, nothing but a fiddler!'

Reluctantly, I knew in my heart of hearts that she was right. It was the end of my career as a musician. In the meantime, I was still teaching in Dulwich. Although the school was an improvement on the previous one, I continued to find teaching exhausting. I was highly relieved, therefore, when one day I received another surprise telephone call from Michel. 'You want to go to Greece?' he asked.

'Definitely!' I exclaimed. I still had money saved from Canada, so, keen to put my failure to become a classical guitarist behind me, I handed in my notice. Three weeks later we flew to Athens, from where we took the ferry to the island of Ios in the Cyclades. The island's *chora*, or main village, consisted of some palm trees towering over a cluster of daz-zlingly white, Cubist-like houses and a minute, blue-domed Greek Orthodox church. It quickly turned into an idyllic period of my life. At the time there was only one discotheque in the village and the only foreigners were a few hippies on their way back from India. For a month Michel and I lived in a sheltered alcove in a rocky peninsula overlooking spectacular Milapota beach. Not far below was a draughty, run-down taverna. Every day I sat by one of the broken windows, where I played chess with Flaco, an emaciated, shaven-headed Ameri-can who had a magnificent, black-and-white Great Dane called Bogart. Now and again the owner of the taverna took us out in his beautiful blue-, yellow-and-white fishing boat.

At sunset, Michel and I used to whistle to two young American women who lived in caves across the bay. They, in turn, would flash their torches at us. During the full moon, we braved the towering waves that crashed down on the golden beach. Once, I had a fleeting affair with a dark, unpredictable, gypsy-like young woman called Maria. One day, she told me she was leaving on the afternoon ferry. I was so heartbroken that I ran the entire flight of steps down to the port to try to stop her, but I never saw her again.

A month later, we sailed back to Athens. As neither of us had any commitments, for a while we were tempted to go to Egypt, which in those days seemed almost as far away as Timbuktu. I forget why – perhaps because it seemed nearer – but we settled on going to Syria instead. We were hitchhiking through Turkey and were just outside Konya, when we learned that war was imminent between Greece and Turkey and they were about to close their borders. Faced with the prospect of being stranded in Turkey or racing on to Syria or Greece, we decided on the latter. At the end of a hectic journey, we got back to the Greek frontier with hours to spare.

From Athens, we again took the ferry to Ios. We had no sooner docked than all the ferry services were cancelled. Unable to leave, we went back to our alcove above the taverna. Every evening we walked round the gently shelving beach to a house in the blacked-out *chora*, where villagers huddled round the radio, listening eagerly to the BBC World Service news. In the minuscule main square, groups of worried young men clustered round the list of those being called up, which was pinned to a tree. Outside the harbour a grey Greek destroyer lay at anchor, to protect the island in case of attack.

When hostilities ceased between Greece and Turkey, I went back to the squat in Crystal Palace. There, as I couldn't face the thought of teaching again in another run-down London school, once more my thoughts turned to Canada. This time I planned to teach English in Saskatchewan, as it was near the Rocky Mountains and I thought the name sounded romantic. A month prior to my departure, Dick and Tony, with whom I shared the squat in Crystal Palace, asked whether I wanted to go with them to Amsterdam for the weekend. Naturally I jumped at the chance, as I had never been there, and it had the reputation of being one of Europe's most exciting cities.

When we got to Amsterdam, we picked up some English nurses in a bar and took them back to our friends' flat in the Achterburgwal, in the heart of the red light district, for 'a party'. Annoyingly, when we arrived outside their door on the fourth floor, we found that our friends were out. In an attempt to get in by climbing through an attic window, I slipped and slid down the precipitous roof. Fortunately, a gulley stopped my fall and, far from having 'a party', my nurse had to swab my badly grazed ribs with methylated spirits instead.

Despite that painful experience, I fell in love with Amsterdam's exquisite canals and cafés to such an extent that I resolved to go and live there. I had no idea how long I would stay; such questions don't arise when you are young. Even so, never in my wildest dreams did I suspect it would be for eleven years. Within days of my arrival, after I collected my few belongings from London, some Dutch friends that I had made in the Achterburgwal asked if I wanted to have the attic of a five-storey, derelict house in the Kerkstraat which they had *gekraakt* (squatted). As soon as I saw it, I accepted on the spot, although it had no floor, no frames in the windows and no tiles on the roof, not to mention no electricity, gas, water or toilet.

The first thing I did, with their help, was to run an electricity cable and a water pipe over the roof from the neighbouring attic, which was also *gekraakt*. Then I laid the floor with planks that I had scavenged, along with badly fitting window frames, from skips at night. These I carried back to the Kerkstraat on the second-hand bike that I had bought, and then in the morning hoisted up to the attic with a hook that hung from the gable outside my window. For heating, I converted a black oil-drum. It was highly dangerous and I had to be careful that when I tossed a match inside to ignite the dripping petrol it didn't explode. For a cooker, I bought a portable camping ring that ran off a gas cylinder. I also bought a chemical toilet designed for use in caravans, which, until the lavatory on the floor below was repaired, I had to carry down four flights of vertiginous stairs. Then, at midnight, when there was no traffic, I had to lever off the manhole cover in the middle of the street and pour the toxic, overflowing liquid into the sewer.

My gekraakt *(squatted) attic in 386 Kerkstraat, Amsterdam*

But nothing could be done about the wooden roof, as retiling it was beyond everyone. Instead, my father, who was staying with my sister and her German husband in their house in Nordrhein-Westphalia, right on the German border with the Netherlands, kindly agreed to come up and help me line it with thick silver insulation. Even so, described by my Dutch friends as 'Robinson Crusoe living in the middle of Amsterdam', I baked in the frequently hot summers and froze in the equally frequent Arctic winters. It was to escape these winters in the Kerkstraat that I started travelling again with Michel. On three separate occasions in the subsequent decade I left Amsterdam in November, and each time we travelled for a year through South America, South-east Asia and Africa respectively.

Michel was the world's best travelling partner. In the whole time I knew him, I hardly ever heard him utter an intelligent word or articulate an informed opinion about anything whatsoever. But it didn't matter. He simply wasn't that sort of person. Instead, he was astonishingly easy-going and content to travel wherever I wished, which was inevitably one step further from where we were. True to his reputation, he was indeed like a Zen master who, instead of resisting, simply yields. As he was so flexible, I tried to be equally pliant in return. As a result, we didn't have a single argument, far less fall out with each other, during the entire time that we travelled together. He was unusually in touch with his feelings and

Me, travelling in South-east Asia

habitually suggested doing things I would normally never have dreamed of. For example, once, we hitchhiked down through the Atacama Desert in Chile. This is one of the driest places in the world, which, paradoxically, runs along the Pacific Ocean. After waiting for hours, we got a lift in the empty trailer of a giant Volvo truck that, miraculously, was going 100 kilometres to our next destination. We were only halfway when, in the middle of absolutely nowhere, Michel proposed that we jump out and go for a walk in the desert. Then, the next day, he proposed that we get out of our lift in a petrol tanker in order to spend the night on a barren, spume-filled beach. Both times I was horrified, but, after I relented, these two experiences of nature at its wildest were among the highlights of our South American journey.

Despite our unrivalled travelling partnership, Michel and I didn't actually have much in common, except that we were both rebellious rolling stones who loved travelling for the sake of it. They were never-to-be-forgotten, carefree years and we only stopped travelling after we began to tire and look forward to going home. When we did return, it was inevitably an anxious period for me. Prior to leaving Amsterdam, I would store my extensive collection of records, which were my only valuable possessions apart from my books, with friends. But as I turned into the Kerkstraat my heart was invariably in my mouth, as I didn't know whether we had been evicted from the house, or if my beloved attic had been pulled down.

Me, hitchhiking with Michel along the Pacific coast, Chile

As usual, whenever I travelled with Michel, I saw the indigenous people and cultures that we encountered on those journeys as mere exotic backdrops. In my early years in the Netherlands, I was too busy writing short stories and half-finished sketches of life in Amsterdam to consider writing about my travels. I also didn't like the idea of drawing attention to places I loved and possibly being responsible for their ruination. Notwithstanding, for the first time our travels were taking us to such unusual places – for example, the village in Bolivia where Che Guevara was killed – that I began to want to share my experiences with others. In addition, I told myself that if readers were prepared to make the same effort to get to these places as we had, they would treat them with respect. So, after I returned from South America, I wrote a manuscript called *The Pavements are Slippery*. This was intended to be a humorous account of our journey there, and contained a lot of immature political diatribes and introspective navel-gazing. Not surprisingly, the publishers it was sent to rejected it, no matter how often I rewrote it. In the end, deeply hurt, I put it under my worn, moth-eaten mattress on the floor and forgot about it.

To finance my writing in Amsterdam I had a variety of casual jobs. These included working on building sites, where I shovelled concrete and demolished the interiors of houses, or picking the tops off strawberries on the fourth floor of the Bijenkorf, Amsterdam's biggest department store. At last I got two regular, part-time jobs. One was washing dishes

Me, near Pokhara, Nepal

Michel, near Pokhara, Nepal

in the basement restaurant of a fascinating, four-storey East-West centre called the Kosmos. The other was working in an alternative bookshop belonging to Alistair, the best friend I ever had, in a large 'underground' arts complex. The similarities between the two of us were uncanny. Although he had been born in Kenya and I had been born in Sussex, he had also been to Edinburgh University, although he had dropped out after studying Social Anthropology for two years. Thereafter he too had spent several years travelling around, especially in India and South-east Asia. The similarities didn't stop there. He too lived in a *gekraakt* house and he too wanted to become a writer. So every Wednesday he came round to the Kerkstraat for one of our 'Doomsbury' evenings, when we discussed interminably how we could improve our rejected manuscripts. We were inseparable, and spent most of our free time going to art-house films, sitting round in cafés playing chess or backgammon, and cycling round the Vondel Park.

But the years rolled by and, no matter how much I adored Amsterdam, at length I tired of the perpetual crowds and lack of space. I tired of the absence of rivers, forests and mountains. I tired of having to speak Dutch instead of English. I tired of being an eternal outsider and not having my own culture. Above all, I recognized that my life in Amsterdam was going nowhere. Living an impoverished existence as an unsuccessful writer in a garret and washing dishes for years on end wasn't good for my self-confidence. The final straw came with the collapse of my torrid relationship with Jenny, a sultry Londoner of Guyanese descent, who also lived in Amsterdam. So one summer, more than a decade after I had gone to Amsterdam for the weekend, I decided to return to Scotland.

Regardless of my initial difficulties in readjusting to Edinburgh's miserable climate, grey buildings and dour citizens, I was brimming with ambitious ideas. At last I was going to get a real, professional career, possibly with Amnesty International or the new, innovative Channel Four on television. I even entertained the idea of studying to become a doctor. It wasn't long before I realized all of these were pie-in-the-sky ideas, as I was either too mature or too unqualified. Once, Alistair, who had been raised in nearby Dunfermline, came over from Amsterdam to see me. His bookshop there had gone bankrupt, and together we explored the possibility of setting up a second-hand one in Edinburgh until we concluded the town had too many already. Yet again, I didn't have the faintest idea what to do. As a stopgap measure, I did a short course enabling me to teach English as a foreign language. Not long after I finished, I was fortunate enough to find a part-time job in a language school and I settled down in the cosy flat that my parents had generously bought me.

But if I imagined my travelling days were over I was wrong. During the ensuing four years, two momentous events occurred in my life. First, my mother, who I adored, despite our often stormy relationship, died of breast cancer. Secondly, Alistair, who had also come back to try to live in Edinburgh again, where he had metamorphosed into an outstanding photographer, died not long afterwards at the tragically young age of thirty-seven. Slowly

My best friend, the one and only Alistair

but surely, with the death of two of the most important people in my life, I began to feel the urge to travel again. First, I wanted to go to China. The language school where I was employed was astonishingly flexible and said I could take as much time off as I liked. For a while I tried to persuade Michel to accompany me again. However, he couldn't be tempted to leave southern Portugal, where he was doing up a ruined farmhouse that he had bought cheaply in the hope of luring his German ex-girlfriend, Sieglinda, the love of his life, to come and live with him.

I found the prospect of travelling by myself in China so daunting that, for two years before I left for Beijing, I tried to learn Mandarin at university evening classes. I also started brushing up my other languages that I thought might be of possible use on future journeys. In my early years, I had never been particularly interested in learning languages, unlike my mother, who loved people and communicating so much that, wherever she went, she picked up languages as naturally as she made her countless friends. However, later on in my life, she was once again a very important influence on me without my being aware of it. At school I had learned French and some Russian. The summer I got back from South America, where I learnt Spanish, I went back to Ios, where I merely swapped my Spanish grammar book for a Greek one. While I was living in Amsterdam, I had learned German as well as Dutch, as, apart from the fact that my sister lived in Germany, for two years I had had a German girlfriend. Finally, while teaching English at the language school in Edinburgh, I had learned Italian, as most of the students were from northern Italy.

Learning Chinese and reactivating these languages gave me confidence that I could handle myself in situations where otherwise I might have been lost. At the same time, as I no longer had Michel to keep me company, I knew I had to communicate much more with people if I didn't want to be lonely. As expected, when I got to China hardly anyone could understand me. But it didn't matter. From that time on, in my wanderings I started to be really interested in people and their cultures. The difference was remarkable. I began to have unexpected encounters everywhere, which I would never have had if I had been travelling with Michel. In fact, travelling by myself became one of my most defining experiences and I realized that finally I had found my way of journeying through life.

II
SOME OF MY JOURNEYS

CHAPTER ONE

Latin America

'Soon the full moon came out and climbed high above the stern, turning clouds into blankets of gleaming silver.'

ARGENTINA: BORGES

From the moment I crossed the bridge spanning the border between southern Bolivia and northern Argentina, a new reality awaited me. Dusty and dishevelled after travelling, like most Bolivians, in cattle trucks for four unforgettable weeks, I stopped at the first restaurant after Immigration. It had clean, plastic tabletops, and the barman, who was the first white man I had seen in a fortnight, was surly and unfriendly. I cleaned myself up as much as possible in the toilet and had a coffee. Then, after discovering the train south had just left and there was no bus for hours, I decided to walk to the military checkpoint on the outskirts of town and try to hitch a lift.

Five minutes later, I heard a shout. Looking round, I saw a khaki-clad soldier lounging against a parked car, beckoning me to accompany him. Despite being quite an experienced traveller, I was still rather naïve about events in Argentina. I had good reason to be. I knew, naturally, that it, like most of South America at the time, was ruled by a brutal, right-wing

Reed canoes, Lake Titicaca, Peru

military regime. However, soldiers at the ubiquitous roadblocks in the rest of the continent, where I had been travelling for months, had given me no trouble. Even Chile, of all places, had been problem free, although that was because, three years after the overthrow of the democratically elected president, Salvador Allende, by General Pinochet, most of the opposition was either dead, in prison or in exile.

I traipsed after the soldier down a side street to a building where a striped blue-and-white Argentine flag flapped in the stiff breeze and another soldier stood idly by the door, polishing his rifle. Inside, a photograph of a mousey-looking man in a uniform, with a prim face and thin moustache, hung on the wall. It was General Videla, the leader of the ruling three-man Junta, which was rumoured to be responsible for paramilitary death squads, torture and the disappearance of countless civilians.

'Take your hat off and show respect!' barked one of the soldiers in Spanish.

A sergeant sitting on a swivel chair muttered something I didn't understand to the soldier, who, without warning, seized my two leather saddlebags and emptied their contents onto the floor. 'What are you doing here?' growled the sergeant, glancing distastefully at my beard and shoulder-length hair as he examined my passport.

'I've . . . I've been travelling through South America and I'd like to see Argentina,' I stammered in Spanish, taken aback.

'Well, we like respectable-looking tourists, not escoria [scum] like you!' he spat contemptuously, handing me back my passport. 'Get out!'

Stunned, I picked up my belongings from the floor before walking slowly to the checkpoint, where a thick, barbed-wire fence surrounded a guard-post and an iron barrier blocked the road. This time, though, a soldier merely flicked through my passport and told me not to hitchhike near the barrier. Beyond, the tarmac road petered out and a dirt track stretched into a seemingly limitless plain broken only by a row of telegraph poles. A strong wind was getting up and, over the top of low hills, a threatening black thundercloud was forming. Shortly, a truck braked in a cloud of dust and, as the cabin was full, the driver offered me a lift in the empty hold. For two hours the truck drove into the horizon, where a thinly drawn line separated land from sky. Flashes of lightning played over the tops of distant hills, and rain drove into my face as I crouched in a corner of the jolting hold under grimy plastic sheeting I had found in a box. I'd nodded off when the lorry shuddered to a halt, and the back of the hold swung open.

'Military! Get out and bring your bags into the checkpoint,' a harsh voice ordered.

'Not again!' I sighed, clambering to the ground. A soldier with a thin moustache – most Argentinian men seemed to have thin moustaches – marched me to a hut in a cluster of bungalows at the foot of a hill. Above the entrance, 'ORDEN EN DISCIPLINA' (order and discipline) was written on a plaque, and pinned to the walls, under captions of 'SE BUSCA' (wanted), were photographs with the words 'SINDICALISTA' (trade-unionist), 'ESTUDIANTE' (student) or 'ABOGADO' (lawyer) scrawled in ink across them.

'OK, you're clean,' a second soldier glowered, when he had finished inspecting my bags and passport. 'At least your passport is.' He turned to the lorry driver. 'You pick him up, Juan?'

'Yes.'

'Well, let him walk, and don't do it again!'

Swallowing my anger, I went outside. The driver grimaced apologetically before roaring off in the lorry. I set off for the last of the bungalows. Opposite, in a railway siding, a goods steam engine hissed. A solitary tree bent into the wind and rain teemed from the gloomy sky. I consulted my map whilst trying, in vain, to keep it dry. Jujuy, the first sizeable town, was still forty kilometres away; despite there being no traffic, I decided to put as much distance as possible between the checkpoint and myself. Five kilometres later, I was pounding along in the middle of a desolate plain when I heard the roar of a powerful engine behind me. It was a mud-streaked, streamlined bus, with the word 'JUJUY' at the front. I ran into the middle of the track and flagged it down. To my relief, it ground to a halt and the driver, a young man with a beard, leaned out the window and smiled at me.

'Got a seat?' I asked hopefully.

He turned and spoke to someone behind. There was a brief discussion until he poked his head out the window again. 'Come on, you look wet,' he replied sympathetically.

I clambered in. A hostess with dark tan stockings and a mini-skirt showed me to a plush leather seat at the back. She pushed a button and it swished into a reclining position. 'Try to get some rest,' she murmured. I dried myself in the toilet, returned to my seat, and tried to relax. The lights in the corridor had dimmed, and there was silence as the bus accelerated into the gathering darkness. I dozed off, waking occasionally to see the bus gliding through streets of small towns, although twice we had to stop at roadblocks and soldiers searched everyone's luggage before allowing us to continue.

At 8 p.m. the bus entered Jujuy. Unlike the narrow, dark, cobbled alleys of Bolivia's stunning colonial towns, the streets were wide, modern and well lit. As the rain had stopped, I slid the dark glass window open and stuck my head outside. It was a warm, damp night, and the bus was passing rows of squat bungalows, outside which sprinklers sprayed rhododendron bushes and lush green lawns. It wasn't long until ugly apartment blocks loomed ahead, and the bus pulled into a terminal where queues of passengers were waiting patiently for buses. The kiosks were full of magazines, some of which, unbelievably, had swastikas on their covers. Sleek cars, hooting impatiently, slid past pavements overflowing with prosperous-looking white citizens out for the *paseo* (evening stroll), and the shops were overflowing with fashionable shirts from London, dresses from Paris, televisions, washing machines and refrigerators.

I found a *pensión* in a back street run by an Italian who had been a prisoner of war in England. He was friendly, although his English was poor and his Spanish worse. 'I was in

Sweendon,' he announced proudly in English, as I put my bags down.

'Where?'

'Sweendon, near London.'

'Ah, you mean Swindon!'

'Si. England is good. 'Here, i militari . . . Mah, it is dangerous to talk. You like vino?'

'Of course.'

'OK, I getta glass.'

The next day I accidentally met Jorge Luis Borges.

I was having breakfast in a café near the railway station, where I'd just bought a ticket for the midnight train south, when the headline of the local newspaper on the next table caught my eye. 'BORGES EN JUJUY!' it screamed. I shot bolt upright. At that time, he wasn't well known outside of Argentina, but he was a cult figure in European literary circles where many considered him to be one of the world's greatest living writers. An improbably well-read intellectual and scholar, he was also my favourite author and I'd devoured every word of his exquisite essays and short stories with their recurring themes of fate, infinity, and the circular, dreamlike nature of history.

On reading the newspaper further, I discovered he was giving a lecture on The Role of Myth in World Literature at eight o'clock that evening in the Auditorio del Ministerio de Bienstar Social. According to my map, it was only four blocks away. With mounting excitement, I calculated that I could hear the lecture, have a meal and still have time to catch the midnight train south. Abandoning my coffee, I set off immediately to get a ticket. The lecture hall was at the end of a street lined with orange trees. As there was no one in the ticket office or the foyer, I pulled open the lecture-theatre door, ignoring the 'No Entry' notice. Inside, it was dark but at the foot of a steeply banked auditorium two technicians were helping an elderly, blind man with a white stick mount steps to a floodlit stage. A thrill ran through me; I would recognize that face anywhere – it was Borges himself.

I slipped into the back row and was just about to sit down when I found I had nearly sat on someone. 'Sssh!' a reproachful male voice whispered, 'or we'll be thrown out.'

'What's going on?' I breathed softly, finding the adjoining seat.

'It's a trial run for this evening – to get him used to the stage, I suppose.'

A slide projector was flashing images onto a screen behind Borges' head, and the loudspeaker system crackled. Borges sat down at a table. He was in his late seventies, bald, and his skin was white and ghostly. As he spoke, his mouth showed a row of what looked like perfect false teeth while his white eyeballs stared vacantly ahead. 'Uno, dos, tres,' he murmured into the microphone, tapping it gently.

Hoping the technicians wouldn't notice I crept down to the front row for a better view. I'd hardly been there a couple of minutes when a voice at the back of the auditorium shouted 'Lights!' and the hall was flooded with light. One of the technicians turned round and spotted me. 'Hey!'

I can't imagine what possessed me, but, to my surprise, I found myself stepping over tangled microphone cables and climbing the steps to the table on the stage. 'Hello, Señor Borges,' I said in English. (I knew he spoke fluent English as in his work he often mentioned how much he admired the English canon, which he read in the original.)

There was a silence until a smile flickered momentary over his pallid face. 'That wouldn't be an Englishman speaking, would it?' he replied, in the overly correct, formal-sounding English of non-native speakers.

'Not really. I was born in Sussex, but brought up in Edinburgh,' I answered, trying to ignore the technicians who were glaring furiously at me.

'Ah, I know it well!' he went on in a mock Irish accent. 'Edinburgh and Geneva, two of the loveliest Calvinist cities in Europe. Did you know that the name Edinburgh might have originated in Northumberland?'

'No, I didn't . . . '

'Well, some say that Edwin, the king of Northumbria from 616 to 632 AD, built a new town on the River Forth which became known as Edwin's Burgh. Over the centuries the two words fused, if you will permit me using such a word, to become Edinburgh.'

'Really!' I exclaimed. Borges was famed for his erudition, but still . . . Thankfully the technicians, satisfied that I didn't constitute a danger, had retreated to the front row of the auditorium to unload boxes of sound equipment.

'Northumberland – now there's a magnificent county!' Borges continued, reverting to his English accent. 'All those Danish and Viking names. You wouldn't be acquainted with Bamburgh, would you?'

'Why, I spent my summer holidays there as a child!'

'Ah, I remember that great windswept beach, although the intervening years may have blurred my memory . . . So how did you like my Scottish accent?'

'That was Irish, not Scottish!' I said, laughing.

'Forgive me.' He began reciting the first few stanzas of a poem in a language I couldn't make out. As his voice rang through the hall, the technicians stopped clattering around and listened in awed silence. 'I wonder if, by chance, you can tell me what language that is?' he asked.

'No, I can't. Hebrew?'

'No, it's Saxon. That was *Beowolf*, of course. You are probably aware that Saxon, or Old English, comes from Friesland.'

'Yes, actually, I am,' I nodded. 'I've been living in Holland for the last four years and . . .'

'Ah, so many fine Scotsmen!' he carried on, paying no attention. 'Hume, Adam Smith, and . . . who was it that wrote *The Confessions of a Justified Sinner*? His name escapes me, although I should know, as I've translated his work.'

'So should I. De Quincey?'

'No. He was the author, if I am not mistaken, of *The Confessions of an English Opium Eater*. And he was English, of course.'

I was still thinking about it when, out the corner of my eye, I saw two soldiers walk menacingly down the aisle towards us. 'You know, every time I see the name Argentina I think of you,' I volunteered quickly.

'You are too kind. Have you read my stories?'

'Of course! All of them.'

'I have done my best, but I must apologize for their quality.' Borges was renowned for his humility, real or otherwise.

'No, really, you're too modest.'

All of a sudden a mischievous expression flitted across his face. 'Perhaps you are familiar with the story of what happened when Goethe visited a brothel in Hanover?'

The two soldiers were hovering, unsure what to do. 'No. But I'd love to hear it,' I said.

The long, complicated tale, which I have now forgotten, lasted for more than five minutes. Afterwards, he questioned me about my writing – I told him that I was living in a garret in Amsterdam, trying to finish a novel – and my journey through South America. After what seemed a lifetime, a man in a grey suit came down the gangway, climbed the steps and leant over him. 'It's time to go, Señor Borges. You have an appointment at three.'

'Very well,' replied Borges grudgingly. Clutching the arm of the man in the grey suit, he rose unsteadily to his feet while his hands searched empty space. To my dismay, the two soldiers, who I had forgotten about and who had been sitting in the front row, were once again advancing towards me.

'You will give my greetings to Robbie Burns, won't you?' smiled Borges, as the man in the grey suit led him down the platform steps and guided him up the auditorium. Desperate to retain the link with my protector, I followed closely behind. Then, as he and the man turned left through a door, I stumbled into the bright sunlight, and, watched by the two soldiers, I walked up the street.

Still hardly believing what had happened, but realising I had forgotten to buy a ticket, I returned to the same café for a stiff drink. It had all happened so quickly – with Borges one minute and back travelling in South America the next. I looked around. It was exceedingly hot. A fly buzzed and settled on the counter. A mirror on the wall reflected rows of red and green wine bottles on a shelf and my dictionary and black hat which were lying on the table. Through the open saloon door an overheated sky loomed over the railway station's ornate white façade. I took out a pen and my notebook. The waiter, who was a tall youth in a white jacket, bent over my shoulder.

'What are you writing?' he asked.

'About what's just happened.'

'What's that?'

'I've just met Jorge Luis Borges. You heard of him?'

The youth stared at me. 'Of course!' he retorted. 'Everyone in Argentina knows Borges. And you've been talking to him?'

'Yes, twenty minutes ago.' Still incredulous, I found talking about it made it seem even more unreal.

'What was he saying?' The young waiter sat down at the next seat, gazing at me awestruck.

'Well . . . ' I began.

I looked up and caught a view of us in the mirror: a young boy talking to an unknown young writer at a table; twenty minutes previously, the unknown young writer talking to a famous old writer at a table; the young boy captivated by the tale of the unknown young writer; the unknown young writer captivated by the tales of the famous old writer. It felt like something from one of Borges' stories about the cyclical nature of history.

At half past seven that evening I was back at the Salon Auditorio, where I managed to get one of the last tickets before I entered the hall. Although there was still half an hour to go, it was almost full. The first five rows were full of high-ranking military officers with clusters of medals pinned to their smart, olive-green uniforms. Behind, wealthy-looking men in dinner jackets sat next to women wearing long evening dresses, pearls and sparkling jewellery. I found a seat in the middle of the back row, where two intimidating soldiers with Kalashnikovs stood at a door, eying me suspiciously. Every few minutes, the door opened, whereupon the entire audience, thinking it was Borges, rose expectantly to its feet, and a sea of excited faces swivelled round, only to discover it was merely another officer. At the foot of the stage, television cameramen adjusted arc lights and photographers fiddled with lenses.

I had been sitting there for a few minutes when I heard a hostile voice say ominously, 'You with the bag, come with me!' I looked up. A weedy-looking man in plain clothes was standing at the end of the row, flashing an identity card. His jacket was open, and in a holster at his waist I could see a revolver.

'Oh God!' I groaned under my breath as, red with embarrassment, I made my way to the aisle. Outside the hall, two more plain-clothes agents were waiting. The weedy-looking man pointed to the adjacent toilet. 'Go inside and open your bag!' he commanded. I pushed the door open reluctantly until it slammed behind us, leaving the four of us standing alone next to the urinals.

Ignoring the alarm bells ringing wildly in my head – I could be beaten to a bloody pulp, or even shot, and nobody would be any the wiser – suddenly I saw red. 'Look, I'm a journalist for *The Times* of London!' I shouted, oblivious, given my unkempt appearance, of the sheer improbability of such a claim. 'Believe me, I'm going to describe in exact detail everything that's happening in this shit-hole country of yours!'

Disregarding my violent outburst, the weedy-looking man silently inspected my bag and passport and then handed them back to me. 'You may return to the hall, Señor Richardson,' he said politely.

Still quivering with anger and feeling utterly humiliated, I went back into the hall. I was a third of the way along the row when Borges abruptly emerged from a side door next to the stage. Accompanied by the man in the grey suit I had seen earlier, he had hardly taken a step before the entire auditorium rose to its feet, applauding wildly, while, at the foot of the stage, television cameras whirred, cameras clicked and flashlights popped.

Two minutes later, Borges, who by now had been shown to the table in the middle of the stage, lifted a hand. 'Gracias, señors y señoras,' he motioned, trying to quieten the tumultuous applause. When he had finally succeeded, he groped for a glass of water, his pale face gleaming eerily in the glare of the television lights. 'Tonight, I want to dedicate this lecture to our brave military, which has fought so hard to save us from the subversion that is threatening to overwhelm us,' he began. 'Our country . . . ' The rest of his introduction was lost amidst another thunderous ovation as, yet again, the audience rose to its feet.

When everyone had settled down, I sat back, calmer now. So this was the other side of Borges . . . For several years the literary world had speculated it was only his right-wing views that prevented him winning the Nobel Prize for Literature. Indeed, only the previous week I had read a magazine interview with him, in which he was quoted as calling for a military coup in the USA in order to 'stop the Communists taking over'. Suddenly, I couldn't take it any more. I didn't care what I missed; I wanted to remember the delightful, blind old man I'd sat with, alone at a table – not the mouthpiece of a vicious military regime responsible for the disappearance of thousands of people. I stood up, pushed my way impetuously along the row to the aisle, and, to the astonishment of the three agents, stormed out the building.

Outside, the lowering sky was again filled with thunder and lightning, and drops of heavy rain were falling. I hurried back to the *pensión*, where the Italian was drinking a glass of wine in the kitchen with friends. On the table the headline of the newly arrived national newspaper blared, 'TREINTE COMUNISTAS MUERTOS EN MENDOZA!' The Italian looked up. 'Mierda, es horrible!' he exclaimed, as his eyes followed my gaze.

Two hours later I packed my bags and, with a deep sense of foreboding, walked reluctantly to the station. Although the train wasn't due to leave for an hour, the three brown carriages standing by the overflowing platform were almost full. As I threaded my way through the compartment to my seat, dozens of well-dressed, European-looking passengers suspiciously eyed my beard, crumpled clothes and dusty travel bags. I'd scarcely sat down when I was swept by a fresh wave of doubts. Why was I doing this? Surely only a masochist would travel through a country that was plainly in a state of civil war? On the other hand, I really wanted to see Argentina. Confused, I pulled a coin out my pocket – heads, I'd continue my journey south through Argentina, tails, I'd return north and perhaps go down the

Amazon instead. It was tails. That decided it. I clambered down to the platform, where I tore up my ticket and tossed the pieces like confetti onto the track.

The next morning, I took the train back to Bolivia.

ECUADOR: THE VALLEY OF VOLCANOES

As our bus pulled into Aqua Verde, a bustling town on Peru's border with Ecuador, the main street was awash with attaché cases, cowboy hats and low-slung holsters. Half the population seemed to be money-changers, the other half military. I and other passengers to Ecuador were corralled into Immigration, where a mean-looking lieutenant with a John Wayne moustache sat, his legs splayed nonchalantly over his desk.

'One day in Ecuador for every ten dollars,' he began aggressively in Spanish.

'Right,' I replied. I knew T-3 tourist cards were for either thirty or ninety days.

'How much you got?'

'Nine hundred.'

' 'Kay, that's thirty days.'

'Hey, that's not right!'

'You got anything for me?'

'What?'

'All right, get out!'

At least, geographically, Ecuador was how all countries should be when first visited – immediately different. Behind mouldy corrugated rooftops, tropical forests climbed foot-hills of mist-enshrouded mountains. The packed bus pulled out along a potholed road lined with banana trees and thatched houses on stilts, where children, cooling themselves in the oppressive midday heat, splashed in puddles.

Eventually the road started to ascend, leaving the sweltering coast behind. By nightfall we'd reached a high pass and the bus clung to the mountainside as its headlights searched for bends and yawning chasms. Trapped in the back seat, I was increasingly uneasy until finally, after the bus teetered over yet another precipice, I couldn't bear it any longer. At the next village I struggled out the rear window of the bus. It roared off into drizzle, leaving me alone on an empty gloomy street.

Footsteps ringing on deserted cobbles, I found a *pensión* where, in a deserted dining room with an abandoned jukebox, a woman was examining her son's head for fleas. I sat down and within minutes she plonked an unsolicited plate of rice in front of me.

'That's all we got,' she said, as a cockroach fell off the ceiling and landed on the floor with a clunk. 'Your room's above.'

Shop in Quito, Ecuador

Still, it was better than the bus.

By day, to my surprise, I found Santa Isabel was rather pleasing. Coconut and palm trees reared up through fuchsias and lilacs in a miniature square. From my balcony, the hillside, dotted with papaya plantations, fell away to cornfields in the valley below, where distant crumpled ranges rose into the crisp blue sky.

I caught the first bus, which wound down the mountainside through sleepy villages until it reached a broad, fertile valley dominated by baroque spires of the colonial city of Cuenca. I found a room overlooking the market, prior to exploring the whitewashed streets with their wooden balconies and squares overflowing with Spanish churches and monasteries. Everywhere, barefoot *ecuatorianos* wandered about wearing colourful skirts and Panama hats.

Curiously enough, these hats originate in Ecuador. The confusion as to their origin apparently began in the 1850s when itinerant gold miners, returning from California to New York via Latin America, were asked where they'd bought their unusual straw hats. 'Panama,' came the mistaken reply. To some, it seems, banana republics are confusingly similar.

As ill luck would have it, it was the rainy season. I'd hoped to see the famed volcanoes, but I was disappointed. By late morning, clouds had closed in and by afternoon the first drops fell until the skies opened. Soon, pounded by hailstones the size of pound coins, the streets were turned into raging torrents.

Nor did I have better luck with Cuenca Museum, which was shut. In any case, the well-known Crespo stones, named after an odd local padre who claimed the Phoenicians sailed up the Amazon to settle in Ecuador 3,000 years ago – and described by von Däniken in *Chariots of the Gods* – were reportedly in a private collection.

It wasn't until I was on the bus for Quito that the skies briefly parted and there, finally, was Chimborazo. It was my geography master who had first mentioned it; I had vaguely thought that he was talking about chimpanzees. Now, as the bus dipped towards the valley, a breathtaking volcano, 6,029 metres high, was framed by the windscreen, its perfect cone jutting into the sky, and dazzling white snow sparkling on its symmetrical flanks. Nor was it was the only one. That morning I understood why in 1802 German explorer Alexander von Humboldt called this the Valley of Volcanoes; there are thirty, including Cotopaxi (5,896 metres), the world's highest active volcano.

In next to no time we arrived in Quito, which, at an elevation of 2,800 metres, is the world's third highest capital. Overshadowed by slumbering Volcán Pichincha, the old part was full of red-tiled colonial houses and twisting, cobbled alleys. Far below, in the seventeenth-century plazas, the cries of shoeshine boys mingled with church bells. Quito was Inca until claimed by Pizarro, although it was Pedro de Alvarado who marched south to occupy it. Meanwhile yet another *conquistador*, Francisco de Orellana, was the first white man to cross the continent; while prospecting for *El Dorado*, he drifted down Ecuador's Río Napo in the jungle to the east until he reached the Amazon's mouth.

Still, I didn't plan to stay long in Quito. Interested in indigenous weaving, I was headed for Salasaca. Originally from Bolivia, until the Incas conquered them in AD 1400, this community of 2,000 had been untouched by the outside world until the twentieth century. Now, still off the beaten track, Salasaca's inhabitants reputedly made remarkable *tapices* (weavings with decorative bird and animal designs).

The next day I got off the bus as suggested, 150 kilometres south of Quito, to find myself alone in a deserted plain. The question was – where was Salasaca?

I trekked along a dusty track lined with cacti until I saw figures with white floppy trousers, blue ponchos and round straw hats scuttling about in fields like Alice in Wonderland rabbits. I rubbed my eyes; it looked as though a haystack was approaching.

'Bueñas dias,' began a droll-looking man, appearing round the back of a heavily laden donkey. 'Ignatius Cavelli, at your service. Are you lost?'

'I'm looking for the village,' I replied.

'What village?'

'Salasaca, of course!'

Ignatius looked dumbfounded and waved his arms around vaguely.

'But you're looking at it!'

I glanced round. Beyond a ridge, the brown plain receded into the distance.

'I see,' I said, trying not to appear stupid.

Ignatius seemed reassured. 'You're not from here?' he asked.

I told him where I was from.

'They make tapestries there too?'

'Not really. But,' I persisted, 'do you live in the village?'

'Oh yes.'

'Which is, eh, where did you say?'

'Let me tell you a local joke.' he asked, leaning towards me confidentially. 'They say our weaving technique's never been copied. Know why?'

'No. Why?'

'Because no one can find our village!' Ignatius doubled up with laughter, and hurried away with a cheery wave.

Returning to Quito, I was grimly determined not to miss Otavalo, thirty kilometres to the north, so easily.

The *Otavaleños* are legendary throughout South America. For centuries their ability as weavers – back-strap looms have been used here for 400 years – was harshly exploited by the Spanish and Ecuadorian landowners until 1917, when a local weaver started copying fashionable Scottish tweeds. This, allied to the 1964 agrarian reform and their shrewd business sense, has made the *Otavaleños* the most prosperous indigenous community in South

Ignatius Cavelli, Salasaca, Ecuador

America. They produce striking wall-hangings and tapes used to bind their long hair, as well as beautiful patterned belts.

The Imbarra-bound *autoferro*, which looked like a converted bus on rails complete with steering-wheel, driver and hooter, descended towards a fertile green valley dominated by two massive volcanoes. The famous Otavalo Saturday market was just beginning, with thousands of *Otavaleños*, surely one of South America's most colourful peoples, pouring in from outlying villages with everyone, including babies, in traditional dress. The men had single long ponytails, calf-length white pants, rope sandals, reversible grey or blue ponchos and dark felt hats. The women wore immaculate white blouses embroidered with roses, long black skirts and shawls, folded navy head-cloths and string upon string of gold beads.

I hiked along a dirt track to a village on the mountainside where teams, watched by spectators falling about with laughter, were playing volleyball. Others lay contentedly on grass, playing cards for maize seeds. A girl, her neck draped in layers of gold beads, picked her way through tall maize carrying *chicha* (beer) and waved to women returning from the market.

It was sunset, and the white roofs of villages tucked away amongst patchwork fields on the opposite mountain glinted in the sun's dying rays. Far below, amongst rushes, cows grazed contentedly by a meandering river. I looked at the volcanoes. Legend suggests Mama Cotacachi (5,000 metres) awakens with a fresh covering of snow after she's been visited by Papa Imbabura (4,609 metres) during the night. I was lost in another myth; I felt as if I was in the Garden of Eden.

COLOMBIA: THE LLANOS ORIENTAL AND BOGOTÁ

Although long before I arrived from Ecuador I knew of Colombia's shocking reputation for drug-trafficking, violence and lawlessness – it's the world's biggest cocaine producer and has the continent's longest guerrilla insurgency – never in my wildest nightmares could I have dreamt what awaited me there.

Not that there hadn't been early warning signs; the German traveller next to me on the bus had told me how, on an overnight coach to Bogotá, he'd awakened to find his trouser leg slit open and his money belt removed. When I arrived in Pasto it was dark, and dingy streets outside the bus station were lined by hustlers with narrow trousers, rakish moustaches and greasy hair. I had to find a hotel, so, pursued by furtive eyes and brazen offers of 'Cocaína, marijuana?' I set off into the murky night and found a seedy backstreet *hostelaje*, where I pushed through crowds of pimps and women in minuscule mini-skirts to a stubbly man slouched against a coffee machine.

'Wan focky focky?' he offered wearily. Many cheap Colombian hotels can be rented by the hour or the night, depending on use.

'Just a room,' I replied, before climbing stairs after him to a shabby top-floor room smelling of sweat and cheap hair oil. Through cardboard partition walls came the sound of men moaning in ecstasy.

The next morning I set off on the Popayán express up the Pan-American Highway, a route notorious for armed gangs masquerading as police or military, which hold up buses at fake checkpoints.

Christopher Isherwood, in *The Condor and the Cows*, described terrain round La Unión, perched on its sheer-sided ridge, as resembling 'violently crumpled bed-clothes, with the road scribbled wildly across tremendous valleys, while tilled fields on opposite mountain-faces look nearly vertical'. Still, nerves jangling, I couldn't really concentrate on the scenery. After 320 kilometres and a long, grinding descent, I was elated to arrive seven hours later in Popayán, the country's most appealing colonial city.

Founded in 1537 by Pizarro's lieutenant Sebastian de Belcázar, and known as 'Colombia's Burgos', it was meticulously restored after being severely damaged by the ruinous 1983 earthquake just as the much-celebrated Maundy Thursday religious procession was departing. Now it's once again awash with classical Spanish architecture, with whitewashed, two-storey colonial mansions, church spires and monasteries overlooked by the snowcapped volcano Puracé (4,267 metres).

Soon I began the seven-hour bus journey over the Cordillera Oriental to San Augustín, one of South America's most significant archaeological sites, which is famous for its pre-Columbian burial mounds and statues. The mountain road was rough and prone to frequent landslides, but it was spectacular, climbing to wispy mountain peaks until it wound down vertical gorges covered with tropical forests to a village nestling in a green valley.

San Augustín's pre-Columbian culture, which some archaeologists link to the Pacific's Easter Island, developed between the sixth and fourteenth centuries AD. By the time the Spanish arrived it had died out – perhaps, like other Andean civilisations, falling victim to the Incas – and it wasn't until the eighteenth century that the sites were discovered. These are circular, underground caverns where torchlight reveals walls and pillars covered with intricate red, white and black criss-cross designs. But it was the stone heads which were most striking – with rectangular, flattened noses, jutting square chins, staring eyes and open speechless mouths, they were like eerie beings in stone, trapped forever in some horrifying existence.

They were so intriguing that I stayed a week. Every day, hoping the men playing cards on overlooking verandas wouldn't laugh at me, I wrestled with an amiable, but reluctant, hired nag before I cantered up red tracks into the deserted green hills to investigate scattered statues of sacred eagles, jaguars, frogs and stylised, six-metre-high masked monsters. This is ranching territory and everyone travels by horseback; it was peaceful, with only grazing cattle and horses for company. Little moved, except for the Río Magdalena meandering through the dozing valley.

At midday I would return to San Augustín and idle away afternoons leaning against shady street corners, drifting into stores full of candles, leather polish and machetes, or hanging out with teenagers at the pool hall. Occasionally, buses or riders trailed dust clouds along the sun-baked road. In the evenings I'd sit by candlelight in the dark – there was no electricity – on my farmhouse balcony, watching silvery moonlight bathe the yard and listening to crickets humming in the creaking banana trees.

Then it happened. I'd spent the whole day descending to tropical lowlands near the Amazonian rainforest. Now I was in a roadside bar in a Wild West shanty town, watching a cowboy with a ten-gallon hat and leather chaps gallop up to the sidewalk in clouds of dust. He'd just tethered his lather-flecked horse to the grocery store's post when a khaki-clad soldier with a Kalashnikov hanging casually from his shoulder suddenly materialized and aggressively demanded my 'papers'.

'What papers?' I replied; I knew this was a notorious marijuana-growing area, but no one had said anything about needing papers.

'Right, come with me to the police station,' he ordered.

It was a cramped building on the tiny square, where a disreputable-looking young lieutenant with a pockmarked face, lanky hair and a David Niven moustache sprawled behind a desk groaning with forms. Including military roadblocks, this was the fifth search that day, so I watched unconcerned as, smirking oddly, he instructed soldiers to search my bags. Just as they'd nearly finished, one pulled out a bag of marijuana.

'Look what I found!' he exclaimed, grinning broadly.

The lieutenant's eyes narrowed. 'Fancy that!' he drawled, turning accusingly to me.

'This is OUTRAGEOUS!' I gasped, unable to believe my eyes. 'He just planted that!'

'Shut up and strip!' he barked. 'Let's see what else you got.'

'You're crazy!'

'STRIP!' he roared, unfastening his holster.

Protesting violently, I undressed until I was stark-naked, except for the money belt around my waist, which contained $2,000.

'Take it off and put it on the table.'

I did as commanded, and stared helplessly as, eyes glinting, he pulled out fifteen $100 bills. 'Right,' he smirked, stuffing them into a grubby envelope, 'these stay. You can go.'

'You can't do this!' I cried disbelievingly.

'Watch me,' he growled. 'Get out, or I'll arrest you for possession.'

Throwing my clothes on, I staggered into the scorching midday sun, where I sat shell-shocked, desperately wondering what to do. After some deliberation, I decided to try to contact the British Embassy in Bogotá. A boy I'd asked to take me to the nearest phone led me to the local church. It was closed for lunch, but after I knocked on the door the padre, a bearded young Italian, invited me inside. He'd been reading a book on liberation theology as he ate a bowl of spaghetti, but he listened sympathetically as I poured out my story. He wasn't surprised; the lieutenant, apparently, was notorious for corruption as well as rumoured to be involved in drug-trafficking and gun-running.

Half an hour later, the padre rose. 'Right, come on,' he ordered. I accompanied him as, warmly greeted by everyone, he threaded his way through backstreets until I found myself outside the police station. When we entered, the lieutenant, even if he rose respectfully, looked less than pleased. It wasn't long until the two men, who clearly detested each other, were arguing furiously. I never discovered exactly what the padre threatened as his Spanish was too fast, although I picked out the words 'denunciar a las autoridades católicas'; all I know is that twenty minutes later, when the lieutenant heard the word 'excomunión' he paled, went to a safe, took out the envelope and pushed it across the table.

'Hijo puta!' he snarled at me. 'Get out!'

Unable to believe my luck, I snatched the envelope and hurried outside, quickly followed by the padre. 'Right,' he whispered urgently, 'I want you to do two things. First, get out of town! Secondly, make a contribution towards, er, those struggling to help Colombia's poor.'

Without hesitating, I pulled out $200. 'I'll never forget this,' I said.

'I'm sure you won't,' he replied, before he was gone.

Incredibly, the daily San Andrés bus was just leaving. I jumped on and fled back to the crossroads at Altamira where I flagged down an Espinal bus that was racing 200 kilometres north. Then, after changing buses again, as a fat mellow moon rose into the sticky darkness, I sank back for the first time, feeling as safe as one can on Colombian highways, on the overnight express to Bogotá.

The name Bogotá, for me, has always been synonymous with exciting futuristic architecture and modernity. But I'd got it wrong; Colombia's capital was in fact my idea of urban hell. After I transferred on arrival to a packed local bus, where I could feel hands fumbling at my bags, I suffocated silently as we headed through shanty towns into smog hanging low over towering skyscrapers. Shortly, a maze of ring roads and flyovers swept us downtown to faceless concrete canyons where vehicles trailed clouds of choking fumes and irate motorists pounded their horns. Overwhelmed, I got off the bus and wandered along refuse-strewn pavements littered with legless beggars, destitute street urchins and sleazy men loitering on graffiti-ridden corners. Eventually I asked passers-by to recommend the nearest cheap hotel.

'Well, it's not safe to go beyond the tenth carrera,' one shouted above the cacophony. 'Try Carlos the Fifth.'

Overlooking a dual carriageway, it was a squalid dump squeezed between a gaping hole and a car park – all that was left of once-stylish colonial terraces. Determined to escape Bogotá as quickly as possible, I immediately set out for the Avianca offices, where I managed to get a ticket for the early-morning Amazon flight. The next chore was the bank, where gum-chewing guards fingering submachine-guns eyed me jumpily as I descended through forbidding steel doors to underground vaults and tellers counting piles of dog-eared notes. Then I retreated to the Museo del Oro, one of the world's key gold collections, where I tucked myself away in top-floor strong rooms, examining some of the 33,000 exquisite pre-Columbian gold pieces – ornamental sticks, crosses and weird Cauca men-birds.

The following morning, after a dawn call by the desk clerk, a taxi whisked me through deserted streets to the airport where I checked in and a smiling stewardess glanced at my ticket as I boarded the plane. Two hours later we taxied to a stop in a deserted airstrip surrounded by crumpled, but oddly familiar-looking, green mountains. It was attractive, but, judging by the lack of tropical forests, it wasn't the Amazon.

'Where do I change for Leticia?' I asked the stewardess, annoyed, as we walked across the tarmac; no one had mentioned having to transfer planes.

She stared at me as if I was deranged. 'In Bogotá, of course,' she replied.

My jaw dropped. 'But we've just come from there!'

We looked at each as mutual comprehension dawned. 'Then you've taken the wrong flight,' she said.

Returning on the same plane, two hours later I was back in Bogotá. I'd covered nearly 2,500 kilometres, flown halfway down Colombia to Pasto, where I'd originally started my journey, and back again, and it wasn't even eleven o'clock. Seeing that there wasn't another Leticia plane for two days, I took a taxi straight back to the Carlos the Fifth, where the desk clerk looked at me, astounded. 'I thought you were leaving for Leticia?' he remarked.

'So did I,' I agreed.

'Didn't you go?'

'In a manner of speaking, yes.'

For an hour, desperate to get out of Bogotá, I toyed with his recommendation of going to Tunja, an attractive colonial town two hours north where Simon Bolivar defeated the Spanish in 1819. But while I was getting food for the bus at a store opposite, an *El Commercio* billboard caught my eye – armed bandits had just ambushed the Tunja bus and shot two passengers.

'Changed your mind?' the desk clerk enquired pleasantly, as I returned to the hotel.

'Yes,' I replied, 'I thought I'd read instead. And no need to disturb me until my plane leaves in two days' time.' I returned to my room, double-bolted the door and went back to bed.

Campesino *(peasant farmer) chewing coca leaves, the northern Andes*

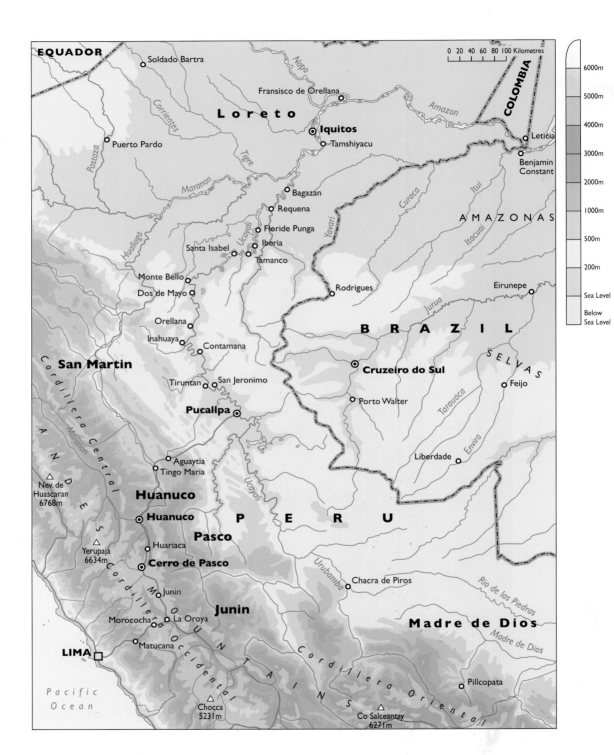

EQUADOR

Soldado Bartra

Fransisco de Orellana

Corrientes

L o r e t o

Napo

Amazon

COLOMBIA

Leticia

Benjamin
Constant

Iquitos

Tamshiyacu

Tigre

Maranon

Puerto Pardo

Pastaza

Bagazán

Requena

Curaca

A M A Z O N A S

Floride Punga

Iberia

Ucayali

Yavari

Itui

Itacuai

Santa Isabel

Tamanco

Huallaga

Monte Bello

Dos de Mayo

Rodrigues

Jurua

Eirunepe

B R A Z I L

Orellana

Inahuaya

Contamana

San Martin

Cordillera Central

Tiruntan

San Jeronimo

S E L V A S

Cruzeiro do Sul

Feijo

Porto Walter

Tarauaca

Pucallpa

Ucayali

Envira

Liberdade

Aguaytia

Tingo Maria

△ Nev. de
Huascaran
6768m

A N D E S

Maranon

Huanuco

P E R U

Huanuco

△ Yerupaja
6634m

Pasco

Huariaca

Cerro de Pasco

Chacra de Piros

Urubamba

Rio de las Piedras

Junin

Junin

Morococha

La Oroya

Madre de Dios

Matucana

C o r d i l l e r a   O c c i d e n t a l

M O U N T A I N S

LIMA □

*Pacific
Ocean*

△ Chocca
5231m

Cordillera Oriental

△ Co Salceantay
6271m

Pillcopata

Madre de Dios

0 20 40 60 80 100 Kilometres

6000m
5000m
4000m
3000m
2000m
1000m
500m
200m
Sea Level
Below
Sea Level

58

PERU: THE AMAZON RIVER

The first day I was in Leticia, a village on the Amazon on the border of Peru and Brazil, I sat dreamily on a quay by the huge river and watched life pass by.

Even although it was 3,000 kilometres from its mouth, the river was two kilometres wide, and dwarfed the river-steamers, barges and freighters lining the banks. Behind corrugated-iron roofs, thick green jungle came down to the muddy water. A long narrow canoe with a thatched canopy glided in and two men unloaded oil drums. An old woman stared idly at a giant tree trunk floating lazily downstream.

I walked over the ramp to the Amazonas bar, which squatted comfortably on stilts above the water. A crowd sat playing cards and drinking beer. A shifty-looking man behind the bar who was chopping papaya with a machete looked up and wiped the blade on a dirty towel.

'What's yours?' he asked. 'Coke, dope or a drink?'

It wasn't the only clue I was in Colombia; the red-, blue-and-yellow striped national flag hung limply from the mast of a paddle-steamer rising and falling gently in the swell. Sweating workmen stripped to the waist and with cloths wrapped round their heads rolled barrels down the gangplank of the boat.

'Fruit juice is fine,' I said.

I stayed until dusk, and the sun settled into clouds stretched like elastic over the flat horizon. An aged steamer, its black hulk silhouetted against the sunset, sidled up to the quay, with a green light on its mast tingeing the tranquil water. A frog belched like a bleary drunk and swallows darted through the village in a hollow in the jungle behind. In the bar, cigarette tips glowed through the darkness and candles flickered, attracting myriads of crazily dancing moths and insects until a generator hummed and a bulb flared in the darkness.

It was still so hot the heat hit you like a punch in the face.

In the end, people drifted home and only a boy was left. He leaned outside and lowered a tin can into the black water before he poured the contents over his glistening body and threw the rest back into the river. It shattered the reflection of moored paddle-steamers into a thousand fragments. A few traces of blue still remained in the sky and I could see the darkened shape of a canoe setting out across the river.

It was night in Leticia.

Not long after I arrived I decided to go to Benjamin Constant, the first settlement over the Brazil border, an hour downriver. The steamer, the *Diez Canseco*, was already tied up at the jetty in Leticia. She was fifty years old and reminiscent of a miniature Mississippi paddle-steamer with verandas, carved balustrades and a tall, pencil-thin funnel. Soon the rust-stained anchor was raised and she slipped out into the calm, muddy water that stretched away like a polished mirror into the distant horizon.

The *Diez Canseco* turned a loop in the river and nosed into midstream, picking her way through thick green floating foliage and rotting tree trunks sailing majestically downstream. The river broadened past Tabinga, a handful of shanties clustered round an iron jetty, and the sun blazed down on the thick awning of the paddle-steamer as she chugged along lazily, passengers dozing fitfully in the heat.

The steamer drew up by a wooden jetty at Benjamin Constant, a jumble of shacks grouped around a church spire. Canoes lined the red clay bank and fronds of banana trees swayed gently in the breeze. Naked children were kicking a football around in the fluid way only Brazilians can until the ball splashed into the river and they hurled themselves screaming into the warm water.

I got off and strolled up the solitary main street. Inside shops painted blue, yellow and pink, shelves were laden with bottles of liquor, tins of meat and condensed milk. Further along in a billiard parlour I could see swarthy, dishevelled men with thick black moustaches. The sound of clinking glasses and the low hum of conversation drifted out the doorway.

I continued past a church until an earthen track disappeared into the jungle. A soldier, green trousers tucked into heavy black boots, a gun strapped to his waist and a cowboy hat pulled low over his face, slouched against a doorway on a porch and watched me idly through narrow eyes.

I wandered back to the billiard parlour and went to the bar.

'Un jugo,' I said. In the Amazon, fruit juices such as *guayaba*, *guava*, *lulo*, *guanbola*, *mora*, *papaya*, *curaba*, *copuazu*, *gan-horia* are an art form, each more exotic than the last.

Later I sat on the prow of the steamer as we fought our way upstream back to Leticia. This time the boat clung closely to the bank where tall, silver-stemmed trees jutted over the jungle. Wispy smoke seeped from thatched villages where dug-outs were moored in the shallows, and women looked up from cooking pots and washing hung out to dry. Sometimes long narrow canoes, blunt paddles dipping into motionless water, glided out through dense reeds until they too were left behind, swaying wildly in the swell.

A parrot with a bright yellow chest, a black beak and an azure blue back sat on the shoulder of the man next to me. It glared at me, let out a loud indignant squawk and closed its eyes. In the wheelhouse, a young boy whittled a piece of wood. The engine puttered contentedly. There was silence and the smell of salty fish. The sun, an orange ball, sank slowly over the jungle roof.

Leticia seemed to be only for those with time on their hands. There was not much to do, although there was always the market on stilts over the river. It was the hangout mainly for crowds of unruly parrots, gangs of feral dogs and swarms of kamikaze flies. The stalls sold piles of stale cakes and oxidized tins of condensed milk, while remains of decomposing apples, unripe oranges and lurid green bananas swilled around under planks in the water below.

The main source of excitement for the locals was the planes. There were three a week: a

Brazilian DC4, its fat belly groaning with supplies and medicines for distant jungle villages as it struggled gamely into the sky, almost clipping the tree-tops; TANS, the Peruvian military jungle flight which accepted passengers for Iquitos, 600 kilometres upriver in Peru; and, by far the most crucial, the red-and-white Avianca jet from Bogotá.

Every Wednesday afternoon, anxious faces scanned the sky prior to a tremendous roar like a pride of lions. Armies of startled parrots would take off from coconut trees by the jetty and a great screaming bird banked low over the lazy river until it landed – just – in a squeal of tyres at the tiny airstrip on the edge of the village. For a while Leticia seemed more like Wall Street than some tin-pot shanty town in the upper Amazon, with people leaping from rocking chairs, hammocks and porches and racing to the *El Espectador* office. The newspapers had arrived.

But the main attractions for me were the elements. The river, for example, was never the same – sometimes smooth and glassy, and sometimes choppy and turbulent when it hurled warm muddy water into the tossing prows of heavily laden canoes. Often the opposite bank was invisible until the sun cleared the banks of dripping mist, and the sheet-like expanse of water could again be seen bearing down in a gigantic loop until it seemed it would sweep you away.

There were also the skies. The heat built up around lunchtime, and the sky was pregnant with fat rainclouds until they evaporated in the afternoon. Then the sky, dotted with puffy men-of-war, became turquoise blue. In the waiting tropical stillness I could see kilometres upriver until the jungle merged with the horizon.

Best of all, though, were the sunsets. Some nights the sun set fire to the sky and streaked it with pink, duck-egg blue, scarlet and orange. Soon it seemed as if the jungle itself was ablaze, with the silver reeds and the bottle-green foliage blending to give an eerie, surreal translucence only quenched by the darkness. The last canoes flitted across the river like fireflies, bats fluttered between river-steamers swaying gently with the swell and parrots swarmed over the jungle.

Most activity centred on the Amazonas bar where the regulars, including the *porte capitán*, lazed around the terrace. The most influential person in Leticia, he always wore a freshly laundered shirt and epaulets dripping with insignia. If you wanted a boat to Manaus, over a thousand kilometres downriver in Brazil, or to Iquitos, or to Puerto Asis in Ecuador, he was, supposedly, your man.

'Si, seguro, mañana,' he would smile, but days would drift past with no boat until it would appear, take three days to unload, and flatly refuse to budge.

'The bomba's gone,' the *capitán* would explain comfortingly. It was always the *bomba* (pump); in fact, either he hadn't the faintest idea about anything or, more likely, he turned a blind eye to what was going on. Hanging round the jetty, which was the only real way to find out about boats, quickly revealed that Leticia was riddled with marijuana, cocaine and gun-smuggling; you wanted it, someone could get it.

There was no point getting upset about the boat situation, but after two weeks even my patience gave out and I decided to try the Peruvian military flight to Iquitos, my next destination.

The next morning I found a canoe crossing to Ramón Castille on the opposite bank. It picked its way through giant floating tufts of grass and decaying tree trunks until it bumped gently against a jetty. In a steaming jungle clearing, a pink flamingo was perched on top of a bungalow on stilts. Someone was banging a metal tin and hammering rang through the stillness.

'LA OFICINA DE COMUNICACIÓNES, SEGUNDO DIVISIÓN, CUARTO ESCUADRÓN LUCHADOR, FUERZAS AÉREAS DE PERU' was a cupboard-sized room behind the lavatory. An orderly with head-phones was yelling excitedly into a radio receiver.

'Hubo un accidente!' he shouted, swivelling round. 'El avión se ha estrellado en las jun-glas!'

Just my luck; the plane had crashed in the jungle.

'Nobody killed, I hope?' I ventured apprehensively.

'Si! Las siete personas han resultado muertas!' Calming down, he shook his head sor-rowfully. 'Mañana . . . . '

That night, as I sat nursing my horror of planes – all seven dead! – over a stiff drink in the Amazonas, heavy thunder hung in the air and the sky was split by dazzling streaks of lightning, illuminating the jungle like thousands of searchlights.

Then, accompanied by violent gusts of wind, it came sheeting down, as if a giant curtain was drawn over the sky. Outsize hailstones hammered on the tin roof as water came pour-ing through holes onto the tables, sending torrents gushing down the gutters to the river. Suddenly the lights went out and there was total blackness until the reflection of the moon burst through heavy clouds and danced merrily on the inky water.

Four days later I had luck at last. A red Fuerzas Aéreas flying boat skimmed low over the river, her floats clipping the glassy water like a high-speed duck as she taxied to the land-ing stage in Ramón Castille.

Along with the six other passengers, I clambered across the wing of the wildly rocking plane. The door swung shut, engines roared and we surged away onto the open river. In next to no time we were airborne, climbing fast until we could see the curve of the earth. Below, the Amazon and dozens of unknown tributaries stretched to the horizon, snaking their way in gigantic loops through unbroken jungle.

Two hours later the plane banked and, carved out of the jungle, I could see a town on a bend in the river. Paved, crumbling streets lined with graceful tiled buildings gave way to a shanty town perched on stilts: Iquitos, 'the pearl of the Amazon'. I was in Peru.

*

I found a room in flaking Tarapaca Hotel on Malecón, the decaying promenade overlooking the riverfront of Iquitos. Nearly 4,000 kilometres up the Amazon, it was lined with run-down mansions, their once-elegant facades decorated with cracked blue-and-white *azulejos*, the handmade tiles specially imported from Portugal by rubber barons who had built up Iquitos, by 1900, into the main trading centre of the Amazon.

After I made myself at home, I wandered downtown, parts of which – except for battered Buicks – also looked like nineteenth-century New Orleans, with pavements lined with stores, billiard parlours and warehouses, and billboards advertising cotton, silk and hardware.

Known as the Amazonian Venice, Belén, the floating shanty town of Iquitos, was perched on stilts in the shallows like a flock of herons. It too seemed stuck in a time warp. Naked children splashed like hippopotamuses in the muddy water, oblivious to floating coconut-husks, banana stems and rotten pineapples. Canoes edged up to the jetty to unload crates of candles, salted fish, sugar cane and mosquito nets before returning to villages on the opposite bank.

But that wasn't the whole picture. Iquitos was founded in 1750 by a Jesuit mission as a base to fend off attacks by marauding indigenous tribes, and as late as 1870 it had only 1,500 inhabitants. With the introduction of the rubber tree, its population of rubber loggers, poor mestizos and enslaved tribesmen exploded and Iquitos boomed with rubber barons vying to build increasingly opulent residences; even Eiffel, of Eiffel Tower fame, designed a building – the Iron House – here.

But the bubble quickly burst. After sending rubber-tree seeds to Malaysia, British entre-preneurs discovered it was cheaper and easier to collect rubber from plantations than from wild trees. By 1914 trade had collapsed and the rubber barons departed, leaving Iquitos and its mansions stranded in the middle of the jungle.

Slow and steady decline began, in spite of the development of logging, agriculture (Brazil nuts, tobacco and *barbasco*, a poisonous vine Indians hunt fish with) and the export of insects and rare animals to Western zoos. In 1960 'black gold' – oil – was discovered; now Iquitos has the second biggest airport in Peru and is, apart from Manaus, 2,000 kilometres downriver, the biggest port on the Amazon.

One afternoon I got talking to the Tarapaca's owner, Señor Morez, who was sitting in a wicker chair on the balcony overlooking the river, reading an article. He was a dignified, kindly man with silver hair, glasses and a perpetual glint in his eye.

I glanced at the title, *The Pulmonary Consequences of Chronic Cardiac Thrombosis*.

'Got a problem, have you?' I asked.

'No, no,' he replied, astounded. 'I'm a doctor. Have been for thirty years. The hotel's just a hobby.'

I thought nothing about it until the next evening, when I saw a dented Ford parked outside the hotel. Painted on the sides were the words: 'SECOND-HAND SEWING MACHINES – SEÑOR J. MOREZ, TEL. 114730'.

I was standing on the veranda mulling this over, when Señor Morez himself sauntered up, bottle in hand. 'Drink?' he asked.

'Don't mind if I do,' I replied. It was excellent, tasting of some sweet exotic fruit with a dash of rum. I looked at the label. 'Chichifanga, produced, bottled and distributed by Señor J. Morez, Iquitos', it said.

'Señor Morez!' I exclaimed.

He pre-empted me. 'Just a medicinal drink I invented,' he went on modestly. 'It's good for the heart and lungs.' He tittered. 'It's also an aphrodisiac.'

But the biggest surprise was yet to come.

I was enjoying a lukewarm drink that Doña, the Tarapaca's alluring – and flirtatious – thirty-year-old receptionist had fetched from a rusty fridge, when the subject of Señor Morez came up.

'How on earth does he do it?' I asked incredulously.

'Do what?' she replied, closing the creaky door.

'Get time to do all these things?'

She glanced at me coquettishly. 'Oh, Julio's got lots of energy for a man his age!' she exclaimed, fluttering her eyelashes. 'He's invented this well-known drink. It's done wonders for our relationship, if nothing else. You should try it sometime!'

I put Señor Morez out of my mind as I sat on steps overlooking the market behind Belén, planning my trip to the jungle to investigate the Yagua, a tribe famed for their metre-long blowpipes and red-painted faces. It wasn't easy to concentrate. Below, gossiping women in stalls were selling dried frogs, armadillo shells and piranha teeth. A skeletal dog carrying a bloody fish-bone growled at black vultures with ugly yellow beaks, mean eyes and huge talons, as they swooped from a tin roof to tear at piles of putrid garbage.

The trip into the jungle wasn't to be, though. While investigating Morono-Cocha, the jetty for river-steamers, I found the *Andresito* leaving for Santa Isabel, three days upriver and halfway to Pucallpa, my next destination. I didn't delay; in the Amazon people wait weeks for boats and can't be choosy.

I'll always remember the first evening on board as Iquitos receded. It was sunset and the jungle was a burning maelstrom of orange and yellow while the last rays of the sun splattered the river with sparkling light. Soon the full moon came out and climbed high above the stern, turning clouds into blankets of gleaming silver. A fish broke the metal water and dived again, leaving rippling rings to break the jungle's reflection dancing on the river.

Daybreak found the *Andresito* skating over the river with the jungle that lined the banks reflected in the water like a mirage. Languid leaves hung motionless over walls of bamboo sprouting through undergrowth, and giant reeds splayed over the water's edge. Nothing moved except the *Andresito* and shadows of the sky and jungle reflected in her wake. Save for the echo of chattering parrots, there was silence.

I spent the next three days swinging in the hammock I'd bought in Iquitos. It was covered with mud and stank of stale fish. At sunset I would shift to sit on an orange box at the prow, where I'd gaze, mesmerized, at the apparently limitless expanse of sky and water as the late-afternoon sun sank low under the jungle's roof and bathed the white bark of trees in amber light.

Then it was dark, and the boat's penetrating lights searched the river for floating tree trunks and dangerous bends. Torrents of stars seemed to pour from the pitch-black galaxy into the jungle, while deep in the trees, lamps flickered and mysterious, shadowy figures flitted in the night.

My reverie was broken only when the boat stopped at villages which were just thatched huts, tin shacks and a church clustered round a jetty. We would tie up, and the boat would rapidly empty as the passengers poured into waiting crowds of eager people selling parrots, monkeys and crocodile skins. Yet within minutes the upper deck would again be heaving with clamouring bodies, colourful hammocks and cooking-oil tins.

Sometimes, though, the water was too shallow to berth, so canoes would glide out from reeds to the waiting boat, where they would fill up with boxes of dried milk and manioc sacks. Then they'd return to the bank where, accompanied by barking dogs and gaggles of pot-bellied children, people triumphantly carried off their spoils like war trophies into the jungle.

It was only the boat's food, or lack of it, which brought me back to earth. Twice a day shouts from the kitchen, a black hole in the stern, precipitated a stampede to the table above the shuddering engine, where *quaki* (boiled river water with a stray floating banana) was lovingly served. At first I was too slow to get any, but after I did manage to taste it I couldn't face eating it. Instead, I stayed in my hammock, suspended from the roof like a giant cocoon, and subsisted on a precious store of unripe oranges and green bananas I had managed to buy ashore.

Three days later we pulled into Santa Isabel.

It was night as I walked up a track lit by a row of dim light bulbs to a grassy glade surrounded by huts on stilts, where squatting families were eating. I found a stifling room in a tiny *pensión*, the only two-storey hut in the village, and when the flickering candle gave out I took off my stinking clothes and tottered onto a smelly mattress on the floor. As there was no mosquito net, I pulled a soiled sheet over my head, but it was useless; that night, as rain hammered down on the tin roof, I tossed and turned, scratched my bites and tried to ignore the scuttling cockroaches, unexplained rustlings and small, unknown things crawling in my hair.

The next morning, peering blearily outside, I could see a little river-steamer tied up at the deserted jetty. I ran down the bank. The boat had an orange hull, a white top-deck and, hanging next to three cabins and hammocks, a notice saying 'SANTA ISABEL–PUCALLPA. HOY. ACCEPTA

The riverboat Ariadna Quinta, *Río Ucayali, Peru*

CARGA E PASAJEROS'. I couldn't believe my luck, as the thought of another night being eaten alive was unbearable, and hours later I sailed out of Santa Isabel on *Ariadna Quinta*.

Gaunt, unkempt and dripping with sweat, I lay in my hammock for the next three days as we chugged upstream. I couldn't remember when I'd last combed my matted hair, my clothes lay in a damp heap on the deck, and my body was covered with festering bites. But I didn't care; at least I'd escaped Santa Isabel.

The river, which by now was the Río Ucayali, the longest tributary of the Amazon, was always changing. Sometimes, engine purring and creamy brown water swishing by the prow as she powered her way upstream, *Ariadna Quinta* clung so close to the riverbank she'd brush overhanging creepers and vines; sometimes, when she came to a bend, she skimmed like a gnat to the opposite bank; sometimes, alarmingly, she took a short cut through channels in reeds, and it seemed she'd be swallowed by water lilies until she'd burst victorious onto the open river.

It was still a huge, lazily floating body of muddy brown water, although the glassy surface often boiled where currents burst to the surface, sending green water lilies dancing round eddying whirlpools. Only the wildlife was disappointing – just continuously screeching parrots and monkeys – although, once, the boat disturbed a flock of pink birds wading on tall spindly legs in the shallows and they took off, fluttering through the air like shredded paper, towards mushroom clouds billowing over the flat horizon.

This time there were few passengers apart from the boat's *capitán*, a swarthy man with gleaming gold teeth and a silver medallion dangling over his hairy chest, who stood at the wheel singing contentedly like some Italian opera singer: his cheerful wife, a stout woman with gigantic white thighs who, when she wasn't cooking, was always darning shirts; and his son, a grinning deaf mute, whose lips were often pursed as if trying to whistle.

Three days later *Ariadna Quinta* slipped into Pucallpa, a bustling frontier town on the edge of the Amazon, at the end of the road from Lima. Navigable by 3,000-ton vessels, the port was lined with hardware stores selling machetes and snake-bite vaccines. Old buses trailing clouds of choking dust picked their way through gaping holes in the red earthen road.

But it wasn't a place to linger, as Maoist revolutionaries Sendero Luminoso (Shining Path) had controlled it after killing the mayor in a shoot-out with the police, so, almost immediately, I took a canoe downriver to the village of San Francisco to visit the Shipibo, a matriarchal tribe noted for pottery and weaving.

The women were very colourful, with tight-fitting orange-, red-and-yellow blouses, black skirts, brightly coloured beads and hand-woven wristbands, while the men, who were small and bow-legged, with flat, oval faces and jet-black fringes, were naked apart from brown loincloths.

Then I rested up at nearby Yarinacocha. Formerly part of the Ucayali, now it was a landlocked, freshwater oxbow lake renowned for exotic wildlife: dolphins, *perezosos* (a kind of sloth), long-toed tropical wading birds, and green Amazonian kingfishers.

Cerro de Pasco, Peru

Soon it was time to face the bus to Lima. The road passed through Tingo María, one of Peru's main drug-running centres, which was also in Sendero hands. But, providing you survived, it led in only two days from the Amazon to Cerro de Pasco, one of the highest towns in the world at 4,380 metres, and then down to an astonishing desert running along the Pacific until it reached Lima. That sounded a lot more interesting than travelling there by plane.

CUBA

Los Aquáticos

At first, when I travelled to Valle de Viñales, 212 kilometres west of Havana in the spectacular Sierra de Los Órganos, I felt decidedly uncomfortable.

As soon as we left the capital, our luxury Viazul bus arrived on the country's sole *autopista*. It was in excellent condition and there were three lanes in both directions. But, apart from our bus, there was no traffic. Instead, crowds of people sat patiently under flyovers daubed with revolutionary slogans. Sheltering from the midday heat, they were waiting for a lift in the occasional overloaded truck; because of severe petrol shortages caused by the US blockade, there were hardly any buses, far less cars. After the extraordinarily dilapidated streets of Havana, it was another shocking reminder of the island's desperate economic plight.

As our modern, air-conditioned express, which was full of foreign backpackers, raced past at 100 kilometres per hour, I guiltily averted my eyes from the stranded crowds; everyone could travel on Viazul but tickets had to be paid in US dollars, which few Cubans had access to. Instead, I tried to concentrate on the flat countryside, where there were endless sugar-cane fields and hardly any villages or towns.

Three hours later I saw the first signs of the 175-kilometre-long Cordillera de Guaniguanico. Soon we pulled into the attractive town of Pinar del Río for a brief stop. There was only one old bus in the shabby station, where waiting crowds milled behind segregated fences and rusty grills. They gazed longingly at the well-dressed young backpackers trooping off the bus until we set off again. The empty road twisted up into rolling countryside increasingly studded with *mogotes* (small, sugar-loaf limestone mountains). These were very dramatic and, with their sub-tropical vegetation, reminded me of Guilin in southern China.

Soon, five hours after leaving Havana, the bus arrived in Viñales. It was minuscule, with a population of only 4,000, but it was very pretty. The main street was lined with pine trees and pink or blue houses, where people on verandas sat in rocking chairs. Jangling horse carts and antiquated Chevrolets drifted past on their way to the main square, which was overlooked by a graceful, Spanish-looking church and old, honey-coloured colonial buildings. Noisy birds chattered in the dried-up fountain. Under flaking colonnades, gossiping old men with straw hats smoked cigars, and muscular men with black moustaches flirted with sensuous young women.

I walked up earthen backstreets to a row of wooden bungalows looking north to the *gorgotes*. They were *casas particulares,* i.e. private houses. Since 1993, when it became legal for Cubans to have dollars, their owners have been licensed to accept paying foreign guests. The *casas* are much better value than the poor quality state-owned hotels, and are an excellent way to meet Cuban families. But, at $15-20 a night, they aren't cheap – little in Cuba is. Running one is also a gamble for the owners, who have to pay a $150 monthly licensing fee whether they have guests or not.

The next day I hired a bicycle, as Viñales was reputedly great cycling territory. Five kilometres north was Cueva de San Miguel, the first of the region's famous karst caves. At the entrance to a vast cavern, which was dwarfed by overhanging rock, there was a disco bar. There I asked the barman to guard my bike, before I entered one of the electrically lit passageways into the cave. It plunged deep into the mountainside and came out at a restaurant on the other side. It was rather uninspiring, so I retraced my steps to the disco bar, picked up my bike and started cycling up the road.

I'd hardly gone fifty metres before the pedal arm fell off. Within seconds, two apparently helpful boys suddenly materialized out of thin air and offered to assist me. When I accepted, they led me to an old Dodge that, luckily, was parked nearby. The boot was crammed with oily tools, and five minutes later the bike, seemingly, was fixed.

I was very grateful to them, so I gave them a generous tip. As soon as they pocketed it, they vanished as quickly as they had appeared. I had only gone a kilometre before the pedal arm fell off again. When I examined it, I saw that a crucial bolt was missing. It was only then I realized that, of course, I had been set up and that they had deliberately sabotaged the bike. Musing that Cuban ingenuity extended far beyond the famous capacity to patch up anything mechanical – there were hardly any spare parts owing to the US blockade – I pushed the bike five kilometres to Cueva del Indio, the next cave.

Previously inhabited by Indians, it was only discovered by Cubans in 1920. Now, advertisements told me, boats plied 400 metres along an underground river until it emerged near a waterfall. To my disappointment, the cave was a tourist trap awash with souvenir vendors, serenading musicians and guides telling you to imagine that the stalactites were snakes. Deciding to give it a miss, I pushed the bike, cursing and swearing, the ten kilometres back to Viñales.

That night my *casa particular* offered to cook for me. I accepted without hesitation, of course, as the food the *casas* offer was far better than in the dire, state-run restaurants, and in Cuba finding food elsewhere could often be a problem. Sure enough, soon a feast of rice, cabbage, tomatoes, cucumber, chicken, pineapple, banana, grapefruit and orange slices awaited me on the dining-room table.

Afterwards, in the simple but comfortable lounge, Maria, the owner, switched on the television. On it, Fidel Castro, who faced four journalists at a studio table, was giving one of his celebrated discourses. At first I was thrilled to see the legendary *Líder* speaking in his own country, though I learned later that it was difficult to avoid him as once a week all programmes on one of the country's two channels are cancelled to enable him to talk for as long as he likes. His record is seven hours.

This time he was exhorting everyone on the need to eradicate mosquitoes, not because of malaria, which was eradicated in 1968, but because they cause dengue fever. With hardly any notes, he reeled off interminable statistics; he was rightly proud of Cuba's medical facilities, which are easily the best in Latin America. But I quickly found the obsequious nodding of the silent journalists – who were supposed to be interviewing him – irritating. Soon Fernando, Maria's husband, sat down. He was a slight, middle-aged man whose job was to co-ordinate local tobacco farmers. He was a committed Communist, and he also belonged to the Committee for the Defence of the Revolution, one of which is on every street corner.

'Doesn't anyone ever interrupt Castro?' I asked.

'Oh no!' he exclaimed. 'There's no need. They used to in the old days, but he just made mincemeat of them.' Like him or loathe him, Castro was an astonishingly well informed, highly articulate and intelligent man who was held in genuinely high regard, especially by the generation of Cubans who grew up with him. The young, however, I found to be different: like their counterparts the world over, they were impatient for more freedom, especially the ability to travel abroad, and tired of the lack of consumer goods. In fact, I found that trying to reach a balanced opinion about Castro and *la revolución* was one of the most interesting aspects of visiting Cuba.

Casas particulares also organize horses and guides to investigate the nearby *Aquáticos*, an unusual mountain community who worship water. They lived in the mountains, three hours away by horse, so I set off early one morning, accompanied by a guide called Pablo, before it was too hot. Our two horses meandered up red-dirt trails that led out of Viñales into a narrow valley. Everywhere *mogotes* terminated in vertical red cliffs, and tall green tobacco plantations were dotted with thatched kilns. Occasionally there were fields where straw-hatted *vaqueros* (Cuban cowboys) plodded behind wooden ploughs drawn by lumbering oxen. Overhead, ubiquitous hawks circled endlessly. Once, we turned off to a shack where a friend of Pablo's downed the machete he was using to cut sugar cane before he made us steaming cups of coffee.

At last, after the horses gingerly picked their way up steep rocky paths, Pablo dismounted 500 metres up the mountainside. 'This is it,' he said, as he tethered the horses to shady trees.

'But where are the *Aquáticos*?' I asked, stiff and saddle-sore; I had been expecting to see a village, at the very least.

'Why, all around!' Pablo exclaimed, gesticulating vaguely. 'This is just one of their houses.' I followed him up to a green, one-storey bungalow on a ledge overlooking the valley. On the veranda, the owner, a thin shrivelled woman wearing dirty grey clothes, emerged to greet us. Her name was Margarita and she was only seventy, although, with her long grey pigtail, thick varicose veins and sad smile, she looked much older. As we sat down, all I could hear was the creaking of our rocking chairs and the ticking of a grandfather clock coming from inside the bungalow.

She was obviously rather shy, so, after I told her how much I admired the panoramic view over the valley, I asked if I could have a quick look round the house, and left her and Pablo to have a chat. Inside, the rooms were divided by blue partitions to allow air to circulate. On walls in the corridor there were photographs showing a family clustered round a drained, middle-aged woman. She had her dark hair parted in the middle and wore a thin dress. A gurgling baby sat on her knee.

After I returned to the veranda I asked Margarita if the photographs were of her family.

'Oh no, that's Antoñica Izquierdo!' she exclaimed enthusiastically in Spanish, referring to the woman who founded the *Aquáticos* in 1943. Soon Margarita, who was one of the oldest surviving members of the community, was explaining more.

'Antoñica was very poor, like all the *campesinos*,' she said. 'She was married to a local peasant and had seven children. One day, one of her daughters fell ill with meningitis. She had no money to pay for medical assistance or medicines, so, in her despair, she carried the child into the front yard and lifted her to the sky, begging God to help her. There she heard a voice saying that if she bathed her daughter three times in pure, flowing water the child would be saved. So she started bathing her in the local water, which comes directly from the mountain behind and is exceptionally pure. To her amazement, the little girl was healed. Shortly afterwards, others started doing the same with members of their family who were also suffering ailments, and the same thing happened again. So people, realising the local water had spiritual power, became *Aquáticos*. Now there are only twelve families left, but we still bathe ourselves three times a day.'

'And do you all enjoy better than average health?' I asked.

'Of course! The oldest *Aquático* is ninety-two!'

'What happened to Antoñica?'

Margarita smiled sadly. 'Unfortunately she came to the attention of the authorities and doctors, who thought she was insane. They forced her to take medicines, and she died in a psychiatric hospital in Havana at the end of the Second World War. But her memory lives on and she has become famous. They've even made films and written books about her.'

All too quickly it was time to leave, and soon our horses were carefully wending their way back down the precipitous rocky path to the baking valley floor. When we were nearly there, Pablo turned round and looked at the diminutive figure standing motionless on the veranda far above. Then our horses clattered round huge boulders and Margarita was gone.

Santería

Dusk is the best time to arrive in Trinidad, 400 kilometres east of Viñales. One of the world's best-preserved Spanish colonial towns and a UNESCO World Heritage Site, it consists of a labyrinth of narrow cobbled streets climbing a hill to the Plaza Mayor. There a beautiful baroque church overlooks ornamental gardens full of graceful palms and marble statues. On the other three sides are orange houses with blue wooden verandas covered with bougainvillea. Inside the ornamental gardens, whose entrance is flanked by stone greyhounds, girls play with dolls and boys chase each other.

For a while I sat there, watching the shadows gradually lengthen and flocks of swallows screech low overhead while the sinking sun turned the church walls roseate. At last, as elegant, old-fashioned lamps came on, the plaza emptied and, reluctantly, I had to find a bed for the night.

Helpful boys offered to show me to a *casa particular*, so I followed them as they meandered through side streets lined with houses where women sat in rocking chairs in run-down, once-gracious rooms, working at embroidery. Behind the Plaza a yellow bell tower dominated a miniature square. The boys knocked at the door of a nearby house, which was opened by a friendly, stunningly attractive woman. Inside, she led me across a patio dominated by an orange tree to a cosy room. From the bed, which filled the doorframe, only the faded bell tower could be seen rearing up into the starlit sky.

The next morning I awakened to the sound of cocks crowing and horses' hooves ringing on cobblestones. By the time I'd finished my breakfast in the patio, old men were sitting on benches outside, idly smoking cigars. In a corner, schoolchildren wearing white blouses and red revolutionary neckties clustered like bees round their teacher, sketching the bell tower. A lonely-looking fat boy, his right hand encased in an enormous baseball glove, was throwing a ball against the wall of one of the houses. It had barn-like doors and huge windows covered with black wrought-iron grilles. By 10 a.m. it was so hot that only gossiping, black-skinned women remained under shady trees alive with birdsong.

Puzzled why Che Guevara T-shirts were hanging for sale on the massive oak doors of the bell tower, which looked like a church, I decided to have a look. The former eighteenth century convent of San Francisco de Asís was in fact the Museo Nacional de la Lucha Contra Bandidos (National Struggle against Bandits). Off palm-filled courtyards were rooms containing maps, weapons and the remains of a US U-2 spy plane that had been shot down over Cuba. They also had dozens of glass cases with sad photographs of bearded, black-bereted local volunteers who died fighting counter-revolutionary bands that operated in the nearby Sierra del Escambray in the 1960s.

Near the entrance, steep stairs climbed past signs saying 'Don't play the bells!' to the top of the bell tower. Below, Trinidad was a sea of orange-tiled roofs and compact courtyards interspersed with palm trees. To the west, sun-dappled forested mountains soared into the cloudless blue sky while, to the south, tree-lined plains stretched away to the flat, curving Ancon Peninsula and the shimmering Caribbean.

The town, which seemed to be frozen in time since the 1700s, had countless other museums. Perhaps the best of these magnificent old converted mansions was the neoclassical Museo Romántico on the Plaza Mayor. Once owned by Dr Justo Cantero, a German who acquired vast sugar estates by poisoning an old slave trader and marrying his widow, it contained outstanding collections of Regency furniture and porcelain. Down the hill, the Museo Histórico Municipal had spacious courtyards and tasteful rooms with immense mirrors, chandeliers and charts showing the history of slavery.

But far more interesting than the town's architecture or museums was the Casa Templo de Yamayá, the centre in Trinidad of *santería*, Cuba's fascinating animist religion. Brought by slaves from West Africa between the sixteenth and nineteenth centuries, *santería*'s worship of ancestral spirits and Yoruban *orishas* (deities) was hidden behind a Catholic veneer. Since the slaves were prohibited from practicing their native religions, they secretly superimposed Catholic saints on the *orishas*. Thus it looked like they were praying to a saint or to the Virgin Mary, though they were also invoking one of their *orishas*.

However, Fidel Castro has openly encouraged Afro-Cuban culture as an important part of the island's identity, and now *santería* is more popular than ever. It has also has been instrumental in slave liberation movements, and has greatly influenced music such as salsa and Latin hip-hop, as well as Latin American literature.

I was drifting along backstreets, looking for the Casa Templo, when, under a cavernous archway, I spotted people with curious white hats sitting on benches. One of them glanced up. 'Come in, come in!' he shouted in Spanish, beckoning. They were all chatting away, oblivious to a sheep's innards being cleaned on adjacent tables. In an earthen yard beyond, a lamb was tethered to coops packed with hens, while a lifesize black Madonna in blue robes stood in a corner vault. She was Yamayá, the goddess of the ocean and mother of all *orishas*. Suddenly I realized that this was the Casa Templo that I had been looking for all along.

Over cups of scalding black coffee, the chubby man told me that *santería* protects believers from sickness and brings good luck. But he became very animated when I asked if, with its ritualistic animal sacrifices, *santería* is similar to voodoo. 'Not at all!' he cried indignantly. 'They drink blood, we don't!' He pointed to a room behind dirty, bloodstained sheets, from where there came the sound of singing. 'Go in and see for yourself.'

Inside, swaying people surrounded a young man dressed in white. He was a *santero* (a *santería* priest) and his cheeks were daubed with blood. On the ground, pots overflowed with feathers and mangled remains. Without warning a man carried in a squawking cockerel. Before I knew it, the *santero* decapitated it with a knife and let its blood pour into one of the pots before he anointed everyone's foreheads with its still-jerking neck. Horrified, I waited until the *santero* went to fetch the lamb. Then, unable to watch it being castrated before its throat was slit, I fled.

The next morning I hired a moped and rode out to Valle de los Ingenios, which, like Trinidad, is also a World Heritage Site. Situated only eight kilometres to the east and overlooked by the Sierra de Escambray's jagged ridges, this peaceful valley was a patchwork of lime-green fields dotted with palm trees, grazing cattle and the ruins of small, nineteenth-century sugar mills (*ingenios*). Most were destroyed in the wars of independence, before the focus of sugar-growing moved westward to Matanzas.

Nevertheless sugar was still cultivated here and antiquated trucks laden with *campesinos* puttered up red tracks before being swallowed by tall plantations. Some haciendas were still standing, such as Manaca Iznaga, whose 43-metre-high tower was used to keep an eye on the cane-cutters. From the top there was a magnificent view of the valley which features on practically every Cuban postcard.

After I left the Valle de los Ingenios, I drove across to the other side of Trinidad, where a deserted country road wound twenty kilometres north-west past Pico de Potrerillo (931 m.), the highest peak in the Escambray Mountains, before reaching the 'health-resort' of Topes de Collantes. It was an eerie experience. Without warning, in the middle of sub-tropical forests, a vast, decaying, concrete monstrosity loomed.

It was the Kurhotel, a Ceauşescu-era fantasy built by dictator Batista in 1937. Originally a tuberculosis sanatorium, it was later used to house militias fighting counter-revolutionaries. In the 1990s it was converted into a hotel spa, and now endless corridors led to locked doors behind which a range of different 'treatments' were supposedly offered. In the dining room, guests, who were mainly vacationing army, trade union and government officials, looked up at me curiously from dirty tables heaped with half-finished plates of mince, rice and potatoes. Outside, past the cracked, drained swimming pool, trails led through coniferous forest to atmospheric caves and cascades.

That evening, back in Trinidad, I went to meet Elio Vilva, whose surreal, sexually charged *santería* paintings, some of which I had come across in the Museo Romántico, have made him one of Cuba's most famous artists. Fascinated by the fierce-looking *orishas* surrounded by fish, serpents, crocodiles, turtles, eyes, phalluses and astrological signs, I had tracked down the locally born artist to a shabby house in broken-down backstreets, where he'd invited me for dinner.

In his early fifties, he was a thin, lean man with a black moustache. Before he became a full-time painter, he had been a schoolteacher and then provincial director of culture. Despite having had exhibitions in New York, Los Angeles, Belgium and Italy, he was, like most Cubans, obviously very poor. Over a meal prepared by his young wife, he explained how he became interested in *santería*.

'I had a Catholic upbringing, and used to dream a lot,' he said. 'They were both major influences, even though for a while I painted only Che Guevara. For many, of course, he was a saint. Then, in 1981, I received Eleggúa, the *orisha* of destiny, into my life, and I started painting *orishas* instead. Actually it wasn't such a big transition, as they're really *santería*'s equivalent of saints. They originate from sorcerers who had magical powers and understood the secrets of plants, the power of animals, the influence of the planets and the spirit of ancestors on people. Human beings can't experience *orishas* unless they're possessed, but this is in a familiar, friendly way, and the *orishas*, although they are deities, are more like relatives or family friends.'

He had a drink of rum. 'Of course, Trinidad played an important role in my fascination with *santería*,' he continued. 'It was an important settlement of black African slaves, especially in the Valle de los Ingenios. For me, it's full of forests, rivers and mountains on the one hand, and whips, sweat and the blood of slaves on the other. In my paintings, with a bit of imagination, one can hear the sound of the drum, the groan in the sugar-cane fields and the cry of freedom.'

I was tucking into delicious chicken when the sound of high-pitched squawking came from the backyard. Reminded of the bloody, twitching neck of the cockerel I had seen being sacrificed at the Casa Templo de Yamayá, suddenly I was repelled by the thought of what was on my fork. Looking in the direction of where the sound was coming from, I asked him nervously, 'That's not another chicken being sacrificed, is it?'

'Oh no!' he replied reassuringly, 'it's just the old woman next-door cackling.'

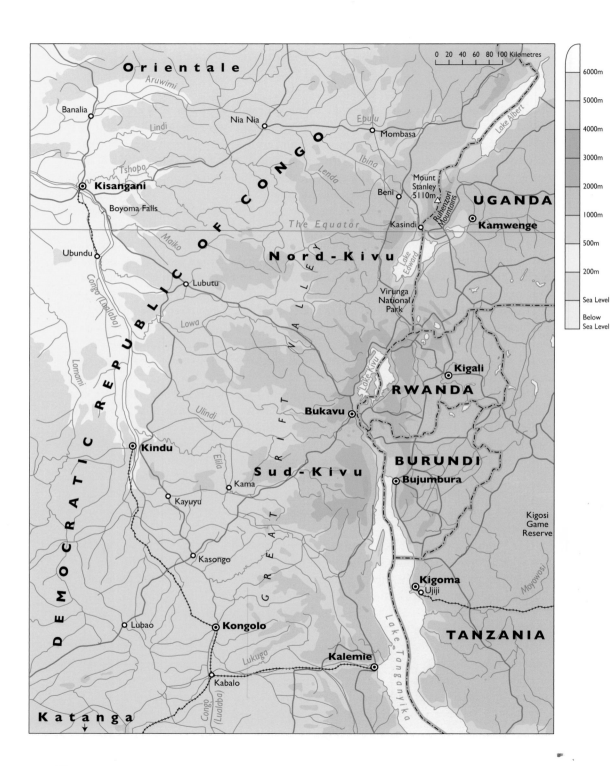

Orientale

Banalia

Aruwimi

Lindi

Nia Nia

Epulu

Mombasa

Tshopo

Lenda

Ibina

Beni

Mount Stanley 5110m

Ruhenzori Mountains

UGANDA

Lake Albert

Kisangani

Boyoma Falls

The Equator

Kasindi

Kamwenge

Maiko

Ubundu

Congo (Lualaba)

Lubutu

Nord-Kivu

Lake Edward

Lowa

Virunga National Park

Lomami

Ulindi

GREAT RIFT VALLEY

Lake Kivu

Kigali

RWANDA

Bukavu

Kindu

Elila

Kama

Sud-Kivu

BURUNDI

Kayuyu

Bujumbura

Kigosi Game Reserve

Kasongo

Kigoma

Ujiji

Moyowosi

Lubao

Kongolo

TANZANIA

Kalemie

Lake Tanganyika

Kabalo

Lukuga

Katanga

Congo (Lualaba)

6000m
5000m
4000m
3000m
2000m
1000m
500m
200m
Sea Level
Below Sea Level

76

CHAPTER TWO

Africa

'Then it was like a slow-motion dream . . . I don't remember almost being swept off the train's roof . . .'

ZAÏRE (DEMOCRATIC REPUBLIC OF THE CONGO): THE CONGO RIVER

Even before recent tragic events, when the eastern part of the country became a battle-ground between warring Hutu and Tutsi tribes spilling over from Rwanda, Zaïre, now the Democratic Republic of the Congo, was nightmarish.

I hadn't paid much attention – although I should have – to stricken lorries which had been overturned by yawning craters in the dusty red track; I was still shaking from the shock of the khaki-clad soldiers brandishing Kalashnikovs, who had exploded out of mud huts in the deserted no-man's-land between Uganda and Zaïre. They had drunkenly yelled about passports and the 'rezzolution', so I had apologized, and hurried on towards the frontier's rusty roofs. Now, minutes later, I was in Zaïre talking to truck drivers transporting coffee from Kisangani to Mombasa. They had been waiting two weeks for documents and for armed guards to escort them through Uganda. 'Not healthy place here, bwana,' one

The drunken soldiers, Uganda–Zaïre (Democratic Republic of Congo) border, Central Africa

volunteered. 'Last week patrol cross at night, shoot peoples. Better move on.'

I was delighted to oblige. My journey had originated in Rwanda and Burundi, countries with terrible histories of tribal genocide, and I was still nervous after travelling through Uganda – now relatively stable, unlike during my previous trip there when my looted Kampala hotel room had reverberated nightly to gunfire as truckloads of teenage soldiers careered through eerily deserted streets.

Zaïre too has had an uncomfortable history. The country was dominated in the thirteenth century by the Kongo empire, which extended over vast territories, each headed by chiefs responsible for collecting taxes in goods, cloth or slaves (primarily criminals and prisoners of war). But the Portuguese, who arrived in 1482, began sending out their own raiding parties – in the sixteenth century alone they shipped out 60,000 slaves – and by the eighteenth century the Kongo empire had been replaced by the Luba and Landa kingdoms to the south, with fine towns full of palm trees and decorated houses. In the mid nineteenth century, slave-trading Arabs from Zanzibar invaded eastern Zaïre, bringing with them all the luxuries of European life: beds, furniture, candles, silver, glass goblets, silk and satin.

Other European powers remained uninterested until Stanley's historic voyage down the Congo in 1874 when, despite losing half his men through smallpox, starvation, crocodiles and battles with local tribes, he proved there were over 1,700 kilometres of navigable waters below the lower Congo's rapids. However, Belgium's King Leopold didn't delay, and in 1884 the Berlin Conference awarded him the Congo Free State, in reality merely a franchise for the exploitation of land and mineral rights. This demanded tremendous quantities of labour, which resulted in even more barbarous slavery. Tribesmen who didn't fulfil rubber quotas were maimed, and baskets of their smoke-cured hands were presented for inspection to their bosses, inspiring Kurtz, Conrad's central figure in his novel *Heart of Darkness*, to exclaim 'The horror! The horror!'

The hideous atrocities ceased after they were discovered by disgusted Europeans, but the exploitation continued as Belgium, playing tribes off against each other, did nothing to develop the Congo. Political parties weren't allowed to exist until 1955 and at independence, after Patrice Lumumba, who was standing for all-Congolese unity, was overthrown and murdered by the army for his increasing allegiance towards the Soviet Union during the Cold War, the Belgian Congo had only six African university graduates.

But as keen as I was to escape the Uganda–Zaïre border, it wasn't easy. With no public transport in eastern Zaïre, only a few trucks set out through the rainforest to faraway Kisangani on the Congo River, in the heart of Stanley's 'Dark Continent'. Inevitably there were battles to board the vehicles at dawn, when they left before the heat became too strong. Nevertheless, I had learned to be patient in Central Africa, and two days later I set off on a lorry that was heading north. The 900-kilometre journey took four days in the dry season and four weeks in the wet, when torrential rains turned tracks into quagmires and lorries had to be towed out of the mud; my visit was during the dry season, supposedly, but I'd rarely seen such rainstorms.

I was so relieved to see the frontier recede that I barely noticed when, only an hour into our journey, we broke down crossing a precarious timber bridge. Instead, I relaxed, looked down through gaping planks at muddy water lazily winding through primeval jungle, and listened. The track ran through Virunga National Park, which was among Africa's greatest game reserves and was home to one of the world's largest concentrations of mountain gorillas. Still, although I imagined hearing hippos yawning in the shallows, I didn't expect to see much – poachers had wiped out most big game and what was left had retreated deep into the virgin forest. In fact, all I could hear was devastating silence broken by occasional birdcalls.

It was midday, with the heat steadily building, before we were ready to set off again. By nightfall we'd covered the 100 kilometres to Beni, a fly-blown village of thatched huts with two main streets lit by the first – and outside Kisangani practically the last – light bulb I saw in Zaïre.

Early the next morning, as mist slowly cleared from roofs, I looked east to the snowcapped active volcanoes of the Ruhenzori range (nicknamed 'Mountains of the Moon' by Greek geographer Ptolemy, who mistakenly thought they were the Nile's source) and, below, over unbroken jungle stretching 2,000 kilometres to Africa's west coast.

At sunrise I found a truck that descended steeply all day into dripping jungle. Giant fronds clipped me as we drove, and blotted out the pregnant rain clouds. I was hoping rain would provide relief from the intense humidity but none came. I suffered silently until midnight, when we pulled into another moonlit village. I found a muggy room for lorry drivers and gulped down the inevitable rice and beans from a roadside stall before I collapsed onto a moth-eaten mattress, too weary to sleep. In any case, it was only three hours until I had to find the next lift and I was looking forward to travelling through the Bambuti (pygmy) heartland, which occupies sizeable parts of eastern Zaïre.

The hold of the solitary truck I found at sunrise in the marketplace was bulging with cattle, so I wedged myself between petrol drums above the cabin's wooden alcove and soon I was clinging on desperately as we plunged into craters on the track. It wasn't, therefore, until several hours – and only thirty kilometres – later, when the driver stopped and strolled up to semi-naked people in perfect proportion to thatched huts, that I realized we were among the Bambuti.

After we set off again the muddy track deteriorated even further and the hold swayed alarmingly as the bellowing cargo was thrown from side to side. When the flimsy timber superstructure began swaying 45 degrees until reluctantly righting itself, it dawned on me that the corroded bolts were going to snap; I was readying myself to jump even before the truck dipped, like a duck cautiously testing water, into that last yawning crater.

I don't remember hurling myself into undergrowth as the groaning hold gathered its final fatal momentum, or hearing the crash as it toppled sideways like a pack of cards, but I do remember desperately scrambling clear, thinking it was collapsing on top of me. There was a deathly silence, broken only by the trapped animals' ghastly bellowing. Miraculously, tiny figures – Bambuti – suddenly emerged from the jungle to help the driver, who was sitting in shocked disbelief in the still-upright cabin. He and I pulled unharmed cows out the wreckage, while the Bambuti crawled nimbly underneath and finished off the wounded beasts with machetes.

Badly shaken, I saw many more Bambuti during the next two days as I inched towards

The driver surveying the overturned hold of the cattle truck, Zaïre (Democratic Republic of Congo)

Kisangani on other trucks. Referred to as *les premiers citoyens de Zaïre* by locals, and said to be Zaïre Army's fiercest fighters, they were friendly people, smiling warmly and waving with disarmingly childish delight as I passed through villages along the 100-kilometre route between Mombasa and Nia Nia. While most still live a traditional nomadic existence, many wear Western-style shirts and trousers. They also live increasingly in permanent settlements, and cultivate clearings. But they're proud, fierce and sensitive, as I discovered when I tried to photograph them from a truck near Epulu despite being told not to do so by other passengers. As I lifted my camera, machetes appeared below us like lightening. I didn't try again.

From Nia Nia to Kisangani is 300 agonising kilometres. The flat, impenetrable rainforest is oppressive, tedious and dangerous. Often I couldn't see over the jungle roof, and had to lie flat to avoid being hit by overhead bamboo raking the cargo. Fearing crashes at every crater, after another three days my nerves were shattered; I had diarrhoea and was grubby and weak. Twice I had to sleep under dripping awnings hastily pulled over the cargo as lightning illuminated the pitch-black jungle like fireworks and terrifying storms churned tracks into knee-deep morasses. It seemed months since there'd been brick houses, far less towns, and I desperately willed the lorries on as we crept nearer to Kisangani.

At last we were passing boarded-up buildings and pulling into a dimly lit square overgrown with weeds. Although it was twilight, I ran down embankments strewn with decomposing garbage to the mighty Congo River, which is second only to the Amazon in water volume. For a while I just sat there, watching dug-out canoes setting out for the opposite banks which were lined with falling-apart sheds and abandoned gantries.

Kisangani lies more than 1,700 kilometres upstream, just below the famous Stanley (Boyoma) Falls, which make large-scale navigation upstream impossible. The town has a long and notorious history going back over a hundred years, when it was founded by Stanley (hence its former name Stanleyville). But, far from remaining the primitive trading post portrayed in *Heart of Darkness*, it flourished after 1900 to become the second city of King Leopold's Congolese empire, with spreading colonial mansions built on clearings hacked out of the jungle. Notwithstanding, when the 1950s spawned African nationalism, Kisangani's wealth and power made it a target for pent-up frustration as tribal intrigues, military plots and international conspiracies proliferated and white mercenaries supporting the secession of mineral-rich Katanga raged up from the south. It was then the first massacres, expropriations, and exodus of white inhabitants began. These continued until 1992, when unpaid soldiers from local garrisons rioted in orgies of looting, rape and murder. Finally came the recent terrible events when over 80,000 fleeing Hutu refugees – many of them responsible for massacres of Tutsis in Rwanda – were attacked by Laurent Kabila's Tutsi-dominated advancing forces and either disappeared, were massacred or starved to death until the remainder were airlifted to safety by the United Nations.

Now Kisangani, littered with bullet-ridden buildings and burnt-out cars, has only a few run-down shops and hotels, mostly dominated by Indians and Greeks. Maria, the chubby proprietor of my hotel, was one of the latter. Although raised in Cairo, she was from Athens and spoke six languages. Regardless of being exiled three times and having had coffee plantations, road-haulage businesses and flour mills expropriated, she remained phlegmatic about Zaïre. 'Anyway, what choice I have?' she asked rhetorically, her face rippling with determination. 'My home and family is here, and I am too old to start in another place. Kalá, they are stuck with me!'

Her hotel, the Pericles, was a tiny enclave fighting to keep Africa's harsh reality at bay. My room's antiquated fan didn't work, the torn sheets were soiled and cockroaches scuttled under the flooded lavatory basin. At the open-air restaurant things were better, if not exactly paradisaical – even the gaily chattering parrots there were bald. Strong black-coffee fumes mingled with the scent of wisteria growing on whitewashed patios; backgammon pieces clattered; voices babbled at tables where Club Hellenica was holding its monthly tournament and perspiring waiters with crumpled shirts and squint bow-ties hovered as bouzouki music beat into the night.

I eagerly scanned the menu, which offered the first real food I'd come across in weeks, until I remembered in disgust that I was trying to starve out diarrhoea and couldn't eat anything. At least the company was intriguing. The distinguished, but lonely-looking elderly man sitting at my table, with silver hair, creased khaki shorts and knee-length white socks, claimed he was a retired count who had emigrated to Zaïre thirty years previously. He had built up a diamond estate that had been nationalized after independence. Now, his wife dead and his married son living in long-forgotten Europe, he'd been in the Pericles for years, with no reason to stay in exile but no reason to leave either. Zaïre seems to abound with such people.

Shortly, it was time to confront the journey's next leg. Theoretically, I could take the Tuesday train 100 kilometres through jungle to Ubundu, from where I could catch a weekly riverboat following Stanley's route along the upper Lualaba (which for a long time Livingstone was convinced was the source of the Nile) for the five-day journey to Kindu. From there I was hoping to catch the express train to Kalemie, 600 kilometres away on Lake Tanganyika.

The men wilting underneath timeworn photographs of antiquated steam engines in Zaïre Railways' stifling office weren't encouraging. 'No train, bwana,' one said casually, mopping his brow. 'No fuel for diesel, but hope coming one day.' I stared at him disbelievingly and pointed to the photographs; I'd read about trains leaving every Tuesday, romantically described as 'antique locomotives stopping hourly for wood'.

'Got diesel,' he proudly pre-empted me.

As the implications of this alarming news sank in – it was unthinkable to return along that unspeakable road to Uganda, so I had no choice but to wait in Kisangani for God knew how long – suddenly I couldn't stand Zaïre any longer. 'What's the use of engines without fuel?' I cried.

He looked at me reproachfully. 'Zaïre poor country, bwana, fuel cost much money. Still,' he brightened, 'you check next week, eh?'

Ashamed, I settled down reluctantly in Kisangani, a town bang on the Equator. It's hard to imagine a hotter place and I could only manage quick dashes to the market before retreating to my suffocating room to sweat it out until mid-afternoon deluges cleared the air. But my patience was rewarded. Four days later fuel shipments arrived, and so at 5 a.m. the next morning I clambered eagerly into one of the *pirogues* (canoes) ferrying people over the gloomy river to a train wailing mournfully on the opposite bank. The crossing felt like a journey over the Styx to Hades; little did I appreciate how near to the truth this would be for some, for it was on this same hellish train that over a hundred Hutu refugees would later be crushed to death trying to escape besieged refugee camps during the civil war.

Although I was hours early for the train, teeming crowds swirled round the blackened carriages that stood engineless in a disused goods yard. Determined to find a seat for the six-hour journey, I battled my way into the darkened compartments until I was knocked off my feet by a struggling mass of humanity. I picked myself up from where I'd been dumped like flotsam outside the disgusting lavatories and wandered across litter-strewn rails to watch a diesel rooting around like a sow in a derelict shed. Three hours later it emerged without warning – wheels squealed, couplings clanked and off the train lurched.

I leapt onto carriage steps along with dozens of others and hung on elated as we clattered through the jungle at 20 kilometres per hour, the maximum speed the buckled single tracks allowed. Soon I was chatting away to a man standing on my foot. 'Train derailed not long ago, three peoples killed,' he confided to me cheerfully, and explained that he too was making for the boat, and tropical Lubumbashi, Shaba Province's distant capital on Zambia's border, where he hoped to find work in the mines.

'Good luck,' I remarked. He'd need it; for most, work in the mines, like emigrating, is a pipe dream. It's one of a few ways to get a pitiful share of Zaïre's enormous wealth, most of which vanished into the pocket of the seriously corrupt Sese Seko Koko Ngbendu wa za Banga ('all-powerful warrior'), better known as General Mobutu, Zaïre's president until he was deposed by Kabila when the civil war was over.

Three hours later my arms were almost wrenched out their sockets, and my feet were so bruised trying to retain perilous toe-holds that I decided, to my new friend's disapproval, to join people lining the roof. 'Ooh, dangerous for wazungu [white people]!' he cautioned as I climbed rungs above jolting couplings. I'd no sooner found space amongst welcoming crowds when we had to flatten ourselves as we entered tunnels of viciously cutting vegetation, before re-emerging into dappled glades.

Then it was like a slow-motion dream – the massive looming branches, the terrible mistake of instinctively drawing up my knees to protect my face, the heavy blows on my legs and head, the splintering of reality and the blackness. I don't remember almost being swept off the train's roof, or being caught by frantically clutching hands and lowered unconscious to carriages below, but when I regained consciousness someone had used frayed cloths to staunch the blood from a two-inch deep gash in my leg. 'You having big cut, but Ubundu not far away, where hospital and stitching,' voices said.

That's what *they* thought.

Suddenly, an hour later, brakes grated on a bend and everyone was sent crashing to the floor. I stuck my head groggily out of the window as the carriage tilted crazily into the jungle. I sank back, unable to believe it; we'd been derailed. The consequences were unthinkable; God knew how long it would take for news to reach Kisangani – I'd seen hardly a telephone in Zaïre – let alone for Zaïre Railways to find fuel, a breakdown wagon, a spare engine, a driver and mechanics, and dispatch them halfway to Ubundu at twenty kilometres per hour. I'd miss the weekly Kindu boat, the Kalemie train and the Ujiji boat . . .

As dusk fell, candles threw shadows in the teeming carriages, smoke billowed from trackside fires and pots hissed until it was night. Finally, people settled down to sleep by the dying embers and children's chatter gave way to cicadas' chirping and the sounds of the hushed jungle. I lay awake on the roof – refuge from the carriages' cockroaches or the slithering creepy-crawlies by the track – numbly watching distant lightning and paranoid about my throbbing leg, which I was assuming would go gangrenous in the humidity and squalor and have to be amputated . . . I was dozing fitfully when terrific explosive bangs jolted me awake. Blinding streaks tore the blackness apart, apocalyptic thunderclaps burst overhead and waves of torrential rain drenched me. It took another two hours before I fell asleep huddled miserably under the saturated sleeping-sheet I had lashed to swaying branches.

The next morning, certain I was dreaming, I was awakened by the sounds of hoots echoing cheerfully through the jungle. When I looked, to my amazement I saw a ramshackle breakdown wagon trundle into view. Miraculously, by mid-afternoon it had jacked the carriages back onto the rails, and at twilight that same day we trundled into Ubundu. To my dismay it was only a village; I wasn't taken aback, therefore, after I discovered the hospital was shut till morning, to find that there were no hotels. Unable to face the thought of joining the hordes of people sleeping on the railway platform who were also waiting for the boat, I decided to try the local mission. Still stunned by everything that had happened, I struggled after helpful naked children, past a church's charred ruins being swallowed by jungle and darkness, to a bungalow where myriads of hypnotized moths danced round a light bulb on the porch. I knocked, and the first of many missionaries I was to meet in Central Africa opened the door.

Like many mainly Belgian or Dutch White Fathers, he was a cheerful little man in his sixties, with silver hair, glasses, a goatee beard and – essential for Zaïre – an unexpected sense of humour. While cleaning my wound he told me that the gutted church had been torched by secessionist rebels before he added it had needed a new roof anyway. He omitted to mention, as I later discovered, that the nuns and missionaries, including his brother, had been raped or tortured, locked inside and burned to death.

Obeying instructions for the hospital, I limped the next morning along paths through tall elephant-grass to a crumbling annex, where I peered through cobwebbed windows at the padlocked wards. At last, at the end of decaying long corridors, I saw swollen-bellied women and children covered with sores sitting despondently on the floor.

'Belgians built hospital before independence to clear conscience,' a young black doctor in a smudged white coat told me as he examined my leg. 'But at that time things work. Now only two of us left, no money for needle-stitching and, anyway, your cut infected. I clean and bandage at least.' When finished, he rummaged in drawers containing empty cartons and handed me two crumpled Elastoplasts and a cracked phial of antibiotic powder. 'Have only these. Take please, you'll need for cattle boat.' I wasn't sure what he meant but, patched-up and proud of having survived the train, I was in good spirits as I hurried down to the jetty, thinking I was as ready for the boat as I'd ever be.

I was hobbling across sidings to an antediluvian steamer moored by a surprisingly deserted quay, wondering where everyone was, when further up I noticed jostling crowds surrounding a moored barge. Judging by the uproar coming from inside, its cargo sounded suspiciously human. Closer investigation and the daubed painted sign saying 'Ubundu–Kindu' confirmed my growing fears: the steamer had been laid up by fuel shortages. With a sinking heart I crossed the gangplanks to a narrow door and fought my way through the dim interior, where a sea of sweltering people were crammed into wooden stalls separated by eroded metal bars. So that's what he meant by cattle boat . . .

It was noon before a rusty tug's hawser hauled us midstream, past half-sunken wrecks beached in the shallows. At this point, the captain invited me, to my relief, up to the wheelhouse. 'White guest welcome!' he beamed. I didn't need asking twice – in Zaïre only the insane refuse privileges – and I stayed until twilight as we powered upstream, enthralled by the immense river and scanning empty banks for crocodiles. At sundown, when the blistering corrugated iron cooled, I stretched my legs along the roof until powerful searchlights raked the darkness for deceptive river bends and the crew requested me to go below.

'Falling overboard in dark, get eaten!' they said, laughing. I didn't object; heat from paraffin lamps was relief from the wringing dampness and kept mosquitoes away, and families cooking on charcoal braziers in neighbouring stalls shared their meagre meals of rice and beans with me. All the same, such generosity couldn't continue indefinitely and I realized I'd shortly be suffering severe food shortage; thinking there'd be food available on the steamer, I had brought no provisions for the five-day journey apart from an emergency tin of sardines.

85

Half-sunken boat in the Congo River, Zaïre (Democratic Republic of Congo)

Passenger boat on the Congo River, Zaïre (Democratic Republic of Congo)

I'd idle on beaches, chatting with locals and watching the lights on the bobbing fishing boats as they cast their nets.

On Christmas Eve, the day prior to my departure by boat for Ujiji, where the historic encounter between Stanley and Livingstone took place in 1870, I stood behind crowds thronging the mission church for mass. Over the heads I could see avuncular, bespectacled fathers in white robes seated by the altar. A choir of girls in daffodil-yellow dresses swayed to rhythms of pounding drums, chanting in Swahili until the congregation rose and voices thundered to the rafters. Suddenly I was overcome by compassion for everyone condemned to living in the purgatory called Zaïre, as well as bizarre feelings of loss; the most difficult, but challenging, journey I would probably ever make was finally over.

MALI
The Dogon Country
Celebrating my birthday in Timbuktu seemed a good idea at the time . . .

I'd fly to Mali, travel 600 kilometres east by road to medieval Djenné, with its unique World Heritage mosque, and by foot explore nearby Dogon cliff-villages, the most famous in Africa, before catching a passenger boat from Mopti down the Niger River, water level permitting, for the two-day journey north-east to Timbuktu.

The Foreign Office wasn't encouraging.

'Travelling in Mali is risky,' it had cautioned, 'owing to armed Tuareg nomads fighting the military government for an independent homeland, as well as bandits attacking road and river traffic, and muggings in Bamako.' At least they'd heard of Mali's capital, unlike the staff at airport check-in.

'Where?' they'd asked incredulously.

Now, sweating profusely – at 11 p.m. it was still an unbelievable 34°C – after stepping off the plane into the suffocating blackness enveloping a tiny, ramshackle terminal, I felt intense foreboding. My antiquated taxi trundled along a potholed highway towards Bamako's distant glow until it jolted interminably through shadowy, earthen alleys in a fruitless search for lodgings.

Finally I couldn't stand it any longer. 'Can't you find the centre?' I asked irritably in French.

'This is the centre,' came the reply.

After I hammered on a Catholic mission's gates, I trailed after sisters to a dormitory, where I lay gasping in a mosquito net under a creaking fan. There I tried to ignore the Dutch women explaining to an exhausted Spanish traveller – who, although from Elche (Europe's hottest city), was unable to stand Mali's heat after only three days – how they'd just been mugged. I didn't care; I was grateful for a bed.

At first glance, Bamako had metamorphosed next day into a sprawling village, with backstreets full of playing children and tall, slender women carrying pots on top of colourful headscarves. The bustling centre, which was dominated by decaying colonial buildings, was a spreading, open-air market squeezed into a maze of narrow lanes.

But it was desperately poor – Mali was amongst the world's least-developed countries even before the 1970s droughts and the Sahara's remorseless march south – and the crumbling railway station, where an antiquated engine and carriages sat abandoned on grassy rails, was surrounded by a sea of corrugated-iron shanties and impoverished humanity. Nor was there any escaping the ubiquitous hustlers, reputedly mild by African standards, who hovered everywhere like vultures and relentlessly stalked me even to the mission's sturdy gates, behind which I increasingly sought sanctuary.

I spent the next three days gathering information from other travellers and drinking countless pineapple juices in a losing battle against the insufferable heat. Eventually I discovered that, as the Tuareg insurrection had just been crushed, road and river traffic was moving freely again and, although the Niger was too low for passenger boats, I could probably catch a *pinasse* (large motorized canoe) from Mopti to Timbuktu.

I was almost ready to leave, and escape from the hustlers, the crowds and the choking motorbike fumes, when I had my first brush with the military.

I had joined throngs in a side street watching a terrific band – drums, bongos, guitar and kora (African harp) – playing at an open-air party where, seated under a shady baobab tree at tables groaning with food, a group of women in colourful dresses was celebrating a local singer's marriage. Mali's music is world famous, and the legendary Salif Keita still sometimes plays with the 'Rail Band' at the shoddy Hotel Buffet de la Gare, where he first performed.

I was reluctantly putting my camera away as it was too dark for photography when a boy tapped me on the shoulder and pointed to a heavily armed soldier in olive uniform beckoning me. Threading my way through the crowd, I accompanied him uneasily across a yard to a hut where, after a harangue about permits, he demanded the film.

I never argue with a gun, so I handed it over although it was empty; I also grudgingly admitted street parties were 'sensitive' and agreed to give him a 'donation'.

The next morning at daybreak, sighing with relief, I took a taxi across the traffic-clogged Pont de Martyrs over the river to the bus station. The sun, a fiery crimson ball, was heaving itself up through thick pollution. Soon, my money hidden in shoes just in case, I was off.

Once past mango groves, Mali's main highway runs deserted save for the occasional bus, military roadblocks and cattle, through flat, semi-arid desert to Gao, 1,200 kilometres to the east. We'd been travelling for six suffocating hours when I glimpsed a tantalizing blue, watery strip – the Niger – through the bush. Shortly afterwards, we entered a gracious-looking town full of falling-apart colonial buildings, palm-lined streets and donkeys pulling carts. Unable to resist, I jumped off the bus and ran joyfully down to the great river, where I spent the afternoon under a thatched hut on the shore, watching *pinasses* unloading wood at a quay and naked children playing in the shallows.

Segou, 240 kilometres east of Bamako, is Mali's second-largest town, and was formerly the capital of an eighteenth-century empire stretching from Timbuktu to Senegal, where captured enemy soldiers were traded as slaves for firearms. The town became a strategic French outpost and headquarters of Office du Niger, which unsuccessfully attempted, by clearing and irrigating huge areas, to provide food for French West Africa and cash crops for France.

That evening, relaxing for the first time, I joined people strolling along the bank to watch the sunset. Apart from softly spoken *bonsoirs*, it could almost have been Banares and the Ganges; accompanied by crescendos of chirping cicadas, girls skipped under banyan trees, boys played in the dust and half-naked women washed clothes by ghats in the river, its placid surface broken by spreading ripples of jumping fish and reflections of *pirogues* drifting to the opposite bank. Then, after the sun sank into the bush, pots glowed on the embers inside flaking houses with green shutters and a new moon glinted on the river.

The following day, still marvelling at Segou's friendliness, clean air and lack of hustlers, I wandered to the old quarter. It was criss-crossed by red earthen tracks, where rows of stately, disintegrating buildings stood in overgrown gardens dotted with bougainvillea. I was photographing a particularly attractive pink one when a tall, arrogant-looking young man in civilian clothes marched menacingly towards me.

'Who permitted you to take photographs?' he barked, pulling out an officer's military pass.

'Not again,' I groaned under my breath, and, aloud, 'Sorry, I didn't realize I needed . . . '

'Give me the film!' he ordered belligerently.

'Please,' I begged – there was an almost-finished reel inside – 'it's only a building . . . '

But no amount of charm or pleading would make him relent; it wasn't until, after a brief stalemate, he demanded my passport that I realized the situation was escalating out of control. Apart from complying, I'd only one option left.

I took a deep breath. 'Absolutely not!' I replied, before striding off, and turning round only to see him storming back to the mansion.

Suddenly aware of what I'd done – I've never deliberately disobeyed the military – I zigzagged panic-stricken through side streets to the main road, flagged down the first bus, leapt off at the hotel, hurled everything into my bags, paid the bill, commandeered a taxi to the bus station, barged onto a just-leaving Mopti bus, pulled down the window curtain and, heart pounding, buried my head behind a newspaper.

It was only as we slowed at a barrier, five minutes later, that I remembered that I'd forgotten about roadblocks.

Horrified, I froze while the driver disappeared with my passport and the passenger list into a command post. Soon paranoid scenarios were flashing through my mind – the officer had phoned ahead, I'd be arrested, camera and film confiscated, I'd rot away in some jail . . . Then the driver was returning, and heading straight for me.

'Yes?' I said desperately, hardly daring to look up.

'Here's your passport,' he beamed. 'Nice photograph.'

I was still trembling six sweaty hours later when, rather than continue 200 kilometres to Djenné via Mopti, I got off in the gathering twilight at a deserted crossroads to try hitching a forty-kilometre shortcut. Given I'd seen only three vehicles all day, that seemed unlikely, and I wasn't looking forward to sleeping in the mosquito- and possibly bandit-infested bush. Luckily, soon a skinny horse drawing a heavily laden cart and a withered old man magically materialized.

After half-hearted haggling – I was more concerned about the horse's health than the price of the journey – I persuaded him for an extortionate sum to take me to the river, and as the sun turned the bush lurid red, we began clopping past occasional hamlets and miniature mosques sketched against the dying light. As the horse flagged and night fell, I lay flat in the cart, bewitched by a gleaming, silvery creek running parallel to our track and looking up at the panoply of stars littering the heavens. Once, dark figures loomed ominously, but the voices were friendly, and by midnight we'd reached a hut on a muddy sandbank where, after lengthy, torchlit negotiations, a water-logged *pirogue* poled me, legs dangling in silky water, across a tributary of the Niger to another, rapidly harnessed, horse and cart. We'd hardly set off towards a faint shimmer when we were crossing a narrow causeway to the gate of a small, darkened walled town on an island. There was no electricity and I was led through a labyrinth of winding passageways, with candlelit shadows flickering on tall, forbidding walls, to a compound, where I tumbled exhausted onto a mattress on the roof.

Djenné.

One of the oldest and most picturesque towns in West Africa, it was founded in AD 800 and remained a Bozo settlement until its king converted to Islam in the thirteenth century. Afterwards, like its twin, Timbuktu, it began profiting from trans-Saharan trade in gold and ivory until it was incorporated into the Mali, Songhai and Moroccan empires.

It was still prosperous when, just before it was conquered by France, nineteenth-century explorer René Caillé passed by, reporting in his *Travels through Central Africa to Timbuktu* that 'Its inhabitants, who live in three-storey houses decorated in Moorish style, have plenty to eat, can read, and seem usefully employed.'

Now Djenné is literally a backwater, although it is still renowned for goldsmiths, wood-carvers, batik and its unique mosque, the world's best example of Sahalian mud-architecture. Built in 1905 in the style of the eleventh-century original, which was demolished by

After the market in Djenné, Mali

Woman at the market in Djenné, Mali

the French, it's a remarkable construction. Inside, forests of wooden pillars support it, and its red clay walls have to be renewed annually against the rains.

At dawn I ambled down to the dusty marketplace to watch traders erecting stalls until donkeys and carts groaning with members of the Peul tribe – whose wealthiest women wear earrings the size of rugby balls, gold neck pendants and large silver bracelets – poured in from surrounding countryside for the well-known Monday market. It was fascinating. I stayed long after the crowds had departed, listening to the *muezzin*'s plaintive cry from the mosque, outlined black against the dusk like a monstrous winged bat, and watching swallows swoop. Under the trees, tattered figures loitered in lamplit shacks, selling tea and torches.

Two days later, zealously guarding my seat, I waited in a rapidly filling Mopti *bâche* (bush taxi) in the empty marketplace. Boys in ragged blue robes, Muslim apprentices learning the Koran at one of the *madrassa* schools in Djenné, begged for alms until we lurched off. Although soldiers at a roadblock began insisting on seeing a travel permit I didn't have, after I admired their paratrooper badges and bestowed them with another 'gift' I was gaily waved on.

Now an experienced Mali hand, I was heading towards Timbuktu.

Reaching Sanga, gateway to the inaccessible Dogon Country, wasn't quite as difficult as I'd feared. Rather than wait all day at deserted crossroads outside Mopti for shared *bâches* to fill up, despite the expense I'd hired my own to the dusty market town of Bandiagara. There, instead of hanging around forever for a lift – in Mali traffic is exceedingly sparse – and being harassed by the town's notorious touts, I jumped at a moped owner's exorbitant offer of a lift and clung on desperately as the machine rattled 100 bone-shaking kilometres along ruts through the bush. Inevitably we broke down, but hours later we triumphantly pushed the moped into a Dogon village hidden amongst escarpment rocks.

My luck continued at Sanga's hotel; within minutes I'd found the chief's son, Serrou, the highly recommended guide I'd been seeking, who was not only free to leave immediately on a three-day trek, but was, rare in a land overrun with intimidating hustlers, amongst the most modest, gentle and dignified men I'd ever met.

Extending 135 kilometres north to south, the baking, red Bandiagara escarpment has been home to the Dogon people, famous for their complex animist culture, art and rock villages, since they migrated from plains to escape Muslim persecution in AD 800. In turn, they expelled the Tellem, pygmy-like cliff-dwellers who lived in rock fortresses so vertical that they are virtually inaccessible today.

After loading up with supplies and water, we set off in the cool of dawn across the boulder-strewn escarpment, dipping into rocky gullies and dried-up riverbeds until we scrambled at midday halfway down steep rock faces to a compact village of conical, thatched roofs. Here, under trees in his compound, I was introduced to the local chief.

Dogon village, Mali

Tellem rock fortresses in the Dogon Country, Mali

Dancers wearing masks in the Dogon Country, Mali

When the pleasantries were finished, I lay my mat on the flat mud roof and slept in the shade until the searing heat had subsided. Afterwards, Serrou, who was greeted everywhere like a long-lost son, took me up to the tiny, thatched *Casa de Palabras* (House of Words), where warring parties meet in front of elders to settle disputes; the first to lose their temper and stand up will bang their head on the deliberately low, three-foot ceiling and lose the case.

I spent the next three days in a lost, timeless world: off at dawn hiking along trails along the bottom of vertical cliffs where birdsong echoed eerily through motionless baobab trees and, surrounded by bellowing cattle, men in parched fields hauled leather pouches from wells. We would rest up in the compounds of villages till dusk, when the chief's wife cooked meals on blazing log fires.

I'll never forget the last night when, bathed by the full moon, I sat high up in a solitary compound on a ledge, like an eagle's eyrie, directly underneath Tellem caves. There I listened to darkened figures talking quietly by candlelight and looked down over the ghostly plains; I lay on the roof, awestruck at the immense cliffs dangling overhead. When I woke up at sunrise the rock faces were pink; half-naked women with water buckets on their heads were climbing steep paths below, and the sounds of barking dogs and laughter were bouncing around the echoing canyons.

All too quickly, like a dream, it was over and Serrou and I ascended the *falaise* back to Sanga, where his moped took me to Mopti to try to find a *pinasse* to Timbuktu.

The Niger River and Timbuktu

Even if it's home to Mali's most aggressive touts, Sanga is one of West Africa's most compelling places, a bustling port positioned on the Niger River's extraordinary inland delta, and a major crossroads of its peoples: Bamana, Songhao, Fula, Tuareg, Moor, Bozo and Dogon.

I found a peeling room in a seedy brothel, with women loitering around the dark landings and dingy corridors, and spent the evening in the red-lit bar buying drinks for an impoverished, bearded young German, the only independent traveller I met, who had just hitchhiked across the Sahara. The following morning I walked past the rusting *Timbuktu*, the regular passenger-boat that was laid up for the winter, and along embankments to the colourful port.

It was swarming with heavily laden *pinasses* and taxiing *pirogues*, and it was there, after enquiries, that I first saw *Petite Baba*. At 200 tons and 80 metres in length, she was the river's biggest and fastest *pinasse*. She was only loading for the 600-kilometre journey to Timbuktu in four days' time, but, as she was already crammed with passengers and cargo, I immediately bought a ticket and reserved a mat in the upper deck's bow fo'c'sle. After watching her suspiciously for forty-eight hours, as boat schedules here were temperamental, I loaded up with provisions and moved aboard.

Sure enough, a day early, and without warning, *Petite Baba* was off.

Pinasse *(large motorized canoe) on the River Niger, Mopti, Mali*

Tattered flag whipping in the scorching dry wind, she slipped past thatched mud-hut villages, where palm trees waved over diminutive mosques and children bathed in glittering green water. Then she powered past drifting dhows with billowing white sails, and headed towards the huge river bends curving lazily towards the horizon.

My elation was short-lived: within hours we were aground.

Unconcerned at first, I watched, fascinated, as crew leapt into the astonishingly shallow river and splashed playfully before levering us off with thick, wooden poles. Then we drifted downstream to reload the floating sacks – which were indistinguishable from curious hippos' snouts – jettisoned for draught. But by the second day, and the umpteenth time we had been grounded, the experience palled, especially when I realized that at this rate – we'd only covered forty kilometres – it would take two weeks, not two days. In addition, as my bottled water was almost finished, quite apart from my dwindling food supply, I'd have to start drinking from the bilharzia-infected river.

Strictly rationing myself, I settled into a routine of dozing, reading and making perilous visits along the scalding, viciously torn, corrugated-iron roof to the lavatories in the stern below. Soon I discovered the coolest place was at water-level amidships, where traders lay on sacks in strong cross-breezes, mercilessly baiting an unfortunate madman, who was trussed like a slave in the hold.

At twilight, as we tied up at the riverbank, I returned to the roof, where I watched men in flowing robes pray towards Mecca before they settled round teapots on glowing charcoal-burners. Once the throbbing Arabic cassette-music ceased, I slept, bones quickly adjusting to the corrugated-iron grooves, in a filthy heap in the silent fo'c'sle.

On the fourth day, aghast that *Petite Baba* was continuing to accept cargo, I was reassured that the river's shallows were over. I was still sceptical as we slid through narrow channels in tall, thick rushes, watched silently by impoverished villagers lining floating reed-hamlets. Yet, after emerging into an immeasurable inland sea – Lake Debo – even I couldn't believe it when, with no land in sight, we ran aground again, being freed only when passengers and half the cargo were temporarily transferred onto passing *pinasses*.

The next night, when the lake narrowed again into a myriad of twisting channels, *Petite Baba* began making up lost ground by ploughing into the blackness for the first time. My relief only lasted until 3 a.m., when I was awakened by a mighty crash, accompanied by horrific screaming. Thinking we'd hit another *pinasse*, and cursing the stupidity of navigating without searchlights, I fumbled for my torch and first-aid kit, ready for grisly scenes, but when I asked if anyone was injured, people only pointed to the cowering, badly shaken madman, who had untied his ropes and fallen from the roof into a *pirogue* loading alongside.

'Only him,' they said, laughing, 'and that's in the head.'

On the seventh afternoon I saw the first Tuaregs. Scrub dotted with palms had been giving way to yellow dunes, when I noticed the banks were lined with round, yurt-like tents. Behind, herds of cattle and horses grazed in sweltering plains. As the sun sank, swallows darted low over the glassy river, and tall, graceful nomads in long, blue robes were silhouetted against the violently red sunset. Soon a sliver of moon and a solitary star hung low in the sky.

Before I knew it we were arriving at Kabara, the port for Timbuktu since its port silted up in 1900. We glided through silky darkness towards figures round glowing lamps in poplar trees, where we disembarked next to moored *pirogues*. It was eighteen kilometres to Timbuktu, and after failing to negotiate down a jeep's ludicrous fare – as a white Westerner, I was being charged twenty times the usual rate – I began the journey on foot. Parched, filthy and famished after five days in temperatures of 45°C with only three litres of bottled water to drink and some biscuits to eat, I trudged past Tuareg camps lining the road. Soon, just after frogs belching thunderously in gleaming marshes, it curved away towards a distant glow in the night.

I'd been walking for hours, intrigued by throbbing music floating from surreal, white trees, but bitterly regretting my impulsiveness – the glow never seem to grow any nearer

– when at midnight a pick-up stopped; within minutes I was in a seemingly abandoned ghost-town, criss-crossed by sandy tracks. One of them led to Hôtel Bouctou on the desert's edge, where I rattled padlocked gates. Then I traipsed after a sleepy caretaker across a sand-filled, Moorish courtyard full of arches, and along empty, echoing corridors to a room. I was in Timbuktu.

Derived from the Arabic for 'place of dunes', even if others claim it refers to an old woman who was left in charge of the first Tuareg settlement in AD 1100 and means 'mother with large navel', from the Crusades onwards it was West Africa's main gold entrepôt. The city was so influential in the fourteenth century that, when passing through Cairo on pilgrimage to Mecca, Mali's emperor gave away so much gold that its price slumped for decades. In 1494 the well-travelled Spanish Moor, Leo Africanus, recorded in his *History and Description of Africa* that 'Timbuktu has a great store of doctors, judges, priests and other learned men, bountifully maintained at the Emperor's expense.'

After Moroccans invaded in 1590, decline set in, with the city's wealth caravanned out, and scholars executed or exiled to Fez. This was merely a prelude to devastating assaults over the subsequent centuries, during which Mossi, Fula, Tukulor and Tuaregs pillaged it. By 1828, when René Caillié, the first of lemming-like waves of European explorers who lived to tell the tale, arrived there, it was a shadow of its former self. 'Everything is enveloped with sadness,' he reported. 'There is great inertia, and heavy silence hangs over the town.'

But it was the Sahara's remorseless march south and droughts of the 1970s that sealed the once-magnificent city's fate. The population is now only 14,000, as compared to 100,000 in the fifteenth century; this excludes the destitute Tuaregs – still proud, although dependent on charity after losing their livestock – who are encamped on the surrounding, ever-encroaching dunes.

Now Timbuktu is almost isolated, except by air as, although furrowed tracks wind through the fiery desert 420 kilometres eastwards to Gao, and occasional *pinasses* like *Petite Baba* stop at Kabara, anything that moves is often attacked by the fighters of the Tuareg independence movement. The only traffic, except for rare four-wheel drives, is camel caravans carrying salt from the remote Taoudenni oasis, 700 kilometres away in the desolate northern Sahara.

The next morning I watched dawn breaking over low, flat rooftops outlined black against the sunrise and, lost in a time warp, listened to lonely bugles sounding reveille from parade grounds formerly occupied by Foreign Legionnaires. Later, I slogged through deep, sandy troughs – there are no paved roads – to get a vital passport stamp from the police *commissariat*, housed in a decaying colonial building on the Place de l'Indépendence.

After a visit to the post office, which was bare save for an archaic radio-receiver, cardboard phone booth and a rickety typewriter, I wandered to *le grand marché*, a falling-apart hangar where gaunt men sat selling mountains of dates. Outside, women squatted under straw matting by piles of rotten tomatoes and huge salt-slabs.

I was returning through a backstreet maze of crumbling alleys from Timbuktu's oldest mosque, built in 1327 by Andalucian architect El Saheli, when I stopped to admire thick, heavily studded wooden doors which, like the clay ovens for the city's famous wholewheat bread, are everywhere. Behind the doors, naked children were playing forlornly in rooms empty of furniture and full of sand. In one of them, a white-bearded man slumbered in shadows until he spied me.

'Lovely doors!' I observed hastily, embarrassed at witnessing his poverty. 'Against the heat, of course?'

'No,' he murmured, stirring slowly, 'against history.' Then he went back to sleep.

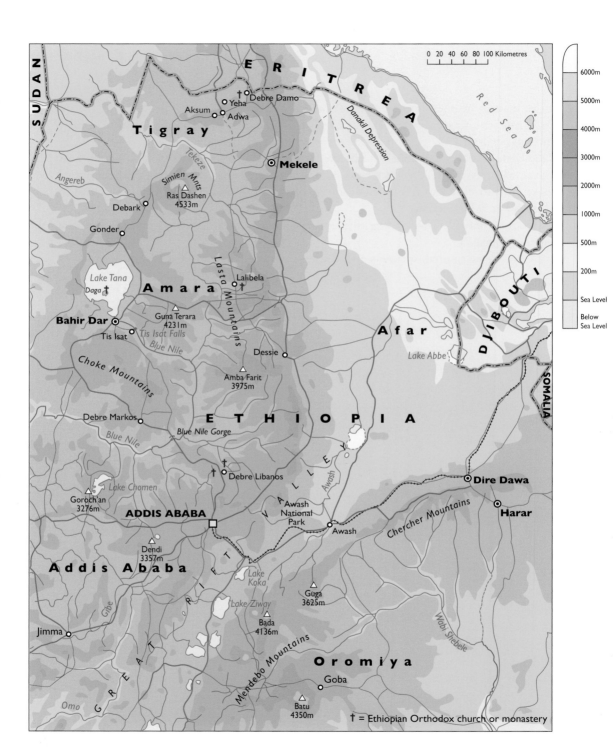

Map labels

SUDAN

ERITREA

Red Sea

0 20 40 60 80 100 Kilometres

✝ Debre Damo

Yeha
Aksum
Adwa

T i g r a y

Danakil Depression

⊙ **Mekele**

Tekeze

Angereb

Simien Mnts
△ Ras Dashen
4533m

Debark

Gonder

Lalibela ✝

A m a r a

Lasta Mountains

A f a r

Lake Tana
Daga ✝

△ Guna Terara
4231m

Bahir Dar ⊙

Tis Isat ○
Tis Isat Falls
Blue Nile

Dessie ⊙

Lake Abbe

D J I B O U T I

SOMALIA

Choke Mountains

△ Amba Farit
3975m

E T H I O P I A

Debre Markos ○

Blue Nile

Blue Nile Gorge

✝
✝ Debre Libanos

Awash

Dire Dawa ⊙

△ Goroch'an
3276m

Lake Chomen

ADDIS ABABA □

Awash
National
Park

Awash ○

Chercher Mountains

Harar ⊙

Addis Ababa

△ Dendi
3357m

Gibe

*Lake
Koka*

V A L L E Y

Wabi Shebele

Lake Ziway

△ Guga
3625m

Jimma ○

△ Bada
4136m

G R E A T

R I F T

Mendebo Mountains

O r o m i y a

Goba ○

Omo

△ Batu
4350m

✝ = Ethiopian Orthodox church or monastery

Elevation scale

6000m
5000m
4000m
3000m
2000m
1000m
500m
200m
Sea Level
Below
Sea Level

ETHIOPIA
Lake Tana

'What on *earth* are you going there for?' my friends asked incredulously.

Let's face it; Ethiopia has an image problem. The name, of course, is synonymous with desert, drought, famine and war. Still, as hostilities with neighbouring Eritrea over a twenty-kilometre strip of barren border – described as 'two bald men fighting over a comb' – were finally over, I set out to see for myself. It was a revelation. True, it *is* desperately poor, and its primitive infrastructure makes travel exceptionally hard. But, if you can survive, there's more to Ethiopia than beggars, battered buses and dirt-track roads. How many people know for example that in the fourth century AD this ancient country was among the first to adopt Christianity? How many are aware that the northern half is in fact a peaceful, fertile, 2,500-metre-high plateau the size of France, or have heard of the fascinating 'Historic Route' that runs through it?

The trail starts just north of the capital, Addis Ababa, and winds for 800 kilometres north-west through the plateau to Lake Tana, the Blue Nile's source and site of island monasteries containing unique Ethiopian Orthodox Church frescoes, until it disappears north. The long, three-day overland journey along the route wasn't easy. Every morning at five o'clock, white-garbed crowds, phantom-like in the moonlight, thronged padlocked gates before pouring into compounds and onto the antediluvian buses. The frantic battle to board the day's only public transport along the route was just the beginning of the ordeal. The bus, its overheated engine screaming, ground along the dusty, rutted roads, hour after bone-shaking hour. In wayside villages, open-mouthed crowds would goggle at *faranji* (foreigners), and countless ragged children along the roadside continually shouted 'you, you!' If anything, nights in dingy, fly-blown hotels were even worse, with the panting of men and women behind paper-thin walls making sleep impossible.

Nevertheless, it was intensely rewarding. Each day revealed biblical scenes. Streams of donkeys and barefoot, scrawny-legged peasants trudged along the roadside. The men wore smudged, ragged *gabis* (long white robes) and had wooden staves slung across their shoulders or immense bundles of wood on their heads. The women carried black umbrellas, and clay water-pots on their backs. Everywhere motionless children stood in dry, yellow fields, tending herds of humpbacked Zebu cattle or sheltering from blistering midday heat under clumps of shady eucalyptus. Thatched villages dotted the gently rolling hills. Occasionally, distant figures on horseback trotted across the brown plains, which were broken only by horizontal, spreading acacia. Aboard the bus, behind the driver, a sea of faces wrapped in headscarves nodded rhythmically to cassettes of religious songs as we rattled ever westwards into the blood-red sunset.

The highlights of the trail were unforgettable. A hundred kilometres north of Addis a side road branched off to Debre Libanos, Ethiopia's most holy monastery. Deserted, apart

Man near Lake Tana, Ethiopia

from families of playful gelada baboons, the road ran along the rim of a gigantic escarpment and wound down through trees to a village. In the main street, which was lined with stalls, pilgrims pored over religious bric-a-brac and bibles in Amharic, Ethiopia's lingua franca.

Past a huge tree, where pitiful cripples and beggars huddled, was the metallic silver dome of the monastery. Perched on plunging cliffs, it dated from the thirteenth century, although Emperor Haile Selassie rebuilt it in 1961. During the Italian occupation, it was a suspected hotbed of rebel activity and the scene of one of the Fascists' worst atrocities. After an attempt to kill him, notorious Viceroy Graziani ordered 387 monks to be executed and, satisfied, informed Mussolini that 'The monastery is closed – definitively.'

Not long afterwards on the route was the Blue Nile Gorge, which is one of Ethiopia's most stupendous sights. Without warning, the bus reached the edge of a precipitous escarpment, beyond which layers upon layers of red rock plunged thousands of metres to the valley floor below. In the distance, the whole of Ethiopia seemed to stretch as far as the eye could see. Trailing clouds of dust, the bus zigzagged down to an elegant, single-span

Timkat (Epiphany) Festival in Gonder, northern Ethiopia

Priest carrying tabot on his head during Timkat procession in Gonder

Young men during Timkat procession in Gonder

merge in the main square. On the priests' heads, protected from the blazing sun by glittering umbrellas, were trays wrapped in red, green, blue and yellow velvet. Underneath lay holy *tabots*. Soon the multitude, preceded by youths wildly pounding drums, streamed down to Fasiladas' Baths, an idyllic spot two kilometres west of Gonder.

Here, in the middle of a grassy, overgrown enclosure, was a two-storied fort that resembled something out of Mogul India. Behind it, ringed by spreading juniper canopies, was a large rectangular sunken pool. With the *tabots* on their heads, the priests crossed a narrow bridge to the fort, where they prayed and chanted all night. At five o'clock the next morning, when it was still dark, the pool was already lined with eager crowds. At the front, rows of girl novices in pale green tunics and red capes with yellow crosses clapped, sang and swayed gracefully to beating drums. As dawn broke, the priests emerged onto the fort's balcony to bless the crowds and the pool, before naked boys hurled themselves into the water, now transformed into a riot of splashing bodies.

A few kilometres along a rutted dirt track outside Gonder, I found Wolleta, the once-renowned Falasha (black Ethiopian Jewish) village. For centuries Judaism was north-west Ethiopia's dominant religion. Nonetheless, after Christianity's adoption as state religion in the fourth century, the Falasha were persecuted remorselessly. Finally, during 1985's catastrophic famine, they were offered the chance to escape to Israel. In the dramatic 'Operation Moses', which was kept secret to avoid undue publicity hampering the mission, 7,000 Falasha people trekked through the Sudanese desert to Khartoum, where the survivors (a third of them had died along the way) were flown to Jerusalem. When civil war racked Ethiopia six years later, 'Operation Solomon' ensured that most of the remaining 14,000 were airlifted out in only thirty-six hours.

At first there was scant sign of any – far less Falasha – life in Wolleta, which consisted seemingly of a pottery stall by the deserted roadside. Notwithstanding, a slim young man with a wispy moustache and beard shortly wandered along. He was Eli, a 24-year-old Falasha, whose family had been plucked from the brink of famine in Wolleta and airlifted in 1985 to Israel in Operation Moses. After spending his childhood in Jerusalem, he had moved to New York and was now visiting Ethiopia for the first time since he left as a young boy. 'Though we weren't as badly persecuted as elsewhere, all Falasha wanted to go to Israel,' he said. 'The problem is that many people there can't accept we're Jewish, because of our black skins. But that's their problem.'

As word spread that a rare *faranji* and a Falasha had arrived and were looking for the former synagogue, two boys materialized like genii. For a small fee, they showed the way up paths to an octagonal hut hidden in eucalyptus copses. There a woman came out of an adjacent thatched shack and, after trying to sell Eli coins bearing Emperor Haile Selassie's head, unlocked the synagogue's door. Inside, the building was empty, with only blackened rafters and red and black Aboriginal-looking painted dots on the walls, but it felt alive with spirits.

The Simiens

A week later, I arrived in the village of Debark, 900 kilometres north of Addis Ababa, to organize a five-day trek into the reputedly stunning Simien Mountains, one of Africa's highest mountain ranges. I had planned to arrive there by midday, leaving the afternoon to get fixed up with the handful of recommended guides or the sole trekking agency, the official National Tourist Commission (NTC). But the morning bus from Gonder broke down twice on the rutted dirt road, and by the time it pulled into Debark it was 4.30 p.m. and far too late to organize anything that day.

Within seconds of getting off, I was surrounded by the usual gaggle of shouting children and jostling youths insisting they were experienced guides. Pursued relentlessly, and worn-out after a month's hard travelling, I set off up a slope for Debark's cheapest hotel. To my dismay it was a fleapit doubling as the bordello, with straw-strewn floors, ear-splitting music and a dim interior lit by red light bulbs. Unable to shake off the pack of youths, I returned to the dusty main street, only to discover the other 'hotel' wasn't much better, and, anyway, was full. Suddenly I could no longer stand the continual shouting of 'you, you!', which was ferocious even by Ethiopian standards, let alone the prospect of two nights in that dreadful dump. I decided to abandon the trek and continue to Aksum, the little northern town that claims to have the Ark of the Covenant.

I was wandering back along the main street, bracing myself for the sleepless, bedbug-ridden night in store, when I met Omar. Dressed in worn fatigues, he was a hardy, good-looking, twenty-year-old Israeli with Byronesque wavy black hair, a beard and piercing brown eyes. After I explained my feelings about Debark, he told me he was returning from the NTC, which had just finalized his eight-day trek to Ras Dashen, at 4,543 metres, the country's highest mountain. 'For Ethiopia they're really efficient,' he told me in his guttural accent, 'and, what's more, they're still open.'

I hurried along to a tumbledown shack on the outskirts and, unbelievably, within an hour the man behind a rickety wooden desk had not only organized the obligatory scout, but also a cook (the only English speaker), a horse and a horse-handler – and everyone ready to leave at dawn.

That night I went down to meet the cook, Hailu, in order to make the final arrangements. Owing to power cuts, there was no electricity, and the main street was dotted with dark, drifting shapes. While he negotiated the hire of a tent, sleeping bag and mat, I haggled with furiously arguing youths over an exorbitantly priced *gabi* (a thick, multi-purpose shawl worn by Ethiopian men, which Hailu said I'd find invaluable for the frosty nights ahead). Afterwards we stocked up on rice, flour, porridge, tinned tomato sauce and biscuits in paraffin-lit shacks, before drinking in a bar to the success of the mini-expedition.

Above: View of the Simien Mountains from the escarpment, northern Ethiopia

Left: My armed scout in the Simien Mountains, northern Ethiopia

When I arrived the next morning at 7 a.m., everything was indeed ready. Our party consisted of Hailu, myself, the scout, who, to my surprise, carried a rifle, and the horse-handler. Soon we set off. Passing through the market, we ran into Omar, who was also leaving. As he, his armed scout, mule and muleteer were taking the same route for the first three days, we decided to join forces. The track climbed through baked gullies towards the distant plateau. Streams of ragged peasants passed by, descending to Debark with donkeys laden with millet. It was a long, slow, strenuous ascent, as we were already at an altitude of 2,500 metres. That afternoon we reached the top, but, disappointingly, instead of the spectacular mountains I'd been expecting there were only high, undulating plateaux.

But that was before we arrived at the escarpment's rim. It was as sensational, if that's possible, as the Grand Canyon. A thousand metres below, a sea of plunging buttresses and pinnacles dropped to sheer cliffs, which in turn fell away to countless canyons, chasms and gorges. To the left, halfway down a mountainside, two lammergeiers soared effortlessly. To the right, the escarpment's 61-kilometre-long serrated ridge was stretched out against the blue sky. All I could hear was the buzz of insects and the flutter of butterflies.

Not long afterwards we joined the new dirt track being pushed east towards Ras Dashen. Without warning, a dilapidated Land Rover drew up in clouds of dust. It was the park warden, who offered Omar and me a lift fifteen kilometres to Sankaber, the first camp. A trained biologist, he told us that the Simien National Park had been established in 1969 to protect the three mammal species indigenous to Ethiopia: the walia ibex, the Simien jackal and the gelada baboon. After a while I asked why the scouts carried rifles, as the few villagers we'd seen seemed friendly enough.

'Mainly against poachers,' he replied, 'but also because of the highlanders. They're still suspicious of each other and, as they've all got rifles, there are often bloody feuds.' He laughed. 'Until recently, if someone from another village offered you water, you asked them to drink first in case it was poisoned!'

Set back from the rim, Sankaber consisted of three stone huts with green, corrugated-iron roofs. As these were for park administration staff only, when Hailu and the scouts caught us up they established camp behind some sheltered knolls and made a fire. Omar, who had forgotten to break in his new climbing boots, tended to the alarming blisters on his feet until he and Hailu began preparing the respective evening meals. When we had eaten, everyone huddled in their *gabis* round the flickering flames. While the Ethiopians laughed and joked in Amharic, Omar told me that he'd just finished his military service, and spent the last two months backpacking through Ethiopia. Once the trek was over, he intended to head overland to South Africa, to 'catch up on some sex and drugs', until he started training, somewhat surprisingly, to become a cook.

Although the Simiens aren't far from the Equator, their average altitude is 3,050 metres and evening temperatures in winter often fall below zero. That night we both almost froze in our tents, as my sleeping bag was far too thin and Omar, who didn't have much money and wanted to keep costs down, had only his cheap *gabi*. But our discomfort was nothing compared to that of the Ethiopians. When Omar and I woke up, we saw to our dismay that they had no tents at all, and had slept by the dying fire. Nevertheless, when we set off and the sun came up, everyone thawed out. The path wound through gnarled, lichen-draped trees clinging to the mountainside. Three hours later it arrived at a breathtaking waterfall: the Jinbara River, which plummeted 1,000 metres into Geech Abyss, an apparently bottomless canyon cut into the escarpment.

A few kilometres later we climbed to Geech, a hamlet where Hailu told us his cousin wanted to invite us for coffee. Her thatched hut was dark inside, with a tall roof supported by a central beam, animal skins over the earth floor and crumbling mud partitions. Shortly, she produced handfuls of coffee beans for us to inspect. Hailu, who, like many of his countrymen, claimed coffee originates in Ethiopia, smelled them expertly. Then she toasted them on a blackened dish over the fire, before proudly handing round cups containing the best coffee I'd ever tasted.

In the afternoon we continued the taxing ascent to the second camp, which we didn't reach until dusk. Located on a bitterly cold, exposed flank on the hill-top above Geech, it consisted of two ruined stone huts destroyed in the civil war and giant lobelia plants silhouetted against the sunset. After camp was established in their lee, Omar again sat near the fire tending his blisters, which were now bleeding badly. When he had finished, he disappeared with Hailu into the sooty huts, where they cooked a joint meal on his miniature Calor gas cooker. An hour later, they re-emerged with gourmet dishes of rice, potatoes, and chicken that Hailu had bought in Geech. After the meal was finished, the Ethiopians chatted happily round the glowing embers, and we lay on our backs, gazing at the immense canopy of glittering stars that seemed to engulf us.

That night both Omar and I slept well, with blankets and a thicker sleeping bag Hailu had managed to borrow in a village near Sankaber. When we woke up we washed in a freezing stream, and set off on a two-hour detour to Imet Gogo, a spectacular, 3,924-metre-high promontory. Omar was limping badly by the time the trail dipped sharply and meandered over cactus-dotted plateaux to Chenek, our third and final camp.

As twilight fell, I sat on the escarpment edge. Nearby, chattering gelada baboons groomed one another, while Mohala, the horse, grazed contentedly. Next to the tents, there was the by-now familiar sight of Omar, who had decided to abandon his trip, bandaging his feet in preparation for the painful two-day journey back down to Debark. Further away, the Ethiopians joyfully cooked the sheep we had bought them in the traditional gesture to celebrate a trek's end. Far below, soft evening light crept over the flank of a mountain spur, where two thatched villages nestled in the yellow fields and the faint echo of children's voices drifted upwards. To the east, gigantic tabletop mountains towered into the roseate sky, while ridge after shadowy ridge fell away to the north and Eritrea.

According to Homer, the Simiens were 'the playground of the Greek gods, who came here to play chess'. Rosita Forbes, the formidable traveller who arrived here in the 1920s, continued the analogy: 'Here the gods must have turned pieces of the chessboard into mountains,' she wrote, 'for we saw bishops' mitres cut in lapis lazuli, castles with the ruby of approaching sunset on their turrets, and far away a king crowned with sapphire.' I couldn't have put it better myself.

Aksum: The Ark of the Covenant

Those who think that after Gonder the best of the Historic Route is over are misinformed. Situated at 2,630 metres in the rugged Lasta Mountains, two hundred kilometres inland, is Lalibela. Known as 'Africa's Petra', this isolated village is Ethiopia's most outstanding attraction. Sited high above plunging canyons and ravines, at first sight it appeared to consist of a main street, where goats and sheep meandered, and a jumble of shanty huts and corrugated-iron roofs tumbling down the hillside. But halfway down was one of the Christian world's greatest historical sites – thirteen rock-hewn churches dating from King Lalibela in the thirteenth century. Álvares, the sixteenth-century Portuguese writer, observed that they were 'edifices the like of which cannot be found anywhere else', and recently they were described as a present-day wonder of the world.

I went to visit them on a Sunday. Beyond gates thronged by pitiful beggars, muffled crowds in ragged robes congregated on flat rocks overlooking a deep, moat-like trench. From almost under their feet, plaintive wailing issued from a colossal Greek-like temple. Measuring thirty-three by twenty-three square metres, with its roof supported by thirty-six immense square columns, Bet Medhane Alem was the world's largest rock-hewn church. White-clad pilgrims stood with foreheads pressed against its red exterior, murmuring silently as they read from dog-eared bibles. Hundreds of pairs of shoes were piled against the massive oak doors. Inside the jam-packed church it was dark, except for naked light bulbs and light slanting through narrow crosses hewn out of the rock walls. At the front, novices held umbrellas over priests with crowns on their heads as they recited verses in Ge'ez. Shabby rugs covered the rocky ground, which had been worn smooth by centuries of shuffling feet. In alcoves were three empty graves reputedly prepared for Abraham, Isaac and Jacob. Everywhere there were smells of beeswax candles and incense.

Outside, a labyrinth of underground tunnels through the rock connected Bet Medhane Alem with other, smaller churches. Nearest was Bet Maryam, the walls of which were painted with exquisite Ethiopian Orthodox frescoes, while the capitals and arches were covered with beautifully carved birds, animals and foliage. At the front was an out-of-bounds column wrapped in cloth where Christ is supposed to have appeared in a vision to

King Lalibela. Opposite Bet Maryam was Bet Meskel, a miniature blackened chapel where hermits still inhabited straw-filled caves. Further away was Bet Giyorgis, the apogee of the rock-hewn tradition. Separated, like Bet Medhane Alem, from the surrounding plateau by a fifteen-metre trench, it had a flat roof forming an enormous Greek cross. Down below, white-bearded monks pulled back curtains covering canvases of St George and the dragon.

After Lalibela the Historic Route trail crosses the Simien Mountains and ends at Aksum, near the Eritrean border.

In Tigray Province, 800 kilometres north of Addis Ababa, this dusty overgrown village not only claims to possess the Ark of the Covenant (the Tables of the Law, which God allegedly gave to Moses on Mount Sinai), but also is to sub-Saharan Africa what the pyramids are to North Africa. In the first millennium BC a unique African civilisation arose in Ethiopia's highlands with its capital here. By the first century AD the kingdom of Aksum had become one of the ancient world's most extensive empires, dominating sea-borne trade between Africa and Asia for centuries until it declined mysteriously and Ethiopia became, as Gibbon described it, 'the land that, for 2,000 years, history forgot'. Apart from ruined palaces, underground tombs and stelae everywhere, I found it hard to believe it had been the centre of a great empire. In the sleepy main square, from which earth alleys radiate, men lazed under a giant banyan tree. Sheep and donkey carts drifted by and youths wandered around half-empty shacks selling soap and Vimto bottles.

Notwithstanding, Aksum continues to serve as an unofficial religious capital and many kings have been crowned here. At the end of the only paved street, inside an arid compound, I found St Mary of Zion Church, a Byzantine-looking domed edifice built by Emperor Haile Selassie in 1961. On steps outside impressive front doors a man was addressing a multitude of listeners. Seated under sequinned claret umbrellas, he wore a pale yellow crown and was flanked by priests carrying outsized, ornate gold crosses and dressed in gorgeous robes. Under the shade of lilac trees, tattered pilgrims listened intently. Pigeons cooed and bells tolled. 'It's the Bishop from Addis,' whispered Haile, the local museum's archaeologist, who doubles as tour guide. 'Today is St Mary Day, and you're lucky to see him.'

Adjacent, between a seventeenth-century crenellated ochre fort and empty ornamental pools, was a small, unpretentious, granite building, which was the carefully guarded sanctuary reputed to possess the Ark. Surrounded by an impenetrable fence, it had a flaking, green-tiled cupola crowned by a cross and burgundy drapes hanging over the tantalizingly open front door, where white-robed novices hovered. 'You don't *really* believe it's there?' I asked Haile sceptically.

'Of course!' he retorted indignantly, convinced, like all Ethiopians, that it was.

'No chance of getting in, I suppose?' I enquired hopefully, knowing full well that only the guardian inside (an elderly and especially holy monk) was allowed to set eyes on it.

'Not unless you want to burst into flames!' he said, laughing, and referring to the Old

Testament fate, allegedly, of those who approached it too closely.

The *Kebra Negast*, the national fourteenth-century epic, confirms Aksum's claim to the Ark. This maintains not only that the Queen of Sheba was Ethiopian, but also that in 1000 BC she visited Israel's King Solomon. He immediately wanted to make love to the enchanting virginal queen, but assured her he would take nothing from her so long as she took nothing from him. Nonetheless, after eating his specially prepared spicy banquet, that night she drank a glass of water that the crafty king had placed by her bedside. Solomon demanded his side of the deal and Sheba returned home bearing his child, future King Menelik. Still, she had her revenge; twenty years later Menelik visited his father in Jerusalem, before making off with the Ark and establishing the Solomite dynasty that reigned for 3,000 years until Haile Selassie's overthrow in 1974.

On the other side of the road was Aksum's remarkable Northern Stelae Field, containing 120 stone obelisks erected in north-east Africa millennia ago. The stelae were used by local rulers as tombstones-cum-billboards to proclaim their power. Sculpted from a single piece of granite, complete with windows and doors, some resembled mini-skyscrapers. The 33-metre-high Great Stele, which, at 500 tons, is the largest stone block humans have ever attempted to erect, now lay broken on the ground after toppling over. To Haile's intense regret, the Rome Stele, at 25 metres high the second largest, was no longer among the obelisks. 'It's disgraceful,' he spluttered. 'It was shipped to Italy by Mussolini in 1937 during the occupation, where it's been ever since, in spite of all our requests for its return.'

Afterwards, Haile led me to the Queen of Sheba's Bath, a 2,000-year-old rock reservoir where naked boys were splashing and women were washing clothes. Beyond were paths that climbed two kilometres to brown plateaux and, overlooking Aksum, King Kaled's sixth-century ruined palace, with its barely excavated underground vaults and sarcophagi. 'Va bene?' ragged children shouted from nearby thatched huts. 'Those are the only Italian words young people know these days,' explained Haile, as we explored the vaults. Then he pointed proudly to distant rocky pinnacles. 'But over there was battle of Adwa in 1895.' At this battle, Emperor Menelik II inflicted on Italian invaders the biggest defeat suffered by a colonial army in Africa, thus saving Ethiopia from the Europeans until the arrival of Mussolini.

Two days after I arrived in Aksum, I hired a driver and decrepit four-wheel drive Toyota and set off to spend the night in remote Debre Damo, Ethiopia's most famous monastery. The rutted dirt road wound east through dreamy, mist-shrouded valleys to Adwa, a little town at the foot of the peaks, where we bought coffee and honey (the customary gift for the monks). Thereafter the track zigzagged interminably upwards until it passed near Yeha. Ringed by protective mountains, this village was the birthplace of the country's earliest civilisation, and its ruined third-century Temple of the Moon, with its immense red walls, resembled forts straight out of the Yemen. Then the road crossed parched plateaux dotted with camels until, sixty kilometres later, a rough track branched off, descended to dried-up river-beds and climbed steeply to the foot of vertical crags.

'Debre Damo,' said the driver, gesturing vaguely at the azure sky.

Dating back to Aksumite times, the monastery is renowned for its impregnable position on a tiny, 2,800-metre-high, flat-topped plateau. Access is only by leather rope, which, after being tied round visitors' waists, two of the eighty monks haul up a daunting, 25-metre-high rock face. Spread over half a square kilometre on the cliff-top above, the sixth-century monastery, forbidden to women, consists of Ethiopia's oldest church, with an outstanding collection of superbly illustrated manuscripts, and monks' humble dwellings which are almost indistinguishable from a maze of boulder alleys.

The tricky rope ascent successfully completed, I hurried over to the precipitous western rim to catch the sensational scarlet sunset. Not far away, a serious-looking, bearded young man wearing a monk's black hat was seated on rocks, chanting prayers. Soon he looked up, startled. 'You, where sleeping?' he asked, obviously a mind-reader – the visitors' quarters were nowhere to be seen – before extending an invitation to stay in his 'house'. From outside, it appeared to be just a pile of boulders, but inside it was a surprisingly cavernous, dark barn with a solitary candle throwing long shadows over earth floor and walls. His English was basic, but he was keen to learn, and soon he asked me to correct his exercises from his well-thumbed beginners' grammar book. We shared my spare biscuits and the honey, which he devoured ravenously until he led the way up rickety steps to a blackened inner sleeping quarter.

Here, by torchlight, he opened a chest and lovingly dug out his prize, and almost sole, possession. It was a handsome bible written in Ge'ez, which he began reading aloud. He read quickly, only stopping occasionally to look up for encouragement. Riveted, I sat, eyes half-closed, on the threadbare mattress. Aeons later, seemingly, he closed the bible and motioned me to go with him outside. There everything was silent, and the sky was littered with galaxies while forlorn plateaux below were bathed an ethereal white by the moon.

At length we returned inside and he barred the creaking door before he retired to his sanctum. Lying on top of the carefully prepared spare 'bed', a wooden table covered with moth-eaten cowhides, I couldn't sleep; I was too moved by this generous monk's humble spirituality and overwhelmed, yet again, by the grandeur of this tragic land.

Harar: Rimbaud

The road to Harar, the old walled town in eastern Ethiopia the great nineteenth-century French poet Rimbaud made his home, is long and hard. From Addis Ababa, astonishingly the world's fourth-highest capital at 2,400 metres, our antediluvian bus gradually descended

200 kilometres east to Awash National Park. Trapped between conical volcanic craters and shimmering Lake Beseka, the Rift Valley was littered with black lava-flows. By the roadside, slender Kereyu girls with Rastafarian-like ringlets sold baskets of charcoal and lanky, barefoot shepherds in ragged fawn robes tended flocks of goats. It wasn't long until savannah gave way to semi-arid desert, the road deteriorated into tracks, and camels stood motionless watching occasional lorries drift past in flurries of dust.

The bus ran parallel to railway tracks and shortly reached the fly-blown village of Awash. To the north stretched the desolate emptiness of the Danakil Depression, one of the world's hottest places, where in the 1920s Wilfred Thesiger explored the Afar's murderous culture. Soon the rutted road climbed into the cool, moist air of the Checher Mountains. Everywhere villages were dotted with green-and-white missile-like mosques. Terraces of *khat*, the mildly intoxicating leaf chewed in the eastern Horn, covered the hillsides. When the bus made a rare, hurried stop, outstretched hands thrust torn, almost worthless, notes down at children holding trays of apricots. Finally, two bone-shaking days after we left Addis, Harar, the fourth-holiest town in Islam, hove into view.

At first, despite being a UNESCO World Heritage Site, it didn't appear promising. Indeed, in 1854 Richard Burton, the eminent English explorer, who was the first European to enter the forbidden town, observed that it looked like 'a pile of stones'. For centuries it spearheaded Islam's penetration into sub-Saharan Africa, and by the eighteenth century it was a key centre of Islamic scholarship, with flourishing handicrafts such as bookbinding, weaving and basketry. All the same, it suffered a severe blow in 1902, when the newly constructed Addis–Djibouti railway was diverted to the neighbouring town of Dire Dawa, leaving it an isolated backwater.

Once through the seven gates into the old town, it was fascinating. Surrounded by imposing five-metre-high ramparts, hundreds of labyrinthine alleyways meandered down through low, whitewashed houses to Horse Market square. Dominated by the nineteenth-century Ethiopian Orthodox Medhane Alem Cathedral, the square was formerly the site of the grand mosque until conquering Emperor Menelik arrogantly had it demolished. Behind it towered thirteenth-century Al Jami, Harar's biggest mosque, near which was Emir Nur's tomb, just one of 300 minuscule sanctuaries devoted to Muslim saints. Further down the hill was the Muslim market, where Harari women with braided hair, ornate silver jewellery and colourful traditional costumes – orange headscarves, and black red, yellow or purple dresses worn over trousers – squatted in the dust next to their wood piles.

Tucked away off Makina Girgir, a rocky passageway where the heads of tailors were bent over outmoded sewing machines, I found 'Rimbaud's house'. Overlooking a courtyard protected by tall white walls, it was a grandiose, wooden, two-storey lodge that resembled something from a Himalayan hill-station during the Raj. Recently converted into a museum, it had half-empty, musty, ground-floor shelves containing his books, writings and photography,

CHAPTER THREE

Europe

'There, intoxicated by lunar madness, I inched towards the crater's rim before shrinking back involuntarily . . .'

ICELAND

Far from Iceland's world-renowned attractions to the south, such as the tourist-thronged waters of the geothermically heated, open-air Blue Lagoon, lies the West Fjords, one of the most unspoilt areas left in Europe. An area of 8,600 square kilometres situated on the remote north-west tip of the island, it has only one town, Ísafjördur, which, with a population of only 2,900, is little more than an overgrown village.

Surrounded on three sides by flat-topped mountains soaring over Skutulsfjördur fjord, Ísafjördur is a peaceful place, with blue, red or yellow timber houses and a harbour full of fishing and whaling boats. Nearby, in four of Iceland's oldest, eighteenth-century timber buildings, is the fascinating Maritime Museum, whose highlight is a touching, hour-long video showing the traditional life of Icelandic fishermen and their spiritual relationship with the sea before industrial fishing methods destroyed the link forever.

But Ísafjördur's main attraction is its proximity to the bleak, uninhabited Hornstrandir Peninsula. This area offers exhilarating hiking, provided the visitor is fully equipped to deal with Iceland's notoriously fickle weather and can read a compass. I was in Ísafjördur during the summer, so one afternoon I took the daily launch that makes the short journey across the bay to the ruined settlement of Hesteyri. Founded in 1894, eighty people once lived here, dependant on a Norwegian whaling station until it closed in 1940. Shortly afterwards, Hesteyri was abandoned, as was the entire peninsula, although several cottages have been renovated as summer homes and the house of the doctor, which is unchanged from when he left in 1952, is a hostel.

Unbelievably, for Iceland, the weather was almost Mediterranean, and it was hot enough to sunbathe by the heartrending little graveyard overlooking the imposing Drangajökull glacier opposite. Then I adjourned to the hostel for coffee and cakes before the launch returned at 5 p.m.

South of Ísafjördur, the road headed south around six deeply indented, deserted fjords where more tabletop mountains plunged dramatically into the sea. It was a time-consuming journey, as, like driving around the fingers of a hand, in my hired car I had to travel over a hundred kilometres in order to advance by twenty. Afterwards the road crossed a high plateau to the sleepy fishing village of Hólmavík (population 450).

The only settlement of any size on the lonely Hornstrandir coast, Hólmavík was home to one of Iceland's most enthralling museums, the Museum of Witchcraft, which was painted all in black. Appropriately enough, given their long-standing association with magic, two

Hot springs, the Blue Lagoon, southern Iceland

oversized black ravens squatted motionless on a perch by the entrance. At first I thought they were stuffed, then one of them squawked indignantly and tried to enter the building through the front door. Konrad, the friendly teenager behind the ticket desk, who, like most young Icelanders, spoke excellent English, told me about them as he vainly tried to shoo it away. 'Every year local farmers kill the ravens as they attack the sheep. So we rescue the young from their nests and feed them until they're ready to be released into nature. But these two, who are brothers called Sera Pall and Brynjolfur Biskup [after an eminent local reverend and a bishop], are so tame we can't get rid of them!'

The museum tells the story of Hornstrandir's history of sorcery. Viking superstition continued here longer than elsewhere, and even today the locals have a reputation for being overly cunning. During the late 1600s, twenty-one people were burnt at the stake. 'Unusually, twenty of them were men,' said Konrad. 'In those days the land was owned by six rich families, and to get rid of the troublemakers, who were usually the poor, they accused them of sorcery.' But the museum's most unusual, and gruesome, exhibit is its *nabrok* (necropants), which were worn as a supernatural means of getting rich quick. The practice involved a sorcerer gaining the permission of a living man to dig up his body after death and skin the body from the waist down. Then he stepped into the skin and placed a coin on the dead man's scrotum – an act that, it was believed, would continually draw money from other living people.

From Hólmavík a potholed road led along the coast to the isolated hamlet of Djúpavík. It was a hazardous journey, as the dirt track often looked as though it was about to be swept away by landslides from overhanging mountains. At last, positioned at the top of Reykjarfjördur fjord, where a waterfall tumbled over a sheer cliff, Djúpavík came into view. Surrounded by jagged peaks not unlike the Cuillins on Skye, it was highly atmospheric, consisting of seven houses and the Djúpavík Hotel, as well as the remains of a huge, derelict factory towering over a rusty ship's hull beached on the shore.

Hedinn, the hotel owner's 25-year-old son, gave me a tour of the factory, which his family also owned. 'When it opened in 1935 it was Iceland's biggest herring processing plant and Western Europe's largest concrete structure,' he began, as we gazed up at the broken windows and giant, corroded machinery inside the vast, echoing building. 'At the height of production in the 1940s, several hundred people lived here. What's now the hotel was the hostel for the women, who worked on the dockside or the factory, while the men lived in the *Sudurland*, the 100-year-old former passenger and cargo ship outside. Mysteriously, in 1949 the herring vanished and never returned, and in 1955 the factory had to close. When my father bought it, it cost too much to demolish. He tried to start a fish-farming factory here, but it wasn't successful, so now he wants to turn it into a museum.' The tour ended on the other side of a towering boiler, where an evocative exhibition of black-and-white photographs illustrated a culture that seemed long since gone, although it was merely half a century ago.

As luck would have it, that Friday the hotel was holding the first of two evenings of the annual festival, where people from the few remaining farms all come together. The programme consisted of a trumpet player, two portly, bearded men singing a medley of Icelandic folk songs accompanied by their guitars, and a 'mystery guest', who failed to appear. But it was a jolly affair, as the thirty-odd people seated at the long table knew all the songs and sang along gustily. One of them was Olaf, a wiry-looking man in his fifties, who had returned to his birthplace especially for the event.

'When I was a boy we had to go by boat round the headland to school in Arnes, as in those days there was no road,' he told me. 'My father was caretaker of the factory after it closed, and my mother still owns one of the houses here, although now she lives in Reykjavík.' He was highly educated, and had studied at university in Canada as well as in Reykjavík, where he now worked as a marine biologist. When I asked him about what happened in 1949, he said simply, 'the shoals just moved on. Herring are like people – they're very unpredictable!'

Eighteen kilometres to the north-west round the fjord, which, like all the others, was strewn with logs washed up from the not-too-distant Siberian forests, was the hamlet of

Landscape near Nordurfjördur, north-west Iceland

SCOTLAND: BARRA

I found travelling to the island of Barra a magical experience. An hour late for the boat, our train from Glasgow shuffled to a halt under the blue Victorian girders of Oban Station. The twin red funnels of the Caledonian MacBrayne ferry, moored by a wooden jetty, hooted impatiently until, passengers safely aboard, the ship hurried across the bay. Yachts, keeled over by a brisk breeze, bobbed like seagulls in the boiling wake as the ship slipped between Mull and the long arm of the Ardnamurchan Peninsula, which was swathed in bottle-green forests. For a moment the white lighthouse on Lismore Island and the dark silhouette of a fishing boat against the sparkling water revived my memories of Greek monasteries and turquoise Aegean seas.

In next to no time the ship reached the open ocean. To the south, islands whose horizontal summits terminated in precipitous cliffs were strewn like giant boulders hurled by an irate Cyclops. To the north, the mountains of the islands of Eigg and Rhum rose up. Past Coll, smeared flat over the curving horizon sixty-five kilometres to the west, were the faint outlines of the Outer Hebrides. The journey took five hours, which was time enough to scan the skies for the area's famous cormorants, gannets, guillemots, petras and terns. Dozing off, before I knew it we were in Castlebay, Barra's main village.

It wasn't particularly handsome, with sprawling, squat cottages at the foot of a hill that, turning its back on the ocean, protected a small, enclosed bay. But, on an offshore rock, the formidable battlements of fifteenth-century Kismail Castle (the seat of Clan MacNeil) were very eye-catching.

Barra has a long history. Reputedly named in honour of St Findbar of Cork (AD 550–623), who converted the inhabitants to Christianity, it was controlled by the Vikings after AD 850. By the sixteenth century, when people from Barra continued to sail to Ireland for religious festivals, the pre-eminent MacNeil clan was established. It was a Barra man who joked there were no MacNeils on Noah's Ark because they had their own boat, and tradition maintains that their herald proclaimed from the castle, 'Hear, o ye people, and listen ye nations, the great MacNeil having finished his meal, the princes of the earth may now dine.'

During the Jacobite uprising in 1745, Spanish money and arms were hidden here, and Redcoats landed, searching for Bonnie Prince Charlie. In the 1840s the population of Barra was decimated by the Clearances, shamefully assisted by the local Protestant minister who found the natives 'still to be incorrigible Catholics'.

That apart, not much on the island seemed to have changed. Groups of boys and girls sized each other up as the ferry nosed alongside the pier. Squawking seagulls squabbled above blue-and-white fishing boats moored round the fortress, its reddish battlements rosy in the setting sun. The church clock dominating the main street still stood at quarter past nine, and sounds of Gaelic, laughter and clinking glasses issued from Castlebay Hotel, where only a sheepdog was listening to the fiddler's band.

Standing at the bar was a rugged seadog with a leathery, weather-beaten face. Like many Barra men, he had sailed the seas and earned enough to return to his beloved island to buy his own lobster boat. Nor, again like most of them, did he have much time for the outside world. 'Mechanization has ruined it,' he stated cheerfully. 'People have lost touch with things. Here we still work with our hands. It's harder but at least it's real.' Yet, outside, it didn't seem real. It was usually coffin-black by 4 p.m., although darkness doesn't fall in summer until 11 p.m., but now the fortress was ghostly white in moonlight, and the phut-phut-phut of a fishing boat echoed through the deafening silence.

The next day was a stormy Sunday, with grey mist swirling over the hill-tops and gales gusting across the bay. A Customs and Excise officer, on a rare visit from Stornaway, suspiciously scowled at a survey launch clinging grimly to the soaked, windswept jetty. He told me he depended on information from the locals, but I suspected they give as little away as in 1941, when the whisky cargo of a freighter that foundered off neighbouring Eriskay was washed ashore and vanished, giving the inhabitants of Barra a fiery start to spring. The event, and indeed Barra itself, was immortalized by Compton Mackenzie in his book *Whisky Galore*, which was later made into a film.

The watery eyes of a shrivelled old man, idling by the heater in a cramped shipping-office on the pier, glowed at the memory. He chuckled gleefully through his few remaining teeth, although he wouldn't reveal to me how many crates he rescued. 'Anyway,' he cried indignantly, his emaciated hand clutching a forgotten cigarette stub, 'the Customs were also at it!'

Suddenly the weather became calm again, and every one of the island's few cars, it seemed, was in a funeral procession that wound along a glistening single-track road to bleak hillocks divided by sheep fences. Beyond a white cottage, where a girl shooed a playful lamb off the road, the crests of Atlantic breakers thundered onto a white, deserted beach. At one end, sheltering in sand dunes, an old man was sitting by the roadside. Still built like a bull at eighty, his eyes were failing but, even if he told me he couldn't hold his water, he could certainly hold his drink. Despite the empty whisky bottle he offered to share, he seemed stone-cold sober. 'Don't think I'm finished yet!' he roared ferociously in a lilting, almost Irish, accent. 'Nosh a tol! Here you're a youngster at ninety!' He tugged his shock of white hair. 'Why, I've more up here than that sheep's got wool!' He raised a concrete-like fist. 'Feel those wrists!' he bellowed. 'They're sixteen inches thick!' His voice dropped and he grinned. 'You know, I've always been a fighting man,' he confided softly. 'When I was young I'd fight my own shadow!' He gave me a playful nudge, which I knew would leave a bruise for weeks to come. 'And when I'm drunk they *still* have to ban me from every pub on the island!'

The narrow road continued up the west coast and picked its way through fields of buttercups. Then it passed whitewashed crofts, remote beaches, rocky promontories and standing stones. Tradition says these stones mark where a Viking was killed in a duel with a local man, and some time ago, when the site was excavated, a skeleton and ancient Nordic armour was indeed found.

Later the track curled inland, past fortified towers and solitary moors where skylarks hovered. Just near a rare clump of trees it divided, with one road running north to the airstrip at Traigh Mhor – a deserted beach – and the other leading thirteen kilometres down the east coast to Castlebay. Meanwhile, on a rock in a sheltered inlet full of drifting seaweed, some black gannets, with their heads erect like bewildered cobras, glared at a lobster boat chugging out to sea. Near a chapel was a trickling waterfall. Women's voices drifted from a croft window, where a motionless cat watched the wispy chimney smoke.

I found it particularly difficult to leave Barra. Everything had quickly become so familiar: the lobster-pots cluttering the jetty; the statue of Our Lady of the Sea, arms outstretched, atop the mist-enshrouded peak that brooded over Castlebay; the inscrutable fortress, attended by respectfully bobbing fishing boats; and the two aged men, cackling toothlessly at memories of past triumphs or boxing blindly away at enveloping shadows.

Then the ship was borne by a gentle swell out into the shimmering sea, where spiralling clouds loomed over the empty horizon. Looking back, I saw that, like a mirage, Barra had vanished, and all that remained was the suspicion of a line squiggled faintly on the horizon.

FRANCE: THE PYRENEES

Far above me, vertiginous dark summits disappeared into boiling clouds. Opposite my hired car, separated by emptiness, the flanks of 2,785-metre-high Canicou, one of the eastern Pyrenees' highest peaks, plunged thousands of metres to the valley floor. Also far below, clinging to the mountainside I had just come up, was Py, the traditional village where I wished I had had the sense to stay. But it was too late. As the hair-raising, single-track road zigzagged remorselessly upwards into the gloom, there was nowhere I could turn the car around. I pressed on, peering through the rain-splattered windscreen, praying nothing came the other way, and concentrating grimly on steering away from the plunging chasms.

Just as I wondered how much longer this could continue, and how much more perilous the narrow road could become, I reached the top of a high pass. Sighing with relief, I stopped, opened the door and battled into swirling gusts to admire the view. It was awesome. On the other side, a high, mist-shrouded valley shrank away from a wall of sombre mountains – the Porteille de Mantet summits, which mark the Spanish frontier. But there was no time to dawdle, as, almost immediately, there were apocalyptic thunderclaps and threatening flashes of lightning until the heavens burst open. After retreating back inside the car I drove on, descending through cataclysmic cloudbursts. Almost vertically two hundred metres below, the tightly winding road ran out at a cluster of grey stone houses. This was Mantet, which, through the guidebook photographs, I recognized with relief as my final destination.

Past the hamlet, at the end of muddy tracks, there was a farmhouse. At the foot of the adjacent, steeply sloping fields, a good-looking man with white hair was rounding up frisky black-and-white goats, helped by barking sheepdogs. Saturated, but impervious to the pouring rain, he looked up quizzically and shouted something inaudible, before pointing to a sign on the fence saying 'gîte'. It is only then I realized that here, at what seemed the end of the world, was the address I was looking for.

A petite woman with flour-covered hands answered the door. Her name was Angeline Cazenove. Friendly and chatty, she was in her late forties, with short wavy red hair, pouting lips and dark brown eyes. Leading the way, she hurried through the deluge to a draughty outhouse next to a barn strewn with mouldy saddles and rusting farm implements. The room inside was cramped, with a low ceiling and a bunk bed covered with thick blankets against the evidently freezing nights.

After she departed, I was leaning out the window when two bearded middle-aged men in soaked hiking gear ascended the steps winding up through the village. Sheltering under the gîte's overhanging roof, they explained in French that they were friends who have been coming here from Paris with their wives for ten years. 'This is our secret hideaway. How on earth did you find it?' one enquired, almost resentfully. Then, mollified by my answer that an acquaintance had recommended it, he looked relieved. 'Wait till you've tasted Angeline's Muscat [a local aperitif] and heavenly home cooking!' he enthused, wringing out his soggy cagoule.

Before the evening meal, I strolled along the muddy track past the barn, as the rain has eased off. Inside, in one of the cattle pens, the tired-looking goatherd was seemingly asleep on his feet, with his arms cushioning his head against iron bars. Not wanting to disturb him, I squelched on into the gathering twilight, accompanied by the sound of goat bells. I was focusing on avoiding puddles and admiring forests of Scots pine on the opposite mountain-side, when without warning what appeared to be two Mongolians on horseback cantered past. They wore Genghis Khan-style hats and claret tunics fastened at the side of the neck, with long, trailing sleeves. Incredulous, I blinked, but by the time I opened my eyes they had vanished. Worried that I was hallucinating owing to the altitude, I turned to check that Mantet was still there. Sure enough, the hamlet, with its thick stone walls, grey slate roofs and lazy smoke curling from chimney pots, was nestling against the protective mountain-side. Shaking my head disbelievingly, but resolved to find out later at the farmhouse who they were, I continued down to a rushing, boulder-strewn stream. Higher up, the path climbed to empty corrals and cows with alpine bells staring lugubriously from the edge of thick forests. Past here, the track wound up a vertiginous pass before it was swallowed by mountains piled against the seething sky.

That evening, by the time I returned to the farmhouse's cosy dining room, the two couples, who looked so at home they could have been family, were already seated round the dark wooden table. In fact, almost everything was dark wood, including the low ceiling, its beams, the floor and the stepladder up to the attic. On the walls were a stuffed fox, a stag's head, a gun, jars of homemade honey on a shelf and ladles above the blackened fireplace. Mathilde, the Cazenoves' eight-year-old daughter, had just fallen down the stepladder and hurt her back, although not seriously. She was a beautiful child, with deep liquid pools for eyes, and she sat quietly on her mother's comforting knee, tears streaming down her face until Angeline got up to attend the pots steaming in the cramped, white-tiled kitchen.

I had stepped straight into the daily life of the Cazenove family, and within minutes I felt as though I had been there forever.

After a while Angeline's husband, Richard, joined us. He was a tall, handsome fifty-year-old who, with his stubbly white beard, short silver hair and olive skin, looked like a Roman emperor. Suddenly I realized he was not only the weary goatherd I'd seen, but also the fiery-looking young man with shaggy black hair and a beard in some of the photographs on the wall. He went off to shower and, completely rejuvenated, re-emerged wearing pale blue jeans and an open-necked shirt. With his youthful good looks, deep voice and infectious laugh, he was definitely a charmer. 'Lucky you women weren't around today – those billy goats were out for sex!' he quipped flirtatiously as he flipped through an issue of *Terre de Vins*, a Languedoc magazine for food and wine connoisseurs. He stopped halfway through. 'Look chérie,' he called proudly through to the kitchen, 'the article has finally appeared!' Inside was a highly flattering report about Angeline's cuisine, especially her fish soup, duck with orange sauce, and pork with mushroom.

Over the meal, the Cazenoves began telling me about themselves. 'Previously Richard was a civil servant and I was a school supervisor,' Angeline said. 'When we arrived in 1982, there was nothing apart from two shepherds. At first we wondered what we were doing but we calculated we could survive. Three years later we started breeding goats and not long afterwards the government installed water and electricity. Now there are only twenty permanent residents, yet there's even a subsidized taxi to take Mathilde and the only other child to school in the valley. Of course, it's not easy. Richard rarely sells more than 150 goats each Christmas, and we couldn't survive without the gîte and our market garden near Perpignon.' She paused. 'But our lives are rich compared to before, and we haven't regretted coming here for a second.'

They were both from Languedoc, while Angeline's parents were Catalans who had fled Franco's Spain, vowing never to return. Nevertheless, her mother had gone back some time later to visit relatives, while her father, who had never done National Service, had to wait until the dictator died. There has been illegal, cross-border traffic here for years. During the Second World War, when the Nazis expelled Mantet's villagers, many Jews and Resistance fighters escaped south over the pass opposite the window. In fact, the Porteille de Mantet Mountains had played a large part in Richard and Angeline's relationship from the beginning.

'When I first asked Angeline out,' Richard said, laughing, 'I suggested she meet me at the hostelería at the frontier. I assumed she knew which one I meant, like everyone in my village. But she didn't, as she was from another one. So, seeing that the frontier is the Porteille de Mantet, which stretches for kilometres, she waited at home. I didn't know her address and it took weeks to find her!'

As the fire died down, the conversation turned to Roussillon, Richard's almost incomprehensible dialect, and Catalan, which Angeline still spoke. At one stage, he got up and fetched two fascinating, and astonishingly weighty, tomes – Roussillon-French and Catalan-French dictionaries. Just when everyone was preparing to retire, I remembered to ask about the horsemen I had seen.

'No, they weren't an illusion,' Richard confirmed, chuckling. 'One of the villagers has stables. Every year he goes to Mongolia, and those horsemen you saw were just friends he's been inviting over since the collapse of Communism. They love it here. Perhaps it reminds them of Mongolia – after all, Mantet does feel like the end of the world.'

ITALY
Naples

One evening, I battled through cosmopolitan opera-goers thronging Teatro San Carlo and braved the apoplectic traffic clogging fashionable Via Roma to dive into one of the dark alleys that escaped up the hill into the night. Here I discovered the old, but often forgotten, Naples of yesterday.

True, the fabled mandolin players, hurdy-gurdies, black-and-gold rococo hearses, mules bedecked with bells, and vendors of glow-worms and tortoises had gone. Nevertheless, in the maze of backstreets that comprises the working-class quarter of Quartieri Spagnoli, which was originally built to house troops during the seventeenth-century Spanish occupation, the traditional life and culture of Naples lingered on.

Women with babies hung out of windows, chatting to neighbours in labyrinthine tenements opposite. The narrow alleys were festooned with drying sheets that billowed like the white sails of Elizabethan galleons. Aged men sat on chairs outside open doors of *bassi* (street-level, single-roomed dwellings with only a door for air and light), whiling away the warm evening. Inside tiny rooms crammed with furniture, crucifixes and posters of the latest football idol, old women in black were fussing over countless grandchildren. Further up, in the shadows, a fat woman selling chestnuts poked embers in a rusty tub nestling in a pram. A *venditore di volante* ('seller of flying things'), his striped blue-and-yellow balloons bobbing at the end of a stick, rested wearily on the pavement. Bands of noisy boys juggled footballs, and girls with rings in their ears skipped nimbly over hopscotch squares they had chalked in the street.

At corners there were *presepi* (miniature marble Nativity scenes) set like grottoes in the wall, where curling photographs of treasured ones, along with dead flies, vases of plastic flowers, and toy cherubs gazing with adoration at portraits of the Saviour, were encased behind glass. On doors there were amulets, shaped like twisted red peppers, to ward off the evil eye. Naples, after all, is the city of San Gennaro, the saint who was martyred near Naples in AD 305. Tradition holds that two phials of his congealed blood liquefied in his hands when his body was transferred back to the city, which he is believed to have saved from disaster on numerous occasions ever since. Every year huge crowds gather in the cathedral where he is buried in the hope of seeing his blood miraculously liquefy again. But the miracle failed to occur in 1941 when Mount Vesuvius erupted; Montesquieu's theory – that heat generated by the crush of frantic Neapolitans and their candles simply melts it – cuts no ice here.

The name Naples comes from the Greeks, who called it Neapolis ('New City') in 6 BC. While it may lack Rome's grandeur – Anthony Blunt wrote that its architecture, like its citizenry, was 'lively, colourful, and with a tendency not to keep the rules' – its innumerable baroque palaces and churches testify to a long cultural tradition. It was here that Emperor Nero made his theatrical debut and Virgil wrote the *Aeneid*. In the fourteenth century it attracted poets and artists from all over Italy, including Boccaccio, Petrarch and Giotto and, later on, composers Gesualdo, Scarlatti and Leoncavallo. It has been conquered by, amongst others, the Spanish Habsburgs, the Bourbons and Joseph Bonaparte; thus the popular Neapolitan saying *e megli cummana che fottere* (domination is sweeter than fornication). Goethe, who should know, commented that a man who has seen Naples could never be sad.

Shortly, it was time to continue up the hill. Before I climbed interminable flights of steps towards the massive, floodlit Castel Sant'Elmo, which seemed suspended – like the ubiquitous moon – over every street, I decided to stop at a pizzeria, where two bakers encrusted with flour lovingly tended their glowing ovens. For a while I sat eating mouth-watering pizza, which in Naples is an art form, and watched life go by – up here there were few of the city's notorious traffic problems. Even a hundred years ago, Mark Twain remarked about Naples, 'Why a thousand people are not run over every day is a mystery no man can solve' – and he was only talking about the horse-drawn carriages. When it became mandatory in Italy to wear car seatbelts, it was in Naples that someone thought up the idea of a T-shirt with a seatbelt sash printed across it.

The night echoed to the din from the dimly lit workshops of carpenters, dressmakers, tailors, joiners, shoemakers, silversmiths and blacksmiths. Naples' markets are more like souks, and Scarfoglio, the eminent nineteenth-century journalist, observed that 'This is the only Western city where there is no European quarter.'

Mopeds driven by swarthy young men, their waists tightly clutched by girls with paper carnations in their hair, cruised proudly up and down. Sometimes I saw nearly an entire family on a single Vespa. Yawning dogs and cats slinking in the gutter scattered as three-wheelers rattled past, laden with boxes of red and green peppers. Canaries sang in cages in grocers' shops where packets of spaghetti, tuna tins, crates of figs and bottles of olive oil were stacked up to the ceiling. There was the smell of roast almonds and fresh bread in the air.

It looked so romantic – what Henry James, describing Naples, called 'the picturesqueness of large poverty' – that it came as a shock to remember I was in the heart of Camorra (the feared Neapolitan mafia) territory. For, behind the deceptive facade, the notorious slums of Naples were still very much in existence, with their legendary overcrowding, poverty, infant mortality and disease. As early as 1884, *Cook's Tourist Handbook* commented that Naples was an 'ill-built, ill-paved, ill-lighted, ill-drained, ill-watched, ill-governed and ill-ventilated city', and, unbelievably, the last cholera epidemic was as recently as 1973. These, of course, are the classical conditions for organized crime, but, curiously enough, the only sign of it was the notice 'Centre for the Committee of Courageous Mothers against Dangerous Drugs' on a backstreet building, and the sign in the local Banco di Napoli. There, inside three electronically operated, self-locking doors, a notice advised 'No Dogs or Guns', and the clerk confided to me that while the bank itself hadn't been robbed, during rush-hour his car had been held up at gunpoint three times in ten years.

Not surprisingly, few foreigners come to this part of Naples, although visitors would probably have less trouble here than in similar areas of most British cities providing they don't dress ostentatiously or thrust expensive cameras in the faces of the locals. Nor was there any sign of the notorious *scippatori*, who scoot about on their souped-up Vespas on the lookout for unsuspecting women with handbags to pinch; the pickings downtown were obviously more lucrative. In any case, crime in Naples is not new: 250 years ago Casanova was robbed of twenty silk handkerchiefs in a month.

Within a few minutes, I reached the summit. Far below, over the baroque Carthusian monastery of San Martino to the east, and over the television aerials and tenement rooftops crowding down to the harbour, I could see giant cranes, ships at anchor and distant Vesuvius silhouetted by the moon. To the west, shimmering lights illuminated the palm-lined promenade that followed the gentle curves of the bay, where crowds dotted with sailors and couples took their evening stroll. In-between, an almost intangible line divided the twilight zone of Quartieri Spagnoli from elegant, cultural Naples, where fashionable society meets amidst colonnaded piazzas, where there are countless museums, and where tourists gawp at the magnificent Capodimonte Palace and the Royal Apartments with their sweeping marble staircases, gilded mirrors and red velvet thrones.

However, that was beyond.

Stromboli

The lonely volcanic island of Stromboli is the most northerly and the most easterly of the Aeolian Islands, which are quite young in geological terms (40,000 years) and, like all wayward youths, still have to learn how to settle down and behave.

First inhabited by the Greeks in 580 BC, they are named after Aeolus, the Greek god who kept the fierce and temperamental winds shut tight in one of the islands' many caves. According to Homer, Odysseus stopped here and was given a bag of wind to help him home, but his sail opened prematurely and, annoyingly, his ship was blown back to port. Even in 200 BC Pausanias was commenting succinctly, 'On Strongyle you may see great fire coming up from the earth.'

The constant eruptions were, finally, too much for many people; thereafter saw only steady decline, leaving the islands to become a haven for pirates and exiles, right up to the twentieth century when the Fascists dumped their political opponents here.

Fifty years ago on Stromboli, the volcano, which continues to belch threatening black smoke and petulantly hurls giant boulders into the air, exploded without warning. It is claimed that the force of the explosion even caused the sea to retreat. No one, at the end of the island I was visiting at least, was killed, as the entire village was at a funeral in the graveyard, but here, with the outlines of Sicily faint on the horizon, forgiveness has always been in short supply.

The village of Ginostra, clinging tenaciously to the foot of the black volcano, is almost forgotten now. It seems to look down longingly over the sea, past the other islands, to the west, still dreaming of sons and daughters long-departed to the New World or elsewhere. Where hundreds lived previously, just a handful of people remain, and everywhere there are only shuttered houses and decaying alleys. Further up the slopes are the neglected olive groves and terraces of vineyards that, owing to the rich volcanic soil, used to provide some of the most subtly flavoured wine in southern Italy.

When I visited Giovanna, the last surviving matriarch of the once-extensive Lo Schiavo family, and Maria, at ninety now stubbornly refusing to leave her bed, both seemed nearly ready to join their forebears in the cemetery. Their line continues . . . just. Mario Schiavo, the shopkeeper, shipping agent and ferryman, has two children, while Paulo, the postmaster, waiting hopefully in his empty office for mail that never came, has none.

Nothing in the village moved, except for darting lizards and the occasional donkey nibbling at weeds in the cracked flagstones. Sometimes I saw Gaetano, who rents out

147

houses to summer visitors, happily wandering in the previously busy alleys, his baby daughter gurgling with delight on his shoulders, or Gianluca proudly marching with his new schoolbag to join his solitary classmate in the empty schoolroom. All I could hear was a distant voice calling, a cat meowing and, somewhere, water dripping in a well. A balmy breeze rustled the tall bamboo and a smell of sulphur wafted down from the sullen volcano brooding overhead.

It's not surprising that Stromboli, although briefly a household name in 1950 (when Rossellini made his *cinéma vérité* film of the same name here), is a secret place and that the few who come here are a hardy, solitary species. It's not easy to reach, or leave, come to that. Often the sea is too choppy for Mario's rowing boat to connect with the newly introduced *aliscafo*, the twice-weekly ship from Naples, and the inter-island ferry bringing much-needed supplies. Nor is it much easier once you are here; as there are no roads, the only way to get from Ginostra to the village on the other side of the island is by boat or, using the shortcut, up and over the volcano.

Life, consequently, is basic. There is seldom fruit, bread or vegetables, while few people I spoke to remember the days of fresh milk or meat. As there's no electricity, there's no television, far less restaurants, bars or discos. There aren't even golden sandy beaches on which to sunbathe, or from which it is possible to slip into the plunging, seemingly fathomless waters to observe the turtles, sea horses and swordfish with which the sea abounds. Instead, the coastline is littered with black, sharp-edged rocks that are dangerous to walk on.

Although not to everyone's taste, there are, though, compensations.

For example, one day I went to the neglected church and climbed the broken concrete steps behind it, which wound to the top of the village. Here, roofless ruins, their balconies tangled with vines, stood amidst volcanic rubble strewn everywhere. An overgrown track led through untended fig groves and cacti encrusted with cobwebs to the walls of the cemetery, where I slowly opened the creaking gate. Flies buzzed, a solitary bird sang in a motionless cypress tree and a harmless snake slithered through rows of lava-filled graves that lined the slopes.

When darkness fell the village was pitch-black. Inside the houses, oil-lamps or candles flickered in cavernous kitchens with blue-tiled floors, dusty cooking ranges and white clay ovens. Outside, thunder frequently rolled round the horizon and sizzling flashes of lightning split the darkness. Then curtains of rain drummed like horses' hooves across the sea.

One night, by the light of the full moon, I climbed the volcano.

A faint path struggled through the thick, prickly undergrowth until it petered out in the lava-strewn flanks. A thousand metres higher up, it re-emerged to cross a ghostly, surreal desert just below Serra Vancura, the summit. There, intoxicated by lunar madness, I inched towards the crater's rim before shrinking back involuntarily; only thirty metres below was the glowing mouth of the volcano.

My knees trembled uncontrollably as the mouth sucked avariciously at the smoke-filled air. An enormous fountain of fire whooshed heavenward, like a gushing Roman candle in a gigantic fireworks display. Molten lava and hellish black slag poured down the smouldering mountainside in a glowing river known as the Sciara Del Fuoco (Fiery Trail). I didn't stay long.

The next day, as I stood by the plain war memorial overlooking the rocky harbour, I wondered whether it had all just been a dream. It seemed a normal enough day. A donkey with empty panniers, a Dalmatian and a group of villagers waited patiently on the quay, their faces turned out to sea. On the water, a tiny rowing boat, inside which Mario was bent over the oars, was returning from the *aliscafo*, now skimming away like a gnat over the glassy expanse.

Suddenly there was a threatening rumble behind me, like the warning growl of a pride of lions. I turned, expecting another storm, but it was the volcano, even angrier than usual. A shiver ran through me; earth, water, fire and air, the elements weren't to be taken lightly here.

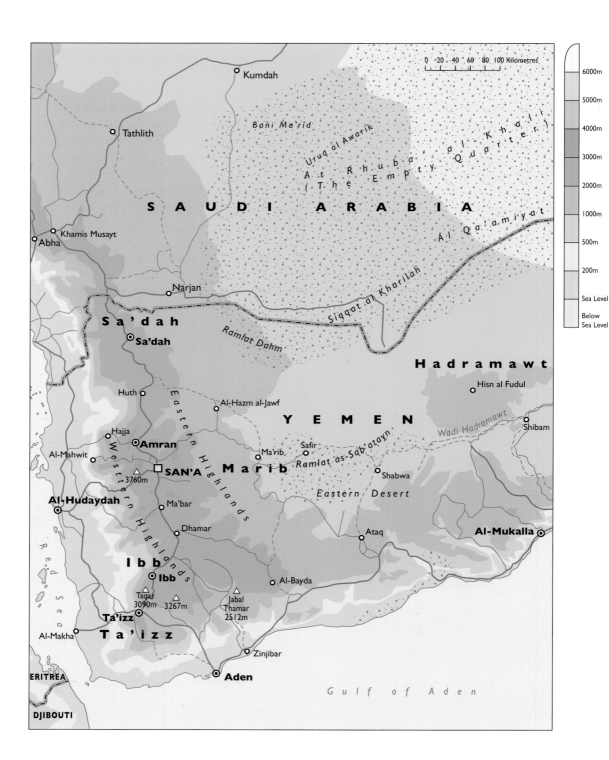

Kumdah

Bani Ma'rid

Uruq al Awarik

At Rhuba al-Kharij
(The Empty Quarter)

Tathlith

S A U D I   A R A B I A

Al Qa'amiyat

Khamis Musayt

Abha

Narjan

Siqqat al Kharilah

Sa'dah

⊙ **Sa'dah**

Ramlat Dahm

H a d r a m a w t

Huth

Al-Hazm al-Jawf

Hisn al Fudul

Y E M E N

Wadi Hadramawt

Shibam

Hajja

⊙ **Amran**

Ma'rib

Safir

Ramlat as-Sab'atayn

Al-Mahwit

△ 3760m

□ SAN'A

M a r i b

Shabwa

⊙ **Al-Hudaydah**

Ma'bar

Eastern Desert

Dhamar

Ataq

Al-Mukalla ⊙

I b b

⊙ **Ibb**

Al-Bayda

Taqar
3090m

△ 3267m

Jabal
Thamar
2512m

Red Sea

Ta'izz ⊙

T a ' i z z

Al-Makha

Zinjibar ⊙

ERITREA

⊙ **Aden**

G u l f   o f   A d e n

DJIBOUTI

0 20 40 60 80 100 Kilometres

6000m
5000m
4000m
3000m
2000m
1000m
500m
200m
Sea Level
Below
Sea Level

CHAPTER FOUR

Asia

'For a millisecond it occurred to me that this would be a spectacular way to die . . .'

YEMEN: THE EMPTY QUARTER

I met Fiona, the hardiest female traveller I've ever encountered, on Hotel Golden Daar's roof garden overlooking San'a, Yemen's medieval capital, where she'd been studying architecture for months. Dressed all in black, like a Yemeni woman minus the chador, and with long dark hair framing her tanned face, she was a forty-year-old grandmother from Islington. By an uncanny coincidence – she was the only foreigner I came across – she too wanted to follow the Incense Route across the southern Empty Quarter, the great Arabian Desert explored by Thesiger in the 1930s, to the legendary city of Shibam in Wadi Hadramawt. Without her, I don't know how I would have done it.

As expected, everyone had said it was crazy going to the Yemen immediately after the civil war and the Saudi border dispute, and the Foreign Office had warned of troops massing on the northern border, mined areas in the south, and four-wheel drives being attacked everywhere. Fiona wasn't bothered.

Facades of houses in San'a, the capital of the Yemen

'Let's just go to Ma'rib,' she said casually. Ma'rib was the 'Wild East' town, notorious for heavily armed rebel tribesmen, on the desert's edge. 'I've a contact there called Mohammed who I bet can arrange transport.'

Two days later, after leaving details of our passports, route and next-of-kin at the fortified British Embassy in San'a, who had said 'go at your own risk', our collective taxi descended from a 2,500-metre-high plateau through a winding pass in austere mountains to arid, baking desert known as Ramlat as Sab'atayn at the Empty Quarter's southern extremity. For hours the road ran straight towards the empty, billiard-flat horizon, where an occasional camel or lorry shimmered like a mirage. I was hanging out of the window, blasted by hot air and wondering how people could exist in such a furnace, when I saw a clutter of buildings: Ma'rib.

First mentioned in an Old Testament description of Queen Bilqus' visit to King Solomon, it had been the kingdom of Saba'a's capital in 700 BC, when the great dam was built and sustained a population of 50,000 through irrigation until, surviving several breaches and a siege by Roman general Aelius Gallus in 24 BC, it burst catastrophically in AD 570. The inhabitants fled, as the incense trade had long vanished, and Ma'rib was forgotten until oil was found in 1980.

Hill-top fortress in northern Yemen

We found a hotel, which was full of swarthy men smoking hubble-bubbles on worn carpets; within an hour we'd tracked down Mohammed, a shifty-looking character at a stall selling rifles in the local souk. There, after interminable haggling helped by a bag of *khat*, the mildly intoxicating leaf chewed everywhere, Fiona reached a deal: $300 for the two-day journey. This included $100 for the Bedouin to guarantee safe passage, a four-wheel drive and driver, Mohammed himself, and a tent so we could camp overnight in the abandoned ruins of once-mighty Shabwa.

Mohammed tried to be reassuring. He said that he had good Bedouin contacts and knew the desert, and although neither he nor Khalid the driver was a mechanic, the four-wheel drive was a new Toyota serviced by Bedouin, whose cars 'never broke down'. Nor, as far as he knew, had there been any problems since two Dutchmen had been kidnapped six months ago and held to ransom by Bedouin trying to raise money for a hospital.

'All in a good cause,' I'd commented caustically.

However, as we left to load up with provisions, to our amazement the dimly lit souk was overflowing with savage-looking tribesmen. Armed to the teeth with daggers and Kalashnikovs, they were all angrily milling around olive four-wheel drives where soldiers edgily fingered machine-guns. There was a buzz of expectancy, as government forces had just killed eighteen tribesmen in a nearby shoot-out. I was wandering back down a dark alley, nerves jangling, when I accidentally dropped my can of orange juice with a clang against the back of a parked truck. Suddenly a safety catch clicked and a drowsy figure swung a Kalashnikov through the window.

I didn't hang around.

The next morning, as we waited for the vehicle, Mohammed blithely announced he wasn't

Above, left: Tribesman in Ma'rib, northern Yemen. Right: Daggers in a shop in Ma'rib, northern Yemen

coming. 'Khalid doesn't speak much English, but you'll be okay,' he added nonchalantly. 'He knows the desert and is well connected, as his uncle's Bedouin.' Then he vanished.

I would have smelled a rat, as we'd just paid him the $300, if I hadn't seen our four-wheel drive already outside. 'Bang goes our interpreter and Bedouin guarantee,' I muttered to Fiona, unsure, as we knew only basic Arabic, which loss was greater.

She didn't even blink. 'Insha'Allah,' she said calmly. 'Our fate's in God's hands.'

At least I liked Khalid. He was thirty, thin, with gaunt cheeks, curly black hair, a Clark Gable moustache and a boyish grin. We loaded up and I climbed into the front seat between his Kalashnikov and cartridge belts, where I stuffed my money into my shoes in case of attack. Then we were off.

We'd hardly left Ma'rib before he screeched to a halt, did a racing U-turn and flagged down a truck towing a wrecked four-wheel drive. After exchanging words with the driver his face fell.

'Friend's car,' he stated mournfully. 'Deaded crash Empty Quarter.'

It was an inauspicious start. I was wondering what objects cars could hit in the desert, when the tarmac road petered out sixty kilometres later at Safir, an army checkpoint with shacks clustered round an oil refinery, and we began following tracks over red sand-dunes.

Apart from a short stop, when Khalid, who was reassuringly a crack shot, practised his marksmanship on stones, we raced at 115 kilometres per hour all morning into the flat void. It was far too fast for me, but he drove well and, lulled by the rhythmic clapping and beating drums of his Wadi Hadramawt cassette, I sat back, enchanted by the desert. It was noon when he veered across a parched plain towards grazing camels and drew up outside a white, round tent.

'Bedouin,' he explained, taking off his sandals. 'Let's say hello.'

I hurriedly removed my money from my shoes, and hid it in the Toyota before I followed him. Inside the tent, a placid old man with a white beard and turban lay on a carpet next to his three wives and astonishingly alluring-looking daughter. Wearing a flowing green embroidered head-dress, she was a young girl with gleaming, jet-black hair cut in a razor-sharp fringe and dark eyes like liquid pools behind a silver veil. Tearing my eyes away from this vision – it was like a dream from *The Arabian Nights* – I tried to concentrate as the old man asked me whether I had camels and what grazing was like at home, while Fiona and the women admired each others' jewellery. In next to no time, raisins, bananas and *khat* were passed around until Khalid broke my fantasies of taking her with us and wrenched me away two hours later.

Then we were off again, racing into desert near the Saudi border. The stark emptiness was broken only by a blackened tank, burnt out in the civil war, and an army check-post consisting of a shanty and a rusting armoured car. The sun was sinking as we arrived at ruins silhouetted against desolate mountains.

'Shabwa,' said Khalid.

'Nowhere,' observed Fiona, correctly.

Its wealth deriving from its strategic location on the Incense Route, it had formerly been capital of the kingdom of Hadramawt. According to Pliny, there had been sixty temples in the first century BC; now only dusty tracks led into the desert. Khalid parked next to two nomad tents in the lee of cliffs.

'Camp here,' he announced.

Watched by two bemused Bedouin boys, we struggled to erect our flapping tent against a swirling wind, but the ground was too hard and even Fiona couldn't understand tortuous instructions about 'red male pins' fitting into 'blue female connectors'. Feeling totally inadequate, we gave up and accepted their invitation to drink *chai* instead.

Shortly, Fiona was squatting over pots with women in the cooking tent preparing food, while the boys, who were twins, took me hand-in-hand on a goat tour. A full moon hung low over the darkened plateau rim. After eating, while Fiona and Khalid quietly chewed *khat*, I listened to the women talking and played with the twins. One was a born comedian, with curly black hair, prominent white teeth, mischievous eyes and cheeky grin. The other was serious, but handsome. In a corner, a silent old man with thick glasses and a half-empty sleeve lovingly stroked his sleeping litter of grandchildren with his one good arm.

The ruins of the ancient city of Shabwa, eastern Yemen

Shibam, 'Manhattan of the Desert', eastern Yemen

After drinking countless cups of tea Khalid rose. 'Sleep,' he motioned.

Dismayed, as I'd hoped they'd let us stay in their tent, I traipsed with him back to the car, where he took the back seat after offering it to Fiona, who opted instead for a ground-sheet outside. After deliberating, I fetched my jacket from the tantalizingly empty front seat, tucked my trousers into my socks and smeared my face with mosquito repellent. After all, if she could sleep outside, why couldn't I? Lying next to her, trying not to think of scorpions and snakes, I listened to the roaring silence and watched the moon, which hung low over the plateau rim. Soon the desert was flooded with ghostly white light.

I woke up only once, startled to see a spectral figure towering over us. At first I thought I was dreaming that Bedouin were attacking us, but it was just Khalid in his white *djellaba*, who was bringing us blankets against the freezing cold night. When I woke up again, covered in sand, the sun was coming up over the plateau, bathing the tents in soft pink light.

After fond farewells, we were off again, speeding through vast nothingness between tabletop mountains towards Jebel al Tukhmayn, an area with huge pinnacles rising like mighty chimneys from the desert. We had been travelling for hours when I noticed Khalid eyeing his rear mirror apprehensively. I swivelled round; another four-wheel drive, which had emerged abruptly from an oasis, was pursuing us. Khalid accelerated, trying unsuccessfully to outrace it as it closed upon us. Finally, he stopped, climbed out with the Kalashnikov, and menacingly stood his ground.

However, after the other vehicle slewed to a stop in a flurry of sand, he relaxed. 'Only local *khat* man,' he sighed with relief.

I quickly lost sense of time, so I don't know how long we'd been running parallel to mountains into an ever-narrowing plateau when we saw at the foot of cliffs. Dismayed, I realized that the desert was over. As we wound through villages and green fields fringed with palm trees into Wadi Hadramawt, I nursed a tremendous feeling of loss. Soon a forest of jostling, mud-brick medieval skyscrapers rose, atoll-like, vertically from the valley floor. It was Shibam, our final destination.

Hadramawt's capital after Shabwa's fall in the third century AD, Shibam is the Islamic world's best example of traditional desert architecture and was the recipient of a $40 million UNESCO World Heritage grant. Here, 500 brown-and-white, seven-storey skyscrapers are crammed into one square kilometre, earning the city its nickname 'Manhattan of the Desert'.

That evening at dusk we sat quietly on steps, watching families picnicking and boys playing football in clouds of dust in the wadi that separated Shibam from the plateau above. As the sun sank over palm trees and darkness fell, we wandered through the walled city's gate into a biblical world where sheep, goats and shadowy figures drifted through the maze of dimly lit, earthen alleys separating the dark, silent skyscrapers.

'We've done it,' murmured Fiona quietly.

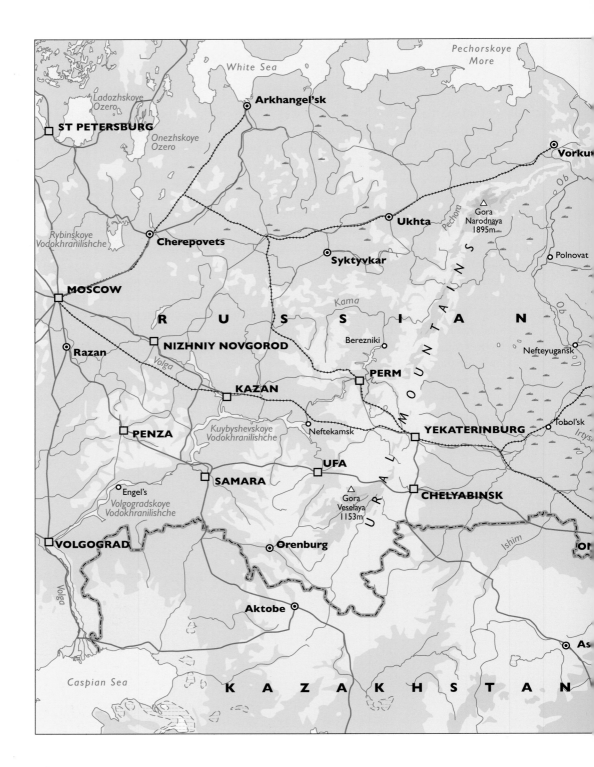

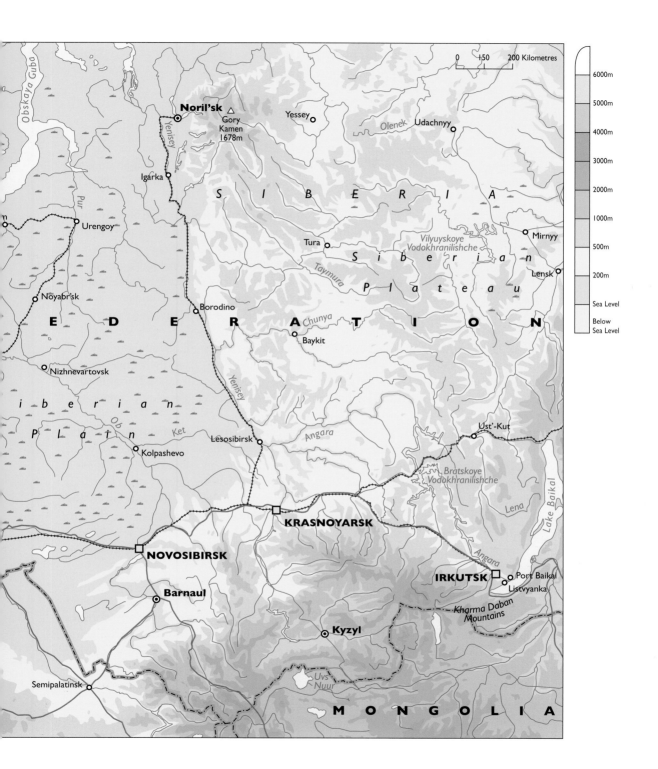

0   150   200 Kilometres

6000m
5000m
4000m
3000m
2000m
1000m
500m
200m
Sea Level
Below
Sea Level

Noril'sk △
Gory
Kamen
1678m

Yessey

Olenek   Udachnyy

S I B E R I A N

Igarka

Mirnyy

Tura   *Vilyuyskoye
Vodokhranilishche*

Lensk

S i b e r i a n

Taymura

n

Pur

Urengoy

P l a t e a u

Noyabr'sk

Borodino   *Chunya*

F E D E R A T I O N

Baykit

Nizhnevartovsk

Yenisey

i b e r i a n   *Ob*   *Ket*

Ust'-Kut

P l a i n   Lesosibirsk   *Angara*

Kolpashevo   *Bratskoye
Vodokhranilishche*

Lena

Lake Baikal

□ **KRASNOYARSK**

□ **NOVOSIBIRSK**

Angara

IRKUTSK □ ○ Port Baikal
○ Listvyanka

Barnaul

*Kharma Daban
Mountains*

Kyzyl

*Uvs
Nuur*

Semipalatinsk

M O N G O L I A

Obskaya Guba

Yenisey

159

RUSSIA: THE TRANS-SIBERIAN EXPRESS

I was thrilled to see 'Moscow–Vladivostock' signs on the bottle-green carriages of train No. 1/2 waiting impatiently in Moscow's frosty Yaroslavl Station. Fulfilling a lifelong dream, I was taking the Trans-Siberian Railway to Irkutsk and Lake Baikal, four days, 5,000 kilometres and six time zones away.

After getting established in a bunk of a comfortable four-berth compartment, I stood in the corridor, watching Russians in dressing-gowns and slippers slop along the carpeted second-class 'hard' carriages, where stern female attendants with Wagnerian exteriors tended outsized samovars, made tea and dispensed bedlinen. Then, pulled by two thrusting diesels, the *Rossia* was off, with Moscow's grim tower blocks replaced by blue-and-red dachas dotted in woods. Sooner than I'd expected, virgin forests and immense wintry steppes stretched away. Occasionally, the antiquated chimneys of dilapidated factories in small towns belched smoke into the blue sky.

In the late afternoon I wended my way along swaying carriages, already impregnated with their distinct smell of sweat and vodka, to the dining car. Over the simple meal, I watched the sunset before returning to my corridor. The racing full moon burst through the tall, dark forests, chasing us along the glinting rails and flooding the snowy countryside with brilliant light.

I slept fitfully, as the bunk was too short, but when I woke up early the next morning it was another stunning blue day. Escaping my hot and claustrophobic compartment, I found sunny tables in the dining car where, apart from returning to my bunk to sleep, I spent a good part of the next four days. Most of the time I read about the railway and chatted in schoolboy Russian to the disreputable-looking waiters who hung out like Mafiosi by the grubby serving hatches, joking, arguing or whispering furtively. Usually they closed the dining car after meals, but, in reward for my attempts to speak their language, I was allowed to stay on and rapidly became as permanent a fixture there as the dusty plastic flowers in the empty drinks cabinet.

Until the Trans-Siberian Railway was completed in 1916, it was quicker to cross the Atlantic, North America and the Pacific than undertake the arduous four-month overland route from St Petersburg to Vladivostok. Spurred by the need to develop Siberia, and aware that the Americans and Canadians had just completed their own coast-to-coast railways, together with the fact that both Japan and China coveted Russia's Far-Eastern territories, Tsarevitch Nicholas laid the foundations for the railway in 1891.

I quickly settled into the journey. In many ways there's not much to see as, apart from the Ural Mountains dividing Europe from Asia, which we crossed by night, the landscape is flat. There were landmarks, naturally: blue-and-gold domes of Trinity St Sergius Monastery at 73 kilometres into the journey; bridges over the Volga River after 282 kilometres;

Yekaterinburg, where Bolsheviks murdered Tsar Nicholas II and his family, after 1,818 kilometres; Omsk, formerly a dumping-ground for exiles, including Dostoevsky, who described his four years here in *Buried Alive in Siberia*, at the 2,716-kilometre mark; blackened Novosibirsk, where cement factories overlooked barges frozen in the Ob River, after 3,332 kilometres; and 4,104 kilometres after leaving Moscow, Krasnoyarsk, closed to outsiders until perestroika, and with top-secret nuclear installations and tunnels rumoured to be ten times the length of Moscow's underground rail system.

Over 5,000 kilometres, that's not much to see, and, once the novelty has worn off, many travellers find the journey tedious. But as we curved slowly round interminable bends I was lost in what seemed, to me at least, to be ever-changing countryside: the impenetrable and foreboding spruce forests which had inspired Chekhov to write 'where they end only migrating birds know'; wispy birch and larch forests, through which white seas stretched away to seemingly boundless horizons; and countless villages straight out of a Tolstoy novel, where Breughel-like figures trudged down water-logged tracks to wooden shacks, and flocks of geese and sodden haystacks clustered round frozen ponds.

There were also my new dining-car friends to keep me entertained. There was flirtatious Anna, the sexy cigarette-and-sweet-trolley woman, who was a fifty-year-old fading rose, with a delicate face, dazzlingly white teeth, slender legs, long grey hair and too-short skirts. Then there was Olga, a ferociously scowling cook with massive thighs, wrists like hams and enough gold teeth to fill Fort Knox. She could have murdered me with one blow, but, after fiercely interrogating me, she melted like butter and adopted me as a long-lost son instead. There was also the football-crazy Andre, the nervous, Slavonic-looking head waiter. He had chewed fingernails, lanky hair, smudged trousers and red eyes, and, as he totted up bills on his well-used abacus, he always looked as though he'd been crying.

Most of all, though, there was Sergei. I had met him one day when, passing compartments crammed with swarthy Uzbeks listening to pulsating Eastern cassette-music, I stopped outside a cramped cabin full of dials. Inside, a middle-aged man in greasy overalls was bent over a chessboard. He was the engineer; he spoke good German, and within minutes he'd invited me to play. Despite having learnt chess when I was five and being no mean player, this was Russia, and he thrashed me. He was a mine of information, except about the past; even though this was glasnost, he clammed up when I mentioned Stalin.

'If you don't know what the future holds,' he murmured, 'it's best to keep your mouth shut.'

Twice a day, usually for only twenty minutes, we would stop. I would rush out to stretch my legs, and pace up and down along the bitterly cold platforms. Beneath the harsh lights – this far north night falls at 3 p.m. in January – hunched babushkas sat on upturned buckets behind broken-down prams, selling dried fish and bottled gherkins. Numb soldiers in long grey coats, fur *shapkas* and black leather boots patrolled the snow; temperatures here drop to –40°C, although many Siberians who go to Leningrad, which is 10°C warmer but more humid, complain about 'glacial weather'.

From Mongolian Altaic language meaning 'Sleeping Land', Siberia has 50,000 rivers and a million lakes. It is wrapped around a third of the northern hemisphere and is big enough to accommodate the area of Europe, Alaska and the USA, with 780,000 square kilometres to spare. From the third century BC until the thirteenth century AD, nomadic Huns controlled it until Genghis Khan, who started as a warlord south-east of Lake Baikal, drove them west. His Tartar Golden Hordes dominated Russia until the sixteenth century, when Ivan the Terrible defeated them. Suddenly, in a parallel to the settlement of America's Wild West, waves of trappers, traders and misfits pushed east through Siberia. Instead of cowboys, there were Cossacks, instead of Native Americans, Tartars.

Siberia is, of course, also synonymous with the exile – Maxim Gorky called it 'the land of ice and chains' – and has been used as a dumping ground for criminals since 1650. By 1890, 3,400 shackled prisoners were passing weekly through the fort of Irkutsk. The most eminent exiles were Decembrists (army officers and aristocrats who bungled revolts against Tsar Nicholas I in 1825), Dostoevsky, Trotsky, Stalin, Lenin himself and Solzhenitsyn.

East of Krasnoyarsk, where the River Yenisey flows north to the Arctic, the bleak tundra was covered with sheets of ice. Snowdrifts swept by piercing winds were piled to the eaves of the increasingly rare villages, in which motionless figures stood at woodpiles, axes in hand and breath hanging in the air, as they watched us pass. By now, with either Moscow, local or Vladivostok time to choose from (some regulars even changed their watches by fifteen minutes every few hours), I was totally confused. Images of never-ending forests and glistening white oceans were imprinted on my mind, and I felt cocooned in a time warp, as if I'd always been on the train, and always would be.

Five days after leaving Moscow we arrived in Irkutsk. With a skyline dominated by the Raising of the Cross Church across the River Angara, it is one of Siberia's most beguiling cities. In the 1880s it boomed after gold was discovered, and became known as the 'Paris of Siberia' because of its classical architecture. Tragically, this is now fast disappearing, although there are still whole neighbourhoods of log cabins with exquisite, lace-like carving. I didn't stay long; I was eager to get to Lake Baikal where, after an hour's drive through *taiga* and traditional wooden villages, I settled into a simple lodge which nestled in the deep-green woods lining the Angara's banks.

Nicknamed 'Sea' by the Evenki tribe and 'The Pearl of Siberia' by the Russians, it's one of the most interesting bodies of water on earth. It is the world's deepest and oldest lake, measuring 1,600 metres kilometres in depth and dating back 25 million years. At 636 kilometres long, it is bigger than Belgium, contains one-fifth of the world's fresh water and, with over 2,000 recorded plant and animal species (80 per cent of which are found nowhere else, or are extinct), is a living museum of flora and fauna. Yet, even here, there are environmen-

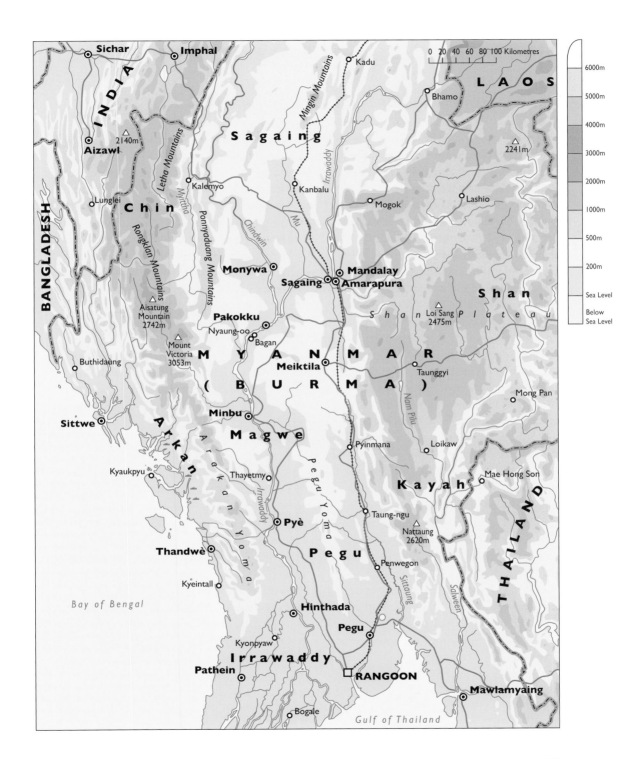

BANGLADESH

INDIA

Sichar

Imphal

Kadu

LAOS

Bhamo

Mingin Mountains

S a g a i n g

2140m

Aizawl

2241m

Letha Mountains

Lunglei

Chin

Kalemyo

Kanbalu

Myittha

Irrawaddy

Mu

Mogok

Lashio

Rongklan Mountains

Ponnyaduang Mountains

Chindwin

Monywa

S h a n

Aisatung
Mountain
2742m

Sagaing

Mandalay
Amarapura

Loi Sang
2475m

P l a t e a u

Buthidaung

Pakokku

Nyaung-oo

Shan

Mount
Victoria
3053m

Bagan

M Y A N

M A R)

Sittwe

Minbu

Meiktila

(B U R M A)

Taunggyi

Mong Pan

Nam Pilu

Kyaukpyu

Magwe

Arakan

Thayetmy

Pyinmana

Loikaw

Mae Hong Son

Thandwe

Irrawaddy

Pegu Yoma

Pyè

Taung-ngu

K a y a h

Nattaung
2620m

Kyeintall

P e g u

Penwegon

Salween

Sittaung

THAILAND

Bay of Bengal

Hinthada

Pegu

Kyonpyaw

I r r a w a d d y

RANGOON

Pathein

Mawlamyaing

Bogale

Gulf of Thailand

0 20 40 60 80 100 Kilometres

6000m
5000m
4000m
3000m
2000m
1000m
500m
200m
Sea Level
Below
Sea Level

BURMA (MYANMAR): THE IRRAWADDY RIVER

For years, only a few lucky travellers have known that Burma, or Myanmar, is one of the world's best-kept secrets. All the same, it's unlikely to remain so for much longer.

Rumours of the country's splendour had filtered through to me in Thailand. Now, during the brief flight from Bangkok, I nervously stuffed dollars I wasn't going to declare into my socks. I had a visa for only seven days, but it was better than nothing; it wasn't long ago that the hardline Communist dictatorship, one of the world's most isolated and xenophobic regimes, hadn't allowed travellers in at all. An hour later we touched down in Rangoon's tiny Mingaladon airport, where heavily armed soldiers surveyed the queues. There everyone had to fill out mountains of forms, even for watches and pocket calculators; it seemed like a scene from *1984*, and in fact George Orwell, whose books also include *Burmese Days* (1934), served in Burma's military police.

Shortly, I emerged into the open air where crowds clamouring for black-market Western goods besieged me. Travellers here had even been known to sell underwear, and I quickly sold my duty-free Johnny Walker's whisky for enough cash to pay for the entire week's travels. Hiding the thick wads of dog-eared notes, I caught a bus into town. The wide, tree-lined boulevards were full of bicycles, trishaws, pony carts and disintegrating pre-war Riley cars. After I located it, I booked into Yangon's famous, but crumbling, Strand Hotel, which would normally have been far outside my budget.

For a while I had tea in the now-shabby lounge where barmaids once served Rudyard Kipling pink gins, then I set off to have a look round the city. The contrast with Thailand was staggering. Instead of prosperous Bangkok's traffic-choked streets and skyscrapers, there were countless decaying colonial tenements. As darkness fell, I wandered through alleys lit by candles – there had been the usual power cuts – and ringing with the sounds of cobblers, blacksmiths and tailors. After independence in 1948, the Communists outlawed private enterprise and launched 'The Burmese Road to Socialism', which reduced Southeast Asia's former rice basket to a place of economic ruin, and Yangon, formerly the region's smartest city, to its most decrepit.

But the people, puffing thick green cheroots, were gentle, graceful and dignified, with slim, delicate-boned bodies accentuated by flattering *longyis* (long loose skirts). Yangon too, with countless reclining Buddhas and shimmering *stupas* (Buddhist burial monuments) seemingly floating above the rooftops, was a treasure trove. Burma's greatest pagoda, the stupendous Shwedagon, dominated the skyline. Started during Buddha's lifetime and containing eight of his hairs, the building is covered in gold plating and topped by weather vanes studded with 5,500 diamonds; not for nothing did Kipling in *Letters from the East* (1898) write 'This is Burma, and it will be quite unlike any land you know about.'

I was at the station at dawn to reserve a seat for the train to Mandalay, 700 kilometres north. There I wanted to catch a boat for the twelve-hour journey down the Ayeyarwady (Irrawaddy) River to Bagan's legendary ruins, which, along with Cambodia's Ankor Wat, are supposedly South-east Asia's greatest sight, before finding transport back to Yangon. The ticket clerk raised his eyebrows on hearing my itinerary.

'Hoping you have time,' he commented. 'Far in only seven days.'

Trying not to share his concern – it was rumoured travellers were incarcerated in dingy cells if they failed to leave the country before their visa ran out – I made my way past barbed-wire fences condoning off platforms; there had been bomb scares after yet another major military offensive against 'bandits', the official name for Karen and Shan ethnic rebels on borders with Thailand, who regularly blow up lines. Despite my protests, I was ushered into a comfortable tourist-only compartment, instead of the carriages full of peasants wearing brightly coloured head-towels. Thankfully my compartment filled up with locals able to pay surcharges, and, after a short delay, we were off.

Soon we were in low swampy countryside dotted with tranquil monasteries, shrines, orange-robed monks, water buffalo and rice fields. I felt as though I were back in Thailand until we entered the arid baking plains of central Burma. Suddenly I was in a pre-industrial time warp, with thatched villages, lumbering oxen yoked to primitive ploughs, peasants threshing wheat in fields full of swirling chaff, and women squatting at slowly revolving waterwheels. When the train stopped, girls selling betel nuts, bananas and rice wrapped in palm leaves swarmed aboard. Gradually, eyelids drooping in the hot air blasting through doors and windows, I dozed off like everyone else.

I slept all night and woke up to find myself in the old, British-designed station of Mandalay. Mandalay! A thrill ran through me at the name, even if I knew that Kipling, who wrote the classic *Mandalay*, never actually set foot here; in fact, his only experience of Burma was limited to a few days in 1889, when his ship stopped in Rangoon, the former name for Yangon. It was amazingly different from what I'd expected: instead of a town with roads, traffic and impressive colonial buildings, it was merely a sleepy village with dusty tracks. As the clock was ticking, I didn't delay; I found a hotel and set off up the town's focal point, 230-metre-high Mandalay Hill.

There, covered stairways wound up the hill past shrines and pilgrims prostrated in prayer. Leaving my shoes behind, I climbed until I came to neglected Peshawar Relics Temple, which contains three of Buddha's bones. Near the top of the temple was the gigantic Shweyattaw Buddha. Legend maintains he climbed the hill, where he prophesied a great city would be built in the 2,400th year of his faith, i.e. 1857, when King Mindon Min did indeed decree the move from Amarapura to Mandalay. At the summit there were glorious views east over the plains to the hazy blue Shan hills, and west over Mandalay itself. It was littered with temples, and stretched all the way down to the shimmering Ayeyarwady, which was dotted with bustling boats, shoals and sandbanks.

Directly below the hill was Mandalay Fort, which previously housed the royal palace. The most Burmese of the country's cities, Mandalay was Burma's last capital until the British took over in 1885. Then the fort became the colony's seat of government, King Thibaw Min was exiled and Mandalay became just another British Empire outpost. In 1945 the royal palace caught fire during fierce fighting between Japanese and advancing British forces. Now all that remained were walls and moats where the Burmese army, who had reoccupied the fort, grew fruit and vegetables to supplement their meagre wages.

Mandalay, with sixty per cent of Burma's 300,000 monks, is the country's religious centre, and close at hand was Sandamani Paya. It was an enormous cluster of slender bell-like *stupas*, where barefoot apprentices with prayer beads padded amongst giant whitewashed guardian lions, carved lotus pedestals and fluttering prayer flags. There was silence apart from the sounds of tinkling wind-bells and distant chanting. The scents of jasmine and

Above left: Stupas at Sandamani Paya in Mandalay, northern Burma. Right: Guardian lion at Sandamani Paya in Mandalay, northern Burma

sandalwood incense, burning candles and fragrant flowers filled the air.

After supper I visited the town's bustling markets. Here the calls of the famous guilds' craftsmen rang through the night as traders sold gems, jade and silk, as well as a wide range of 'nirvana goods' to bring devotees good karma: wood and marble Buddha sculptures, tapestries, folding manuscripts, lacquered scriptures and gold-leaf stickers.

At 3 a.m., after only four hours sleep, I was at the embankment steps, overlooking the muddy shores. Already peasants were washing market vegetables, and water-buffalo mingled with the crowds wandering amongst flotillas of antiquated riverboats. I hurriedly found the small Bagan steamer and battled my way to the upper deck, where I squeezed my mat into a cramped space. Two hours later, as skies turned pink and outlined the darkened city against the sunrise, we slipped out into the silky river. Not far away was Sagaing, once the capital, where regal processions of white pagodas and *stupas* lining both banks caught the early light. Soon we nosed into midstream, along with mammoth rafts made of chained logs – Burma is the world's biggest teak exporter – complete with thatched huts and families cooking amidst piles of earthenware pots.

The Ayeyarwady, which is navigable all year for 2,000 kilometres, was the country's lifeline for centuries, and the main trade route from the Indian Ocean upstream into China. The name itself comes from Sanskrit, and means 'River of Refreshment', but Kipling called it 'the River of the Lost Footsteps', referring to the tragic Anglo-Burmese nineteenth-century wars. At the height of British rule, the Glasgow-owned Irrawaddy Flotilla, which was the world's largest river fleet, carried 9 million passengers annually along the river in colossal steamers. Mainly crewed by Scottish masters and officers, and with giant paddle-boxes emblazoned with gilded coats-of-arms, they were 100 metres long and could accommodate 4,000 deck passengers. These lasted until the Second World War, when the Allies, in a desperate stand against the all-conquering Japanese, hastily dispatched them to Mandalay; over 100 were scuttled. I was aboard one of the T-class replacements, which, paradoxically, had been donated by the Japanese. Now fifty years old, these vessels still ply the notoriously shallow river, carrying up to 400 passengers and 60 tons of vegetables, livestock and teak.

Despite there being little to see apart from sandy wilderness, as the river was wide with flat banks, and villages were set well back because of flooding, I adored the journey. Motionless herdsmen stood silently on the sandbanks, watching their oxen wading happily in the shallows. Sometimes we glided over to groups patiently waiting on banks, and passengers would descend on precarious gangplanks, before hordes of women selling cheroots and sweetmeats swarmed aboard like invading pirates. One of the passengers, Aung Win, an elderly bespectacled Inland Transport Board inspector, spoke excellent English. He told me about the river, which he had been travelling for years.

'It's never the same,' he explained. 'One minute there are 300-foot channels, next day they're silted up. But captains read the river like a book. For example, the width of the eddy tells the depth. Twelve-inch eddies means the bottom's only four feet away, and five-foot eddies means twenty feet. They also listen to the sound of the bow wave. When it's soft it means the water's getting shallow, when it vanishes it means you're in trouble.'

Early in the afternoon, as blistering heat turned the sky and the river searing white, we passed the confluence with Burma's second huge river, the Chindwin. I couldn't wait for sundown, and when it came we tied up at the diminutive town of Pakokku for the night. I slept badly, as I was kept awake by battalions of kamikaze mosquitoes, barking village dogs and the cold. I was glad to take up my favourite position at dawn near the prow, where I watched pole men with long bamboo sticks call out the depth measurements.

We'd only been going for an hour when they began shouting urgently as their poles hit the bottom near biscuit-coloured cliffs. I watched alarmed as, engines churning the muddy water, the captain ordered full ahead, sending us inching closer and closer to ominous-looking sandbanks.

'What's he doing?' I muttered to Aung Win. 'Shouldn't we be going astern?'

'Don't worry,' he said, 'he knows what he's doing.'

I hoped he was right. Half an hour later, with the crew frantically running around and heated words being exchanged between the pole men and the captain, the engines stopped completely.

'What's happening now?' I asked Aung Win, who had been listening intently.

'We've run aground.'

I groaned. 'So what now?'

He shrugged philosophically. 'We wait to be pulled off.'

With merely two days left in the country, it was just what I didn't need. I settled down reluctantly on my mat and passed the time reading, dozing or hanging out with Aung Win at the food stall, which sold bananas, onion cakes and single cigarettes.

That afternoon I heard uproarious laughter, so I drifted curiously to the stern, where a crowd had gathered round a skinny young man who was telling stories. I sat down, and, although I understood nothing, I stayed for hours, listening to one of the most eloquent, entertaining and expressive storytellers I'd ever heard. It was like watching the performance of a great Shakespearean actor.

Sixteen hours after we ran aground, an antiquated tug with a pencil-thin smokestack chugged alongside us, laboriously attached rusty hawsers and towed us off the sandbank. At dusk we arrived in Bagan, a village on the bend in the river. There, in an empty hotel with torn mosquito nets and creaking overhead fans, I found a room and watched the sunset in abandoned gardens overlooking the river.

Early the next morning, with no time to lose, I pedalled a squeaking bicycle to the village of Nyaung-oo, which was the best place to start exploring Bagan. Suddenly I was confronted with the unbelievable sight of 2,200 whitewashed *stupas* and huge crumbling

Temple in Bagan, central Burma

temples, scattered for forty square kilometres over an arid plain.

Bagan, showing unmistakable Mahayana, and possibly Tantric, influence similar to Buddhist temples in north-east India, was built between 1057 and 1287. The eccentric monarch Narathihapate, whose nickname was 'the swallower of 300 dishes of curry daily', abandoned the city after his army – 2,000 elephants and 60,000 soldiers, according to Marco Polo – was put to flight by Kublai Khan's Mongolian hordes, leaving it to become the world's most fabulous ghost town.

I spent the day climbing the cracked overgrown temples, many of them capped by tinkling silver bells. The dark interiors were full of peeling murals, bat droppings and soot from fires lit by Burmese hiding from the Japanese during the Second World War. That evening I ate in a cramped candlelit shack in the village before I cycled back to the hotel. Then, at dawn, I squeezed into the back of a crowded pick-up heading for distant Yangon. Fifteen hours later, I arrived, dusty and exhausted, back in the capital, with only six hours left until my plane departed and my visa expired.

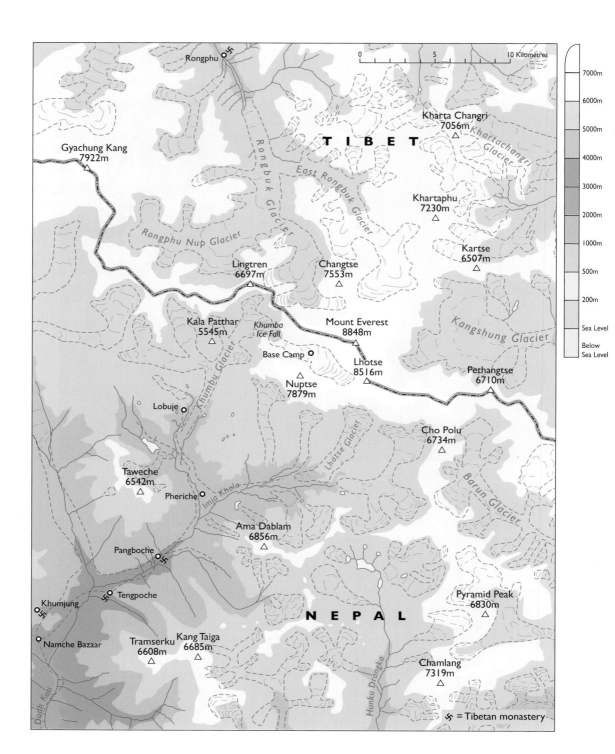

Rongphu ⚕

0   5   10 Kilometres

7000m
6000m
5000m
4000m
3000m
2000m
1000m
500m
200m
Sea Level
Below
Sea Level

Gyachung Kang
7922m △

Kharta Changri
7056m △

Kharta changri Glacier

T I B E T

East Rongbuk Glacier

Rongbuk Glacier

Rongphu Nup Glacier

Khartaphu
7230m △

Kartse
6507m △

Lingtren
6697m △

Changtse
7553m △

Kala Patthar
5545m △

Khumba
Ice Fall

Mount Everest
8848m △

Kangshung Glacier

Base Camp ○

Lhotse
8516m △

Pethangtse
6710m △

Nuptse
7879m △

Khumbu Glacier

Lobuje ○

Lhotse Glacier

Cho Polu
6734m △

Barun Glacier

Taweche
6542m △

Pheriche ○

Imja Khola

Ama Dablam
6856m △

Pangboche ○⚕

Khumjung ○⚕

⚕○ Tengpoche

Pyramid Peak
6830m △

N E P A L

○⚕
Namche Bazaar ○

Tramserku
6608m △

Kang Taiga
6685m △

Hunku Drangka

Chamlang
7319m △

Dudh Kosi

⚕ = Tibetan monastery

To my delight it was the weekly market, when Sherpas flock in from neighbouring villages. Nick and I split up for the day, and I spent all morning exploring the winding stone alleys. Toothless shrunken men sat cross-legged on blankets selling flour, and women in traditional Sherpa dress – a long sleeveless tunic with a gaily striped apron and a coloured blouse – spun yak wool. There were also many lowland porters, who carry goods from villages up to ten days' walk away before racing back down to warmer valleys below.

That afternoon I made the stiff one-hour climb past Hillary's original school to neighbouring Khumjung, whose monastery claims to possess a yeti's skull. Unluckily, it was closed, so I wasn't able to see it. In Tibetan *yeh* means 'snow valley' and *teh* 'man', and yetis are reputedly elusive, man-like animals living at high altitudes on the Himalayan snowline. They've never been photographed, but footprints have been found by many expeditions, while the mountaineers Don Whillans and Reinhold Messner claimed to have seen one in 1970 on Everest and one in 1986 in Tibet. In Mustang, in western Nepal, people even reported seeing an entire herd in 1992. Hillary, himself, who maintained that it is impossible to divorce yetis from the Sherpas' supernatural beliefs, was sceptical, especially after scientists declared Khumjung's skull, which he took to America in 1960 for examination, to be antelope skin.

The night was exceedingly cold and we woke up repeatedly, not helped by local clocks (made from empty oxygen cylinders) striking. We were glad to be on the move again at dawn, when we made the steep two-hour ascent to Tengpoche. This is Khumbu's largest and most active *gompa* (monastery), which is spectacularly situated in meadows surrounded by firs and rhododendrons, in the shadows of snowcapped Kang Taiga and Tramserku. Buddhism was introduced to Khumbu in the seventeenth century by Lama (monk) Sange Dorje, the fifth reincarnation of Rongbuk Monastery's lama, Red Hat, who, according to legend, flew over Everest and landed on rocks at Tengpoche. Only completed in 1919, the monastery has been rebuilt twice, after being destroyed by an earthquake in 1934 and a fire in 1989.

That evening, we found lodgings in the New Zealand-built Sherpa Lodge and slipped unobserved into the temple's prayer hall, where expeditions used to receive the lama's blessings, for the evening ceremony.

It was a sublime experience; shaven-headed monks in purple robes chanted mantras, clashed symbols, banged drums and blew three-metre horns underneath original *tankas* (hanging silk scrolls depicting Buddha's life) full of writhing demons and Bosch-like visions of heaven and hell. When it was finished I wandered past young apprentices turning prayer wheels in the courtyard. Snow was gently falling from clear, starlit skies, and I could see the Yugoslavs' fires flickering in the darkness.

At 6 a.m. the next morning, we picked our way past the expedition's yaks grazing in meadows which sloped down steeply to the thunderous Dudh Kosi River far below. Then we tramped along the well-beaten path that ascends the valley opposite breathtaking

Ama Dablam (6,812 metres), where the path descended steeply through groves of twisted junipers and green lichen-laden birch trees. There we came to a swaying bridge, and we crossed the rushing Imja Khola River before climbing past carved *manis* (stones covered with Tibetan prayers) and *chortens* (Buddhist funeral mounds) to Pangboche. This was the mountain's 450-year-old *gompa*, the oldest in Khumbu, which housed yeti 'relics' until they were stolen in 1991.

Tracking the Imja Khola, which led up directly north-east to the Khumbu Glacier and Base Camp, we reached the tundra, which in summer is covered with edelweiss. Further up was Pheriche (4,200 metres), a straggling village with single-storey Sherpa tea-shops, where we spent the next two days acclimatizing. Each afternoon we toiled 450 punishing metres up to ridges from which there were staggering views of four of the world's thirteen peaks higher than 8,000 metres, including Makalu and Cho Oyu. After we descended, as

Young novice outside Tengpoche Monastery, with Mount Everest in the background, Nepal

the clinging mist closed in at dusk, we sat with Sherpas round blackened stoves. There we listened to the howling winds and the crackle of Radio Delhi, as well as the tales of the American doctors from the all-important Himalayan Rescue Association aid post, who all insisted that the five-week experience had changed their lives forever.

At last Nick and I set off for Lobuje, the last inhabited settlement before Base Camp. It was a shattering climb, with the track zigzagging steeply across boulders and streams onto the Khumbu Glacier's jumbled terminal moraine. Worried about my headaches, sleeplessness and lack of appetite, which are all classic signs of altitude sickness, I let Nick go ahead, although I was fairly sure that my symptoms were probably because I was wearing my contact lenses for longer than normal. Along the way, I paused at sad little memorial bridges that had been erected by the parents of trekkers who had died.

The trail curved round the valley's arid western flank, reportedly the habitat of snow leopard and yeti, to the lee of mountains. Here, we pitched our tent with considerable difficulty in the hard ground next to herders' scattered stone huts, and watched the Sherpas, yaks and Yugoslavs straggle into Lobuje. That night we crowded round smoky fires in cramped draughty rooms, which were not much more than byres, where asthmatic old Sherpas prepared the meal. I stayed until late, but eventually, unable to stand the smoke and the conversations of New Zealand trekkers discussing porters' prices, I stumbled outside for fresh air.

A brilliant full moon had just emerged from behind Lhotse, looming into the star-scattered skies. Suddenly a dark shape stirred in one of the stone corrals – I'd disturbed the entire yak herd. A cowbell rang, and another, and yet another as more and more yaks woke up, until dozens of cowbells were tinkling harmoniously like an immense orchestra tuning up for some great cosmic concert.

That night temperatures fell to –20°C. We hardly slept, as we huddled in freezing sleeping bags and tossed and turned on the rock-hard ground. At daybreak, unshaven, hungry and filthy, we set off in the ambitious attempt to reach both Everest Base Camp and Kala Patthar, where there was nowhere to stay, before returning to Lobuje that night. The alternative was to take two days to make this journey, which meant having to repeat our footsteps or bivouac at a freezing 5,500-metre altitude.

The path was rough and, apart from the yak droppings, difficult to find as it descended to loose moraine criss-crossed with glacial streams. For the first and only time, as my beloved, but soaking, gym shoes started to split, I wished I had proper climbing boots.

It was also highly dangerous; after we scrambled down to the shimmering green Khumbu Glacier, several times as we crossed ice-fields we found ourselves within metres of yawning crevasses. We carefully picked our way through melting, fifteen-metre-high ice pinnacles and, avoiding broken glass, rusting cans and plastic bottles, arrived at group of orange tents and fluttering prayer-flags at the foot of the stupendous Khumbu Ice Fall. It was Everest Base Camp (5,360 metres).

It was an extraordinarily busy scene, as the advance party of the Yugoslavs had already been there for a week. We watched goggled Yugoslavs and Sherpas in colourful gear pottering around amongst oxygen cylinders for a while, before we began the final push up to Kala Patthar, a 5,600-metre spur of 7,100-metre Pumori, and the best vantage point for viewing Everest. Leaving Nick behind, as he'd just been violently sick, and convincing myself at each step that the Herculean effort was worth it, I set off up the last two-hundred-metre stretch. It was a killing ascent, and as I dragged myself up over boulders, head throbbing and lungs gasping for oxygen in the rarefied air, I didn't dare stop in case I never started again. Two hours later I reached the summit where, body screaming in pain, I finally turned round.

It was, arguably, the world's most awe-inspiring sight. Through five kilometres of yawning emptiness directly opposite was the Khumbu Ice Fall, which was like a great frozen city composed of vast blocks of ice. Above, past towering buttresses, fluted walls, serrated arêtes and fractured fissures flanked by the West Shoulder and precipitous Nuptse, a bare, black pyramid soared another 3,500 metres above Base Camp into the royal-blue sky. Long snow plumes whipped by ferocious winds streamed imperially from its aloof and forbidding summit.

It was mighty Everest, or Sagarmatha in Nepali, and Chomolongma in Sherpa and Tibetan.

Mount Everest from Kala Patthar, Nepal

Overwhelmed, I lay amongst rocks in the warm sunshine, listening to the intense silence, which was broken only by occasional rumbles of avalanches collapsing thousands of metres down Nuptse. It was one of the most spiritual experiences of my life; I felt like Adam, the only person on earth, or God just after the birth of Creation. As I closed my eyes against the dazzling glare of the sun, my mind was flooded with concepts of The Absolute – Alpha, Omega, The One – before the Tibetan Buddhist prayer *Om Mani Padme Hum* came to me.

An hour later, Nick arrived, also half-dead. Then, when we'd both recovered, we set off back down to the world of mortals far below.

INDIA: KASHMIR AND LADAKH

At first, as I stepped off the bus into the walled terminal in Srinagar, Kashmir's capital, I thought I was going to be lynched. It was dusk, and the police escort, who had given up waiting for us, had left open the gates of the normally sealed compound. Now a mob of clamouring houseboat owners, desperate for customers, besieged the handful of Westerners foolish enough to have travelled to Kashmir. Just two years earlier, Al-Faran, an unknown group of separatist Muslim guerrillas, had kidnapped six foreign trekkers, beheaded one of them and vanished.

I was worn out after the rattling, ten-hour journey up from Jammu's railhead in north India, but I managed to fend off clutching hands and, chased by only the most persistent hustlers, hurried through the deserted medieval town. It was a frightening experience, as everywhere there was barbed wire, Indian Army barricades and burnt-out houses, so I didn't stop until, at Dal Lake, I'd shaken them off. As the hour of military curfew approached, I arrived at lakeside steps and randomly selected one of the pleading *shikara* (gondola) owners, who paddled me through lush, floating gardens to a magnificent houseboat's intricately carved stern.

It was an astonishing Edwardian time warp, with comfortable armchairs, bleached chintz curtains and silver-framed Raj photographs. Mohammed, the dignified, elderly owner, was hospitable and courteous. That night, over sumptuous courses lovingly served on cracked Chippendale, he told me that the road to my destination, remote Ladakh, 320 kilometres east, was still cut off by snow.

The next morning, therefore, I joined two travellers wintering on his cheaper, basic boat moored opposite. Karen was a moody, bad-tempered 26-year-old from Yorkshire. Her long-suffering boyfriend, Rob, was a bearded, bespectacled Australian with a much-needed sense of humour. Reluctantly, I settled down to wait.

It was easy to see why Kashmir, enclosed by the snowcapped Himalayas, has been called a modern-day Garden of Eden. It's not surprising that tourism started here a century ago,

My houseboat on Dal Lake, Kashmir, northern India

when the British, eager to escape the baking hot Indian plains, but forbidden by Kashmir's rulers to own land, built houseboats on Dal Lake. Later it became a popular holiday destination for India's prosperous middle classes, and a stopover for hippies travelling overland to India in the 1960s.

Every morning, awakened by Karen haranguing Rob, I'd prop open side hatches to watch graceful, flower-laden *shikaras* glide by before I breakfasted outside in the wintry sunshine. After I'd fed Percy, the lovable chicken we'd bought to stew until we grew too fond of him, I would paddle at the stern, crouched Kashmiri style, through the maze of waterways to the local shops, which were just houseboats tucked away among weeping willows. There I'd buy freshly baked chapattis and drift back via the floating gardens, marvelling at the monstrous cabbages and carrots; I had never realized what human manure could do for vegetables.

The evenings were also magical. At dusk we would cook on our spluttering paraffin stove before we visited Kashmiri friends on neighbouring houseboats. They squatted in carpeted corners, smoking hubble-bubbles and nursing 'winter wives' (urns of glowing coal) under long woollen cloaks. When I returned home, I'd lie on my mattress on bare floorboards, watching my candle flicker in the inky night. Outside, ripples slapped the hull as *shikaras* nosed silently like sharks through the velvety water.

Sometimes, of course, we went ashore. We'd shake off the touts clustered by the *shikara* steps, and stroll along the promenade to Nishat Bagh. Here the Mogul art of formal gardens reached its greatest heights after the visiting Emperor Akbar declared Kashmir his 'private garden' in 1589, when it was merged into his empire. Mercifully, the gardens were deserted, except for a few men lazing under shady cedars and women in purple saris and green head-scarves picnicking on now ill-kempt landscaped lawns.

Once, we went swimming in eastern Dal Lake, where, in glades free of the usually ubiquitous clinging weeds, there were wooden rafts. It was here I met Philippe, a gaunt in-tellectual from Paris with a walrus moustache, who worked as a journalist for a Left Bank newspaper. Undergoing a spiritual crisis after spending months with Burmese Karen rebels, he wanted to study Buddhism in Ladakh, so we agreed to travel together the minute the road opened.

Only rarely did I venture into Srinagar. The road ran past old-fashioned, eerily deserted emporiums stacked with exquisite carpets, intricate wood engravings and lacquered papier mâché objects. Further along, in the old quarter's twisting alleyways lining the River Jhe-lum's banks, the atmosphere was even more oppressive, as sullen Kashmiris behind stalls piled with fruit and raisins suspiciously eyed nervous-looking Indian soldiers.

Hindu maharajas ruled Kashmir during the British Raj. However, on independence, in 1947, they opted to join India instead of Pakistan, although Kashmir had a Muslim population. The result has been three Indo-Pakistani wars, turmoil and terrible atrocities committed, according to widely documented allegations, by the brutal Indian Army, who behave like a hostile occupying force. But Pakistan's much-denied covert support for Kashmiri guerrillas rebounded; by 1992 the Jammu and Kashmir Liberation Front were demanding independence from both nations.

As weeks passed, my relationship with Karen deteriorated: on one occasion, after we'd had a petty dispute about expenses, she poured a bucket of water over me. I grew impatient, and gazed longingly east towards Ladakh, far beyond the Himalayan peaks ringing the lake. But then came the rains, breaking up the lake's glassy surface and hanging like curtains over the houseboat. Marooned for days on end, I spent hours talking to Mohammed, who, like many a dogged Anglophile, reminisced about British Army officers he'd taken trekking as a lad. 'God made our bones, but the English made the rest,' he'd repeat ruefully, before bewailing present-day Kashmir's calamitous state.

At last, news arrived that snowploughs had opened the road. A month after I had arrived, Philippe and I set off, overjoyed, on the arduous three-day journey to Ladakh. Tracking the swift-flowing River Sind, our bus passed through valleys dotted with cherry orchards and mud-brick thatched villages. The road climbed to Sonamarg, which, previous to the terrorist activity, had been a favourite base for trekking in the surrounding peaks. Now the falling-apart chalets in the steep valley were locked, and only a few foolhardy, overweight Indian tourists seemed to be interested in the ten-minute pony rides on offer.

Not long afterwards, the bus terminated at Baltal, where tracks branched off to Amarnath Cave. Here, at full moon every July, thousands of half-naked Hindu *sadhus* (holy men) from all over India make the long and dangerous two-day pilgrimage to worship a swollen ice lingam that is believed to be a symbol of Lord Shiva, the Creator.

We waited outside a dusty army compound, where we found a lorry bound for Kargil, 160 kilometres away. Soon we were stuck behind army convoys as we inched towards spiky, snowy pinnacles. This area has had a sensitive history: the Chinese seized parts of disputed east Ladakh during the 1962 Sino-Indian war, and the road was built to enable Indian forces to reinforce the border. Meanwhile sporadic Indo-Pakistani fighting still flares at the controversial demarcation line across the eastern Karakoram, and the area is closed to foreigners.

Near the highest point of the road there were vertical drops to a torrent that, far below, sliced through precipitous ravines. Suddenly we were queuing behind bustling snowploughs through Zoji La Pass, an area of treacherous ice-fields and deep snowdrifts. For centuries, traders carrying saffron and silk crossed through here on their way to ancient Silk Road trading posts in China.

Fifty kilometres later, and badly sunburnt, we were grateful when the road descended to Kargil. Although it's Ladakh's second-biggest town, it has a population of only 8,000, predominantly Shia Muslims who share cultural affinities with Baltistan, and consists of a main street sprinkled with grubby restaurants and garages piled with cannibalized vehicles. For a long time it had been a key trading centre linking Ladakh with Gilgit and the lower Indus Valley and, despite being stranded on the wrong side of the 1947 ceasefire line, only twenty years ago it was still common to see yak trains in the bazaar. A trickle of travellers had also passed through, after the Indian government opened Ladakh in 1974, but even this had dried up, especially following the Pakistani shelling that killed seventeen civilians in October 1997. Now it had an oppressive air, with women rarely to be seen, although mosques dominating the town were swarming with fierce-looking, turbaned tribesmen. I wasn't sorry to leave the next morning, when we hitched a lift with Manfred, a hippy traveller reminiscent of Mick Jagger, who had driven his self-converted 1970s Mercedes bus all the way from Berlin. Shortly, we were climbing into Buddhist Ladakh.

Hidden away in India's remote north-west, tiny Ladakh, with a population of only 130,000, marks the boundary between the western Himalayan peaks and the Tibetan plateau, with which it has close links. First populated by yak-grazing nomads, it wasn't until Indian Buddhist pilgrims passed through on their way to Tibet that settlements were established

led me through a maze of panelled corridors to a simple room that looked out onto a cast-iron bell suspended from the beams of a pagoda. Although there was only a mattress, a tatami mat on the polished floor and a stove for furniture, it was warm and peaceful.

I was lying there blissfully when, to my astonishment, I heard my name called urgently on an intercom.

'Mister Lichaldson, take bath please.'

I didn't need urging, as I was desperately in need of thawing out, so I hurried down to the entrance. A shrunken-looking monk showed me through the kitchen to a steamy bathroom, where I spent the evening luxuriating in a tub of heavenly hot water and trying to erase my nightmarish memories of Tokyo.

It snowed again heavily during the night, and the next day the town was white and sparkling. Soon I set out to do some exploring. Just round the corner was the oldest building in town, Kokubunji, a three-storey pagoda dating from the fifteenth century, although the original was from the eighth, when the Japanese emperor ordered the building of provincial temples across the country as a symbol of his desire for peace. Nearby was Teramachi, a row of eighteen exquisite Buddhist temples and Shinto shrines stretching over three kilome-

Temple in Takayama, Nagano-Ken, central Japan

tres in landscaped gardens, where minute bridges and cedar trees were laden with snow.

I was in Shiroyama Koen, a park from where you can see the Japanese Alps, when I heard chanting coming from Shorenji, a sixteenth-century pagoda reputedly made from a single giant cedar. I crept up a path and peered round immense oak doors. In front of a Buddha draped in yellow silk, a row of women, heads bowed, were kneeling on cushions. A monk with a shaven head, a maroon robe, white socks and clogs was slowly beating a cylindrical red drum. Suddenly there was silence, broken only by the drip, drip and drip of melting water.

Takayama is often cut off by snow in winter, and this, plus the fact that a samurai family ruled it, has meant that it and many traditions have been remarkably preserved. San-Machi Suji, the old quarter, is as it was three centuries ago, when local warlord Kanamori laid out his castle town. The streets run in a grid pattern similar to Kyoto, giving Takayama its nickname 'Little Kyoto'. Later it came under the direct control of the Tokugawa Shogunate, which lasted until the Meiji Restoration in 1868.

The centre is Furui-Machinami, a pedestrian street lined with wooden houses, taverns, inns and shops selling striking woodcarvings, lacquerware and pottery. There are also many craftsmen's workshops and sake warehouses, which are indicated by a ball made of cedar leaves hanging outside. Sake, for which Takayama is famous, needs fine rice, pure water and cold weather. All have long been here in abundance, and the eight breweries in town date from the Edo era (1603–1867).

Two days later I left for Shirakawa-go, a remote mountain region famous for traditional thatched farmhouses built in *kirizuma gassho zukuri* ('hands held in prayer style'), with steeply sloping gable roofs to support heavy snowfalls.

The bus stopped briefly on the banks of the Seto River in the exquisite town of Furukawa. Its narrow streets were dotted with white-walled storehouses and criss-crossed by canals stocked with golden carp. Some time later, the empty bus headed into a raging blizzard. The road ran alongside the rushing, icy-green Shokawa River, through deserted hills and villages piled high with snow. In due course we pulled into a village that looked like a scene from Hansel and Gretel, with thatched roofs peeping above the snow.

'Shilakawa,' stated the driver baldly.

The area was settled in the twelfth century by survivors of the Taira clan who were defeated by the Genji clan in the decisive battle of Dan-no-Ura for control of Japan. The villagers used to earn their living by farming, silk cultivation and burnt-field agriculture. Being surrounded by mountains, they had only a few cultivated fields and, because many hands were required, they were forced to establish the extended family system. All the children, except the eldest son, had to live at home – sometimes single houses contained fifty people – and not get formally married. A young man was expected to visit the house

The minshuku *(guesthouse) in Shirakawa, Nagano-Ken, central Japan*

of his girlfriend's family to make love to her, and children of these couples were raised by the woman's family.

I crossed a mini-bridge over a frozen stream and, obeying the pictorial signs, struggled up a path through an immense snowdrift to the *minshuku*, a traditional Japanese family home that takes guests. It was a long wooden farmhouse buried to its eaves; outside, a shrunken man in a peasant's bamboo hat was cheerfully digging out his sledge.

His wife showed me along a dark corridor full of tools, looms, spindles and piles of logs and bamboo to a room. It was very spartan, with only a mountainous pile of thick bedding on the floor and, at the foot, a plain wooden box.

'Put feet in. Nights cold,' she explained.

Not only nights: the temperature outside was already −15°C, and I was so frozen that, once she shut the sliding panel, I went to bed. There I discovered the bliss of a Shirakawa footwarmer, the plain wooden box that has two electric light bulbs (protected by a cage) left

193

on all night to keep the feet warm.

Later that evening she knocked and announced supper. The dining room was all dark floorboards and sliding panels, and was very minimalist, except for a dresser containing iron cooking utensils, and a kettle suspended by a hook over a fire in a hearth in the middle of the room. It was also smoky and draughty, with smoke going straight through blackened rafters up to the attic, which was used in earlier times for storing farming tools and as a space for silkworm nurseries, spinning and weaving.

The meal, as always in Japan, was immaculately prepared: thirteen miniature dishes, including rice wrapped in a bamboo leaf, tofu decorated with a sprig of parsley, asparagus in hot soya sauce, a steamed plum, spinach, strips of seaweed, salty rice crackers and fresh grilled trout.

The woman spent the evening telling me about Doburoku-Matsuri, an October festival celebrating harvest. When the mountain forests become red and yellow, a huge drum on a float and coloured streamers are paraded through the village. Then young girls in front of the shrine perform 'the lion's dance', and everyone drinks unrefined sake and plays music on samisen or sings folk songs.

After I left Shirakawa, I returned to southern Honshu, where I visited Nara, the former capital of Japan. Most of its famous temples and black and white pagodas were in Nara-koen Park, which had a serene holy lake and was full of tame, grazing deer. The largest

The Todai-ji Temple in Nara, Honshu, central Japan

temple, Todai-ji, contained Japan's largest Buddha, which was housed in the world's largest wooden structure. Then I took the *shinkansen* from Osaka to Hiroshima, where I visited the Peace Park. This, of course, commemorates the dropping of the atomic bomb on the city in 1945, and it was, as I suspected, an overpowering emotional experience, and one that everyone should have.

But, when I left Japan, it was the memories of the dark winter evenings, the little trundling trains and snowy mountains of Nagano-Ken that lingered in my mind.

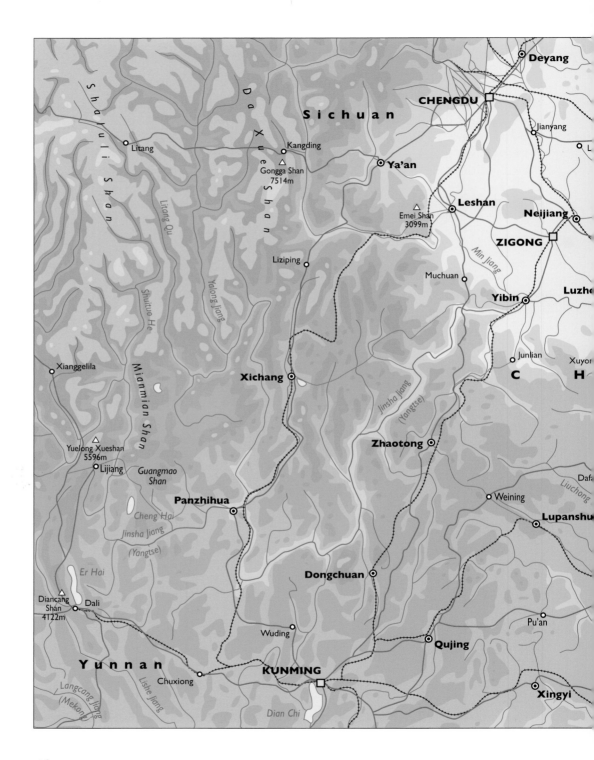

Deyang

Sichuan

CHENGDU

Jianyang

L

Litang

Kangding

Gongga Shan
7514m

Ya'an

Emei Shan
3099m

Leshan

Neijiang

ZIGONG

Liziping

Muchuan

Min Jiang

Yibin

Luzho

Da Xue Shan

Litang Qu

Shuiluo He

Yalong Jiang

Junlian

Xuyor

Xianggelila

C   H

Xichang

Jinsha Jiang
(Yangtse)

Mianmian Shan

Zhaotong

Yuelong Xueshan
5596m

Lijiang

Guangmao
Shan

Dafa

Liuchong

Panzhihua

Weining

Lupanshu

Cheng Hai

Jinsha Jiang

(Yangtse)

Dongchuan

Er Hai

Pu'an

Diancang
Shan
4122m

Dali

Wuding

Qujing

Yunnan

Chuxiong

KUNMING

Xingyi

Langcang Jiang

Lishe Jiang

Dian Chi

(Mekong)

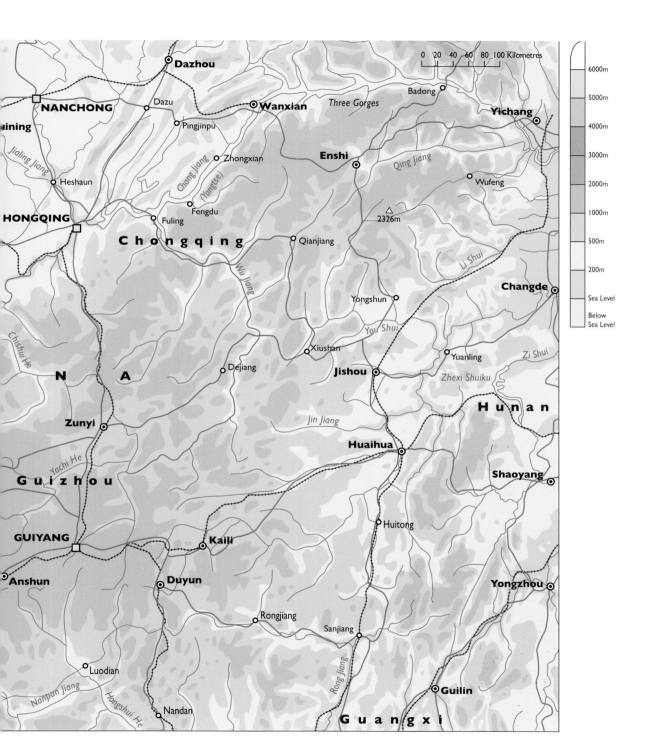

Dazhou

NANCHONG

uining

Jialing Jiang

Dazu

Pingjinpu

Wanxian

Three Gorges

Badong

Yichang

Zhongxian

Enshi

Qing Jiang

Wufeng

Heshaun

Chang Jiang

(Yangtse)

HONGQING

Fengdu

Fuling

C h o n g q i n g

Qianjiang

△ 2326m

Li Shui

Wu Jiang

Changde

Chishui He

N   A

Dejiang

Yongshun

You Shui

Xiushan

Jishou

Yuanling

Zi Shui

Zhexi Shuiku

H u n a n

Zunyi

Jin Jiang

Yachi He

Huaihua

G u i z h o u

Shaoyang

GUIYANG

Kaili

Huitong

Anshun

Duyun

Yongzhou

Rongjiang

Sanjiang

Luodian

Rong Jiang

Nanpan Jiang

Hongshui He

Nandan

Guilin

G u a n g x i

0 20 40 60 80 100 Kilometres

6000m
5000m
4000m
3000m
2000m
1000m
500m
200m
Sea Level
Below
Sea Level

CHINA
Lijiang and Dr Ho

The road north from Dali to the town of Lijiang in Yunnan, south-west China, is beautiful. Once past the head of Erhai Lake, the shallows of which are dotted with fishing boats and nets, the road leaves behind the villages of the Bai people and climbs into uninhabited red hills. Soon there are pine and rhododendron forests, with spectacular views over ranges stretching west to Tibet. The summit is quickly reached and, to the north, there's a new panorama: the Jade Dragon Mountains, with Lijiang nestling snugly in the valley below.

Old Lijiang is also very appealing, with tiny canals, humpback bridges, and cobbled streets crowded with minority Naxi people. The Naxi are descended from Tibetan nomads and believe they come from a common ancestor named Tabu, who helped them hatch from magic eggs. Many Naxi women still wear traditional clothes, namely navy-blue trousers and

The Moon-Embracing Pavilion in front of the Jade Dragon Mountains, Lijiang, south-west China

covered peaks so close you could almost lean out and touch them. Then the descent began, winding down through pine forests until, 600 metres below, surrounded by brown treeless mountains, was a ledge which disappeared into a gigantic canyon.

An hour later, with the Naxi shrieking with delight as the bus bucked like a bronco on the rough track, we arrived in Daju, a village dozing in the baking midday heat. As I looked for somewhere to spend the night, I could see a horse wandering aimlessly amongst the wooden shacks and babies playing in the dust.

The next morning an irritable man rowed me across the narrow Yangtze River to a dusty path that climbed a cliff and disappeared into the canyon. The track wasn't much more than a narrow ledge cut into the vertical mountainside, and I tramped along it with trepidation, hardly daring to look up at thousands of tons of overhanging rock, or down at the dizzying drop into emptiness.

Once, the sound of a landslide ricocheted round the canyon, and I heard a shepherd boy calling his sheep. Apart from that, I could only hear the roar of water far below and a rook cawing. The path was also deserted, save for a wild horse and a ragged, shrunken old man. Although he had no teeth, he was smoking a silver pipe, and he had a tobacco pouch full of twigs.

Six hours later I reached Tiger Leaping Gorge, which was so narrow that, legend says, a hunted tiger jumped across it. Opposite, a wall of black rock soared so vertically I had to crane backward forty-five degrees to see a forest of spiky black pinnacles swirling in mist and blotting out the sun.

I stayed the night in a spartan house a few kilometres further on, where, clinging to a ledge, green terraces rippled down the mountainside until they fell off into the abyss. Inside the house, an aged peasant man played well-known Naxi compositions such as 'The Water Dragon is Singing' and 'Wind from the River' on his flute; the Naxi were renowned for music long before Kublai Khan's invasion in the thirteenth century.

Two days after I'd set off I arrived filthy and hungry at the end of the gorge. Not far away was the First Great Bend in the Yangtze where, under Mao, the Red Army made its famous crossing during The Long March of 1936.

I was exhilarated but thankful I hadn't been in their shoes. My walk, after twenty kilometres, was at an end; they would have had another 3,000 still to go.

Emei Shan
Judging by Baoguo Temple, at the foot of the peak, a stunning experience awaited me as I set off on the two-day pilgrimage up lofty Emei Shan in remote south-west Yunnan – at 3,117 metres, the highest of China's four sacred Buddhist Mountains.

Built in the sixteenth century by Emperor Kangxi, it was set against hillsides covered

Young novices in Baoguo Temple, Yunnan, south-west China

with rhododendrons. Incense burned at a giant porcelain Buddha behind massive maroon doors. At the back of the temple, classrooms were crammed with chanting, shaven-headed novices. Through side arches there were bonsai rockeries, and miniature ornamental bridges led to a lotus-roofed pavilion on a minuscule island. Here, monks lazed about enjoying the hazy sunshine and idly watching an approaching crocodile of noisy kindergarten infants with red taffeta ribbons in their hair and panda-shaped schoolbags on their backs. They peeped at me shyly as they filed past, before admiring their reflections in carp-filled pools.

The beginning of the trail, as it wound up lush terraced hillsides, was also very atmospheric. It was lined with stalls, where shrivelled men with wispy mandarin beards sold herbs, plastic raincoats, handcrafted walking sticks and umbrellas. Further up, past dripping bamboo thickets, cedar tops poked out of the notorious clinging mist, which I hoped would lift, as I wanted to see Emei's equally famous butterflies, brazen monkeys and elusive giant pandas. Soon Wannian, the Temple of Ten Thousand Years, loomed. Built in AD 980 and Emei's oldest surviving temple, it was hemmed in by bamboo groves and tropical vegetation. Under a white domed roof, a bronze Bodhisattva rode a life-sized elephant called Pu Xian, the mountain's protector. Vaults contained statues of Chinese sages, and there were niches lined with 1,000 tiny Buddhas. In gardens to the rear, courtyards were full of roses, bonsai trees and goldfish ponds.

In ancient China, climbing sacred mountains was a traditional pastime: emperors went to make sacrifices to heaven; scholars to draw inspiration for poetry and painting; mystics to become hermits; and ordinary people to pray. By the fourteenth century, Emei, which represents Pu Xian, Bodhisattva of Universal Kindness, had thousands of monks living in 100 monasteries, many dating back to Buddhism's advent in China during the Han dynasty (AD 25–220). By the late eighteenth century, Imperial China had entered a period of irrevocable decline, and now fewer than twenty monasteries remain on Emei Shan. This is also because of fire, the 1895 Sino-Japanese war and, most destructive of all, Mao's Cultural Revolution, when violent reaction against 'feudalism' led to widespread vandalism by the Red Guards. However, Buddhism has been openly tolerated since liberalisation in 1976, and the authorities have recognized the need to prevent further deterioration.

After Wannian, the path climbed through ghostly pine forests to what appeared to be an old barn. Inside, an aged monk sat at a glowing stove while mist swirled round dusty red drums, kettle-lined walls and a Buddha draped with orange flags. 'Ni shi zai nar ren? [lit. You are where person?]' he asked.

'Wo shi Sugelan ren [I am Scotland person],' I replied, keen to dry out in the barn, and practise my basic Chinese, which was still largely incomprehensible, despite two years of diligent study.

'Ah,' he sighed, his face lighting up, 'Shew-en Ken-nai-ray [Sean Connery]!'

Higher up, the mountain seemed like something out of Chaucer's *Canterbury Tales* or a Kurosawa samurai film-set. Indistinct figures of women selling 'divine water' floated around outside bamboo huts. Voices rang out as straw-hatted pilgrims with walking canes descended into the gloom, and brawny young men carrying geriatric women in medieval-looking sedan chairs jolted past. After climbing steeply, the path arrived at an old monastery built on rocky outcrops at the confluence of two torrential streams. About halfway up Emei Shan, it was the Pavilion of Singing Waters, which, according to my map, had a guesthouse. A monk showed me to a spartan dormitory under the eaves, from where echoing corridors led to a precarious balcony on stilts overlooking a courtyard. It was full of drying sheets, and the sounds of beating drums, tinkling bells and chanting drifted up from lamplit windows, along with clouds of sweet smelling incense.

As darkness fell, I joined the monks for the evening meal in the frugal-looking kitchen downstairs. Afterwards, I was wandering along labyrinthine passageways when I heard laughter coming from draughty offices above the imposing main gates. Inside, monks in thick greatcoats were huddled round a brazier as mist seeped through panelling and crooked doors. They were playing cards, but were desperate to practise their English. 'Wish success in modernisation programme,' mumbled one, poring over a yellowing phrase book printed in Beijing.

'Circus fantastic, especially lion dance and trapeze,' announced a second, turning pages as he leant over the first's shoulder.

'Want shampoo, trim, no set!' said a third, humorously rubbing his pate.

I stayed till late, as I'd had noticed earlier that there was only one blanket on the bed in the dormitory, where I'd heard rats scuttling about. Just as I suspected, I passed a sleepless night; even worse, the next morning dawned with the mist thicker than ever. Momentarily, I was tempted to turn back but I decided against it. After all, the weather could improve, and I might yet see the reputedly breathtaking view from the top of the peak – when the sun emerges above a sea of swirling clouds – and perhaps even the 'Buddha's Aureole'. This is a rare phenomenon, when rainbow rings, produced by the refraction of water particles, attach themselves to a person's shadow in cloud banks below the summit – a sight so awe-inspiring that ecstatic pilgrims, thinking it was a call from yonder, used to jump off the Cliff of Self-sacrifice until Ming dynasty officials erected railings.

An hour after I left the monastery, I reached a ruined pagoda at the edge of a mist-shrouded abyss, where sounds of a gurgling river and birdsong wafted up eerily from far below. I was toiling painfully upwards when ragged entrepreneurs appeared at the foot of icy, crudely hewn steps. They were touting antediluvian crampons, which were just rusty iron soles with spikes. At first, I was tempted to hire some but they were ludicrously expensive and, in any case, had to be exchanged every 100 metres. Ignoring the mocking laughter of the entrepreneurs, I inched upwards to the top, only to find that the path emerged onto a dirt track gouged out of the mountainside. It was the road up to the newly constructed cable-car terminal, and hordes of tourists were piling off minibuses into shanty food-stalls.

Fortunately, the route plunged immediately back into the forest. I was tracking footprints in grimy snow, feeling cheated, as it had taken me a hard, two-day slog to do what now tourists can do in an hour, when a grotesque, pink four-storey building reared ahead. Although it looked like a power station, it was the new cable-car terminal, from which crowds spewed onto wasteland littered with sandpits, bricks and pipes. Fearing the worst, as mass accessibility usually means ruination, I hurried on. Sixty metres higher up was Jinding Golden Temple, the last accommodation before the summit, where I had planned to stay the night. Previously famous for its brass tiling engraved with Tibetan script, it had been garishly rebuilt after being gutted by fire and was now awash with teenagers wearing baseball caps and trainers, and carrying blaring portable radios. Nearby, laughing crowds queued by photographers with old-fashioned cameras, before sticking their heads through cardboard cut-outs with titles like 'Buddha's Aureole' and 'Nirvana'. Further up, radio antennae, electricity pylons and satellite dishes poked out of the mist.

For a while I stood at the edge of creeper-covered cliffs, peering into the boiling emptiness and wondering what to do. Then, jealously treasuring those unforgettable memories of cloud-kissing precipices, ethereal monasteries and laughing, bald-headed young monks, I fled back down by minibus to Baoguo.

Leshan

That afternoon, I left by bus for nearby Leshan, a town 2,400 kilometres up the Yangtze, and the site of the Dafo, the world's largest standing Buddha. An hour later, the bus stopped at a jetty and everyone was herded onto a ferry that glided across the river to a compact little town. The old quarter was very eye-catching, with narrow cobbled streets enclosed by embankments. Everywhere there were green- and red-shuttered houses, and tea-rooms with bamboo chairs spilled onto pavements. To my dismay, the only decent hotel was full. I was standing there, looking lost, when a voice said in almost-fluent English, 'You want a ride?' It belonged to a man in his late forties with an intelligent, sensitive face, who was sitting in a rickshaw.

'Know a cheap place to stay?' I asked.

'Sure, OK,' he answered. 'Jump in.'

As he pedalled down streets choked with cyclists to the adjoining 'new' town, which consisted of the inevitable dingy concrete blocks, he introduced himself as Jiajing, a factory worker with an unemployed wife and a fifteen-year-old daughter. After explaining he drove a rickshaw to supplement his meagre wages, he told me that he'd not only read Thackeray and Dickens in English but knew 7,000 Chinese characters. (The average number known by a Chinese-speaker is 2,000.) Intrigued, as we drew up outside a squalid hotel I invited him to meet me the following evening.

The next morning I went down to the old town's quay and joined the crowds aboard a rickety steamer for the day-trip to the Dafo. Soon we were all being swept downriver by the powerful current until it swam into view. For a few minutes the boat hovered in swirling eddies to allow for photographs of rocks covered with hanging creepers, but I was brusquely elbowed aside by the hoards of people with cameras and by the time I'd got to the stern they were gone.

Soon the boat docked at ramshackle paper-mills belching black smoke into the blue sky. After climbing steps lined with tacky souvenir stalls, the disembarking crowds set off on paths that wound up through subtropical vegetation to Wuyou, a Tang dynasty temple sited high above the river. It was also a museum housing calligraphy and painting exhibitions, and had green cobbled roofs topped by yellow dragons. Inside gravel courtyards dominated by imposing Buddhas, monks tended urns full of incense. Thereafter the track dipped to decorative bridges across streams and climbed to landscaped gardens on a promontory, where young women with cameras and tattered albums filled with sample photographs loitered under rose-laden trellises. Nearby, a geriatric-looking man sat in a deserted pavilion, staring

morosely at sandy plains on the opposite bank.

Five minutes further on, next to shabby restaurants, was the top of the Dafo. It was simply colossal. Nestling in red sandstone cliffs and flanked by gigantic, eroded guardians, it was seventy metres tall, with slit eyes, orange lips, squashed flat ears, and toes so enormous – each one was eight-metres long – that families were picnicking on the toenails. To one side, streams of people zigzagged up and down metal stairways cut into the rock. Begun in AD 713 by Buddhist monk Haitong, who hoped its presence would protect boatmen from the river current, the Dafo took ninety years to complete. It wasn't finished until long after Haitong had gouged his own eyes out in protest against funds disappearing into the hands of corrupt builders.

That evening, Jiajing was waiting in the tea-house he'd suggested. It was in a nineteenth-century, wrought-iron bandstand on a roundabout surrounded by seas of cyclists. Waiters in slovenly white jack-

The world's largest standing Buddha, Leshan, south-west China

ets bustled about, and men in bamboo chairs played cards, cracked nuts and puffed long pipes. In a park opposite, boys chased each other through bamboo clumps, or teased gossiping girls, and proud parents watched toddlers being carried round on a rusty miniature railway.

As he sipped tea, Jiajing talked about life during the Cultural Revolution. 'I was only sixteen, and was still at school at the time,' he explained. 'I wanted to go to university but, like others in my class, I was sent to Beijing, where I trained as a Red Guard. Afterwards, we had to go to the countryside. At first, we all thought it was a good idea, as it would help develop China. But it didn't last long. We earned nothing and had to live in overcrowded barns. By the time the Cultural Revolution was finished it was too late to go to university. So, after my father died, I got his job at a heat-treatment factory, where I've been a worker for the last thirty years.'

'Couldn't you have got a promotion?'

He nodded. 'Yes, but you must be in the party, and I'm no longer interested in politics. I just want make enough to lead an ordinary life, read books, talk English with friends and listen to the BBC. Now I'm a Buddhist, and I like to take my family for Sunday picnics to the Dafo.'

Later we strolled along the embankment. Gardens overlooking the river were overflowing with darting swallows, children flying kites and elderly women gracefully practising t'ai chi. Further along, in the old town's stall-lined streets, slippered octogenarians with sticks tapped along pavements, girls played hopscotch and men with fruit-laden prams struggled through hoards of cyclists. Downriver, near the Dafo, a white, seven-storey pagoda on top of Wuyou Hill shimmered in the warm haze.

'So how do you see Mao now?' I asked Jiajing.

'He made mistakes, but he was still a great leader.'

'But surely the Cultural Revolution ruined your life?'

'Only partly,' he replied. 'I was also responsible.' He smiled gently. 'Anyway, there's no point in being bitter. As the Buddha says, life is like climbing a mountain – the view from the top is often very different from what you expect.'

The Yangtze River

It was mega. Gargantuan. Thirty million people in one city; I'd never seen anything like it. Even more astonishing was the fact that I hadn't even heard of Chongqing, reputedly the world's largest city since its boundaries were redrawn. It was from here that I wanted to catch a boat through the Three Gorges, before the Sanxia project flooded them forever.

I'd spent the day heading east by bus through Sichuan, China's most densely populated province. It was very photogenic, with lush, green countryside full of paddy fields, bamboo copses and country roads swarming with blue-clad peasants. But gradually the picturesque, red-earthen hamlets gave way to dreary, grey-brick villages and, as dusk fell, the hazy sun disappeared behind thick sulphurous smog. Without warning, we were on dual carriageways and crossing bridges high above the muddy Yangtze, its leaden banks lined with armies of dismal tower blocks and blackened factories pumping effluent into the polluted river below.

An hour later, stiff and sore after the long journey, I got off the bus to find myself surrounded by a sea of humanity and soaring flyovers. Arm outstretched hopelessly, I stood trying to flag down overcrowded, beaten-up buses as they ground past, belching fumes. Soon I gave up and fought my way down teeming concrete canyons to a roundabout, where I managed to hail an antiquated taxi. Determined to pamper myself after this nightmarish arrival, I asked the driver to take me to the legendary Renmin Hotel. The taxi puttered through frantically honking traffic for all of 200 metres before turning into quiet, secluded gardens, where palm avenues festooned with Chinese lanterns led up to steps at the foot of an immense palace. Inspired by the Temple of Heaven in Beijing, the Renmin Hotel, whose main hall alone seats 4,000 people, had dozens of 20-metre maroon columns supporting a 65-metre dome and wings with gigantic pagoda roofs.

I had already decided to escape Chongqing as quickly as possible, so when I checked in I asked reception to try to phone the port about scheduled passenger boats through the Three Gorges. To my amazement, the receptionist not only got through immediately but was told there were berths still available for the 6 a.m. *Tung Fang Hong No. 41*. Without even seeing my room, I chased after my taxi and within minutes we were juddering through the neon-lit streets that wound down to the harbour. I'd expected to have to wait days or take a foreigner-only luxury boat, but, unbelievably, within the hour I'd collected my second-class ticket in the half-empty 'Red is East' terminal.

Chongqing was opened as a treaty port in 1890, but few foreigners made it to this isolated outpost. In 1938, after the Japanese invaded China, it became the Kuomintang's wartime capital and refugees flooded in from all over the country. A year later, Edgar Snow arrived to find a city living in fear of Japanese air raids, and described how Japanese bombers waited for moonlit nights, when, from their base in Hankow, they followed the gleaming Yangtze up to its confluence with the Jialing, which identified Chongqing in a way no black-out could obscure. The raids didn't stop it taking off economically and now, with countless obsolete-looking mills and smoky chimneys spewing pollution over its sprawling hills, it is south-west China's chief industrial city. Ironically, its name means 'repeated good luck', although, cursed by summer temperatures reaching 45°C, it doesn't have much of that.

At dawn, another taxi took me down to the river. It was a great sight, with ant-like streams of people pouring across the long pontoons that stretched over the river's shallow sandy banks to board innumerable craft moored midstream. I battled through to the *Tung*

Fang Hong No. 41, a green-and-white four-deck ship in berth no. 8, and tumbled into one of the three unoccupied berths in my cabin. Although it had no porthole and was cramped and airless, it was comfortable, with clean, white bedlinen, reading lamps and Thermos flasks for hot water. When I woke up hours later, Chongqing had mercifully disappeared and the Yangtze was flowing through lush green hills dotted with banana plantations and yellow, terraced fields.

The beautiful scenery didn't last long. Within an hour, grubby tugs pushing heavily laden lighters were battling upstream, and along the banks were the darkest, most satanic-looking towns I had ever seen. These included Fuling, which, 2,000 years ago, was the kingdom of Ba's political centre; Fengdu, which was formerly known as the City of Ghosts, with such ghoulish landmarks as Ghost Torturing Pass, Last Glance at Home Tower and Nothing-to-be-done Bridge; and Zhongxian, which, during the Warring States period (475–221 BC), supposedly got its name from a loyal general who cut off his own head rather than surrender three Ba cities to his enemies. Despite their romantic history and intriguing names, they were now black industrial slums, with ducts discharging poisonous waste into the scum-flecked river below.

Not much later, however, we stopped briefly at the impressive Precious Stone Fortress. Built during the reign of Emperor Qianlong (1736–96 AD), and climbing up a thirty-metre-high rock called Jade Seal Hill, the twelve-storey Lanruodian Temple was a striking red pavilion that had tall orange gates decorated with lions and dragons. In the rear hall of Ganyu Palace at the top was Rice Flowing Hole. Legend maintains that, long ago, enough husked rice flowed up through the hole to satisfy the daily needs of the monks until one day a greedy brother, thinking he could become rich, chiselled a bigger hole, and the rice flow ceased forever.

Some time after we'd cast off I withdrew to the second-class lounge overlooking the prow; I was weary of tramping round the bleak, windswept decks and watching rain-splattered barges. In the lounge I got talking to a distinctive-looking couple. Unusually well-dressed for Chinese travellers, they could almost have been American tourists. He was elderly and balding, with horn-rimmed glasses and tobacco-stained teeth. He wore a neat blue pullover, a clean white shirt and sandals. She was a gaunt, sharp, cerebral woman, with a severe face, a humourless smile and no eyebrows. Dressed in a smart grey trouser-suit, she looked alarmingly like Mao's forbidding wife, Chiang Ch'ing.

'Allow me to introduce myself, please,' the man began. 'I am Professor Qing, director of Chongqing Geology Institute. This is my wife, the deputy editor of the *Chinese Journal of Family Planning*. Sorry, she doesn't speak English.'

It was his umpteenth journey through the Gorges, as his work involved studying the Yangtze's rock formation for petroleum deposits, but it was the first for his wife, who was on her way to a conference in Yichang. During the 1960s, they had both been forced to work as farm labourers, so they didn't have much praise for the Cultural Revolution. None-theless, the professor, like many educated Chinese, defended Deng Xiaoping over Tianan-men Square. 'At first, I sympathized with the students, but they went too far,' he said. 'We are a huge country, and we could easily break up.' Now he was proud of China. 'Things are really good. Between 1990 and 1996 there was eleven per cent annual growth in our GNP, the world's fastest after Equatorial Guinea. And forty years ago we were the world's sixth biggest coal producer, but in 1999 we produced 1,397 million tons, and today we're number one!'

'Keen on statistics, aren't you?' I observed.

'Yes,' he said, laughing, 'like all scientists!'

At dusk, I retired to my cabin until the evening meal. Instead of eating in the pricey second-class dining room, I made my way to the ordinary restaurant at the stern. It wasn't a pretty sight. Snake-like queues besieged the brimming galley and slovenly, bad-tempered cooks doled out bowls of sludge-like rice, onions and liver. Seated at a crowded table, and watched by hundreds of incredulous, gawping eyes, I gobbled my food down until I fled back to the second-class lounge.

Later on I returned to the stern, which was the only place on deck to escape the pierc-ing wind. To my surprise, the restaurant had become a disco, complete with flashing strobe lights and couples foxtrotting stiffly round the floor. It was my birthday. Outside, the clear moonless sky was riddled with stars, and, not far away, a passenger ship seemingly sped towards us as we were swept downstream by the raging current. Momentarily I caught a glimpse of a multitude of faces thronging decks ablaze with light before we raced apart into the night.

At 11 p.m., with our searchlights' powerful beams holding the embankments in a vice-like grip, we tied up at Wanxian. In 1926, in the so-called 'Wanxian Incident', two British gunboats bombarded the town, after the local warlord took to commandeering foreign ves-sels to transport his troops. Now, in the dark, it looked atmospheric, with porters staggering up never-ending flights of steps to twisting alleys high above. Nevertheless, I was apprehen-sive of being left behind, as Red is East ships are notorious for departing unexpectedly, so I didn't stay ashore for long.

We were due to reach the Three Gorges at dawn. I slept fitfully until jolted awake by the exasperated voice of the captain, who, using a loudspeaker, was ordering tardy tugs out the way. The professor was also pounding at my door. 'Wake up, wake up, you're missing the scenery!' he cried. My alarm clock, which hadn't gone off, showed 8 a.m. Cursing, I threw on my clothes and ran along to the second-class lounge. It was broad daylight, and the professor was peering through rain-soaked windows at towering black canyons, so tall they almost blotted out the sky. 'Sorry to disturb you,' he said, 'but I know you wanted to see the Gorges, and you've missed the first already.'

We hurried outside for a better view. It was stupendous. The river had dramatically narrowed, and rocky pinnacles rose to strangely formed, mist-covered peaks. 'This is the second one, which is called Witches Gorge,' the professor shouted above the howling gale. 'It's the smallest, but here the cliffs are 900 metres high. Look, there's Facing Clouds Peak, Assembled Cranes Peak and Climbing Dragon Peak!'

Not long afterwards, we passed through Xiling, the Third Gorge. 'This one is seventy-six kilometres long and the most dangerous one!' yelled the professor as we hung on to rails to avoid being blown overboard. 'The captain must pay attention, as the current is really treacherous!' He gestured to eddying whirlpools and rapids shooting through jagged rocks on both sides of the river, which were so narrow two ships could hardly pass each other. After he retreated into the second-class lounge, I stayed for what seemed like hours. I was spellbound – when not having to take snapshots of the professor and his wife, who repeatedly rushed out with their camera to pose woodenly before hurrying back into the warmth. At last, soaked, frozen, but thrilled, I rejoined them, and listened with fascination as the professor pointed out peaks with outlandish names such as Military Books, Precious Sword, Ox Liver and Horse Lung, as well as explaining the geology, which is karst limestone.

To my dismay, just as I was getting used to the Three Gorges they had receded, the river had widened and the mythical-sounding mountains had petered out into featureless foot-hills. I was still feeling a palpable sense of loss when, not long afterwards, forests of pylons and cranes appeared on the horizon and we arrived at Yichang locks. They were right at the foot of the mammoth, seventy-metre-high Gezhouba Dam, part of the world's largest, most controversial hydroelectric project, which will drown 4,000 villages, displace 4.5 million people and create an artificial lake 550-kilometres long. For a while the professor and I stood silently at the starboard rail, staring at crowds lining the decks of a passenger ship as it inched through the lock opposite, or craning our heads at the vertical cement cliffs hanging precipitously overhead. 'Awful, isn't it?' I commented, appalled at how the formerly mighty Yangtze had been so brutally tamed and trussed. 'Especially for you geologists.'

'Yes,' he replied, glumly surveying the concrete jungle of weirs, sluice gates and silt-prevention dikes. Suddenly he livened up. 'But, you know, the dam stops the Yangtze from breaking its banks, which it did two years ago, when it flooded 21 million hectares. And it also supplies 14 billion kilowatt-hours of electricity annually!'

Then we were through Yichang's locks, and China's seemingly limitless plains stretched interminably east into the gloom.

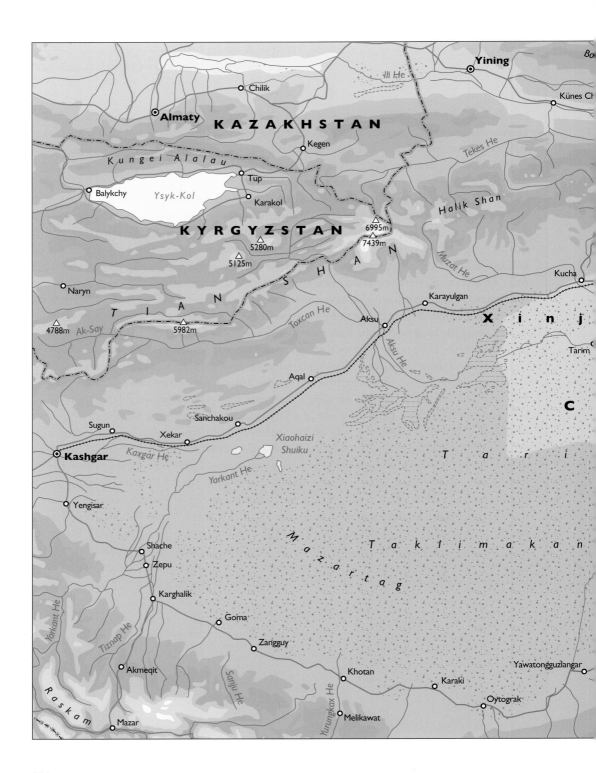

Yining

Künes Ch

Chilik

Almaty

K A Z A K H S T A N

Kegen

Ili He

Tekes He

Kungei Alalau

Tüp

Balykchy

Ysyk-Kol

Karakol

Halik Shan

6995m

Muzat He

K Y R G Y Z S T A N

7439m

5280m

5125m

Kucha

Naryn

Karayulgan

X i n j

Toxcan He

Aksu

4788m Ak-Say

5982m

Tarim

Aksu He

Aqal

Sugun

Sanchakou

Xekar

C

Xiaohaizi
Shuiku

Kashgar

Kaxgar He

Yarkant He

T a r i

Yengisar

Taklimakan

Shache

Mazartag

Zepu

Karghalik

Goma

Zangguy

Yarkant He

Yawatongguzlangar

Akmeqit

Tiznap He

Sanju He

Khotan

Karaki

Raskam

Oytograk

Yurungkax He

Melikawat

Mazar

214

the mountains. On it was a red pagoda, its roof upturned like a flowering lotus.

Two hours later, when I was purple with cold, a pre-war lorry trundled round the corner. I flagged it down, and soon I was heading again for Yining. The road ran along the lake and climbed to a high pass. Suddenly it zigzagged steeply, down past a burnt-out bus in a ravine, to the valley floor far below. Then we entered the fertile Ili Valley, where there were vineyards, fields of rape, and attractive blue bungalows tucked away in waving poplar groves.

Ili's rich pasture lands have been trampled by everyone of any note: the Xiongnu, who were descendants of the Huns; the Tang dynasty, whose army defeated the western Turkic khan in 744, thus strengthening Chinese hold over the new Northern Silk Road; Genghis Khan, who annexed it in 1218; Kublai Khan, who garrisoned troops here; Niccolò and Maffeo Polo in 1260; and the legendary Tamerlane (1336–1405).

Two hours later we passed through the outskirts of an obviously once-appealing town, where I was appalled to see rows of Uyghur houses being demolished.

'Where's this?' I asked a passenger.

'Gulja,' he replied simply, using the Kazakh name for Yining.

Before long I was walking down the main street, where, behind high walls, there were lilac and green decaying mansions, reminiscent of Russian palaces, with white Doric columns and grand mouldings. Yining was under Russian influence – and even occupied by the Tsar's troops during Yakub Beg's independent rule of Kashgaria in 1876 – for much of the late nineteenth century, and again in 1944, when a Kazakh Uyghur independence movement established the Republic of East Turkestan.

My hotel was close by. Ili Kazakh Autonomous County Government was holding its annual conference, and it was festooned with pink and yellow flags. Behind a wall was a statue of Lenin, overgrown gardens and blue bungalows with carved wood window frames hidden in trees. Outside the main entrance, Kazakh deputies in white Mongolian-looking hats with black fur rims stood gossiping or admiring antiquated limousines being polished by servants.

I spent the next morning on the post office steps, watching scribes at desks as they laboriously wrote letters for illiterate, bearded Uyghurs to send to relatives in Russia. In front of them a stream of Han Chinese, Uyghurs, Hui, Kazakhs, Uzbeks and even Russians passed by.

Just round the corner was the park. It was Sunday and it was bursting at the seams. Families picnicked under trees and groups of gypsies listened to throbbing Uyghur music; young bloods, their knives boldly displayed, eyed alluring Uyghur girls in silk dresses, or played chess and billiards at tables in front of the cinema; squatting withered women, their thick skirts nonchalantly hitched up to reveal green, woollen bloomers, admired their innumerable grandchildren or queued for shish kebabs and naan bread; and photographers with old black cameras took photographs of people.

I spent the next day being shown round the Uyghur Mosque, which was built during Emperor Qianlong's reign (1736–96). I also met several imams, most of them shrunken men with flowing beards, brown robes and white caps, who were friends of my guide, a young Hui translator I had met on the bus. The Hui are descended from Muslims who, originally sent as soldiers from Persia to help Genghis Khan, settled down in China instead of returning home.

Unfortunately, soon I had to leave. The bus took the new road south over the formerly impassable Heavenly Mountains and followed the meandering Ili River up a wide, remote valley. Suddenly, for the first time, we were in the heartland of the Kazakhs. Thousands of horses grazed peacefully or stood motionless in shallows of the river. Groups of horsemen trailed clouds of dust to feudal-looking hamlets or to round yurts dotting the plain like some medieval military encampment.

The Kazakhs are descended from Wusan tribes, who became established here in the first century BC. In the summer, up to three generations live in a single yurt, which is divided by embroidered curtains for privacy. They still have 'horseback' schools, where a teacher rides to a group of children, many of who have simple names resulting from the custom whereby, following a birth, mothers name babies after the first thing that comes to mind.

Once the valley was behind, the road climbed into thick alpine forests, snow, mist and bleak, glaciated moors. The next day, running parallel to a rocky river-bed, we plunged into immense gorges and ravines. At last we emerged into the flat Taklimakan desert, where all the Uyghurs on the bus blinked in the weak sunshine and sweated with relief at the familiar terrain. My thoughts, though, lingered over memories of that Sunday in the park in Yining, as well as the Kazakhs and the awe-inspiring Heavenly Mountains.

The Silk Road: The Taklimakan Desert

At first I didn't think much of Shache, the fabled Silk Road town, better known to armchair travellers as Yarkand, 200 kilometres south of Kashgar on the edge of the ferocious Takli-makan Desert in remote north-west China.

I was in elevated company. Marco Polo, passing through in 1274, commented: 'The in-habitants follow Mahomet, they are subject to the Great Khan's nephew, and have one foot bigger than the other, but can walk perfectly well,' before he quickly moved on.

The traveller Peter Fleming, who spent only a day there in 1935, merely noted signs of recent fighting, during which an occupying Chinese garrison had been besieged by fanatical Muslim insurgents. They'd finally surrendered, on condition of being given safe conduct, only to be taken out and massacred in the desert. 'The incident was', he wrote in his classic *News from Tartary*, 'typical of a Province whose history stinks of treachery.'

Now, as a policeman who I'd asked for directions to a hotel led me down a long avenue of what seemed yet another dreary Chinese town, I wondered what I was doing there. Still, things might have been worse: no one knew whether the town was open to foreigners, and as I had no permit the policeman could have arrested me instead of helping me.

Top left: The Taklimakan Desert, Xinjiang, north-west China

*Top right: Jiayuguan Fort on the edge of the Taklimakan Desert,
Xinjiang, north-west China*

Left: Man in a pony cart, the Flaming Mountains, north-west China

Above: Caves at Bezeklik, Xinjiang, north-west China

My spirits rose further as I shooed away a hopeless drunk who insisted on accompanying me to my hotel room – I later discovered he was the manager – and found myself in a rambling shady courtyard, where bungalows were dotted amongst trellises laden with trailing vines.

Later, as I sat on the porch with a glass of red wine – oases round the Taklimakan, fed by melted snow from the surrounding mountains, have thriving vineyards – I reflected on my journey so far.

The road had run through Yengisar, well known for centuries for the knives carried by every self-respecting male of the Uyghur, the predominant minority ethnic group, especially during melon season. Then it had continued along the foot of the snow-covered Pamir Mountains and headed into the Taklimakan.

In the desert, there was no traffic except for occasional buses heaving like ships over the flat horizon and steaming through drifting sand towards us; not for nothing had the great nineteenth-century explorer Sir Aurel Stein described the Taklimakan in his *Sand-buried Ruins of Khotan* as 'a sea of sand curiously resembling the ocean with its wave-like dunes.'

I'd loved the desert, as well as its tiny oases with irrigation canals full of rushing water, and roadside stalls, where women sat patiently selling red-and-yellow hard-boiled eggs to passing buses laden with swarthy Uyghurs. Nor could I forget the swashbuckling young man on the bus sitting next to me, who had an Errol Flynn moustache, a charming grin and a black Astrakhan hat worn at a rakish angle. Going to the bazaar at Shache to sell raisins, he had flirted outrageously with the woman in front, although she was old enough to be his grandmother. Then he had lost interest and spent the next seven hours prodding me in the ribs instead, and asking me where Europe was, what the raisins there were like, and whether it had Muslims.

Boy on a horse at the horse fair, Shache, north-west China   *Uyghur man sleeping in the market, Shache, north-west China*

Once, Shache had been the biggest town in southern Xinjiang and the point from where caravans carried silk, precious stones, gold and furs across the Himalayas to Leh in Ladakh. That was before Kashmiri merchants taught the neighbouring Yarkandis to treat wool, after which Hindus, Pathans, Tibetans, Baltis, Afghans and Armenians flocked to the region.

Now it seemed a sleepy backwater, with youths hanging out by pool tables outside the local cinema or at an intersection that was empty except for jangling horse-carts with rickety red-and-blue sun-awnings.

Ruins of an ancient Silk Road city, Kucha, north-west China

Notwithstanding, twenty-four hours later it was transformed as a torrential flood of carts, sheep, cattle, horses, goats, camels and Uyghurs carrying bundles of wood poured in from the countryside for what was surely the biggest bazaar in China.

I loved the horse section. Overlooked by a lovely, blue-tiled mosque in a leafy cemetery, it was a giant dusty compound where hundreds of horses neighed, tossed their heads and pawed the ground, or were put through their paces by proud Uyghur boys.

The old town was also fascinating: a maze of flat roofs piled with dried twigs, and high mud-baked walls, crumbling alleyways, green ponds tucked away in weeping willows, and little mosques. In vine-shaded courtyards, women hidden under brown veils rocked babies in colourful hand-painted cots, and elderly men dozed on straw mats in the shade.

The next day I left for Khotan, 300 kilometres through the desert on the southern Silk Road, and celebrated for centuries throughout Central Asia for its jade, rugs, carpets and silk.

The bus passed through Karghalik, the assembly point for mountaineering expeditions up the Chinese side of K2 in the Karakoram Mountains. Then it passed through Goma, previously the focal point of the Taklimakanchis, treasure-seeking tramps who spent their lives ransacking remains of old Buddhist temples in the desert.

Legend says sericulture was introduced to Khotan by a Chinese princess who, betrothed to the king over 1,000 years ago, concealed silkworm eggs and mulberry seeds in her head-dress to avoid discovery by officials instructed to guard the national secret.

The industry thrived and it continues to be the centre of traditional hand-woven aid-elaixi silks, which Uyghur women use for their dazzling black-, yellow-, mauve-and-green-striped dresses.

Many distinguished people have been here since: fourth-century Chinese pilgrim Fa-hs-ien returning home from India; Marco Polo, naturally, who described Khotan as 'a splendid city, amply stocked with the means of life'; Stein, hoping to identify Buddhist sites; and Fleming, who described how the city was hand-printing currency on paper made from mulberry and witnessed the arrival by mule of three-month-old copies of *The Times* from Kashmir.

Regrettably, unlike these travellers, I didn't see much.

I was in the bazaar admiring traditional two-storey Uyghur houses, with their intricately carved balconies and floral woodwork, when I felt a spot of rain and the light suddenly faded. Alarmed, I looked up to see the sky yellowing and then darkening, as if a giant black curtain was being drawn over the tree-tops. It was the dreaded Taklimakan *kara-buran*, or sand storm.

I dived for cover just as the squall hit; before I knew it, teacups were flying, awnings flapping, horses panicking, trees bending double and women, their faces wrapped in black scarves, battling into the raging storm until everything was lost in a blizzard of choking sand.

The next morning, to my relief, the sky was deep blue, so instead of visiting a carpet, jade or silk factory I hired a jeep and driver to go to the isolated archaeological site of Melikawat, capital of the Yutian kingdom during the Han dynasty (206 BC–AD 220), thirty-two kilometres south. This was instead of going to the site at nearby Yotkan, which both Sven Hedin and Stein explored. There valuable pottery shards showing Indo-Hellenistic and Persian influences were found, but now it's under rice fields.

A long straight road lined by poplars and gurgling canals led through quiet Uyghur villages before a track branched off into dappled vineyards and green fields running alongside the oasis edge. To the south fiery red mountains flared out of a desolate plateau and beyond were the snowy peaks of the Kunlun Mountains, the beginning of Tibet.

Not much later we dropped down a steep escarpment, and wound through a lush oasis on the banks of the dried-up White Jade River, where jade is still found. Then, watched by curious children, we followed tyre tracks up across sandy desert. After a while the driver stopped and pointed towards the remains of a tall, crumbling tower on top of a sand dune.

'Melikawat,' he explained, and added, unnecessarily, 'There's not much here.'

I walked up and sat at the tower alone, intoxicated by the emptiness and solitude and, lost in time, watched lizards playing in shards strewn in the sand.

There was enough for me.

Ruins of an ancient Silk Road city set against the Kunlun Mountains, Melikawat, north-west China

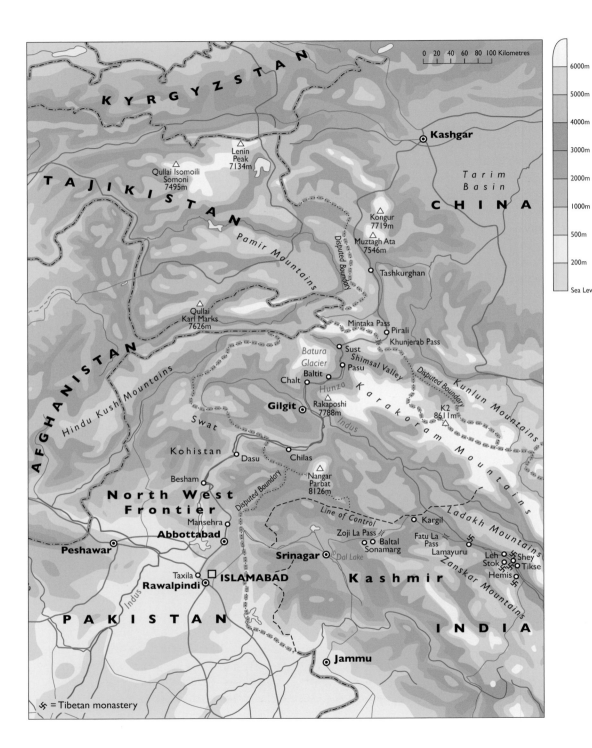

KYRGYZSTAN

TAJIKISTAN

AFGHANISTAN

Kashgar

CHINA

Tarim Basin

Lenin Peak 7134m

△ Qullai Isomoili Somoni 7495m

△ Kongur 7719m

Muztagh Ata 7546m

Tashkurghan

Pamir Mountains

Disputed Boundary

△ Qullai Karl Marks 7626m

Mintaka Pass

Pirali

Khunjerab Pass

Batura Glacier

Sust

Pasu

Shimsal Valley

Disputed Boundary

Kunlun Mountains

Chalt

Baltit

Hunza

Indus

Hindu Kush Mountains

Karakoram Mountains

K2 8611m △

Gilgit

Rakaposhi 7788m

Swat

Kohistan

Dasu

Chilas

△ Nangar Parbat 8126m

Besham

Ladakh Mountains

North West Frontier

Disputed Boundary

Line of Control

Kargil

Fatu La Pass

Mansehra

Zoji La Pass

Baltal

Sonamarg

Lamayuru

Leh

Shey

Stok

Tikse

Abbottabad

Peshawar

Srinagar

Dal Lake

Hemis

Zanskar Mountains

Taxila

☐ **ISLAMABAD**

Kashmir

Rawalpindi

Indus

INDIA

PAKISTAN

Jammu

卍 = Tibetan monastery

0 20 40 60 80 100 Kilometres

6000m
5000m
4000m
3000m
2000m
1000m
500m
200m
Sea Level

PAKISTAN: THE KARAKORAM HIGHWAY

To my dismay, there were long lines of people in Kashgar in western Xinjiang, China, for the bus to Pakistan via the Karakoram Highway (KKH) and the Khunjerab Pass, which, at over 4,500 metres, is one of the highest in the world. A friendly Italian hippy let me jump the queue for the rugged two-day journey; when the road reopens after winter and there's only one bus a week, moral scruples don't matter. Soon we were weaving through jangling horse carts, mud houses, irrigation canals and poplars stretching in green fingers across barren stony plateaux towards the seemingly impenetrable Pamir Mountains. For a while we ran parallel to the Ghez River into ever-narrowing canyons, although once, through gaps, I glimpsed gigantic glaciers and Mount Kongor's white peak floating in the blue sky.

The KKH was begun in 1970, when China and Pakistan started cutting a road following the old Silk Route across the knot of four great mountain ranges: the Himalayas, the Hindu Kush, the Karakoram and the Pamir. The result of a monumental collision 55 million years ago between the Indian and Asian continents, here is arguably the world's highest concentration of glaciers and peaks, including K2, the second-highest point in the world. The Karakoram Mountains are grouped in clusters called *muztagh* (Uyghur for ice mountain), and are characterized by closely packed serrated summits, bottomless gorges and immense glaciers. Not surprisingly, the road, which was built by 15,000 Pakistani labourers (400 of whom were killed) and 20,000 Chinese (figures unpublished), is exceedingly dangerous, as blasting so destabilized the mountains that landslides, rock falls and mudslides still regularly bury it since the road was opened in 1986.

But there wasn't much time to brood: when I wasn't hanging out windows staring awestruck at giant boulders strewn, as if by the Cyclops, next to the road, I was observing the other passengers. They were an interesting group. Most were Pakistani traders returning with cheap Chinese goods. Babbling and joking through a fug of marijuana, they played incessantly with plastic jets they had hung from the roof. Few spoke English, although a distinguished-looking older man with wavy grey hair and an elegant white moustache reminisced wistfully to me about discipline during the British Empire.

Then there were the Westerners: the Italian, all in black, with leather bag, belt and silver rings, who was returning to India; Fritz, a shrivelled German in his forties with manic eyes, a disintegrating sheepskin jacket and a dirty knotted handkerchief to protect his balding head; two tough Geordies with mountainous rucksacks, tattooed red skin, running shorts and bulging muscles, who were on leave from the British Army to climb the Pamir; a striking Danish woman – the only female on the bus – with blue eyes, silky brown hair and a long flowery skirt; and her boyfriend, a skinny intellectual Berlin student, reminiscent of a Weimar cabaret compère, with foppish hair, horn-rimmed glasses and a missing front tooth.

Uyghur man in Kashgar, Xinjiang, north-west China

The bus wound past the Kyrghiz settlement of Bulun Kul and round Muztagh Ata, the 'Father of Ice Mountains'. Then it drove along smoothly contoured valleys full of serpentine streams until it reached the stunning blue Kara Kul Lake, where legendary Swedish explorer Sven Hedin nearly drowned, and a sheltered plateau dotted with windowless adobe houses, ploughed fields and herds of grazing horses. The sun had nearly set as we idled along a single street lined by low buildings and poplars. It was the overnight stop at Tashkurghan, the administrative centre of Tadjik Autonomous County and centre of China's 20,000 Tadjiks.

While passengers milled around a decaying hotel's compound, I hurried to find the celebrated ruined stronghold, dated to the Yuan dynasty, AD 1280–1368, although Greek philosopher Ptolemy mentions it in his second-century AD *Guide to Geography*. But giggling Tajik girls with long pigtails, white veils and colourfully embroidered caps only blushed when I asked directions in the otherwise deserted street so I returned to the darkened compound where the Pakistanis, wrapped in cloaks, were watching the two soldiers vainly trying to persuade the driver to unload their rucksacks from the roof.

Meanwhile the Europeans in the restaurant were gathered round an emaciated London dropout with a pock-marked face, scraggy beard and obligatory fawn cap. 'Man, I've been in Pakistan for years, but though the dope's great there, they say China's far out,' he remarked nonchalantly, looking up from his noodles. I laughed aloud; only the chemically brain-damaged, or those who've never been, believe that.

Sunrise revealed peaks jutting out of green plateaux dotted with shaggy yaks; 'a lean beast grows fat here in ten days', wrote Marco Polo, who passed through in the thirteenth century. Suddenly we were opposite vast, glaciated Mintaka Valley on the border of Tadjikistan and Afghanistan's Wakhan Corridor. Here, British spies disguised as scholars, explorers, merchants and Muslim holy men played cat-and-mouse with Russian agents as they criss-crossed mountains on mapping and spying missions during the nineteenth-century Great Game in order to control the route to India.

I was in love with the Pamir. Inaccessible and desolate, their smooth, rounded summits and olive-, brown-and-orange-dappled flanks looked like something out of Tibet, and did indeed make me feel, as the name Pamir suggests, on the roof of the world. Finally, as the road climbed towards rocky, needle-sharp peaks, there was a cluster of huts and a barrier – Chinese Customs at Pirali, on China's most westerly rim. We all trooped off the bus, and I walked across to a sour-looking Han Chinese Customs officer, who was wearing dark, racy Ray-Bans and a high-peaked military cap. 'Duibuqi [excuse me], can I can change money here?' I enquired amiably, in Chinese.

'You English speak!' he snarled, and strode off to harangue Pakistanis squatting patiently in the road. Three hours later everyone piled on board to collect passports, except the two soldiers, who, reunited at last with their rucksacks, were going to walk back to Tashkurghan, and Fritz. After heated arguments with the Customs officer, he had been refused permission to continue to the Pakistan border, where he'd gambled on getting a visa.

'Macht nichts,' he joked, 'the scenery is nice, and I will try Russia.'

I admired his bravado; it meant returning back to Kashgar, then skirting the fierce Taklimakan Desert, and finally, if the Russians wouldn't admit him, returning over 2,200 kilometres to Beijing.

Then we were off, slowly climbing towards snowy summits, where, as applause broke out from the passengers, signs stated 'KHUNJERAB PASS, CHINA–PAKISTAN BORDER'. The great nineteenth-century explorer Sir Aurel Stein dismissed the pass as 'an excursion for ladies', but intrepid Chinese pilgrim Fa-hsien, passing through it on his heroic fifteen-year journey on foot across Turkestan and the Karakoram to India in AD 400, recorded feelings of vertigo. In addition, Khunjerab means 'Valley of Blood' in Wakhi, a reference to neighbouring Hunza's deadly bandits, who for centuries slaughtered merchants and plundered caravans here.

Soon the descent began into fearsome canyons of Khunjerab National Park, past signs saying 'World Wildlife Fund – protect Snow Leopards'. I didn't realize we were in Pakistan until a battered Ford Transit stopped, and intimidating but friendly North-West Frontier policemen, with berets, moustaches and Kalashnikovs, climbed aboard. Before I knew it we were in Soest, which was merely a few hotels and a barrier in a gorge where an emerald river

Karakoram Mountains, Hunza, northern Pakistan

ing Uyghur, Wakhi, Burushaski, Pushto and Urdu. All around, there were ornate mosques, barber shops and slender minarets from which plaintive *muezzins* called the faithful to prayer. Best of all, though, apart from my lodgings at the Golden Peak Inn, a venerable-looking house set in sunny, overgrown gardens formerly owned by the Mir of Nagar, was the municipal library, a colonial time warp tucked away up a hillside behind leafy cypresses. Former home of the political agents, whose faded photographs – including, inevitably, Durand's – still line the walls, once it had been the hub of British intrigue during the Great Game. Now it was a peaceful sanctuary, consisting mainly of chipped cabinets, antediluvian typewriters and stacks of yellow newspapers. There was the sound of turning pages and, through sunny bay windows, birds chirping in orchid-laden gardens.

Assistant librarian Sherbaz Ali was a tall, gaunt, dignified man in his sixties. He had a long silver beard and wore a grey waistcoat over his long baggy trousers. Even after forty years, it seemed, he continued to admire the British. 'You know, slavery is slavery whatever you care to call it,' he remarked, as we sat with tea in the old wing. 'But even if they did it for their own reasons, the British built roads, schools, bridges and so on. And above all, they were fair. Remember that, until they came, the North-West Frontier was dominated by exceptionally cruel, hard men.'

He wasn't joking; they included Gilgit's last non-Muslim ruler, the barbaric Shiri Badat, who, according to legend, ate a baby a day, and Gauhar Aman, who, after the Silk Road's decline in the fifteenth century when Gilgit became an isolated backwater fought over by local tribe-states, sold sizable parts of Gilgit's population into slavery. In 1848 the British took over and stayed in control until 1947, as much through guile as the Gilgit Scouts (the local militia), who, drawn heavily from local royalty, were raised and dressed in their own tartan. Then came Partition, when the maharaja of Kashmir, now the area's nominal ruler, elected to join Hindu India rather than Muslim Pakistan. Outraged, local Muslim groups, including the Scouts and the Kashmir Infantry, joined in the first Indo-Pakistani war, during which the Indians bombed Gilgit. The 1949 United Nations ceasefire left the region now known as the Northern Areas to Pakistan. Nonetheless, memories are long, and every November the normally reserved Gilgitis celebrate the uprising with music, dancing and week-long polo tournaments, usually won by the Northern Light Infantry, the Scouts' descendants.

The next day, a Suzuki passenger pick-up took me west through a lush green valley full of shady glades and children playing by the lazily winding Gilgit River to Kargah Nala. From here, I followed rushing streams up gullies until I came to an enormous seventh-century AD Buddha carved out of the cliff-face. Along with the unrivalled sculpture trove at Taxila and the petroglyphs scrawled on rocks at Ganesh and Chilas, this is one of the few remnants in Pakistan of the once-fabled kingdom of Gandara. Under the Kushan dynasty, this was the centre of an astonishing flowering of Buddhist culture based on the fusion of

Greek and Indian artistic styles. The former was first introduced by Alexander the Great in 326 BC, and the latter by the Indian King Ashoka (273–235 BC). Following the Silk Road, it spread up the Indus into China and Tibet, and by the time Fa-hsien arrived in AD 403, there were hundreds of monasteries. The White Huns later destroyed these when Islam began replacing Buddhism in the eleventh century.

I left Gilgit a few days later, covered with bedbug bites and crammed into the back corner of a minibus to Islamabad. Sticking my head outside to ease my claustrophobia and verify we weren't plunging off the road proved costly, as the woman in front promptly vomited out the window all over me. When the driver stopped at roadside stalls to buy dried apricots, I squeezed myself out the window and gratefully hauled myself up to join the passengers on the roof.

Although I had to hang on grimly, it was my favourite stretch of the entire KKH. Leaving behind the snowcapped peaks of Rakaposhi, Dubanni, Haramosh and Mishkin to the north, we headed all morning for colossal Nanga Parbat (8,534 metres), believed locally to be a fairy citadel topped by a crystal palace and guarded by snow serpents. The world's eighth-highest mountain, it has killed more climbers than any other; no wonder, considering its north side drops a mind-boggling 7,000 metres to the churning Indus, which travellers see for the first time past a flimsy suspension bridge leading to Skardu and the even mightier K2 (8,687 metres).

Suddenly it was all behind us and we entered another astounding gorge, where in 1841 an earthquake caused an entire valley wall to collapse into the Indus, forming a lake which stretched almost to Gilgit; when it broke, walls of water roared down the valley, sweeping away dozens of villages and thousands of people, including an entire Sikh army battalion at Attock, 400 kilometres downstream. I was still awestruck a few hours later when the driver, who I'd asked to let me off at the Chilas petroglyphs, ground to a halt in the middle of a particularly forsaken chasm, pointed towards a suspension bridge over the Indus and revved off, leaving me standing alone by the deserted roadside.

I crossed the river and was gingerly picking my way over rocks by the riverside, when two fiery-looking, bearded tribesmen with Kalashnikovs and criss-crossed ammunition belts stepped out behind boulders and confronted me suspiciously. I gulped, giggled nervously and started drawing squiggly shapes in the air, until their weather-beaten faces creased into understanding smiles and they took me to boulders covered with battle scenes, long-horned ibex and serene, 2,000-year-old Buddha figures. Proudly clutching their weapons, they posed for photographs and escorted me back to the bridge, where they squatted patiently by the roadside until they waved me off on the first passing bus, two hours later.

Apart from being stopped at the police checkpoint, we didn't linger in Chilas, a sullen sprawl of buildings clustered around a heavily armed citadel, which was first garrisoned by Durand after his 1891 Hunza campaign and is now a police station to control still-anarchic tribesmen. An hour later the KKH crossed from the Northern Areas into the North-West Frontier Province, passing the intended India–Pakistan border drawn by Sir Cyril Radcliffe in 1947 before the agreement was thrown into chaos by the Gilgit uprising. Suddenly the landscape darkened again, as the Indus, which for the first time had been flat and meandering, cut through blackened gorges so deep and narrow it was almost impossible to see the sky.

We were in Indus Kohistan.

Skirting the western end of the Himalayas, which here become the Hindu Kush, its hair-raising, unstable terrain makes this one of the most harrowing passages in Asia; caravans passed it by, and even Fa-hsien, who had seen everything by now, was dumbfounded. Although Kohistan means 'Land of Mountains', its nickname was Yaghistan, 'Land of the Ungoverned', because of its even worse reputation for murderous feuds, brutal lawlessness and bloodthirsty tribal warfare. The British wisely left the area well alone, and it wasn't until after the KKH's forerunner was begun in the early 1960s that the Pakistan government established a Kohistan District, the government of which now relies heavily on the North-West Frontier police and a series of squat strongholds – still regularly attacked – which dot the unruly valley. Needless to say, it's highly recommended that foreigners don't stray off the KKH without escorts or informing Frontier constabulary; for single Western women to do either in this intensely male, oppressive atmosphere, where there's not a female to be seen, is madness.

It was north of Dasu, where more lives were lost during the construction of the KKH than anywhere else, that I experienced my first landslide. The bus had just inched round a blind bend when the road, just a cleft notched into the vertical canyon wall, was blocked by a heavily laden articulated lorry, whose rear wheels were dangling over the edge of a yawning chasm. Piling off the bus like everyone else to see what had happened, I peered into the nothingness where half the road had been until monstrous boulders, gouging out the mountainside, had subsided into the turbulent Indus far below. Fearing another landslide, though no one else seemed to be bothered, I waited uneasily for the next few hours until Frontier Works Organization bulldozers arrived. Soon it skilfully hauled the lorry back from the abyss and, to my intense relief, allowed single-file traffic to flow again.

Late that evening I stopped in Komila, a straggling village high above the Indus, before spending all the next day in the back of a jolting Toyota pick-up. I hung on tenaciously as it raced south past Pattan, the centre of a catastrophic earthquake in 1974 that buried whole villages and thousands of people, and down the now steeply descending, increasingly straight road. By twilight we'd reached Besham, a scruffy frontier transportation hub spawned by the rapid growth of the KKH. It was choked with gaudily decorated buses, honking trucks, seedy all-night bazaars and shacks selling Kalashnikovs. That night I ate my meat and chapattis in grubby tea-houses, too worn-out to register that the surly, heavily armed men wearing loosely wrapped turbans were Pushto-speaking Pathans, a fiercely independent tribe from the Pakistan–Afghanistan border, until I fell asleep on a soiled rope-bed in a cheap, open-air rest stop for drivers.

At dawn, with the KKH's end almost in sight, I took a bus bound for Rawalpindi, now only seven hours away. Soon we passed Kunshe, which was believed by Sir Aurel Stein to be the site of Fa-hsien's Indus crossing at the end of his harrowing Kohistan journey. This is actually in Swat; in contrast to Kohistan, its southern part was a key destination for pilgrims 2,000 years ago, since it contained, as the tireless Fa-hsien noted, a stone at Tirat believed to bear footprints of the Buddha himself.

At long last, there was flat-topped Pir Sar (2,438 metres), where Alexander the Great supposedly fought the tribes of Swat in the third century BC, and the graceful suspension bridge that, with its stone lions and sign saying 'Welcome to the Karakoram Highway', crosses the river to Thakot. Then the road, leaving the Indus and Kohistan, entered Hazara Province and began its gradual descent through gentle, richly forested hills towards the sweltering plains and throbbing cities of lowland Pakistan.

The Karakoram Highway, North-West Frontier, Pakistan

My truck, the Karakoram Highway, North-West Frontier, Pakistan

K

R U S S I A N   F E D E R

○ Edigan

○ Kyzyl Mazhalyk

Bashkausl

R e p u b l i k a   A l t a y

Katun

△ 3976m

Uureg Nuur

Uvs Nuur

U v s

△ 4273m

○ Ulaangom

Haanhö

Achit Nuur

Türgen Uul △
4116m

Hyargas Nuur

○ Uryl

Tsagaanuur ○

Bayan Uul

Ölgii ○

Khovd Gol

KAZAKHSTAN

Tavanbodg Uul △
4373m

Tsengel ○

B a y a n - Ö l g i i

Khoton Nuur

Buyant ○

Cast Uul △
4208m

Burqin He

Tolbo ○

A

l

t

Rashaant ○

Khovd ○

Buyant Gol

Har Us Nuur

Ho Nu

Kaba

△ Chandmandi

Jargalant
Hayrhan △
4373m

◉ **Altay**

a

i

Tögrög ○

○ Burqin

Etrix He

M

K h o v d

Ulungur Hu

o

u

○ Fuyun

Jargalant ○

n

Mönh
Hayrhari △
Uul
4231m

t

Ulunguur He

a

i

n

s

C H I N A

Üyönch Gol

○ Bor Üdzüür

Gurbantuggut Shamo

Manas Hu

J u n g a r   P e n d i

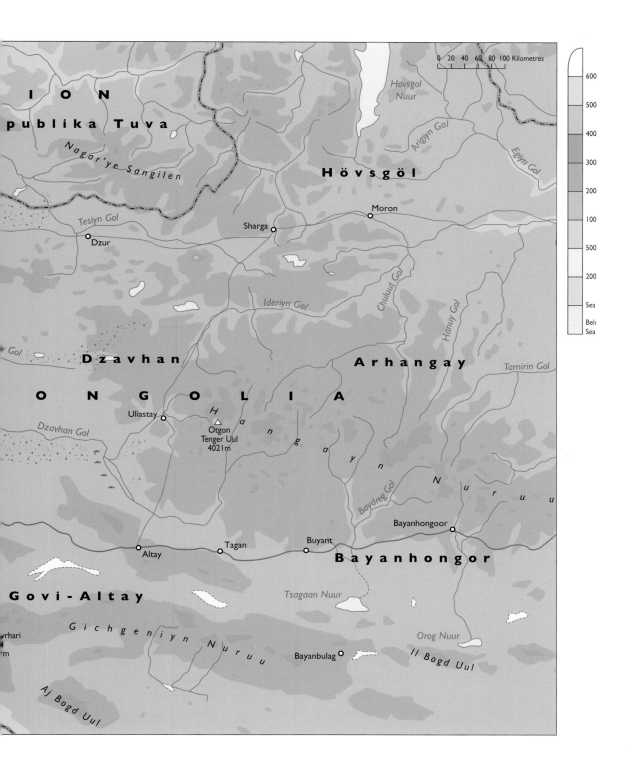

I O N

publika Tuva

Nagar'ye Sangilen

Hövsgöl

Hovsgol Nuur

Arigiyn Gol

Egiyn Gol

Tesiyn Gol

Dzur

Sharga

Moron

Ideriyn Gol

Chuluut Gol

Hanuy Gol

Tamirin Gol

Dzavhan

Arhangay

Gol

O N G O L I A

Uliastay

Dzavhan Gol

H
a
n
g
a
y

N
u
r
u
u

Otgon
Tenger Uul
4021m

Baydreg Gol

Bayanhongoor

Altay

Tagan

Buyant

Bayanhongor

Govi-Altay

Tsagaan Nuur

Orog Nuur

Gichgeniyn Nuruu

Bayanbulag

Il Bogd Uul

rhari
m

Aj Bogd Uul

600
500
400
300
200
100
500
200
Sea
Bel
Sea

MONGOLIA
The Eagle-hunters of Bayan-Ölgii

In the far west of Mongolia, on a hillside above a blue alpine lake reflecting soaring, permanently snowcapped peaks, were two white, round nomad tents, or *gers*. Tucked away in a cluster of pine trees, they belonged to Taikoni, one of this almost-deserted region's Kazakh eagle-hunters, who I was hoping to meet. It was June, during the brief summer, and shaggy black yaks and horses with long, unkempt manes grazed nearby, tails swishing. Separated from Russia and China (whose borders are only three and thirty kilometres away respectively) by the mighty Altai Mountains, this is one of the world's most remote places. The province of Bayan-Ölgii, which is ninety per cent Kazakh, has no paved roads, and the only way to get here is take the four-hour, 1,645 kilometre flight from Ulaan Baatar to Khovd, the desolate main – and practically only – town; thereafter, as there were also no buses or cars, you have to hire a four-wheel drive.

So Nomads, a surprisingly well-organized travel agency in Ulaan Baatar, had arranged for me to fly from the capital accompanied by one of their young Mongolian interpreters and our camping equipment for a month-long expedition, and to be met at Khovd's tiny airport by a non-English speaking Mongolian driver and his jeep. We had collected the necessary permits from the police station, and loaded up with provisions and spares from the dusty market before setting out.

It had been a magical, four-day journey. Following the River Khovd through seemingly countless precipitous gorges, every evening we had camped by streams next to *gers* containing nomadic relatives of Tseveenjav, the wonderfully warm and chatty 67-year-old driver, who had long been settled in Khovd. After receiving an ecstatic welcome, the three of us had cooked the evening meal and he had lovingly polished his antiquated, ex-Russian army jeep before we spent hours laughing and joking with his aunties, uncles, nephews and nieces – who he hadn't seen since winter – in their *gers*. Finally, as we travelled ever westwards, and the handful of *gers* we encountered gradually became Kazakh instead of Mongolian, we had followed meandering grass tracks across high, empty plateaux until we arrived at Khoton Nuur, the last of three stunning, adjacent lakes.

Now, as we approached Taikoni's two solitary white *gers*, my interpreter Tunga, a newly graduated Mongolian medical student who spoke Mongolian, Kazakh and English, shouted the usual warning, 'Nokhoi khorio! [Call off the dogs!]' A man in his early thirties emerged. He was Taikoni's son Madef. Although his father wasn't home yet, he tethered the furiously barking Siberian huskies and ushered us through the *ger*'s blue, hobbit-like wooden door to the guest of honour's place. As I squatted on a miniature stool on the damp grass, a gaggle of snotty-nosed infants gazed open-mouthed at me, as if seeing a Martian, until there was a sudden flurry of activity as Madef's shy little daughters prepared the obligatory welcome for visitors. Mongolian nomads are famed for their hospitality, and soon

Madef's daughter outside the family ger, Bayan-Ölgii Province, western Mongolia

a low table was piled with plates of sweets, cheese, curds, bowls of undrinkable salty white tea, and surely the world's best yoghurt.

While we were waiting for Taikoni, Madef, who also spoke Mongolian, chatted with Tseveenjav about the usual nomadic topics, especially the height of the rivers and the state of this year's pastures. As they talked, I took the opportunity to observe the differences between Mongolian and Kazakh *gers*. Next to baskets of dried yak dung, there was the usual stove in the middle, where smoke curled lazily from a pipe sticking through a circular hole in the roof. There were also a couple of metal bedsteads, a saddle stand, milk churns, and a stereo on top of a pile of shabby suitcases. But, like most Kazakh *gers*, it was taller, wider and more richly decorated, with an attractive black-and-red-striped roof, bright orange homespun rugs around the felt walls, and pink-and-green cupboards decorated with reindeer. Most telling of all were the prints of Mecca, in pride of place on top of a chest with mirrors flanked by porcelain horses and photos of long-dead grandparents.

Not long afterwards, Taikoni himself arrived. He was a sturdy, short man in his late sixties, with a witty face and a white goatee beard. He wore the traditional long black Kazakh corduroy coat, a round, Kazakh cap and knee-length leather boots. Like many nomads, he had alarmingly bandy legs, which, Tunga later told me, are caused as much by Vitamin D deficiency as spending life in the saddle. He had a haughty air, and obviously enjoyed being the family patriarch as well as one of only two famed eagle-hunters in the area. Although his main language was Kazakh, he spoke Mongolian as well, so I decided to try to soften him up. 'Mal süreg targan tavtaiyuu? [I hope your animals are fattening up nicely?]' I ventured, employing the universally understood nomadic greeting, and one of my few Mongolian phrases.

'Tavtai saikhan! [Fattening nicely!]' he replied, smiling for the first time. Encouraged, I continued with other fundamental pleasantries from my phrasebook that, with my tortured pronunciation of Mongolian's fiendishly difficult vowels, I had quickly learned were guaranteed to bring the *ger* down. Sure enough, when I tried to say, 'I don't understand', even he roared with laughter. Five minutes after Tunga had explained the joke to me – I had just said 'I'm an appendix' – he had thawed and, as I hoped, started talking about eagle-hunting.

'I'd like to take you out with me,' he went on, still wiping away tears, 'but we only hunt between November and February, when the pelts of foxes, which are the eagles' main prey, are at their best. But we always catch something, such as hares, marmots and even small wolves. Eagles have wonderful vision, which is eight times sharper than humans and enables them to spot a fox or rabbit up to two kilometres away. We also only use females, which are a third heavier than males and more aggressive. Eagles have always been very expensive – in the past, a good one could be exchanged for up to six camels. Now, of course, you can buy them, though usually I take mine from their nest, or lure them with pigeons and trap them, when they're still young. I bought my present one for $30, when she was only three. I've had her for five years, and when she's ten I'll release her, as I do with all my eagles – even though they can live up to fifty – back into nature.

'But some people sell theirs, as they're in big demand, especially in the Arab world. There, hunting – especially with falcons – is very popular. Since the fall of the Soviet Union, the United Arab Emirates has been the main destination for thousands of them caught and sold illegally for huge sums on the black market. Kazakhstan, alone, is estimated to lose up to 1,000 a year. It's dreadful! It's become so bad that its government has started breeding programmes to try to maintain the wild falcon population. But enough talk! If you want, I'll get my eagle ready and you can come and see her.'

'Of course!' I replied, honoured at this unique opportunity, before he hobbled off.

Eagle-hunting is a Kazakh tradition dating back 2,000 years, even if millennia previously the Chinese mentioned it as an 'activity practised by barbarians living north of the wastes'. Introduced to the West by the Crusaders, it was also described by Marco Polo in his *Travels*. For centuries, previous to becoming a tourist attraction, it was an elite sport in Central Asia; historical chronicles from the thirteenth century record the famous Mongol emperor Kublai Khan's lavish hunting trips in autumn and winter, which involved thousands of people and horses. But among Mongolia's isolated, tightly-knit Kazakh community, the real tradition lives on.

The origin of this small ethnic group remains in dispute: some say that, two hundred years ago, they were pushed here by the advance of troops from the Russian Empire, while others maintain that they came to Bayan-Ölgii in the 1840s to escape persecution by China's Manchu emperors. Regardless, separated from the rest of Mongolia by the Khovd River, and from Central Asia by the practically impassable Altai, these Muslim nomads, who make up less than six percent of landlocked Mongolia's 2.5 million population, have kept their language and identity almost intact.

This is unlike those in China's Autonomous Kazakh Province or the strongly Russified state of Kazakhstan. After the Soviet Union's disintegration in 1990, the first president of Kazakhstan, Nursultan Nazirbyaev, faced the problem of the Russian majority, who came in the industrialization wave of the '60s and '70s and comprised some 54% of the population. To shift this balance in favour of the Kazakhs he appealed to Kazakhs living in other countries to return to their motherland, promising money for resettlement, free housing and jobs. Some 60,000 or more than half of the 120,000-strong community of Mongolian

Above: Nomad, Bayan-Ölgii Province, western Mongolia.
Right: The eagle-hunter Taikoni, Bayan-Ölgii Province, western Mongolia.

245

Kazaks took up his offer, fondly imaging a new, culturally compatible homeland, but most have returned, disillusioned with the way so many of their beloved traditions there have been eroded.

Half an hour later Madef beckoned us to accompany him. Along with some men on horses who had materialized from nowhere – most nomads have binoculars, and word of rare outsiders spreads quickly – we set off past a hutch occupied by a cowering, four-month-old wolf cub that he had caught recently. To my dismay, he told me that they would eat the unfortunate creature in autumn and sell its highly prized bones as good luck charms.

Soon we squelched down the peaty hillside to a stream. There, squatting unconcerned on the boggy ground was Taikoni. On his gloved arm, framed against the alpine lake, towering white summits and azure sky, was a magnificent brown eagle, with a two-metre wingspan, powerful legs and vicious-looking talons. Most striking of all, though, were its large yellow eyes, which fixed me with an unblinking, pitiless stare. Trying hard to ignore them, I concentrated as Taikoni patiently explained how eagles are trained. This requires an intimate knowledge of, and close bonding with, the young birds. At first, the eagle-hunter, who is known as *kusbegi*, keeps them for about a month or two and feeds them with meat from his hand until they become used to his presence. Then, in late summer, he 'breaks' them. This he does by binding their ankles with leather straps and tying them to a block, so that each time they attempt to fly they flip upside down. During this time they aren't given any food; after two days they are so exhausted that they are ready for further training. This consists of being sat on a pole called a *tugir*, and one of the young men pulling a lure made of small animal skins in front of the eagle. When it attacks the lure, called a *shirga*, it is given some meat as a reward.

Suddenly, tired of answering my questions, Taikoni peremptorily put a neat hood over the squawking eagle's head, tied its feet to a post, and imperiously rode back up to the *ger*.

As Madef, to whom Taikoni had been teaching eagle-hunting for twenty years, told us about the hood's purpose – to calm down the eagle – my attention drifted below, where the late-afternoon sun was glittering on the tranquil lake. At its western end, I could almost see the summit of my next destination – spectacular Tavanbodg Uul, at 4,373 metres Mongolia's highest mountain and the only one in Bayan-Ölgii to be permanently covered with glaciers, where, if you sit on the summit, you can simultaneously be in Mongolia, China and Russia. At the eastern end, near the cove where we were camped, mangy Bactrian camels were grazing in fields of buttercups. Not far below, a pale-blue ex-Russian army lorry inched painfully across a swollen steam. It was piled to the top with a dismantled *ger*, and inside there was a nomad family, moving up to high summer pastures. On the shore opposite, scattered among dense forests climbing steep mountainous spurs, were a few puzzling white blobs. They looked like clumps of snow, but careful examination revealed them to be *gers*.

Altai Mountains and Bactrian camels at Lake Khoton Nuur, western Mongolia

Altai Mountains and ger, Lake Khoton Nuur, western Mongolia

Nomad husband and wife, outside their ger

There was the sound of cuckoos, and some of Mongolia's ubiquitous hawks spiralled warily overhead. Gradually, as if I were in a dream and I was trying to perceive reality, my awareness returned to Madef, who was explaining why his family never left for Kazakhstan.

'Why should we?' he asked rhetorically. 'This is our home and we love it. Why not appreciate what you've got?'

The Throat-singer of Chandmani

After Tunga, Tseveenjav and I returned to Khovd, we set off south, where I wanted to see if I could meet a Mongolian throat-singer. I'd first come across throat-singers the previous year when, out of curiosity, I'd gone to hear an exotic-sounding ensemble called Huun-Huur-Tu, the surprise hit of that year's Edinburgh Festival. While queuing for my seat, I had read in the programme that this still-unknown group was from Tuva, a small autonomous mountain republic in Russian Siberia. However, it continued, throat-singing was almost the same as *khöömi*, as it was called in neighbouring western Mongolia whose nomadic, pastoral culture was very similar to that of Tuva. Once the concert began, I had been spellbound by the strange, seemingly impossible sound made by their lead singer, consisting of two harmonics

Girl on high summer pastures, Bayan-Ölgii, western Mongolia

My jeep waiting for me on the road to Mt Tavanbodg (4,373 m.), western Mongolia

and a melody, all sung simultaneously. This wasn't even to mention their bizarre instruments, which included dried horses' hooves and a rattle made of a dried bull's scrotum filled with sheep's knucklebones. When clacked together and shaken, these, along with imitative sounds made by the group's other vocalists, had conjured up wonderfully evocative images, such as horses trotting across windswept pastures, dogs barking and owls hooting.

Yet though their music sounded so foreign to me, its timeless human themes such as longing for home, yearning for a loved one, and sorrow at parting from friends, also seemed deeply familiar. So I had bought their CDs *Sixty Horses in My Herd*, *Where Young Grass Grows*, and *If I'd Been Born an Eagle*, which had only whetted my appetite to learn more about throat-singing and its Buddhist-shamanistic roots. In fact, it was being introduced to the music of Huun-Huur-Tu that was mainly responsible for me going to western Mongolia – which claims to be the home of *khöömi* – in the first place.

Tseveenjav, who seemed to be acquainted with everyone in the province, had told Tunga he knew a famous throat-singer called Davaajav who lived in Chandmani, a remote village about 150 kilometres south-east of Khovd. So, after we passed marshy, emerald Lake Har Us, which was swarming with mosquitoes, we drove for hours and hours across a vast desolate plateau flanked to the south by the snow-covered Altai Mountains.

It was very slow going, because there was just the usual maze of bumpy, criss-crossing tracks, which became increasingly sandy as steppe changed into semi-desert. Once, the half-drunk driver of a dilapidated lorry flagged us down. His was the first vehicle we had seen all day, which was hardly surprising; Mongolia is five times the size of Germany, and, as 1.5 million of its 2.5 million inhabitants live in Ulaan Baatar, traffic in the rural wilderness is practically non-existent. Now, carrying a cargo of cigarettes from Russia, he was hopelessly lost. When Tseveenjav told him he had overshot Khovd, his destination, and was heading for the capital over 1,500 kilometres away, he was so grateful that he pulled out grimy plastic cups and insisted we share the half-empty bottle of vodka from which he'd obviously been drinking.

Once, too, Tseveenjav's beloved jeep broke down in the middle of a limitless expanse. Astonishingly, it was the first time this had happened in three weeks, during which we hadn't even had a flat tyre. At first, after he crawled under the chassis, he looked extremely worried. Tunga and I stood watching anxiously as he hammered the axle with tools from his well-equipped toolbox. But an hour later he re-emerged, his hands, face and clothes covered with oil. 'Fixed!' he told Tunga proudly in Mongolian, and presently we were on our way again. I was full of admiration; I couldn't imagine what we would have done if he hadn't been able to repair whatever was wrong.

At last, just after the first of a series of red sand dunes, we branched off the main track east to the Altai Mountains. Far in the distance, I could just make out some large animals with humps – camels – silhouetted against the skyline. For some time, we ran alongside a swollen torrent dividing us from the foot of hazy hills. Tseveenjav was obviously looking for a place to ford it and when he found one we ploughed through the green, crystal-clear icy water. Then we climbed north through a low pass between the sun-dappled Jargalant Hayrhan Uul and the Bumbat Hayrhan Uul before emerging on the other side.

There an unforgettable sight awaited us. Below the southern flanks of these 3,800-metre-high mountains, which were lightly powdered with snow, herds of horses grazed peacefully on thin, sloping pastures. Further down, just before some low mud buildings, a cluster of white *gers* was dotted among trees. Nearby, a stream wound downhill to lose itself in immense nothingness that stretched away to a silver strip separating land from sky. At first I thought it was sunlight on the horizon, but closer examination revealed what seemed to be an endless, glittering sea.

'Chandmani, the Gobi Desert and Lake Har,' stated Tseveenjav, reading my thoughts.

Halfway down the mountainside Tseveenjav stopped a young goatherd to ask for directions, as it was two years since he had last been here and he couldn't remember exactly where Davaajav lived. After the boy gave him instructions, we jolted over rough ground to one of the *gers*. There we were greeted by the inevitable gaggle of dirty excited children and apoplectic mangy dogs. A small, serious-looking man dressed in blue trousers, a grubby T-shirt and trainers emerged to investigate the cause of the uproar. About fifty, he had a sunburned face and sleepy-looking eyes, remarkably black hair for his age, and a hint of whisker under his lower lip. It was Davaajav.

After he and Tseveenjav embraced each other, he invited us into his *ger*. It was unusually shabby, with paint flaking off the little wooden door, and a dirty black sheepskin mat outside. Inside there was the inevitable chest of drawers, old suitcases, rusty bedsteads, and horses' bric-a-brac. Davaajav, who didn't speak any English, ushered me to the master's stool at the back, as is normal when guests visit *gers*. There I gave him packets of razor blades, a lighter and one of the tins of expensive snuff I had brought from home as presents, along with a large number of trinkets. Snuff is the best gift you can give a Mongolian man and, as soon as he took a pinch of it, his face creased with delight.

'Aaaaaaaah!' he exclaimed, before he broke into a stream of onomatopoetic-sounding Mongolian – if such a thing exists – and closed his eyes, as if in ecstasy.

'He says he's in heaven!' Tunga translated, laughing. Shortly, he pulled out a miniature blue snuffbox and offered me some of his own. He had a deep, throaty voice and sniffed continually – probably a result of indulging in the habit too much like many Mongolian nomads. After I complimented him on the quality of his snuff, I gave packets of balloons and colourful stickers of foals to his two delighted little daughters, who were playing on one of the threadbare mattresses. Then I gave some hair clasps and a much-appreciated set of needles and thread to his smiling, forty-year-old wife.

That evening the dazzling, deep-blue sky clouded over and it started raining. Still, I didn't mind too much, because Davaajav invited us to eat in his *ger*. It was warm, cosy and amazingly watertight, apart from drops slanting through the circular hole for the pipe in the canvas roof and pinging on the hot stove underneath. While the two girls busied themselves stirring basins of noodles, Davaajav told me about himself over cups of milky tea that tasted of mutton.

'Like many boys in Chandmani, I started learning *khöömi* when I was very young,' he began. 'In fact, this is where *khöömi* began, though some minority peoples in the Altai Mountains, as well as Tuva, also sing it.'

To my amazement he had heard of Huun-Huur-Tu, so I told him how I had been to a concert of theirs in Scotland. When I had finished describing how overwhelmed I had been, he said knowledgably, 'Well, you know, Tuvan *khöömi* isn't exactly the same as Mongolian, and in my opinion Huun-Huur-Tu use too many instruments. Also, traditionally, *khöömi* is sung by only one person, so here it's purer. Still, *khöömi* is *khöömi*, no matter how it's sung. Of course, throat-singing takes years to learn, though normally you only practise every two days as it takes a lot of strength and you can damage the throat if you don't train it properly.'

'Have you always been a *khöömi* singer?' I enquired.

'Yes, though I've also been a herdsman, like everyone else. Once, I taught *khöömi* in a college for fifteen years, though I missed my animals so much that I went back to being a herdsman. But I kept singing, and I won several competitions. Now I'm one of the oldest teachers left around here and many young people, especially Japanese, come to learn from me.'

'How did *khöömi* begin?' interrupted Tunga, who was as interested as I was.

'Some say it's as old as nature itself, and started when man made the first melodies imitating the murmur of streams or the echo of voices in the mountains. It's about what we call our "jewels" – our horses, camels, yaks, sheep and goats. But it's also about the beautiful Altai Mountains and longing for one's sweetheart, for example. It's often said that it's the traditional music of western Mongolia, where many people still live in harmony with nature. However, I think it's a musical art form.'

He wasn't being immodest. *Khöömi* isn't just singing; it's using the throat as a sophisticated musical instrument. One tone comes out as a whistle-like sound, the result of locked breath in the chest being forced out through the throat in a specific way, while a lower tone can sound as bass at the same time. There are several different ways of singing *khöömi*, depending on the position of the lips, mouth, palate, teeth and tongue. But, whatever the style, the result is a weird, ethereal polyphonic sound.

'Anyway,' Davaajav was saying, 'I'd like to sing for you, but at the moment I'm tired and I haven't warmed up my voice. Still, if you're here tomorrow night, I'll sing for you then.'

'I'll be here!' I retorted, unable to hide my delight.

'Good,' he said. He pointed to the cupboard, where I could see a bottle with an image of Genghis Khan on the label. 'Now, before we eat, have you ever tried Mongolian vodka?'

The next morning, still nursing a terrible hangover, I woke up to find that, to my dismay, it was raining harder than ever. I could hardly believe it, considering we were right on the edge of the Gobi Desert, which I'd always thought was one of the driest places on earth. The previous evening Tseveenjav had told me that Naadam, the traditional annual festival, was beginning next morning just outside Chandmani. I had planned to spend the entire day there, before returning to hear Davaajav sing in the evening. Instead, I was stuck in my tent waiting for the rain to abate. But at midday, with no sign of it easing off, I set out, regardless.

I followed a path along the stream down to the gravel-covered plain. There, despite the teeming rain, hundreds of soaked nomads in trilby hats and claret or green, long-sleeved *deels* (the traditional national costume) were squelching around in the mud. Next to rows of battered parked jeeps, music blared from huge loudspeakers mounted on the trailer of an antediluvian lorry. Opposite there were crowded rickety stalls selling steamed mutton dumplings, doughnuts and *arak* (fermented mares' milk). Further away, young boys milled round dozens of tethered, shaggy horses. But I didn't pay them much attention; I was too absorbed in the horses.

To my astonishment they looked more like ponies, and I found it almost inconceivable that it was horses similar to these which had been mainly responsible for Genghis Khan being able to conquer the whole of Asia, not to mention most of Eastern Europe. Of course, I wouldn't have said anything, even if I had been able to speak Mongolian; nomads are rightly proud of their exceptionally hardy horses and they're very sensitive to foreigners making foolish comparisons.

Eyed continually by goggling families, I stayed for the rest of the afternoon. Although the wrestling and archery events had been washed out, or had taken place in the morning, I wanted to see the end of what was obviously – judging by the excited, waiting crowd – some kind of race. When it came, I could hardly believe my eyes. Gradually, out of the Gobi's apparently infinite distance, a tiny figure appeared, riding bareback on a cantering horse. It was only when the horse crossed the finishing line, where it was met with huge applause and sprayed with *arak*, I realised that the rider was only about five-years-old.

While I was watching increasingly exhausted-looking, diminutive figures straggle home on their horses, a young man called Galbaatar, who spoke broken English, explained how Mongolian horse races are organized. These are quite unlike those in the West, which consist of short sprints usually not much longer than two kilometres. Races during Naadam, on the other hand, are cross-county events, with races fifteen to thirty kilometres long. Moreover, it's the horse, not the rider that wins the race. The horses are divided into six different classes by age, with the youngest being two years old. The riders, who are always bareback, are children, with the oldest – the young boys I had seen milling around earlier – being twelve years old and the youngest five. After the races, the top five horses in each class earn the title of *airgiyn tav* and the top three are given gold, silver and bronze medals. In addition, the horse that finishes last in the two-year-old class is given a top-five award, in the belief that it will do better in its next race.

On the way back to Davaajav's *ger* I stopped at the spartan shop owned by his son in Chandmani. There I managed to buy another bottle of Genghis Khan vodka – the last on the half-empty shelves – to replace the one we'd finished the previous evening. By the time I arrived at our camp outside Davaajav's *ger* the light was fading fast, though the rain was easing off at last. Soaked to the skin, but still exhilarated by the day's indelible images, I dried myself and changed into my spare clothes. By the time I'd finished it was night, so, following the beam of my torch through the darkness, I hurried across to Tseveenjav's tent where he, Tunga, and Davaajav were telling each other stories. Inside, a burning candle cast their shadows onto the sloping sides of the tent, which was so cramped that they were practically sitting on top of each other.

After I squeezed in, I found that Davaajav had also changed his clothes. Now he wore a

dark-green *deel* fringed with blue embroidery and fastened at one side at the neck by orange beads. On his feet he had decorated, black felt boots with orange turned-up toes, and on his head he wore a dark-green-and-black-hat with an orange peak in the middle. In his lap he had a *morin khuur*, a basic, sitar-like instrument with two strings made of horsehair, and a circular wooden soundbox covered with goatskin.

For almost two hours, as we finished the bottle of vodka I had bought, I sat listening to them laughing and joking. For once, I decided to give the hard-working Tunga a well-deserved rest. She had been an outstanding interpreter, and I didn't want to ask her every five minutes, as I usually did, to explain what everyone was saying. But then, with not the slightest sign of Davaajav getting ready to sing, I began grow restless.

Before I'd arrived in Mongolia I'd read that foreigners are often requested to sing a song when they visit a nomad's *ger*. So I waited for a lull in the merriment before I announced loudly, 'Now, would you like to hear a song?' Then, in the hope my example might encourage Davaajav, I launched into the Beatles' 'When I'm Sixty-Four', which I had specially learned by heart back home.

It was received with enthusiastic applause, but soon they merely started laughing and joking again. Half an hour later, losing patience, I slipped out to the expedition's large communal tent. There, to get rid of my disappointment, I vigorously scrubbed the breakfast dishes, which I had volunteered to wash that morning but hadn't yet got round to doing. After I dried them and stored them away in one of the expedition's large black plastic containers, I returned to my tent, where I decided to call it a day. I had finished brushing my teeth, prior to undressing and getting into my sleeping bag, when it occurred to me it would be most impolite not to tell them I was going to bed.

So, for the second time, I went over to Tseveenjav's tent. I'd been sitting there for a few minutes, waiting for an opportunity to say goodnight, when Davaajav turned to me. 'Now,' he said, reaching for his *morin khuur*, 'as our guest has come from so far away, I want to honour you by singing for you.'

Completely taken by surprise, I made myself comfortable, like the others. There was a long pause, while he tuned his instrument. Then, holding the *morin khuur* in his lap, he started singing. He sang three songs, entitled 'In Praise of Altai Mountains', 'Horse with Light-Grey Coat', and 'Two Little Ducks', respectively. Each lasted only five minutes, but each was a different combination of mesmerising harmonics and haunting melodies, such as I had never heard before. Suddenly, as I sat there, I was swept by a feeling of immense gratitude for my life; never in my wildest dreams had I imagined that, one dark moonless night, I would find myself in a candlelit tent on a mountainside overlooking the Gobi Desert, listening to a famous Mongolian throat-singer singing especially for me and the patter of the falling rain.

Roadside monument, Bayan-Ölgii, western Mongolia

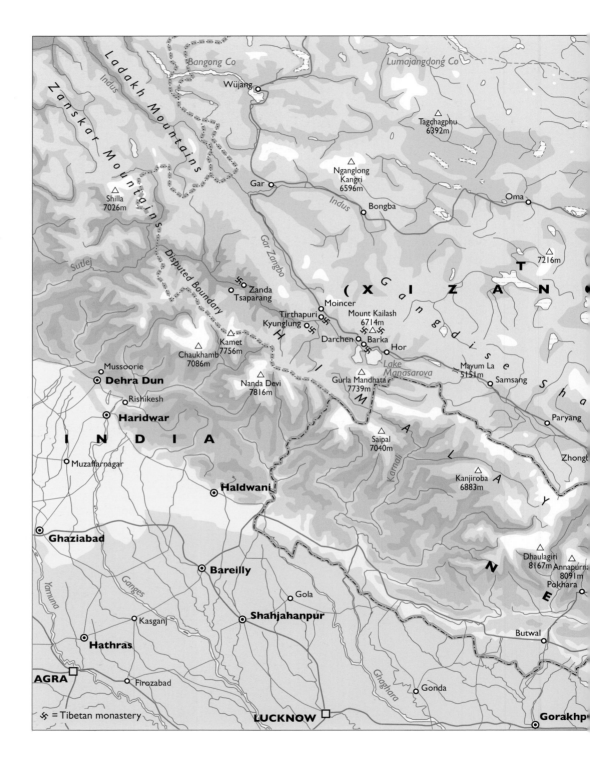

Bangong Co

Lumajangdong Co

Wüjang

Zanskar Mountains

Ladakh Mountains

Indus

Tagchagphu 6392m

Nganglong Kangri 6596m

Shilla 7026m

Gar

Indus

Bongba

Oma

Sutlej

Disputed Boundary

Gar Zangbo

7216m

T

(X I Z A N

Zanda Tsaparang

Moincer

Tirthapuri

Mount Kailash 6714m

G a n g d i s e   S h a

Kyunglung

Kamet 7756m

Chaukhamb 7086m

Darchen

Barka

Hor

Mussoorie

Nanda Devi 7816m

Gurla Mandhata 7739m

Lake Manasarova

Mayum La 5151m

Samsang

Dehra Dun

Rishikesh

H

M

Paryang

Haridwar

I

A

Saipal 7040m

Karnali

Zhongb

I N D I A

Muzaffarnagar

L

Kanjiroba 6883m

A

Haldwani

Y

Ghaziabad

N

Dhaulagiri 8167m

Annapurna 8091m

Bareilly

E

Pokhara

Ganges

Gola

Yamuna

Kasganj

Shahjahanpur

Butwal

Hathras

AGRA

Firozabad

Ghaghara

Gonda

⚕ = Tibetan monastery

LUCKNOW

Gorakhp

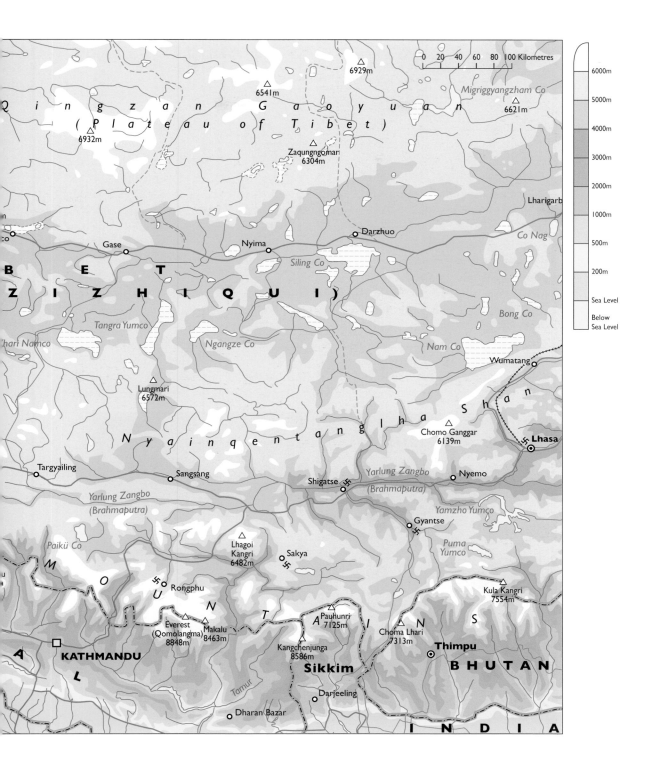

Q i n g z a n   G a o y u a n
(P l a t e a u   o f   T i b e t)

6932m

6541m △

6929m △

Migriggyangzham Co

6621m △

Zaqungngomari
6304m △

Lharigarb

Co Nag

Darzhuo ○

Gase ○

Nyima ○

Siling Co

B E T

Z I Z H I Q U I)

Tangra Yumco

Bong Co

hari Namco

Ngangze Co

Nam Co

Wumatang

Lungmari
6572m △

N y a i n q e n t a n g l h a   S h a n

Chomo Ganggar
6139m △

卍 Lhasa ◉

Targyailing ○

Sangsang ○

Shigatse 卍 ○

Yarlung Zangbo
(Brahmaputra)

Nyemo ○

Yarlung Zangbo
(Brahmaputra)

Yamzho Yumco

Paikü Co

Gyantse 卍 ○

Puma
Yumco

M O U

Lhagoi
Kangri
6482m △

Sakya 卍 ○

Kula Kangri
7554m △

卍 Rongphu ○

N

Everest
(Qomolangma)
8848m △

Makalu
8463m △

T

A

Pauhunri
7125m △

Choma Lhari
7313m △

N

S

KATHMANDU □

Kangchenjunga
8586m △

Thimpu ◉

B H U T A N

A

Sikkim

L

Tamur

Darjeeling ○

Dharan Bazar ○

I N D I A

0 20 40 60 80 100 Kilometres

6000m
5000m
4000m
3000m
2000m
1000m
500m
200m
Sea Level
Below
Sea Level

TIBET
Mount Kailash

Tears came into my eyes when, beyond the fluttering prayer flags at the top of a 5,280-metre-high mountain pass, I first laid eyes on sacred Mount Kailash, one of the world's most remote and legendary destinations, in the far west of Tibet. I had wanted to go to the mystical Himalayan kingdom for decades, but time had passed and after a serious health scare four years previously I had questioned the wisdom of doing so, given its high altitude, isolated location and unsanitary conditions. Eventually, to celebrate my birthday, as well as to prove to myself that I could still do it, I had decided to take the plunge and go on a three-day *kora* (circumambulation) around the mountain after attending Saga Dawa, Tibet's most important religious festival.

My journey had begun 1,200 kilometres to the east in Lhasa, which, at an altitude of 3,650 metres, is the world's highest capital. My doubts about the journey had quickly proved to be well founded. I had decided to be sensible and spend five days acclimatising in Lhasa, but I hadn't expected to have such headaches and sleepless nights. Then there had been the arduous journey westwards. For days I'd sat choked in dust as my hired four-wheel drive juddered across the forlorn 4,500-metre-high plateau. As the flat-roofed, white Tibetan villages gave way to increasingly desolate mud settlements more in keeping with

Girl in Lhasa, central Tibet

Monks' debating session, Sera Monastery, Lhasa

those in Afghanistan, the guesthouses had become increasingly primitive, with revolting toilets and not much to eat except rice and noodles. Before long, like many travellers, I had a raging cold, and had to take antibiotics for such bad diarrhoea that I had begun to wonder whether I would even reach the holy mountain.

To my surprise, I had also been rather disappointed with Tibet. Of course, I had loved the magnificent monasteries, especially Shigatse, Gyantse and Sakya, as well as the vast, treeless, sun-dappled valleys dotted with white or brown yurts and shaggy black yaks. But my guide, Tikki, a squat, 26-year-old woman, and my driver, Chumpin, a would-be cool, chain-smoking young slicker from Lhasa, had been a tremendous letdown. Both had been totally uninterested in Tibetan Buddhism or taking me to meet nomads, unlike Tseveenjav and Tunga, the driver and guide, who had made my Mongolian journey so memorable four years previously. Nor had Tibet's impressive-sounding 5,000-metre-high passes lived up to expectations, as they had merely given way to yet more ranges of arid, crumpled hills, instead of the tantalizing Himalayas that I had expected, and which could be occasionally glimpsed to the south.

Now, finally, although it was 100 kilometres away, the perfect, snowcapped triangle of Mount Kailash rose majestically above the seemingly infinite, bleak Barkha plateau. To the south, on the other side of stunningly blue Lake Manasarova, a wall of white peaks reared up into the sky, including Gurla Mandhata and Kamet in India. Mount Kailash itself, at

6,714 metres, isn't exactly the world's highest mountain, but apart from its mesmerizing presence and special shape (four sheer walls matching the cardinal points of the compass) it is of unparalleled spiritual and geographical significance. Firstly, it is believed to be the axis of the universe by Tibetans, who call it 'Precious Jewel of Snow', and Hindus, for whom it is the abode of Shiva. It is also of crucial importance to followers of Tibet's ancient Bön religion, a precursor of Buddhism, who call it Nine Stacked Swastika Mountain owing to the long cleft resembling a swastika, which is originally a Tibetan good luck symbol, that marks its southern face. Secondly, four of Asia's major rivers originate here: the Karnali flows south before joining the Ganges at Patna; the Indus flows north before turning south through Pakistan; the Sutlej flows west before flowing through the Punjab; and the Yarlung Zangbo flows east and joins the Brahmaputra before flowing through Bangladesh.

As if that isn't enough, some Tibetan experts, such as Charles Allen, are convinced that the area near Mount Kailash is the site of Shangri-La, described in James Hilton's book *Lost Horizon*, unlike those who claim it is in the Hunza Valley in Pakistan.

Four hours after my first, unforgettable glimpse of Mount Kailash, we reached Darchen. It was a scruffy stone village nestling at the foot of the mountain, where young Tibetans played pool outside tiny restaurants and tumbledown shacks selling biscuits and packets of noodles. In spite of there being two days to go to Saga Dawa, which marks the enlightenment of Shiva (Sakyamuni in Tibetan) on Mount Kailash and occurs on the full moon of the fourth Tibetan month (May or June), the village was already full to capacity. Down by a rocky stream there was a sprawling camp of nomads, and the walled compounds of the usual dreary, Chinese-run hotels were choked with dust-streaked jeeps, Indian pilgrims and foreign travellers. Like myself, most of them had arrived early to avoid the scramble to get the necessary permit, buy food, find yaks or porters, and make sleeping arrangements in tents or monastery dormitories.

Soon the great day dawned, and our preparations were complete, though I was disappointed to find that all the yaks had been taken by a 150-strong group of Indian pilgrims, and I had to make do with Norbu, a young local porter. After telling the astonished Tikki the previous night that I didn't need her for the next three days, I set off at 7 a.m. with Norbu on the two-hour walk around the base of the mountain to Lha-chu Valley, where the festival was being held. To my surprise, by the time we arrived it was already in full swing. Apart from dozens of jeeps and beaten-up lorries with painted swastikas above their cabins, there were numerous stalls selling prayer wheels and Tibetan jewellery. In a clearing in the centre, amid a joyful carnival atmosphere and wreathed in smoke from burning juniper incense, excited crowds ceaselessly circled the giant Tarboche flagpole, which lies on its side, draped with prayer flags, before being raised every year.

Further up, the rising sun chased shadows from the dark mountainsides, and ponies with red-, white-and-yellow saddles were tethered outside yurts, where nomad families squatted at cooking pots on yak-dung fires. Apart from being a religious festival, Saga Dawa has an important social function, as it is a rare opportunity for nomads to meet up, and for proud mothers to introduce their doe-eyed daughters, in ornate traditional dress, to young herdsmen.

Midway through the morning, long Tibetan horns sounded, and novices dressed in maroon robes and red Tibetan hats emerged from stone buildings on a slope, holding umbrellas over a procession of lamas. There was an unseemly scrum as Western tourists jostled each other to take photographs, until the lamas and novices led a noisy parade round the flagpole. Then, amid an air of fevered expectation and spurred on by echoing cheers, long lines of men at the end of thick ropes started raising the flagpole, inch by inch. In the end, aided by the pulling power of two lorries, it stood upright, framed against the cloudless azure sky and Mount Kailash. There was a mighty roar as the exultant crowd showered the flagpole with paper prayers before recommencing their continuous circling; how the pole stands is critical, as Tibetans believe that if it isn't vertical the future augurs badly for themselves and the country.

When the festival wound down in the early afternoon, I started on the fifty-two-kilometre *kora*. Most Tibetans, who are accustomed to the altitude and leave at dawn, complete it in fourteen hours. I, like most Westerners and the 600 Hindu pilgrims who had been granted permits by the Chinese government, was going to take three days. The path

Prayer wheel between cairns on 5,000-metre-high pass, western Tibet

Lamas at Saga Dawa Festival, Mount Kailash, western Tibet

wandered past a ridge where there was reputed to be a footprint of Buddha and a Tibetan sky burial site. Here, in accordance with Tibetan beliefs concerning death, bodies of cherished ones are chopped up and left to be eaten by eagles. However, I didn't climb to have a look, partly out of respect, and partly because I knew that, in the past, intrusive foreigners had been pelted there with stones.

Soon the valley narrowed and the path reached the foot of the small Chuku *gompa*, which was perched fortress-like on cliffs above the valley. Blending harmoniously into the mountainside, it had been rebuilt after being wrecked during the Cultural Revolution. Still, I decided to have a look, so I told Norbu to rendezvous with me that evening at stone huts owned by the Dira-puk *gompa*, my first stop for the night, and began the steep, 200-metre climb. Twenty minutes later I arrived, shattered, outside the miniature prayer hall, from where there were spectacular views directly up the west face of Mount Kailash.

There was nobody inside, apart from a lama tending some flickering butter lamps. For twenty minutes I inspected the Buddhas and *tankas* and tried to find Chuku Opame, a revered marble statue that was reputed to talk. Feeling dizzy after the climb, I soon gave up and, savouring the solitude, squatted quietly at the back. However, when I stood up I felt a rush of blood to my head. For a fleeting second I imagined I was having a divine revelation; the next thing I knew I was lying on the earthen floor with the lama's worried face peering down at me. It was only then I realized I had blacked out and hit my head on the ground, where soft piles of prayer flags had luckily cushioned the blow.

After I reassured the lama that I was all right I slowly returned down to the valley. But I felt severely chastened; after all, I was an experienced hill-walker, and had climbed to Kala Pattar above the Everest Base Camp without problems. I also considered myself still to be very fit, despite my unfavourable health diagnosis. Yet here I was, hardly having started the pilgrimage, with another 800 metres still to go and I had fainted already . . .

However, there was no time to dwell on it as I laboured up the valley, tracking the swift-flowing Lha-chu River and a group of overweight Indians on ponies. Once, I paused briefly at a white tea-tent, which was full of guides and porters cooking their own rice and noodles. Four hours later, by the time I arrived at the pre-arranged stone huts on a hillock overlooking Dira-puk *gompa*, darkness was falling.

With flurries of snow and the temperature plummeting, I was exceedingly grateful for

Chuku Monastery looking up to the west face of Mount Kailash, western Tibet

one of the few places in them that Tikki had managed to reserve for me. Overlooking the *gompa*, which sat aloofly on a hillside on the other side of a stream, the huts were sited directly below the windswept west face of Mount Kailash, which towered menacingly above. For a while I watched stragglers arrive and their porters unload heavily laden yaks and set up tents. Then I retired to my hut, where I huddled in my sleeping bag and chatted to the six Indian pilgrims who shared my hut. Eventually I got up and, too cold, unlike some hardy Westerners, to climb to Kangkyam Glacier only 100 metres above, went to see what was happening in the large communal tent.

Inside, guides and porters were crowded round an antiquated, red-hot stove, which had a thin, rusty pipe sticking through the roof. Unable to face the rice and noodles everyone was eating, I sat on a grubby mattress on the ground, flirting innocently with a slender young Tibetan woman called Pema. About thirty years old, she had long black pigtails and wore a pair of worn plimsolls and a smudged, ankle-length skirt with a grimy Tibetan apron. To my surprise – I thought all the porters were male – she turned out to be a porter for a pilgrim from Bombay. For nearly an hour, we playfully swapped ever-smaller pieces of her bread and my biscuits. At the same time, I couldn't help observing the desperately ill-looking Korean woman in a corner, who was suffering from pulmonary oedema and gasping like a dying fish into an oxygen facemask.

The next morning, the improbably speedy Norbu and I set off at dawn on the long haul up Drölma-chu Valley. Soon I was struggling to keep up with him – and, in any case, I found his tuneless whistling unbearable – so I instructed him to go ahead and meet me at Zutul-puk *gompa*, my second stop for the night. Not much later, I drew level with most of the chubby Indians, who had left while it was still dark. For a few minutes we all stopped at Shiva-tsal, where cairns were strewn with piles of discarded garments: pilgrims are supposed to leave their former life behind here, along with an item of clothing to represent it. There was also, allegedly, a footprint of Milarepa, the revered thirteenth-century Tibetan poet-saint. Nevertheless, none of us could find it, so I forged ahead, though not before having to explain repeatedly why I was doing the *kora* alone. 'Where's your group?' the Indians kept asking me. (In Tibet, the Chinese authorities insist that foreigners travel in groups.)

'You're looking at it,' I said, 'a group of one.' I explained that, with my driver and guide, I – just – met the minimum requirements.

At the top of a ridge, I caught up with Pema and her pilgrim. Although she was wearing a soiled white face-mask, I recognized her smiling eyes immediately. For a quarter of an hour she led me by the hand, or I held on to her dangling string of prayer beads. After a while I left them both behind to toil up a long, tedious moraine. I was going recklessly fast, despite the warning from my blackout. Even so, at the foot of the rocky, 200-metre ascent to Drölma-la Pass (5,630 metres), which was the highest point of the *kora*, to my amazement I was repeatedly overtaken by Tibetan porters carrying loads of up to sixty kilos. Finally, half dead and panting from a lack of oxygen, I reached the top of the pass. Festooned with prayer flags whipping in the bitterly cold wind, and surrounded by a circle of white summits, it was a glorious sight. For twenty minutes I sat there alone, watching grey clouds sweep over the crumpled black ridges that hid the north face of Mount Kailash. Then, as a symbolic offering to the universe, I slipped an envelope containing locks of hair of my beloved mother, who had died twenty years previously, into a mound of crumpled prayer flags; I felt highly emotional, as I also knew that, now approximately halfway, I was going to complete the *kora*.

When a party of chattering Westerners arrived, I began the seemingly never-ending descent to the minute, green Lake of Compassion, 400 metres below. Four interminable hours later, the trail met the grassy banks of the Lham-chu Khir River. Forced to constantly hop across boulders, I laboured down the marshy valley, from where there was the only glimpse of Mount Kailash's eastern face. To my relief, in due course I arrived at Zutul-puk *gompa*, my second stop for the night. Although it was small and unassuming, and had also been renovated recently, it was very atmospheric. Almost immediately, a snotty-nosed three-year-old girl wearing a tattered sheepskin coat emerged and took me by the hand round the courtyard, which was deserted apart from two men whitewashing the walls. Then her father, the sole lama, arrived and unlocked the prayer hall for me. Inside there were garish Buddhas and *tankas*, and at the back was a cave where Milarepa was believed to have meditated and to have

Prayer flags on 5,000-metre-high pass, western Tibet

had one of his celebrated confrontations with his rival Bön master, Naro Bönchung.

That evening I joined the lama, his wife and the little girl in the *gompa*'s living room. It was dark, with only one narrow window in the immensely thick walls which overlooked the camp that porters had established for the Indians on the valley floor below. In the middle of the room there was the inevitable hot stove, while burning candles threw long shadows over benches padded with thick Tibetan carpets. For an hour, using my Tibetan phrasebook, I tried to chat with the lama, who, not surprisingly, fell about laughing.

Not long afterwards, Pema and some male porters arrived. I kept my distance, though, and we merely winked at one other as one of them, who could have been her husband, was obviously on intimate terms with her. For a while I watched everyone hungrily gnaw the remaining strips off almost-bare yak bones, until Pema and the porters left and I retired to the adjacent 'guesthouse'. It consisted of four rough stone walls and was empty, apart from a mattress on the earth floor. But it was very peaceful, and that night, when I was the only person in the *gompa* except for the lama and his family, will remain in my memory for years.

Filthy, unshaven and hungry, and feeling as if I had been eating only biscuits and high-energy snack bars for years, I woke up on my third and final morning to find the mountains on the other side of the valley covered with snow. When I walked down to meet Norbu in the camp below, Tibetan porters and Indian pilgrims were milling around, their breath hanging in the freezing air, and dozens of yaks and ponies were pawing the frozen ground. Astonishingly, Norbu had slept the night in the open, like many of the porters; apparently this was standard practice, but, still, I felt guilty as we set off down the valley.

Thankfully the path, which ran parallel to the Dzong-chu River, was now downhill. Once, we passed a Tibetan pilgrim in his early forties wearing a bashed trilby hat, a ragged fur coat and old-fashioned sun goggles. He was doing the entire *kora* prostrate, which involved lying full length with his arms stretched over his head, standing up, placing his feet where his hands were, and repeating the process ad infinitum. Normally it takes three weeks to do a prostrate *kora* round Mount Kailash, with Buddhists travelling clockwise, and devotees of Bön travelling anticlockwise. Whatever the faith, Tibetans consider at least one circuit necessary to wipe out a lifetime's sins, with thirteen the real minimum, and 108 for really committed pilgrims. This guarantees instant nirvana, and a clean slate for those unfortunate enough to have repeated incarnations.

Four hours later I reached the end of the *kora*, where the Dzong-chu River emerged on to the Barkha plain, and ramshackle buses and refreshment tents were waiting for the pilgrims. While I was sitting in one of the latter, wondering whether Chumpin, my driver, was also coming to meet me, an Indian who I'd met at Dira-puk *gompa* invited me for a tea. 'So how do you feel on completing the *kora*?' I asked him, stirring my cup.

For a moment he was silent, then he replied thoughtfully, 'I'm very happy. Like most Hindus, I believe the world is a zero, which it stays whether you take something from it, or add something to it. That zero's filled with light, or Shiva, God, Buddha, Mohammed, call it what you like. But whatever name you use, it's divine.'

He had no sooner gone to his bus than Pema arrived with her pilgrim. Without thinking, as a sign of the pleasure meeting her had given me, I gave her $20 – a fortune for a Tibetan – and she kissed me delightedly on the cheek. Then, with no sign of Chumpin, and taking one last look at Mount Kailash as it vanished from view, I set off with Norbu on the dusty, six-kilometre track back to Darchen.

The Kingdom of Guge

After Mount Kailash, I set out with Tikki and Chumpin for the supposedly spectacular ruins of the ninth-century kingdom of Guge, 180 kilometres to the north-west.

On the way, across a dusty brownish-red plateau, was Tirthapuri ('place of death' in Sanskrit) Hot Springs. Only a few hours drive from Darchen, it is one of the most important power points in the whole of Tibet, and pilgrims traditionally bathe here after completing their circuit of Mount Kailash. Overlooking a tiny white *gompa*, the springs were on a mound where hot white sulphurous water bubbled out the ground and flowed down to the Sutlej River.

There I stopped to make the short *kora* around the monastery. This is named after Guru Rinpoche, who brought Tantric Buddhism to Tibet in the eighth century. At one time it was connected with the important Hemis Monastery in Ladakh, whose unforgettable festival I had been to so many years previously. On the hillside above the monastery the trail was pock-marked by little pits dug by pilgrims in search of tiny pellets of lime. These are swallowed as medicine pills which are said to ease the transition of the spirit after death, known as *bardo*.

Further along, past *mani* stones inscribed with the words *Om Mani Padme Hum*, there was a hole in a rock. Here you were supposed to reach in and pull out two stones: if both were white your karma was excellent; if one was white and one black it was all right; and if both were black you had karma problems. However, as with the Buddha's footprints on Mount Kailash, I couldn't find it so, not unduly worried about the state of my karma, I continued to the *gompa*.

It was locked but, while I was sitting on the steps outside the heavy wooden door, a young monk arrived by chance and let me in. Inside it was exquisite. Behind a miniature courtyard piled with brushwood there was a prayer hall so cramped there was space for only two rows of cushions for monks to sit on. In the centre there were dozens of flickering yak-butter candles, while light from a little cupola in the roof streamed onto beautiful *tankas*. For a while the young monk and I sat in silence before we went to the steps outside, where he taught me some basic Tibetan words and I gave him an English lesson.

Langchen Khambab Canyon, kingdom of Guge, western Tibet

Beyond the *gompa* was a remarkable 200-metre-long mani wall topped with yak horns and skulls. This was said to be the end result of a demon firing an arrow at the guru, who stopped the arrow's flight and transformed it into this wall. Down the embankment was the river, where rows of flapping prayer flags spanned a narrow gorge. Nearby, some Indian pilgrims who were camping in two faded white army tents bathed themselves in the rushing green water.

Some time after we left Tirthapuri the dirt road climbed into barren mountains. As we zigzagged laboriously upwards, their flanks turned different shades of ochre, claret, crimson and maroon. At last, after a small emerald green lake, we crossed the Bogo La Pass (5,900 metres), which is one of the highest in the world, before we emerged onto a high plateau.

The view was staggering. For 180 degrees the massive, snow-capped Himalayas filled the entire horizon from the far right to the far left: the peaks of Ladakh to the west; Mount Kamet (7,756 metres) straddling the Indo-Tibetan border, 80 kilometres away; and far, far away to the east the mountains of Nepal, nearly 150 kilometres distant.

But it was what separated us from the Himalayas that really took the breath away. Below, a brown plateau fell away to the stupendous Langchen Khambab Canyon, which was dissected by thousands of lime-grey gorges, ravines, gullies and crevasses. It was like the Grand Canyon, except that it was overlooked by towering white mountains. In 1948

270

Lama Govinda wrote in *The Way of the White Clouds*: 'Whole mountain ranges have been transformed into rows of gigantic temples with minutely sculpted cornices, recesses, pillared galleries, bundles of bulging cones and intersected by delicate ledges, and crowned with spires, domes and pinnacles.'

Soon we descended into the ever-deepening canyons. We'd been threading our way along the bottom of one of them for two hours when, at the junction of two confusing dust tracks, Tikki cried 'Look, there's Zanda, our base for exploring Guge!' Situated at the foot of a steep escarpment, and on a wide ledge over the Sutlej River, it was a large village tucked away in the first cluster of green trees I'd seen in hundreds of kilometres.

We crossed a small chain bridge to ugly concrete Chinese blockhouses. To one side, the old Tibetan quarter blended into the landscape so perfectly that it was hardly noticeable. At the top of the tree-lined main street – which was baking hot despite Zanda being at 3,650 metres – was a Chinese military barracks. Further down, the street was lined with Chinese shops and little restaurants. They were full of Chinese, with hardly a Tibetan to be seen. At the foot was a hideous Chinese-built square, where an officer was drilling a phalanx of People's Liberation Army soldiers. They wore neat olive-green uniforms, and as they wheeled in perfect unison they shouted aggressively and punched the air. As he barked instructions, a hostile-looking officer eyed me suspiciously. Nearby a few dirty, sad-looking Tibetans circled a vulgar, badly restored *chorten* overlooking the river.

Suddenly, not for the first time in Tibet, I was swept by a sense of outrage; the Tibetans appeared to foreigners in their own land, and the Chinese soldiers looked what they were – an oppressive, alien army of occupation.

On the other side of the square, behind high mud walls, was Thöling *gompa*. Once, when Thöling, along with neighbouring Tsaparang, had been the capital of the kingdom of Guge, this had been most important monastic complex in western Tibet. Now it had been almost swallowed up by encroaching buildings. After I settled into the spartan dormitory of the local hotel, I set off to have a look at the *gompa*, but despite paying a hefty entry fee to a surly monk all I could see inside were courtyards piled with heaps of rubble and earth. In the middle, workers were throwing mud haphazardly onto the cracked walls of the three chapels, which were closed for 'renovation'.

I spent a sleepless night in the dormitory, along with some snoring Chinese, and I was relieved to leave at dawn for Tsaparang, twenty kilometres west of Zanda. A rough track followed the canyon bed and the Sutlej River before it crossed a high plain. I was looking for the Royal Palace, which I knew from photographs was positioned high up on a pinnacle, when, just past a white Tibetan village, what looked like a gigantic termite mound suddenly appeared. At the end of a narrow clay spur, it was honeycombed with holes and tunnels, and at the top was a lonely white citadel so high in the blue sky I had to crane my neck to see it.

The ruins of the Royal Palace perched on top of the 200-metre-high mound, kingdom of Guge, western Tibet

The kingdom of Guge flourished as an important stop on the trade route between India and Tibet. By the ninth century it had become a wealthy centre supporting thousands of people. It was also the powerhouse of the revival of Buddhism in Tibet; the great Guge king, Yeshe Ö, sent the young monk Rinchen Zangpo to study in India, and when he returned he built 108 monasteries throughout western Tibet and Ladakh. The influence of the Guge kingdom, particularly the monastic centre of Thöling, was felt from Kashmir to Assam.

The kingdom prospered until the twelfth century, when the advance of Islam to the north and west gradually reduced both its capacity to trade with its neighbours and its authority. A century later it was overrun by the Mongols of Genghis Khan, and the country's leaders were forced to acknowledge Mongolian suzerainty and pay annual tribute to them.

In the late sixteenth century Jesuit missionaries from Goa reached the remote kingdom, mistaking it for the long-lost Christian civilisation of Prester John, the legendary Christian king who was believed to have ruled over a kingdom in the Far East. However, if their leader, Father Antonio de Andrede, had expected to find Christians waiting for him, he was disappointed. The Guge king agreed to let him set up a Jesuit mission, but it proved to be not only his undoing, but also that of the entire kingdom.

Lamas, furious at their king's increasing enthusiasm for a foreign religion, enlisted the support of neighbouring Ladakhi mercenaries in laying siege to the Royal Palace at Tsaparang. Although he was well entrenched in his hill-top fortress there, the king decided to make a deal with them: he would surrender in return for his liberty and pardon for all his subjects. What happened next is unclear. Some accounts say that the treacherous Ladakhis had no intention of honouring their promise and that he, his court and all the palace's defenders were brutally butchered; others, that he fled abroad.

Whatever, the result was that the Royal Palace fell, the monarchy was overthrown, the Jesuits expelled, and the Guge kingdom disappeared from history and was forgotten about until the legendary Swedish explorer Sven Hedin spent three weeks on the banks of River Sutlej in 1908.

After I told Tikki and Chumpin to come back in three hours, I set out to climb the 200-metre-high mound to the Royal Palace. At the bottom of the hill was a Tibetan compound. When I knocked on the door, a friendly Tibetan caretaker emerged with a ring of jangling keys and unlocked the huge studded doors of Lhakhang Karpo (the White Chapel). The first of four that straddled the hillside, it was very dark inside, as there was no natural light except from that coming in through the door. However, the caretaker's flashlight revealed an appalling sight – Mao's Cultural Revolution had completed what the conquering Mongolian hordes had failed to do. Everywhere there were only the shattered remains of giant

Close-up view of the ruined Royal Palace, kingdom of Guge, western Tibet

View from the ruined Royal Palace towards the Himalayas, kingdom of Guge, western Tibet

Buddhas. By the door were two five-metre-high guardian deities, minus their arms and with great holes gouged out of their torsos. Along the walls, where row upon row of small deities had been destroyed beyond recognition, lay heaps of rubble and plaster that were once heads and limbs.

Further up was Lhakhang Marpo (the Red Chapel), where the caretaker's torch revealed slender red wooden pillars supporting a ceiling painted with intricate geometric designs. Here too was a scene of appalling destruction, but at least most of the stunning 400-year-old gold murals had survived. They showed the consecration of the White Chapel, with tributaries in formal costumes gathered from various parts of the Himalayas: musicians and dancers; the people of Guge seated in rows before their king, his queen and the royal family; and everyone turning in devotion towards Amitabha (Buddha in the Land of Ultimate Bliss), himself flanked by rows of teachers, scholars and monks.

After I had been to the Red Chapel I continued the steep climb to the top. The twisting path passed the ruined mud buildings of the monastic area. Further up, burrowed into the soft clay, was a warren of caves in which monks had lived. Thereafter, steps led up through dark, secret, clay tunnels to the remains of the Royal Palace, perched high above. Now it was only a red, roofless shell, while the Winter Palace, just below, contained three small empty rooms with red columns, blue lintels and yellow windows.

From here generations of kings and queens of Guge must have gazed out across their kingdom, as eagles might look out from their eyries, until the last royal family were overthrown in AD 1630. To the right, I could see down over the ruined mud buildings to the green strip of trees running along the river. To the left, high above the plunging canyon floor, layer upon layer of eroded brown cliffs climbed to still more serrated ridges and the snow-capped Himalayas beyond.

For a while I sat there alone, with my back against a huge ochre *chorten*. On top of it, an orange-and-yellow prayer flag flapped in the hot breeze. A pigeon fluttered, and a lonely hawk circled in the cloudless blue sky. Far below, I could hear the sounds of tinkling goat bells, the cry of a young boy and the murmur of the river.

I felt overwhelmed by the desolate barrenness, as well as the immensity of space and the stillness. I also felt very humble; it had taken nature less than 400 years to reduce the mud Royal Palace to such a state that it was almost impossible to see what was crumbling cliff and what was crumbling building. Rarely had I been so aware of the futility of humanity's attempt to leave a permanent mark on earth; never had been so clear to me that, sooner or later, everything passes into dust.

INDIA: RISHIKESH

It all began, accidentally, in Tibet. I was at the foot of sacred Mount Kailash, watching pilgrims raise the symbolic prayer pole at the start of the annual Saga Dawa ceremony. Suddenly, flanked by orange-clad *sannyasi* (followers), a short, middle-aged Indian guru swept through the crowd. He was obviously also on a pilgrimage, as Kailash is as revered by Hindus as it is by Buddhists, and he looked very impressive with dark flashing eyes, saffron robes, long black hair streaked with white, and a bushy black beard. Then at midday I saw him again, this time in the middle of a throng who were watching people dancing, where he was seated next to high-ranking Buddhist lamas under umbrellas against the fierce sun. He dominated the day's remaining events until everyone left on the three-day *kora* of the mountain. Still, I thought no more of him until, two days later, while staying in nearby Chiu Monastery on the shores of barren, stunningly blue Lake Manasarova, I investigated a rectangular compound tucked away behind high mud walls.

The only building for kilometres, apart from the tiny white village behind the monastery, it turned out to be an ascetic ashram full of Indian pilgrims. One of them, who invited me to eat with them, explained that the ashram was a newly built project financed by Swami Chidanand Saraswati, the guru I'd seen at Kailash, who was due to arrive when the meal was finished. Apparently his main ashram, Parmarth Niketan, was in Rishikesh in India, so, intrigued by the coincidence – I wanted to go there later that year – I waited to watch him sweep in again. I stayed for only an hour, listening to the chanting and singing, before I slipped out unnoticed; I've always had only limited time for Indian gurus. Nevertheless, once back in the UK, I decided to book a room at Parmarth as, quite apart from wanting to do a yoga course, I wanted to experience life in an ashram and it seemed a good base from which to explore the nearby town. Furthermore, unlike most of the other ashrams, it didn't insist guests rise at 5 a.m. to meditate.

Rishikesh (population 71,000) has been a place of pilgrimage for over a millennium, with sages and ascetics stopping here to pay homage to the great Mother Ganges en route to pilgrim sites further north in the Himalayas. Now, six months after I had returned from Tibet, I crossed the swaying footbridge suspended high over the river to Swarg Ashram, the area where most of the ashrams were sited. Two kilometres north of the frantic, traffic-clogged town, and nestling at the foot of the forested Himalayan foothills, it was very tranquil. Instead of Rishikesh's swarming, wasp-like *tuk-tuks* (three-wheel motorized rickshaws) with their incessant strident horns, only sacred cows, *sadhus* and *sannyasi* wandered through the covered alleys, which were lined with tea-shops, bookshops overflowing with spiritual guides, and stalls selling Indian flute music.

Parmarth Niketan, which was right on a bend in the river, was a revelation. Imagining it to be similar to the basic Tibetan ashram on Lake Manasarova, or overflowing with burnt-out Westerners, I was astonished to find it full of Indian pilgrims strolling through ornamental gardens dotted with palm trees, grottos, and statues of colourful Hindu gods and saints. Through a passageway, dormitories in shady courtyards overlooked giant banyan trees, and everywhere there was the smell of incense and the sound of chanting. Only my cold, unheated spartan room overlooking the river was disappointing.

I rapidly established a daily routine. Every morning I was awakened by the sound of banyan leaves being swept in the earthen courtyard and monkeys thundering along the corrugated dormitory roof. Dodging bicycles and meandering cows in the alley outside, I breakfasted on the rooftop of my favourite tea-shop, which had sweeping views over the Ganges. During the day I did a yoga course, before I returned at dusk to the rooftop to watch the sun, a titanic red ball, sink into the town's hazy silhouette opposite. Below, *sadhus* bathed in the green shallow water and the last of the day's wooden passenger boats, crammed as always with women in colourful saris, crossed the river.

At 6 p.m., it was time for the day's highlight, the Ganga *aarti* (river worship ceremony). Even for those sceptical of gurus, like myself, it was very moving. Seated on marble steps on

Ferry crossing the River Ganges to Swarg Ashram, Rishikesh, northern India

the ghats under Parmarth's triumphal arch of Krishna and Arjuna, and accompanied by a harmonium, tabla and violin, Swami Chidanand led 200 swaying, orange-clad *ishikumars* (novices from the ashram's orphanage), in ever-faster chanting, singing and clapping. After its joyous climax, they and hundreds of pilgrims waved flaming golden candelabras in front of the floodlit statue of Shiva offshore, and watched the swiftly flowing river carry off dozens of ornate oil lamps into the darkness. Then everyone dispersed, leaving only beggars in the dark alleyways, where they wrapped themselves in threadbare blankets and bedded down round twig fires for the night.

But there was another, even more impressive, side to Swami Chidanand. He had spent nine years meditating in the forest until he arrived as a novice at Parmarth in 1969. By 1986 he had become a swami, and founded the dynamic India Heritage Research Foundation. This impressive, non-profit-making organization not only aims to preserve India's cultural and spiritual heritage, but also provides free schools and hospitals, and emergency relief for disaster victims, as well as finance for women's vocational training schemes and rural development programmes.

Nor do his activities stop there. He has addressed the United Nations General Assembly, and attended interfaith gatherings with the Dalai Lama, Bishop Desmond Tutu and Mother Teresa. He organizes the International Yoga Festival every March and has published the first-ever, eighteen-volume encyclopaedia of Hinduism. He even provides a service for any

Indian to stay for free in the ashram after the death of loved ones, as well as paying for their ashes to be scattered in the Ganges.

Parmarth aside, there was plenty to do. An hour south-west by bus was chaotic but fascinating Haridwar (population 189,000). One of India's four holy towns, every twelve years it hosts the Kumbh Mela, India's biggest spiritual festival. This is often attended by 70 million pilgrims, who believe that by immersing themselves in the Ganges they wash away their sins and escape the wheel of reincarnation. The ghats, which are positioned at the propitious site where the Ganges leaves the mountains and enters the plains, are invariably crowded, with families bathing in the river or admiring the footprint Vishnu supposedly left in a nearby stone.

North-west of Rishikesh and a steep, two-hour climb by bus through lush forest there was also the hill-station at Mussoorie. Situated at an altitude of 1,921 metres on a fifteen-kilometre-long ridge, and with a salubrious climate, it was founded by Irishman Captain Young in 1827. While he was hunting he immediately recognized its potential. Soon Indian maharajas and British officers were being borne up from the hot plains on ponies, or carried up on chairs by sweating bearers, while bullock carts hauled up such essential items as crystal chandeliers, billiard tables and grand pianos. By the 1880s it had become a favourite British summer retreat, crammed with palatial Victorian hotels and the residences of maharajas. Now they are decayed and falling apart, but it was still a pleasure to breakfast in the rose gardens of the once-gracious Hotel Padmini Niwas. Afterwards, I took a rickety cable car to Gun Hill, 609 metres higher than the town, from where there were glorious views of the Himalayas.

The day before I left, I visited the ashram of Maharishi Mahesh Yogi, which was made famous when the Beatles stayed there in 1967. Located halfway up a hill past Parmarth, four years ago it was abandoned because of a dispute with the government. Now the Maharishi, whose transcendental meditation course costs $2,500, and who is now reputedly worth $3 billion, lives in Holland. After I bribed a surly caretaker twenty rupees to unlock the gates I climbed a path through luxuriant forest alive with chattering monkeys. Pursued by a sad-looking old man who claimed to have known the Beatles, I finally reached the buildings. Derelict but atmospheric, now they were being swallowed up by dense undergrowth.

For a while I sat comparing the Maharishi with Swami Chidanand until I adjourned to an adjacent knoll. Looking out over the gently curving Ganges, I reflected back on the chance encounter in Tibet that had brought me to Rishikesh, playing with the idea that, somehow, it hadn't been quite so accidental after all.

Sadhu *performing* puja *(Hindu ceremonial offering) at the River Ganges, Rishikesh, northern India*

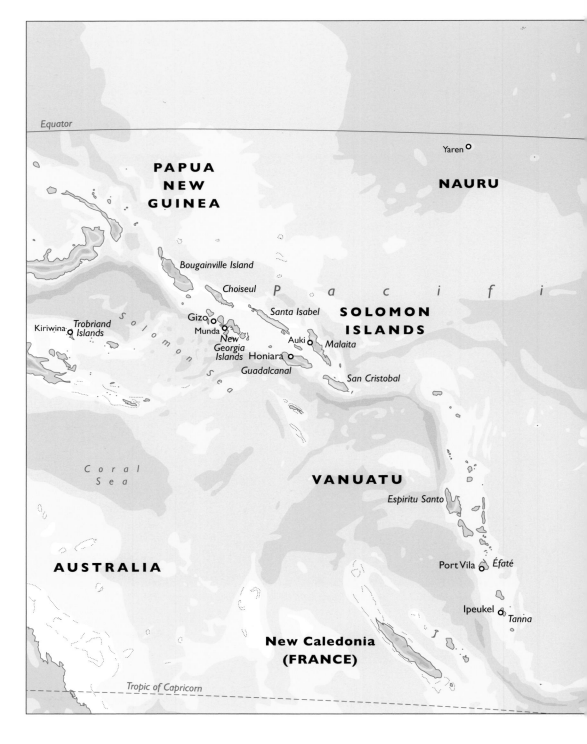

Equator

PAPUA
NEW
GUINEA

Yaren ○

NAURU

Bougainville Island

Choiseul

P a c i f i

Santa Isabel

SOLOMON
ISLANDS

Gizo ○
Munda ○
Kiriwina ○ *Trobriand*
Islands
New
Georgia
Islands

Auki ○
Malaita

Solomon
Sea

Honiara ○
Guadalcanal

San Cristobal

VANUATU

Espiritu Santo

C o r a l
S e a

AUSTRALIA

Port Vila ○ *Éfaté*

Ipeukel ○ *Tanna*

New Caledonia
(FRANCE)

Tropic of Capricorn

280

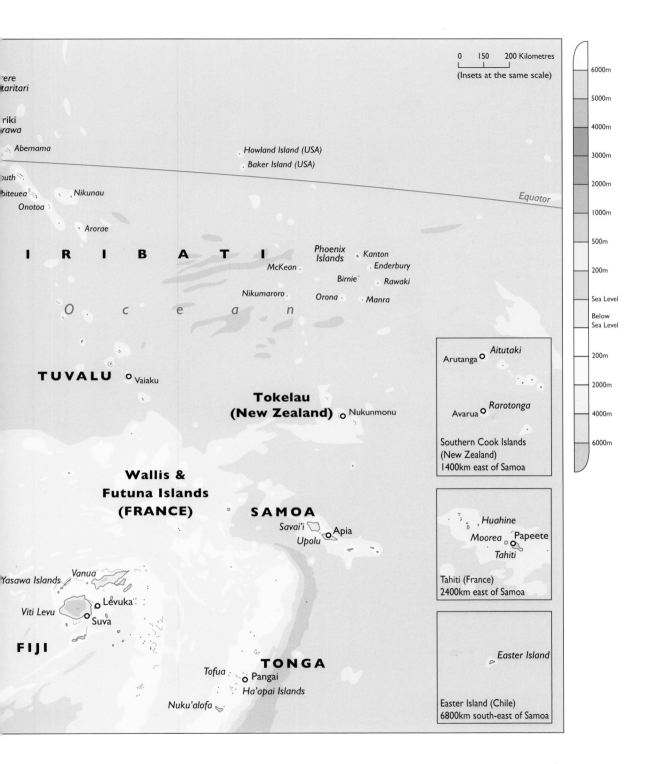

0   150   200 Kilometres

(Insets at the same scale)

6000m
5000m
4000m
3000m
2000m
1000m
500m
200m
Sea Level
Below
Sea Level
200m
2000m
4000m
6000m

rere
taritari

riki
rawa

- *Abemama*

outh

biteuea   *Nikunau*
Onotoa

- *Arorae*

I   R   I   B   A   T   I

Howland Island (USA)

Baker Island (USA)

Equator

Phoenix
Islands   *Kanton*
McKean   *Enderbury*
                Birnie   *Rawaki*
Nikumaroro
            Orona   *Manra*

O   c   e   a   n

TUVALU o *Vaiaku*

Tokelau
(New Zealand)   o *Nukunmonu*

Wallis &
Futuna Islands
(FRANCE)

S A M O A
Savai'i
Upolu o *Apia*

Yasawa Islands   *Vanua*

Viti Levu   o *Levuka*
          o *Suva*

F I J I

Tofua   o *Pangai*
       Ha'apai Islands
T O N G A
Nuku'alofa

Arutanga o o *Aitutaki*

Avarua o o *Rarotonga*

Southern Cook Islands
(New Zealand)
1400km east of Samoa

Huahine
Moorea   o *Papeete*
    Tahiti

Tahiti (France)
2400km east of Samoa

Easter Island

Easter Island (Chile)
6800km south-east of Samoa

CHAPTER FIVE

The Pacific

'... the indescribable feeling of being ... in the most remote place on the planet.'

FRENCH POLYNESIA: HUAHINE

Racing across the grey, windswept south Pacific on the *Ono-Ono* ferry, a powerful modern catamaran, wasn't exactly how I'd imagined sailing to Huahine, the first of the Leeward Islands, 170 kilometres west of Tahiti. Still, it had its compensations. I was standing forlornly at the stern, watching the boiling wake and trying to forget my romantic notions of bumming around in rusty steamers, when I met Jeff.

A tall, innocent dreamer in his thirties, with a lean body, long face and glittering blue eyes, he'd fled Sydney for tiny Norfolk Island, halfway between Australia and New Zealand. There he lived with his Tahitian wife, who was directly descended from Fletcher Christian of mutiny on the *Bounty* fame. Working as greenkeeper for Government House, he'd saved for years to go to Tahiti specially to have his wife's family tree tattooed on his thigh by Polynesia's most celebrated tattooist.

He had just finished proudly showing me the newly completed, Marquesan patterns on his leg, when we saw Huahine for the first time. It was a long, seemingly deserted island, where forested mountains disappeared into the hazy clouds and wild coasts were being pounded by surf. Soon we rounded a sandy promontory and skimmed across a sheltered bay towards Fare, a sleepy South Seas settlement, where people idled on a wooden wharf and children splashed in the azure water.

After we disembarked, I left Jeff, who was going to seek out a fire-eater on the south coast, and wandered along the main street to Hotel Huahine. It was a cracked, two-storey building, but it was a friendly, family-run place. Cockatoos squabbled in mango trees and in the lounge there were faded, nineteenth-century photos of Tahitian maidens wading in a lagoon. The owner, 35-year-old Dolores, a cosmic, New Age mother of three, greeted me like a long-lost friend. Her head in a turban-like towel, she showed me to an empty first-floor room with views out to the reef, before she continued slopping around, breastfeeding her baby.

Captain Cook was the first European to visit Huahine in 1769, and he returned in 1777 to build a house in Fare for Omai, the young Tahitian man he had taken back to Britain. Be that as it may, Omai, whose London stay had given him a taste for grandeur, pronounced it too modest. In 1808 groups of London Missionary Society missionaries began to arrive in Huahine, with the great pioneering missionary William Ellis among them. He wrote *Polynesian Researches*, which was published in England in 1829 and describes early-nineteenth-century Huahine in considerable detail. Fare quickly became a bustling little port that attracted whalers from all over the Pacific, although the wooden shops, most of which were destroyed by fire in 1995, weren't built until Chinese shopkeepers settled here in the 1920s.

I chatted to Dolores about the cyclone that had devastated the west of the island only two weeks previously, and then drifted round the town. I was passing Chez Guynette, a backpackers' hostel next-door, when I heard someone calling my name. It was Jeff, who, unable to find the fire-eater, was staying in the dormitory. We had some beers and strolled along the main street, where there were shops and two supermarkets on one side, and the wharf, a waterside fish market and a white beach on the other. It was peaceful, with only occasional cars or passenger trucks rumbling past.

That dusk we sat on my balcony watching the surf unfurling over the reef as the sun sank below the distant mountainous outlines of the islands of Bora Bora, Raiatea and Tahaa. Soon we went to eat. Despite it being only 7 p.m., it was pitch black, with nothing open except on the wharf, where locals were eating fish and chips at *roulottes* (mobile restaurant vans), and bleary-looking drunkards loitered in the pavilion.

Later we walked back along the waterfront until I returned to the hotel, where I lay in bed, listening to the sound of banjo music drift up from the beach. Suddenly it stopped and waves of torrential rain thundered like horses' hooves across the corrugated-iron rooftops. When I retired to bed I read about Huahine's two connected islands, which, legend maintains, were created when the god Hiro ploughed his mighty canoe into the island, creating Bourayne Bay to the west and Maroe Bay to the east.

The next day I was awakened by the sound of dogs barking, cocks crowing and children splashing in the sea. It was a stunning day with a cloudless sky, and I went to the hostel to collect Jeff with whom I planned to cycle round the island. To my surprise he was still in bed, with his leg up.

'Sorry, mate, can't come,' he grumbled disconsolately, pointing to his badly swollen thigh. 'My thigh's gone septic and I'll have to see a doctor.'

Setting off east by myself, I cycled to Hotel Bali Hai, the island's only luxury hotel, where showcases contained objects found in local swamps. These included canoe anchors, pearl-shell coconut grazers, and flattened club-like weapons made of whalebone. Used only by New Zealand Maoris, these support theories suggesting that apart from there being villages here 1,000 years ago, Tahitians also migrated even then to New Zealand.

Afterwards, I tramped along the deserted road to palm groves where a group of friendly teenage volunteers from Tahiti, who were part of the government Emergency Aid package, were replacing storm-damaged roofs with tarpaulins. I continued along the shores of Lake Fauna Nui, a stunning inlet, until I reached the village of Maeva, Polynesia's most extensive archaeological site.

I began by exploring two overgrown walls that disappeared up into rainforest. The first was built in 1846 by Polynesian resistance forces, which were vainly attempting to repel invading French marines. The second was built during the pre-European era, probably as protection against raiding Bora Bora tribes. Badly bitten by the voracious mosquitoes, I walked to Maeva, where youths were sheltering under shady trees. They invited me to a cup of cheap red wine as they played boules while listening to Bob Marley on a blaring ghetto blaster. Knowing I'd get lost otherwise, I asked one of them to help me find *marae* Matairea Rahi.

A millennium prior to the arrival of Europeans, Maeva was Huahine's seat of royal power, and *maraes* (large foundation stones) are still dotted everywhere, mostly in the rainforest-covered slopes of nearby Matairea Hill. Matairea Rahi is the most notable; it was here the chief sat on his throne at major ceremonies, and it also housed a *fare atua* (god house), where images of Polynesian gods were safeguarded, protected by a 24-hour watch.

In return for a bottle of wine, one of the boys agreed to show me the way. We slogged up steep paths into rainforest until we came to grottoes where, he claimed, sacrificial victims' skulls were crushed. But although he knew the jungle intimately, not long after we passed through glades full of giant, liana-hung banyan trees we lost the tracks, which had become quickly overgrown in the daily downpours.

For an hour he hacked through dense undergrowth with his machete until we emerged jubilantly at the *marae* on a steep, open hillside. Disappointingly, it was merely a terrace of round boulders, but there were spectacular views over the tree-tops to emerald inlets. In a bay, a motionless white yacht was framed against dark, rugged mountains.

I returned to the road and cycled up the steep pass over Mount Turi, Huahine's highest mountain, before I plunged down the Route Traversière to Maroe Bay. Just west of Fare was Fitii Valley. Prior to the cyclone roaring through, leaving a trail of destruction, this had been Huahine's most significant agricultural area, with melon, breadfruit and pineapple plantations. Amazingly, no one had been killed, but now there were only decapitated trees, twisted metal frames and bungalows reduced to matchsticks. Bulldozers were busy removing giant boulders from the blocked roads, and the air rang with the sound of hammering and sawing as people struggled to rebuild their properties.

When I returned to Fare I found Jeff sitting in Chez Guynette's shady back garden, his thigh swathed in bandages. 'How was the doctor?' I enquired.

He whistled. 'Ex*pen*sive! Including antibiotics, it cost me 200 dollars! Or, rather, those damn beers did.'

'What do you mean?'

'She – it was a woman – said alcohol had curdled my blood. So no swimming, and dressings to be changed twice daily. Christ, I can't even sit in the sun!' Suddenly he cheered up. 'Still,' he grinned, 'that's the best-looking doctor who's ever taken my pants down!'

Four days later, Jeff, whose money had run out owing to the unexpected medical expenses, and I were checking the Tahiti-bound *Ono-Ono*'s departure times, when I noticed an antiquated freighter at the wharf. Closer investigations revealed that the *Vaeanu*, which had a dirty white hull, yellow derricks and a green funnel, was not only leaving that evening for Tahiti but also accepting cargo and passengers. Unable to believe our luck, we boarded immediately.

At midnight, five hours late, the *Vaeanu* slipped into the darkness. While Jeff curled up on the upper stern deck, I stood watching Fare recede until, to monstrous thunderclaps, the heavens opened and sheets of rain blotted out the town. Except for solitary lights at the southernmost tip, Huahine was quickly swallowed up by the night and we were alone in the ocean.

Lying on my towel next to Jeff, I tried to sleep but the deck was too hard, all the lights were blazing and the ship shuddered and rattled like thousands of tin cans. I must have dozed off, because the sun was already heaving itself above the horizon when I woke up. I left Jeff snoring loudly and wandered to the bridge. Astonishingly, it was deserted, with no one even at the helm. However, soon the captain, an unshaven Tahitian wearing a singlet and gym shoes, appeared. He told me that the *Vaeanu* was a 5,000-ton, German-built ship, which had previously plied the prize Hamburg–New York route. Now nearing the end of her days, she had been banished to the Pacific, where she carried copra from the Leeward Islands to Tahiti.

Soon a bizarre-looking man I'd noticed the previous night joined us. A handsome, sixty-year-old of European extraction, he had a finely sculptured, droll face. He could have been an ageing film star if it hadn't been for his frayed straw hat and badly bitten bare legs and feet. His name was Albert and he told me he'd been born in New Caledonia before his parents had moved to French Polynesia. He was highly intelligent and articulate, and I was amazed to hear that he'd spent his life working on building sites. Now his wife and son were dead, although his daughter was employed by the justice department in Tahiti, where he was going for injections for his blackfly bites.

'No, I've never been to Europe, far less France,' he continued in a soft French accent. 'But I don't miss it. I have been content here. I know all the islands, from the Tuamotos to the Australs. They're incredible!'

He was very political. 'L'indépendence viendra en cinq ans!' he exclaimed, gesticulating eloquently. 'The French have been a catastrophe! We are taxed to the death and Tahiti is one of the most expensive places in the world. Worse, there's no discipline.' He chortled. 'What we need is a dictator! Gauche, droite, ça ne fait rien, as long as there's discipline!'

Later, I returned to the stern to watch Moorea's spectacular green pinnacles recede. Jeff was examining his thigh after changing the bandages. It was still an unspeakable mess, with black ink leaking into the suppurating sores. 'Healing nicely, isn't it?' he commented cheerfully.

'Sure,' I lied. 'Shame about losing the tattoos.'

He looked at me reassuringly. 'No worries, mate,' he replied, 'once my thigh's healed, I'll redo them myself.'

I was gawping at him when Albert reappeared. 'Know why Hitler was a great man?' he asked, poker-faced.

My eyebrows, and hackles, rose.

He chuckled mischievously. 'Not only was he un dictateur, but he was also from Austria, the land of cette musique fantastique! Écoute!' Suddenly he produced an old mouth-organ and, to our delight, serenaded us with 'Blue Danube' and other Strauss waltzes.

Lulled by Albert's music, as the prow rose and fell in the gentle swell, Jeff and I sat as happy as sandpipers as the seemingly motionless *Vaeanu* chugged towards Tahiti's distant craggy outline. Soon the familiar ugly docks, oil tanks and marinas of Papeete, the capital, loomed larger and larger. But I didn't care; I had found Huahine and my rust bucket, and anyway, in two days' time I was setting out for the Cook Islands, on the next leg of my south Pacific journey.

THE COOK ISLANDS

Rarotonga

Avarua in Rarotonga, the 'capital' of the Cook Islands, was my sort of place. Located on the palm-fringed coast at the foot of tropical green mountains, it was a sleepy South Seas village with wooden trading stores and decaying colonial buildings. Only bikes and the occasional car pottered along the sea front between the parliament (which was housed in a ramshackle bungalow), the harbour and the Seven Coconut Trees roundabout. It was also full of characters.

There was Don Silk, a craggy, white-bearded Aussie who, along with other ex-pats, propped up the bar every evening at Trader Jack's, a converted, corrugated-iron barn on stilts over the ocean, where I went to watch magnificent sunsets on the terrace. He had fled 1950s New Zealand as he found it too claustrophobic, and spent his life on freighters in the Pacific, before 'stopping off' in Avarua, where he'd married a New Zealand Maori and founded his own shipping company.

The first of his three ships had foundered outside the harbour, but he'd prospered and in due course also became harbour master. He'd retired to write his fascinating autobiography, copies of which hung on the tobacco-stained walls, along with photographs of schooners wrecked on local reefs.

'But just because I've been here forty years doesn't mean I've settled down,' he grinned mischievously, downing his umpteenth beer. 'There's life in the old sea dog yet!'

There was also the half-Maori 'Tupui' Henry, who owned 'Maria's', an empty, pink-and-blue, two-storey chalet for rent three kilometres along the coast. Seduced by surf thun-

Hammocks on a beach, Rarotonga, the Cook Islands

dering onto the beach below the veranda, I stayed there for a week. A lean septuagenarian with a pinched face and a vest emblazoned with the words 'Veteran Runners', Tupui was the son of Albert Henry, the first prime minister, who had gained the islands' independence from Britain between 1967 and 1978, and whose lifesize bronze bust, wearing a pair of spectacles and draped with floral garlands, adorned the cemetery of Avarua's white coral church.

Tupui himself had been a cabinet minister until he had resigned in protest at the Thatcherite policies of his cousin, the present prime minister, Sir Geoffrey Henry; politics in Rarotonga was obviously a family affair. Now he pottered about all day in the shady yard of a congested log cabin, where he lived modestly with his wife. Here, he talked articulately for hours about his father, who had been stripped of his knighthood on grounds of corruption. 'He was set up,' he complained bitterly, 'and I won't rest until he's rehabilitated!'

Albert wasn't the family's only distinguished figure. They were all related, like half the island, apparently, to Strickland, Somerset Maugham's main character in *The Moon and Sixpence*, although Tupui claimed that in real life he was a disgraced English aristocrat who had been banished in the nineteenth century to the South Seas.

Best of all, though, was Pa, Rarotonga's celebrated laidback guide and 'natural healer', who took a group of us on a rugged cross-island trek. He was an hour late, but he was worth waiting for. Apart from shoulder-length blond dreadlocks, he looked like a brawny, if thickening, Marlon Brando, with a husky voice, pouting mouth, muscular thighs and tattooed arms. As he drove the minibus around the island collecting everyone, his eyes lit up when he discovered that I loved swimming. 'We must go out together!' he exclaimed. Where do you go swimming?'

'Only in swimming pools, unfortunately. But when I'm in Greece I often go out four kilometres.'

He grinned condescendingly. 'Oh, I was thinking more of forty! I was the south Pacific's long-distance swimming champion, you know.' He turned to Meagan, the attractive young Sydney lawyer behind, and peeled off his shirt to reveal gashes in his burly shoulders. 'This is where sharks attacked me during the Tahiti to Moorea marathon,' he said nonchalantly.

Driving inland up a back road across Ara Metua (Ancient Road), which was originally built of coral blocks in 1050 AD, we passed through lush, fertile valleys and headed into rainforest-covered hills. Gradually the road petered out at the trail, where he commanded us to cluster round.

'First, I want to tell you our traditional way of dealing with mosquitoes,' he began. 'It's much better than expensive repellent. You pick some leaves – any will do – like this, and you whack them, like that!' Everyone laughed. 'But, seriously, our plants are well known for their healing properties. There's Phuanini, which cures diabetes, Morinda, which cures cancer . . . '

'Really?' someone broke in sceptically.

Pa looked upset. 'Of course! I cure people all the time.'

We plunged into dripping undergrowth and hiked along slippery red paths that wound steeply up over tangled tree roots into rainforest. It was a spectacular climb, with glimpses over the jungle canopy to the distant ocean and across ridges to precipitous green peaks in the wild interior.

Sweating profusely, we reached the base of the Needle, a sheer 410-metre-high pinnacle, where Pa, who had bounded ahead effortlessly, was unpacking his heavily laden rucksack. His eyes followed ours upwards. 'Only nine foreigners and myself have climbed it,' he announced casually, handing round mandarins. 'But I was the first, when I was only eight.'

Everyone gasped with admiration. 'It looks so dangerous!' exclaimed a wide-eyed young New Zealander.

'It is,' replied Pa. 'But we were all Leos.'

'Leos?' asked the young New Zealander, puzzled.

'Because only the lion-hearted can climb it,' he explained without blushing.

There was a pause. 'How old are you?' someone asked.

'Fifty-eight.'

Everyone gasped again, as he looked twenty years younger. 'How do you do it?' another burbled.

Pa in front of the 410-metre-high Needle pinnacle, Rarotonga, the Cook Islands

Pa's brow furrowed. 'I keep in touch with my inner spirit,' he said, trying to look sincere.

There was silence. 'Are you married?' asked Meagan tentatively.

'Five times. But I don't chase women,' he murmured, staring deep into her eyes, 'they just come to me. They can sense I've got a big soul.'

When we were ready we began descending the island's south coast, continually re-crossing a boulder-strewn stream that Pa leapt over like a gazelle. Often he waited to help Meagan, who kept falling in. 'Balance!' Don't *fall* in, *tune* in!' he instructed as, his powerful hands always just brushing her breasts, he lifted her over.

Once, we stopped in a dappled glade, where he laid out sandwiches, coconut slices and mango on palm fronds that he had cut with his machete. Suddenly he put his fingers to his lips. 'Ssssh!' he commanded, cupping his ear to the sound of a trickling brook. 'Listen to *real* music!'

As we continued down treacherous muddy paths, I could hear him telling the young New Zealander how much he loved dolphins. 'They're my guiding spirit,' he was saying, 'and when I go swimming, I call them until they come in droves . . . '

An hour later, we arrived at the foot of the mountain near Wigmore's Waterfall, where rutted tracks led past ruins of the derelict Sheraton

Resort, started by Sir Geoffrey Henry but funds 'ran out' – to the island's circular coastal road. Then the waiting minibus took us back to Avarua, where we paid Pa before he strolled off, arm in arm with Meagan.

Aitutaki

Those who say Bora Bora in French Polynesia is the south Pacific's most beautiful island are deceived. It isn't. It's probably Aitutaki, in the Cook Islands, 150 kilometres north of Rarotonga.

A week after arriving in the Cook Islands, my eyes boggled as Air Rarotonga's eighteen-seat Fokker banked over the south of the tiny island (population 2,000), which nestles in a huge surrounding lagoon protected by the outer reef. Exquisite, palm-laden atolls ringed by stunning white beaches shimmered like a mirage in the shallow jade water.

We landed at the 'airport', a deserted thatched hut overlooking an immense airstrip built by the Americans during the Second World War, and I hitched to Arutanga, the island's main village six kilometres south. It consisted of some trading stores, a weathered-looking church and some playing fields next to the harbour. I found rooms in the Tiare Maori Guest House, an airy bungalow full of flowing lace curtains, bibles and stands of the white, broad-rimmed straw hats which the women wear to Sunday church.

'Come in, don't mind my hoovering!' said Mama, a cheerful grandmother with a floral garland in her hair, as she swept the porch with a broom made of palm leaves.

According to tradition, Aitutaki's first settler was Ru, who was escaping his legendary, overcrowded Polynesian homeland, while another ancient seafarer, Ikaroa, from French Polynesia, was supposedly guided here by Are Mango, god of sharks.

Aitutaki's European discoverer was Captain Bligh on board the HMS *Bounty* in 1789, seventeen days before the mutiny took place, en route to Tonga. Captain Edwards on HMS *Pandora* arrived in 1791, hunting those involved, while Darwin also stopped off during the HMS *Beagle*'s epic voyage in 1835.

The following day, I visited Arutanga's Cook Island Christian church, which has monuments to missionary John Williams' landing in 1821, before I set off on a rented moped round the island. The paved road dwindled out north at the airstrip, where, lost in a time warp, I stood imagining heavily laden B-24s lumbering down the runway as they practised bombing Japan.

Then I trudged along dirt tracks running east through clearings in rainforest, where children waved from porches of bungalows, and turned south to Vaipeka and Vaipee, the only other villages, halfway down the east coast.

Shortly afterwards, signs pointed to Tokongarangi, Aitutaki's biggest *marae*, so, branching off the main track, I tramped along palm-frond strewn paths through dark, bamboo tunnels into the bush. To my dismay, the moped quickly became entangled in shoulder-high elephant grass, so I gave up and returned to crossroads where a disintegrating signpost

Lagoon in Aitutaki, the Cook Islands

stated 'NEW JERUSALEM': the famous – some say infamous – religious sect whose isolated settlement is hidden on the island's southern tip.

Intrigued, I zigzagged down through rainforest to the coast until, just after my moped sent thousands of crabs scuttling into their holes, I arrived at deserted thatched huts. Rusting tractors lay abandoned in coconut groves and rotting boats were drawn up on a ravishing white beach that looked out to atolls dotting the lagoon.

I was standing uncertainly by some fish ponds when a woman swinging a machete suddenly materialized out of the blue. I gulped nervously until I realized she'd been slicing coconuts, and was in fact a dignified, graceful woman in her fifties who, with her unlined forehead and wise face, reminded me of Doris Lessing. 'Hello, I'm Emelia,' she volunteered, smiling gently. Within minutes she was telling me about New Jerusalem.

'The Free Church is based on a mixture of Maori and Christian beliefs,' she began, 'and now we're all over the Pacific. There's the Garden of Eden in New Zealand, the Lamb of

Life in Rarotonga, and New Nazareth in Tahiti. We have five Gods: Jesus, Father Joseph, Holy Mother, Almighty and Home, who we believe have already descended to earth and established a new kingdom of Heaven, called Beyond Time World.'

'So where are these gods now?' I asked, fascinated.

'In New Zealand, with John, my husband. Let me explain. He used to be a fire-dancer, but had to give it up when he became increasingly anaemic. I tried everything, unsuccessfully, until someone told me to ring this new movement in New Zealand. I did, and, saying it was punishment for betraying his vocation, unbelievably they cured him over the phone.

'Sadly, it recurred – he actually died three times – but each time they brought him back to life. So in 1986, out of gratitude, he founded New Jerusalem. Now, as we're the longest surviving members, he's gone with everyone to fetch them. Come, I'll show you our preparations.'

I accompanied her to the huts, which were built in traditional Polynesian style. 'John designed these after Noah's son, Ham, gave him the plans in his dreams,' she continued earnestly. Opposite were five newly constructed *fales* on the shore, each with different-coloured wooden thrones and double beds expectantly facing south. 'This is where the gods will stay when they come,' she commented proudly.

I scratched my head. 'And what do the villagers think about all this?'

'Oh, they refuse to come here. They think it's full of evil spirits. But, on the contrary, we're charmed. When Hurricane Sally's tidal wave hit Aitutaki, it parted right here and left us untouched.' She beamed serenely. 'That's proof of our faith. So's William.' She pointed to a hunched old man vigorously digging vegetable plots. 'He's ninety, but, like everyone else here, he's got the energy of a teenager. No, I've no doubt, in time people will come to us.'

An hour later it was time to return to Arutanga. Although she was one of the wackiest people I'd ever met, in spite of myself I couldn't help feeling inexplicably moved. 'Here,' she murmured, handing me coconuts and embracing me lovingly, 'if you remember the gods, they'll remember you.'

FIJI

Levuka

A lover of remote imperial outposts, I had high expectations of tiny, historic Levuka (population 3,000), which had been Fiji's capital from 1874 to 1882. It was late at night, and it had been a long journey by 'express' coach from Suva up the east coast of Viti Levu, Fiji's main island. There I had caught a ferry from isolated Natovi Landing over to Ovalau, where another rattling bus jolted me off into blackness, halfway round the seemingly uninhabited island. Now, through the drizzle, solitary lights loomed ahead.

I got off at deserted Beach Street, where, opposite coconut trees lining the ocean, pillared wooden walkways linked pink, blue and green weatherboard buildings, their headboards proclaiming 'Bank', 'Hardware Store' and 'General Supplies'.

I tramped to the end until, just before a canal emptying into the sea, I found the run-down, colonial Royal Hotel. The oldest in Fiji, it was another time warp – rather how I imagined Kenya to be in the 1850s – with walls lined with masks, spears and bongos. But I was too tired to take in any more properly, so I dragged myself upstairs and collapsed into bed.

The origins of Levuka, Fiji's earliest European settlement, date back to 1806 when sandalwood traders started stopping here for supplies. By 1830, many had married Fijians and, with their chiefs' protection, were building schooners to trade in *bêche-de-mer* (sea cucumber), turtle shells and coconut oil.

Mysteriously, it was razed in 1841, but although the inhabitants of Lovoni, a village high in the island's wild, mountainous interior, continually raided it, by 1850 it had become a popular port for sailors, whalers and beachcombers. Incredibly, Beach Street once had fifty-two hotels. Soon the booming town was flooded with bickering British planters, and it became a centre for blackbirding (slave-trading in the Pacific), with a reputation for drunkenness, kidnapping and violence.

Attempting to restore law and order, in 1874 Britain took over from Chief Cakobau, Fiji's most influential warlord, and proclaimed Levuka the new colony's capital. This didn't last for long; hemmed in by mountains, the town couldn't expand, so in 1882 the government was moved to Suva, and in 1888 and 1905 Levuka was devastated by hurricanes. By the 1930s, with the copra markets on which it relied plummeting, Levuka was rapidly disappearing into the annals of history, but not before it was immortalized by Kipling in his poem 'Sussex': 'the palm-grove's droned lament / Before Levuka's Trade'.

The next morning, when I opened my window's shutters, I saw to my dismay that it was pouring with rain. Down below, by a bridge over the canal, crowds were huddled under a rotunda's corrugated-iron roof. Intrigued and forgoing breakfast in the dark-floored dining room, which was dotted with aspidistras, turtle shells and discoloured photographs, I hurried down to see what was going on. It was the Saturday market, and women squatted in the mud, surrounded by piles of mandarins, coconuts and cassava.

I was watching the rain while drinking tea from a kiosk when I got chatting to a cheery, plump woman with a frizzy orange hairstyle, no shoes and only a few teeth. Along with others from all over Ovalau, she was waiting for fresh fish; astonishingly, she not only spoke fluent English but also was the stenographer for a department of agriculture research station on neighbouring Makogai Island, the south-west Pacific's former leper colony.

'Hi, my name's Liz Taylor, but people call me Cleopatra!' she said, laughing. 'Actually, I'm just a racial fruit salad. My great-grandfather, who was black, came off an American whaler, and I've got Chinese and Fijian blood as well.'

Encouraged by her openness, I asked her about the ongoing ethnic conflict between poorer Fijians and fourth-generation Indian immigrants who, imported by the British in the

four English girls on a gap year, who lay wilting under the burning sun. Further up, young, blond Australian snorkellers trudged along for Otto and Fanny's legendary 'high tea' of homemade banana cake and ice cream.

That night there were only six other guests for dinner. All were New Zealanders who had come for the diving. There was Jeff, a heavily built 35-year-old, with glasses, bush hat, pale skin, freckles and ginger hair, who worked with security systems; Philippa, his chubby, amiable wife, who had spent her childhood in Lautoka, where her father was the town's water engineer; Sam, a monosyllabic computer-science student with a giraffe-like neck, whose favourite word was 'cool'; Jo, his girlfriend; and two men on a newly arrived yacht, which they'd run aground accidentally during the Auckland to Nadi race.

They all liked to talk about beer. They talked about their favourite brand, its cost, who owned it, why they liked it, what its ingredients were, when it was first produced, where they usually it bought it, how much of it they normally consumed and how long they'd been drinking it for. As they prattled away, Harry served the meal. He was a gentle, good-humoured man who loved food and had worked as a chef on the *Captain Cook*. Now he produced gigantic, exquisitely prepared meals twice daily, including spaghetti bolognese, fish, chicken, fresh beans and carrots, fruit salad, pineapple and melon, as well as making the afternoon teas.

He was also very well informed, as we discovered after the meal, when, with all beer-related topics at an end, everyone lapsed in silence. As he cleared the table discreetly, Philippa piped up. 'Come on Harry, tell us something interesting,' she said.

He scratched his balding head. 'Well, you probably don't know, but until recently we were the south Pacific's worst cannibals,' he said, laughing. He wagged his finger in mock disapproval at our plates of half-finished, gargantuan steaks. 'And nothing was ever wasted. For example, the story goes that in 1867 one of Fiji's chiefs borrowed the comb of the Reverend Baker, the Methodist missionary, while he was out. When he returned, Baker mistakenly tried to take it from the chief's hair. Of course, touching his head was taboo, so the locals ate Baker, as well as his shoe leather!'

He wasn't exaggerating. Archaeological evidence shows that cannibalism was a ritualised part of life here for 2,500 years. Captain Cook was already aware of Fiji's bloodthirsty reputation when he stopped off in 1774, but afterwards European sailors wisely gave the islands a wide berth. Now, with the country probably doomed to becoming the south Pacific's Costa Brava, it's hard to believe that, until the late nineteenth century, the delightful Fijians, who are easily the South Seas' friendliest people, routinely either threw their captives alive into ovens, or dismembered them and forced them to eat their own body parts.

Harry had witnessed more contemporary history, as well. 'When I was a boy I remember when the Chief of Taveuni Island arrived,' he reminisced, referring to Fiji's second most-prestigious chief. 'He was so important that he had a food taster to make sure that his food wasn't poisoned. And, of course, I saw his boat being escorted into Tavewa by line of sharks . . . '

'Ah, come off it!' Jeff broke in.

'No, really!' Harry insisted.

I spent the next few days on sun-drenched white beaches at nearby Savutu Point, the island's southern tip. There, swimming in the warm, clear water was like being in a tropical fish tank. As ill luck would have it, the brilliantly blue sky clouded over, despite the fact that the Yasawas are the one place in the south Pacific where non-stop sun is virtually guaranteed. With not much else to do, as Tavewa has no banks, shops, postal or medical services, far less villages, and no boats to other islands, everyone was quickly bored. It wasn't surprising, therefore, that when Harry mentioned vaguely he was going to 'a church fundraising' on Nacula Island opposite and asked if we'd like to come, we all jumped at the chance.

The following morning we boarded his fishing boat, which puttered across the aquamarine lagoon. An hour later, we arrived at the island and tramped after him through coconut trees until we arrived at Malakati, one of the rare villages on the almost-abandoned Yasawas. Harry showed us into a *bure*, which as usual had no furniture apart from suitcases, a double bed, and pictures of Christ on the wall. There he bustled around, handing out *sulus*

Women at the meke *(traditional dance), Yasawa Islands, Fiji*

(long skirts worn by Fijian men). 'In traditional Fiji we still think it rude to enter a village wearing shorts,' he told us.

'Cool,' commented Sam, as he admired the new attire he had been given.

'You look ridiculous!' said Jo disdainfully.

Soon Harry took us to a clearing where musicians with drums and guitars were seated on the ground. Suddenly a procession of men and women dancers in brown-and-white floral patterned *sulus* and grass skirts emerged from a *bure*. To our delight, the church fundraising was a genuine *meke*. This is a traditional Fijian dance that, accompanied by stamping feet, clacking bamboo sticks and beating drums, enacts legends and stories from the past. Formerly, it involved chanting by 'spiritually possessed seers', and was held on essential religious and social occasions, but increasingly the dance is only performed for tourists.

That evening, after we returned to Tavewa, Sam, Jo and I set off to see the sunset from the top of the low hill dominating the island. Tracks wound up through bamboo clusters and tall elephant grass until they reached a grassy knoll. A magnificent sight waited. Beyond the *Captain Cook*, which lay peacefully in the lagoon below, the watery horizon stretched for 360 degrees. To the west, a Saturn-like ball was dipping into the crimson ocean. To the east were Bligh Waters, so-called because here, after the mutiny on the *Bounty*, Fijian canoes chased the notorious captain's rowing boat here before he continued on his astounding 6,000-kilometre journey to the Dutch East Indies. A yellow moon was rising over the water.

'Cool!' exclaimed Sam, trying to give Jo a romantic kiss.

'Oh, don't be so stupid!' she replied, swatting him off like a fly.

A few days later the three of us tramped up the beach to Coral View, the island's backpacker camp round the promontory, to catch the boat back to Lautoka. I wasn't looking forward to it. My guidebook advised, rather alarmingly, I thought, that the trip was quite long and crossed 'a notoriously exposed stretch of water, where weather conditions can quickly change. In the past, passengers have been stranded adrift owing to engine failure, and only rescued hours later'. But it was already spectacularly out of date. A few weeks previously, my short-wave radio had picked up the BBC World Service, which reported that a heavily overloaded boat with twenty-five Western tourists aboard had sunk north-west of Fiji. I hadn't paid this much attention until I heard Harry tell Jo that the boat in question had been taking backpackers from Tavewa to Lautoka, and belonged to Coral View.

Maria, the pleasant thirty-year-old Fijian who sat inside the camp's hut selling boat tickets, wasn't apologetic. 'It wasn't our fault,' she said casually, when I questioned her about it. She gestured to an outmoded motor-launch moored in the shallows. 'That's our boat there, and that's the one that will take you today. At the time of the sinking it had engine problems, so we hired another one. It was the hired boat that sank, not ours.'

'Yes, but it was still your responsibility,' I pointed out. 'And the boat was overloaded.'

'Look,' she announced with a hint of impatience, 'it was the captain of the hired boat who decided how many to take, not us. Anyway, it wasn't such a disaster. No one was injured or drowned. Everyone either swam ashore or hung on to the boat until they were rescued.'

'Yes, but they were in the water for eight hours!' Jo exclaimed.

'True,' Maria said nonchalantly, 'but they were only ten kilometres from land. It's just our competition trying to discredit us. I got so fed up with Radio Fiji and newspapers phoning from all over the world that eventually I just referred them to our Lautoka office.'

The three of us looked at each other; Jo pointed to the decrepit motor-launch. Its stern was so low in the water that it looked like it was capsizing already – and that was with only the two men aboard who were struggling to start the engine. 'And what about your boat?' she asked fearfully. 'It won't sink as well, will it?'

'Oh no,' Maria replied amiably. 'It normally takes twenty people, but because of what happened we're only taking nineteen.'

The nervous backpackers removed their sandals and waded out to the boat. An hour later the engine had been repaired and, with a throaty roar, we were off. As we powered along a few kilometres offshore, I gazed uneasily at the Yasawas' east coast. I was a strong swimmer and I knew that I could reach the shore if the boat sank. Suddenly the boat turned left and surged out to sea until the islands, now probably far outside my range, were only a smudge on the horizon. I crossed my fingers and, lulled by the juddering engine, dozed off. By the time I woke up, Viti Levu's mountains were looming, and three hours after setting off from Tavewa we entered Lautoka's harbour safely.

'Thank God for that!' exclaimed Jo, mopping her brow and shrugging off Sam's comforting arm.

'Cool,' declared Sam, sadly.

TONGA: THE MUTINY ON THE BOUNTY

Newly arrived in Tonga to go by boat to the island where the mutiny on the *Bounty* took place, I was amazed to find the poky airport's concourse heaving with a sea of vast men – Tongans are built like container ships – dressed in black. 'Why's everyone in black, and what are those for?' I asked my taxi driver, pointing to frayed straw mats on top of their *tupenu*s (sarongs).

'The king's brother has just died,' he answered. 'When someone in the royal family passes away, people wear black for months. The mats are *ta'ovalas*. They're traditional family heirlooms – the older the better – worn as a mark of respect.'

The king he was referring to was Taufa'ahau Tupou IV, who, at 1.9 metres and 180 kilogrammes, is renowned for his size (photo-journalists continually try to photograph him beside Tonga's diplomatic vehicle, which has the number plate '1 TON'), and for being the world's last absolute monarch. His mother, the equally overweight and majestic Queen Salote, was even more legendary. In 1953 she earned the undying affection of the British when, despite pouring rain, she rode, unlike Queen Elizabeth II, in an open carriage to the latter's coronation in Westminster Abbey. Noel Coward used the occasion to exercise his customary wit. He knew that cannibals inhabited Tonga's islands until Wesleyan missionaries arrived in 1822. When a bystander asked who Queen Salote's diminutive companion (a retainer) was, he reportedly quipped, 'her lunch'.

The road into Nuku'alofa, the capital twenty-five kilometres away, wasn't pretty. Run-down shacks, corrugated-iron huts, cannibalized vehicles and rubbish-strewn gardens straggled along it. Nowhere in the south Pacific, apart from Tahiti, has vernacular architecture been so destroyed as in Tonga. But the taxi driver was entertaining. 'I'm also a trainer at the gym where the king works out,' he explained. 'I know him well. Everyone does. His limousine goes there three times a week.' He laughed. 'It's only a hundred metres from the palace and it's quicker, and better exercise, to walk. But he works hard, especially on his arms and legs. He even cycles round the National Stadium accompanied by sweating bodyguards, all jogging desperately to keep up.' He sighed. 'Not that it does him much good, as he never loses a kilo. Still, he's friendly and most people like him.'

Soon it was time to leave for the Ha'apai Islands, 100 kilometres to the north. Legend maintains that the demigod Maui, who borrowed hooks from a wizened man named Tonga in order to go fishing, yanked up the islands one by one and graciously named the largest after the old man. In the thirteenth century, fierce Tongan warriors sailed in gigantic catamarans to establish a far-flung Polynesian empire that extended to Fiji and Samoa. But for people with such a nautical history Tongans are remarkably reluctant sailors. I was advised unanimously against taking M/v *Olavaha*, the rust bucket that makes the twice-weekly run. 'It pitches and rolls terribly, and everyone's violently sick,' they warned repeatedly. Yet, that evening, after I had boarded, she slipped gently into an idyllic red sunset; the only hint of violence was on the blood-curdling video *Return of the Serial Killers*, which the crew were watching avidly downstairs.

Daybreak found us sailing past coral islands lined with palm-fringed, white beaches until we arrived at Pangai, my final destination. The administrative centre of Lifuka Island, it was only a village, and was empty after 11 a.m., when people fled from the blistering sun to spend the day weaving mats inside their decaying bungalows. The lethargy was infectious. I settled into Fifita Guest House, a decrepit, two-storey building, and wandered opposite to buy biros in the minuscule Friendship store. A woman idling at the till tried several unsuccessfully until she found one that worked. 'The others are sleeping,' she said, smiling sweetly.

Captain Cook visited here in 1777, when he and his crew were invited to a cannibalistic

'airport', which was a shanty hut by a grassy strip, to return to Nuku'alofa. To my amazement, a gentle giant from Royal Tongan Airlines announced that the tiny plane's departure was delayed because some coconut trees were too tall and had to be cut down.

I was puzzled. 'But they didn't prevent last week's plane taking off!' I objected.

'Well,' he drawled languidly, 'after the recent rain they've grown.'

VANUATU: TANNA AND THE JON FRUM CARGO CULT

I hadn't been looking forward to flying from Port Vila, Vanuatu's capital, to Tanna Island, 200 kilometres south. The previous week, at midnight, a plane from Espiritu Santo Island had crashed into the town's bay during torrential rain. Half the passengers were killed on impact, while, of the eight who escaped the sinking fuselage, only four, who had swum disoriented for six hours in pitch darkness to the nearest land, had survived. As we flew over the crash site itself, one of the passengers told me that the wreck had never been found and that sharks had probably eaten the missing bodies.

To my relief, our eighteen-seat Fokker reached Tanna safely. At the airstrip I hitched a lift in the only vehicle, a battered pick-up whose driver Roy, astonishingly, was going the length of the sixty-kilometre-long island to within a stone's throw of Ipeukel village, the stronghold of the bizarre Jon Frum cargo cult I wanted to visit.

My jubilation was premature; luckily, I didn't know what was ahead.

The rutted road curved through rainforest dotted with thatched huts in roadside clearings. Half-naked ni-Vanuatu people, the indigenous inhabitants of the islands, silently watched us pass. At crossroads near Lenakel the increasingly pitted road climbed inland towards jungle-covered ridges and craggy mountains. Without warning, we reached a high pass. Far below us there was a desolate grey moonscape, where what looked like an atomic mushroom cloud spiralled into threatening, rain-laden skies. This was Mount Yasur (361 metres), one of the world's most accessible and active volcanoes.

We descended a muddy red track riddled with craters, all that was left of the road that British Army engineers had built in 1980, until, at the volcano's foot, we reached Lake Isiwi's barren, treeless shores. Not long afterwards we arrived at Yaneumakel, a hamlet of primitive huts crouching behind adjacent ridges.

Containing Roy's extended family of over eighty people, it was desperately poor, but, seeing dusk was approaching, I accepted his offer to stay the night. I was led to a surprisingly clean mattress in a hut adorned with posters that said 'VANUATU SOSAIETI, BLONG ALL PIPEL – SKUL, WOK, PLEI.' Shortly, I returned to eat in his hut. In a smoke-blackened corner Thelma, his wife, crouched over pots of yams steaming on a log fire. Joined by Sloki, his oldest son, and watched by naked infants who stood at the entrance peeping shyly at me, we ate cross-legged on the earth. For a while we sat by the smouldering embers, staring at shadows cast by flickering hurricane lamps and listening to the volcano. It was disconcertingly close, and its booms and rumbles sounded like jumbo jets taking off.

Like most male ni-Vanuatu, who are Melanesians and resemble Australian Aborigines, Roy was a small, stocky, bearded man wearing only dirty torn shorts. He was the only villager who spoke some French. (The official language of Vanuatu, which was an Anglo-French condominium until independence in 1980, is Bislama.) 'It strange,' he observed, 'the volcano always active during planting. Before, our chiefs walk around it with special leaves to calm it. In those days we worship it – Yasur means God – and we believe our spirits go there when we die. But missionaries come, and everything changes.'

He had no idea when that was, and in fact he seemed to have little sense of time or the past. When I asked his age he replied, 'thirty'. I pointed to Sloki, who was obviously in his twenties. 'No, sixty,' he said, uncertainly scratching his curly black hair. 'All I know, I was born in 1950.' I didn't press him but, trying to change the subject, I asked where ni-Vanuatu's gods came from. A heated family discussion ensued until he announced, 'We born after Christians arrive, so can't tell. Question too difficult. You must ask chief. He's wise, know everything.'

Then, at midnight, I was attacked by a pack of dogs.

I was returning across the pitch-dark compound, having been to the village's only toilet, when I heard barking. Within seconds I felt a dog snapping at my heels. Ignoring it, I continued until I felt my trousers rip, accompanied by an electrifying pain in my right leg. Realising I'd been bitten, I turned furiously and tried to kick it away, but before I knew it I was surrounded by a pack of snarling curs. Horrified, as within my torchlight's radius there were at least twelve pairs of dripping fangs and crazed eyes, I backed away desperately, lashing out with my feet. Shortly, awakened by the uproar, Roy and his brothers arrived and beat them off with sticks.

Examination by torchlight revealed a deep gash under my bloody trouser-leg. 'Dogs don't see many whites,' Roy mumbled apologetically, visibly shaken. 'Even so, this not like them. You should get injection.' While he hastily prepared the pick-up, I performed emergency first aid. When he was ready, we set off past Lake Isiwi and the grumbling crater, but within minutes he skidded to a halt outside seemingly derelict bungalows. Hunting around urgently with his torch, he managed to rouse Jonah, a barefoot, bearded man, who showed us into a squalid room littered with bloodstained swabs. It was the local clinic, where shelves were lined with empty bottles and tables were strewn with medieval-looking instruments. 'No rabies vaccine,' he announced in basic French, 'but you lucky, pick-up's leaving in a few minutes to take pregnant woman to Lenakel Hospital.'

That was forty kilometres all the way back down that appalling track. Paranoid, I urged a driver to hurry as he laboriously readied a pick-up daubed with red crosses. Half an hour later, we set off. Oblivious of the silent woman in the back, I peered into blackness, still picturing those terrifying fangs and praying we wouldn't break down. Although, heart-stoppingly, the engine cut out twice as the driver skilfully negotiated the craters, by 3 a.m. we'd arrived at the coastal crossroads.

The hospital was a long low building, where, to my relief, I found a relaxed young Canadian doctor who was in Tanna on a six-month voluntary placement. After he tended to the pregnant woman in Maternity, which was a mothballed ward full of vacant beds, he listened attentively as I told him my story before he disappeared to consult nurses. Five minutes later he returned. 'They're not certain but they think there's only rabies in Espiritu Santo Island,' he said, smiling reassuringly. 'We've no vaccine either, but as there's no plane for two days there's no point in worrying.'

I did, though, and there was plenty of time for it. I woke up at midday, as we hadn't got back to Yaneumakel until 5 a.m. My initial relief at realising that I wasn't foaming at the mouth was quickly replaced by dismay at the curtains of water hanging from the leaden skies outside my hut. I spent the next three days trapped like a prisoner in the village, where I lay miserably on my mattress, swatting mosquitoes and cockroaches, or gazing disconsolately at tree-tops whipped by stormy winds. It wasn't long until I got bored, so I started visiting other dim, soaking huts, in which women with babies at their breasts cooked yams and wove mats interminably.

After what felt a lifetime the rain relented. Desperate to get moving again, and with another two days until Ipeukel's *custom* (traditional) dance, reputedly attended by all the surrounding Jon Frum villages, I decided to climb the volcano despite my festering lesion. Initially, Roy advised strongly against it, saying that the volcano was dangerously active and, with such low cloud, I wouldn't see much. Regardless, accompanied by William, a French-speaking guide, one day I trudged through dripping bush before I ascended crumbling lava ridges to the crater's precipitous rim.

It was an apocalyptic sight. A hundred metres below, like something from a Hieronymous Bosch painting, the volcano's hellish, glowing mouth sucked greedily, and vomited lava and boiling smoke into the sullen clouds. 'Can't stay long!' William shouted nervously above the deafening roar, as we crouched instinctively at the ominous rumbles and held our noses against the evil-smelling yellow fumes. 'Three years ago, a rock killed two Japanese tourists and their guide. Anyway, the edge can collapse any second.'

The next day, when the rain had almost stopped, I set off for Ipeukel. I descended slippery trails to the foot of a steep, jungle-covered ridge until I came across groups of almost-naked, wild-looking men. Squatting on the ground under trees, they spat continuously as they prepared *kava*, which in Vanuatu is fifty per cent saliva. They were friendly, and a helpful young man called David, who was the chief's son, immediately invited me to stay with him.

Built around a grassy square, the village was the poorest I'd seen in my life. I dumped my bags in a sodden hut and he showed me the Jon Frum 'church', which was merely a wooden roof over a red cross stuck in cinders. There I watched children shrieking joyfully as they played tag on the spare ground with dented tin cans, before I meandered to the volcanic beach. Not far away, a naked old woman with shrivelled breasts sat by some dilapidated outriggers, staring into the surf.

Captain Cook, who had already named Vanuatu's dark, rugged islands the 'New Hebrides' because they reminded him of those in Scotland, landed here in 1774 to investigate the inexplicable glow in the night sky (the volcano). The island of Tanna got its name when, pointing to the ground, Cook asked Paowang, the elderly chief he had befriended, what the place was called. The latter, thinking he wanted to know their word for ground, answered 'tana'.

The nineteenth and early twentieth centuries saw the arrival of fire and brimstone Presbyterian missionaries and European planters, who brought not only harsh, repressive practices but also catastrophic epidemics.

In 1936 the Tannese began talking about a mysterious brother of the god of neighbouring Mount Tukosmera in northern Tanna, who, they claimed, promised a return to traditional values, an end to epidemics, and unlimited wealth. Within a few years, during the Second World War, US troops arrived in Vanuatu. Their numbers included Medical Corps staff and African-American soldiers, who generously dispensed seemingly infinite supplies of free medicine, Coca Cola and cigarettes. Shortly afterwards, concluding the latter were their brothers in disguise, and that their saviour, now known as 'Jon Frum', was American, many people in Tanna began erecting dozens of red crosses all over the island, hoping to intercept the magic which produced such abundance.

When it was explained there was no Jon Frum, this was interpreted as another foreign attempt to deprive the Tannese of their rightful inheritance. They began to examine arriving planes in case he was inside and, keen to receive his latest message, not only made imitation radio aerials out of tin cans and wire but even constructed an airfield in the bush, complete with a replica bamboo aeroplane.

This weird phenomenon has several explanations. Most commonly accepted is that Jon Frum stands for 'John from America', after a US Medical Corps member with a red cross on his sleeve. Some maintain it is a mispronunciation of Jon Broom, i.e. the broom that will sweep Tanna clean of Europeans and their influence. Others claim that African-American US troops told the Tannese about John Brown's nineteenth-century fight against slavery. Whatever the origin, Ipeukel villagers believe that one 15th of February the messiah will return, bringing all the cargo he promised. Every year, on that date, ragged groups of men with 'USA' daubed on their backs hold military parades and proudly march up and down clutching bamboo rifles.

That night, I rested by candlelight in David's darkened hut – even the chief's son had no money for paraffin – until I went to the *nakamal* (communal meeting place) for the regular Friday evening dance. Under the village's solitary hurricane lamp, young men playing guitars and singing childlike songs were surrounded by a crowd clapping and chanting 'Hallelujah! Hallelujah!' With rain keeping the inhabitants of other Jon Frum villages away, it was less spectacular than I'd expected, but, reminded of Southern Baptist Revival meetings, I found it intensely moving, nevertheless. To general hilarity, I joined the tots leaping about like frogs in soft drizzle outside, where young women in yellow, pink, green and red grass skirts swayed rhythmically until dawn.

I was preparing to leave the next morning when I noticed women streaming past, all wearing the same colourful skirts as at the dance, but with elaborately painted faces. Intrigued, I followed them to shady trees overlooking a clearing, where the entire village had gathered, dressed in traditional costume. Soon processions of semi-naked men carrying poles and with grass arm- and knee-bands emerged from the forest, leading a handsome young boy. He wore an ornate crown of feathers on his head and his body was covered with glitter.

Jonah, the friendly man I'd met that dreadful night at the clinic, was standing next to me. 'At fourteen years, young boys are cut,' he explained, pointing between his legs. 'They're taken into bush where they're not allowed to see women or girls. There they're taught how to behave like a man. When they heal, they return for a ceremonial feast.' He pointed to a woman sobbing next to piles of newly woven mats and baskets full of yams. 'Those are gifts, and that's his mother, who won't see him for three months.' As village elders began addressing the crowd, young warriors carried in terrified pigs suspended from poles and started clubbing them. Sickened, I turned away, although that didn't block the hideous thudding sound as they were beaten to death.

At midday I returned exhausted to Lenakel and treated myself to a comfortable bungalow in the Tanna Beach Resort, the island's only tourist lodge along the rocky coast. That afternoon, I cleaned myself up, as I'd hadn't washed or changed my clothes for days, and gorged myself in the open-air restaurant until it was time to join the afternoon tour to Yakel, a famous village where the men wear only penis gourds.

The guide began by telling us how the ten families there shared different responsibilities, for example growing *kava*, coconuts and taro, and then steered us obediently through the rainforest. Once, we passed some mossy, overgrown shanties, which were almost indistinguishable from the dense vegetation. 'Women and girls must come here during menstruation,' he explained.

Not much later we arrived at a hollow tucked away in the wilderness. Here, resigned-looking men wearing penis gourds and women wearing grass skirts waited wearily under giant banyan trees. Soon the traditional dancing started, with young women jumping up and down, whooping and shouting, as the men danced round furiously in circles. When it

The boy at the initiation ceremony, Tanna Island, Vanuatu

Above: Family in Yakel village, Tanna Island, Vanuatu
Left: Boys wearing penis gourds, Yakel, Vanuatu

had stopped, along with the frantic camera clicking, they filed past dutifully, shaking hands and inviting everyone to buy *nambas*. 'If tourists want one, we ask wife for size,' the guide joked. 'Husband always exaggerate!'

Two days later I was back at White Sands airstrip, waiting for the Port Vila plane. Standing next to me was a 78-year-old Catholic missionary called John. Slim and olive-skinned, he'd been born in Malta, and lived in Egypt before being raised in England. He had been stationed in Dunblane during the Second World War until he was dispatched to Tanna. He had never returned, except for a prostate operation and to see his brother. 'I don't miss it at all,' he volunteered. 'I'm retiring next year, and I hope the church'll find me somewhere in Port Vila to see out the rest of my days.'

'And what about the Jon Frum movement?' I asked.

'It's slowly fading,' he went on. 'They've suffered too many hoaxes, and had their expectations raised too often.' He chortled wryly. 'But you have to admire them. If you ask them how they keep going, given the lack of evidence, they reply, "At least we've waited only sixty years – you Christians have waited two thousand."'

PAPUA NEW GUINEA: THE TROBRIAND ISLANDS AND MALINOWSKI

'I know why *you're* going to the "Islands of Love!"' joked the young air-stewardess, sitting down next to me and grinning mischievously. Outside, the mountains of Papua New Guinea receded and the half-empty plane droned across seemingly boundless blue ocean.

'No you don't,' I answered, blushing. In fact, I wanted to learn about the Trobriands, the exotic coral islands 250 kilometres east of Papua New Guinea, which were made world-famous by Polish anthropologist Bronislaw Malinowski in his classic books *The Sexual Life of Savages in North-Western Melanesia* (1929) and *Coral Gardens and their Magic* (1935). Despite both being serious studies of the islands' inimitable yam culture and mysterious *Kula* circle (a ritual trading ring), his astonishingly explicit analysis of the islands' sexual mores – especially those of the sensuous girls with their free and easy manners and short grass skirts – caused a sensation and led to the mistaken perception that the islands were a sexual paradise.

Two hours later we banked steeply over the fifty-kilometre-long main island of Kiriwina, the flat, bush-covered interior of which ended in beaches ringed by coconut trees. Once we had landed on a short grassy airstrip, we taxied to a hut where eager faces crowded behind a fence watching the week's highlight: the arrival of our Saturday flight from Port Moresby.

An elfin-looking Australian, Zak, who had a long black beard and shining eyes, was waiting with his wife, Katie, and two young children for the mail. While they gave me a lift in their pick-up into Losuia, the main village, Zak explained that they'd been on the island,

Men and women at annual traditional festival, Port Moresby, Papua New Guinea

Reception for the government's chief education officer at Okaibona village, Trobriand Islands, western Pacific

lodge built.' He paused. 'Of course, all the heads of state stayed here,' he added casually.

That night, we ate dinner by paraffin lamp in the shadowy dining hall and adjourned to the terrace, where John launched into a lecture about *Kula*. 'You must understand that the intelligent man has to be multilingual, not just with people but also with birds and plants and trees,' he expounded. 'You see, they all have their own language. For example, if you stroll along a deserted beach and see only ribbing in the sand you think no one's been there. But there has! Waves may have erased their footprints, but the memory of everyone who's ever walked there is contained in the ocean.' He flashed his charming smile. '*Kula* means tuning into that, into the Universal Spirit, which is everywhere and nowhere and . . . '

'Sorry, how do you tune in?' I cut in.

'By using your intuition, your senses, your body and your soul, of course!' he exclaimed impatiently. 'Look, for years I was seduced by Western rationalism – I studied law, politics, philosophy and psychology at Australian universities – until I realized that linear thinking leads nowhere. *Kula*'s different. It's spiral. Though some say it's "New Age", it's actually Pacific Old Age. That's why I now spend all my time in the garden. A garden's a meditation, a prayer. It's there that wisdom lies and the soul gets energy, not from the intellect.' Then, with hardly a pause, he was off. 'You see, *Kula*'s a dynamic, fluid, flowing, creative process, and it's about giving, growing, the *quality* of shared experience . . . '

Nonetheless, his belief in *Kula* didn't seem to extend to his wife Mary, who was a kind, considerate, Chinese-Malayan woman. On the second evening, embarrassed at how he peremptorily instructed her to bring the meals before curtly dismissing her, I innocently said 'cargotalki' ('thanks' in Kiriwian). John glared at me. 'In *Kula* the word means "thank you for giving food to my spirit",' he said, rebuking me sharply. 'You shouldn't use it so lightly.'

When she had cleared away the dishes, she always reappeared immaculately dressed in a kimono, only, completely ignored by John, to depart unhappily again five minutes later. On the third morning, as he vanished as usual towards the yam plantation, she could restrain herself no longer. 'There he goes again, just wasting more time and money!' she burst out bitterly.

Not knowing what she meant, later that day I returned to the VBA where Elizabeth, who always had her finger on the island's pulse, seemed equally disenchanted with him. 'No one trust John any more,' she pronounced disapprovingly. 'I'm not tricking you. For years he full of foreign schemes to bring money to the island, but not a kina arrive, or, if do, it disappear. He even imprison for a year on corruption charges, along with paramount chief.' She was almost as hard on Mary, who apparently had owned several shipping and logging businesses until they had lost their licence through John's dubious business activities. 'She a good woman,' she continued sternly, 'and has plenty reason drink too much, as John spend most her money. Still, chief's wife shouldn't be drunkard. Whole island scandalized.'

Shortly, it was time for the celebrated 'cricket' match. Introduced by missionaries to take the islanders' minds off less salubrious activities at the end of July's yam harvest, it had, as my guide book intriguingly commented, 'developed in a style not exactly as the MCC [Marylebone Cricket Club] intended'. But, as if by conspiracy, the skies unseasonably opened, and every day the match had to be postponed. Dismayed, for days I sat around Zak's bungalow, or, dodging non-stop deluges, hurried down to the jetty. There I sheltered in the market shed, and watched friendly men with blackened teeth who hung out at the betel nut stall.

By late afternoon the rain had usually cleared up, and an expectant crowd gathered, keenly scanning the watery horizon, which was empty apart from D'Entrecasteaux's distant mountains, for signs of the day's fish catch. In due course tiny, billowing sails grew larger and larger and there would be stampedes into the bay's ankle-deep muddy water, where clamouring hands besieged the primitive outrigger canoes.

Miraculously, only two days prior to my departure, the sun finally shone and Zak

Cricketers at Yalaka village, Trobriand Islands, western Pacific

drove me through bush to Yalaka, where the match with a neighbouring village had already started. It was worth waiting years for. In a grassy clearing, surrounded by thatched huts and watching crowds, over 100 barefoot, half-naked, highly decorated warriors formed an intimidating square around two visiting 'batsmen'. The warriors had red sashes round their waists, straw pouches over their genitals, white paper stars or feathers in their hair, yellow floral garlands draped rakishly over their heads, and their backs were covered with glitter. Every time one of the 'batsmen' was bowled out, the warriors would advance threateningly on his successor, yelling bloodcurdling cries and waving silver tinsel sticks festooned with yellow streamers. Then, leaning backwards, slapping their thighs and stamping the ground like angry bulls, the square reformed.

Forty-eight hours later I found myself waving through the window of the Port Moresby-bound plane until Zak and Katie, who had come to see me off, were dots far below. In next to no time the airstrip and coconut trees had receded, and once again we were droning high over the ocean.

THE SOLOMON ISLANDS
Ghizo

'The Solomons? They're some experience, I can tell you,' Bill, the good-looking, blond Australian, pronounced cryptically. 'By the way, that's your ship, the *Iuminao*, down there. Good luck; you'll need it!'

It was Sunday and, after I'd arrived at dawn at the deserted, minuscule Henderson Airport, he'd given me a lift in his pick-up to Honiara, the capital, where I was rushing to catch the boat for the two-day journey to Ghizo Island, 100 kilometres west. Soon we reached a dusty town overlooking a bay where some tramp freighters lay at anchor.

Unsure what he meant, I walked down earthen lanes off the empty main street, and there, besieged by crowds in a dock, was the filthiest rust bucket I'd ever seen.

For a while I sat watching aghast as the *Iuminao* settled lower and lower in the water until her hold's entrance had almost sunk below the jetty. Nonetheless, my mind was made up to board, especially when the harassed but obliging Wings Shipping manager, who I'd phoned from Fiji, confirmed at the chaotic pier gates that he'd got me the only cabin.

Pushing aside mental images of overcrowded boats that periodically capsize in the west Pacific, I battled aboard to the purser's office, where Whitney, the sweating, overweight purser, was engulfed by a clamouring, ticketless mob. Finally, giving up ordering them ashore, he seized a megaphone and, as if announcing a Club Med cruise bellowed, 'Halo, welcum, welcum!' in Pijin, the English-based lingua franca which supplements the country's sixty-three languages. He led me across a deck already littered with bodies and boxes to a padlocked cabin under the bridge.

'Desfella bilong iufella!' he beamed proudly.

With cobweb-covered windows overlooking the prow, it was bare except for two moth-eaten mattresses on wooden bases full of ants' nests. Cockroaches scuttled over rotting floorboards into the stinking, overflowing lavatory. But at least it was my own space and, with the archaic air-conditioning making the suffocating humidity tolerable, it was better than below decks, where passengers were crammed like battery hens next to the juddering engines.

Three hours later, under lowering skies, we made our way along the coast of mountainous Guadalcanal, its misty summits covered with bottle-green jungle, and out into Iron Bottom Sound. The name derives from the sixty-four Allied and Japanese warships, which included battleships, cruisers and submarines, sunk here in some of the Second World War's fiercest fighting; twice I saw the blackened hulls of Japanese transports beached offshore.

I was perched on the stern rails when I met Ross, a stocky Solomon Islander wearing a Budweiser baseball cap. Previously he'd been a Honiara taxi driver. 'Bifoa, mi drive Japan ol fella look dai comrade bodi,' he said. 'Find, hem hav parti, go-go ash Japan. Plenti tearful.'

Now he worked as the driver for a Malaysian logging company on Rendova Island.

'They have a bad name,' I commented, referring to the controversial South-east Asian companies now moving into the Solomons, eighty per cent of which are still covered with virgin rainforest. 'How do the islanders feel about them?'

'Hem no laek hem,' Ross replied. 'Mi too. Hem take plenti, no replanting.' He sighed. 'But mi workim.'

Not much later we'd left Guadalcanal behind and were alone in the vast ocean. Two hours later, we passed the Russells, which consisted of dozens of thinly populated, wooded islands amid pristine green lagoons. I was admiring a particularly beautiful atoll when I was got chatting to Guy and Peter, two skinny young Peace Corps volunteers lying on mats on the crowded deck. The only other foreigners aboard, they were going for a well-earned break to the famous Marovo Lagoon, after spending two years in Malaita Island.

'It's wild!' Guy exclaimed, answering my question about life there. 'Especially the Kwaio, who are a tribe living in the mountainous interior. They believe their ancestral spirits are everywhere, and they hardly allow government troops in, far less us. There are also Laulasi's shark callers. Until 1972, they used to be able to call sharks, which boys would ride around the lagoon. Honestly, it's well documented!'

It sounded like nonsense to me, so I didn't go into it. That afternoon I joined the bare-foot, impoverished-looking teenagers who, to escape the bedlam below, had shimmied up the stern railings onto the curved roof. Returning home for school holidays to some of the archipelago's 992 islands, which are spread over 1.4 million square kilometres, they were surprisingly Westernized, with frayed jeans, torn Bob Marley T-shirts and Rastafarian caps. I was so engrossed in conversation with Joseph, a seventeen-year-old schoolboy, I hardly noticed that night had fallen and that, as the *Iuminao* began rolling in strong winds, the others had long since gone below.

We carefully made the now-perilous journey back down to the stern; as there were no rails, one slip and you were treading water as the boat disappeared into the blackness. But death would've been quick; during the Second World War, when 15,000 Japanese alone perished in naval battles, the Pacific's nickname here was Sixty Second Sea, referring to the time it supposedly took for torpedoed sailors to die in frenzied shark attacks.

Once safely back in my cabin, I managed to sleep despite loud, alarming, metallic bangs as the *Iuminao* lunged into choppy seas. It must have been midnight when I was awakened repeatedly by Whitney shouting 'Al ticket blu!' through loudspeakers above the door, accompanied by streams of incomprehensible Pijin.

Unaware these were instructions for passengers disembarking at stops in the Marovo Lagoon, the largest world's island-enclosed lagoon, I attempted to disconnect the wires until I gave up and lay miserably on my mattress, scratching my itchy hair and listening to unnerving scuttling. I must have dozed off, because in the morning I woke up to find us gliding up swamp-lined creeks to Viru Harbour, a hamlet on eighty-kilometre-long New Georgia Island, where hopeful villagers were waiting at mango-, fish- and rice-stalls for the twice-weekly boat.

Fishermen in the Vonavona Lagoon, the Solomons

Hugging the island's mangrove-fringed coast, next we headed to tiny Munda, renowned for its *nzunguzungus* (carvings inlaid with pearly nautilus shell), and the scene of more frantic Second World War fighting. Stopping outside the unnavigable lagoon, the *Iuminao* was met by hordes of canoes for the mass exodus.

Before long, we entered ravishing Vonavona Lagoon, with its dozens of coral-encrusted atolls, sandbars and emerald shoals. I was back on the roof when I met twenty-year-old Mohammed, a young draughtsman returning home to Kolombangara Island, whose towering volcano dominated the western horizon.

Although he looked destitute he was astonishingly well informed, and for hours he told me about the Baha'i faith, which he'd joined two years previously. He also told me about how the Solomons achieved independence from Britain in 1970, as well as its perennial crocodile problem. 'As hav plenti, plenti,' he continued, 'but nao, no plenti Kolombangara.' He laughed. 'Tu yeah bifoa, siks people dispeah, as laugh Niu Georgia head-hunt again. But, hem dis crocodile, hem run gut, hem savvy laek human.'

After we stopped at Nono, a small port with a tuna-canning factory, only a few wild-looking people were left on board. Most were women with tattooed faces and orange mouths discoloured by betel nuts, who sat breastfeeding babies and picking nits out of their children's hair. The remainder were Aboriginal-looking men with dark, brooding eyes, who laughed hysterically when I looked at them and spent the rest of the time eyeing me suspiciously. After we paused briefly at Kolombangara's Ringgi, which was just a collapsing quay at the misty volcano's foot, we headed towards the little town of Gizo, on Ghizo Island opposite.

Although it was the second-largest town in the Solomons, it had a population of only 4,500 and was not much more than a village, with a stall-lined waterfront, copra boats drawn up by a rickety wharf, and an earthen main street with half-empty, Chinese grocery stores. I struggled ashore through crowds flooding aboard for the return trip, and found rooms up a hill in two-storey Paradise Lodge, which overlooked rooftops and Kolombangara's looming cone.

That evening, as dusk fell, I wandered along the darkened main street, where there was hardly any electricity, to Restaurant PT 109. Named after the patrol craft which, captained by future American president J.F. Kennedy, was sliced in two by the Japanese destroyer *Amagiri* in 1943, its porch had spectacular views. Despite unbearable mosquitoes, I stayed on when my meal was finished, watching canoes flit through the bay's reflections of a magnificent pink sunset.

I was idling at waterfront stalls the next morning when I found myself beside four shoeless people with the blackest skin I'd ever seen. Curious, I discovered the three men and a woman were from Bougainville in Papua New Guinea, only five hours away by boat. Maggie, the woman, told me she'd come to attend Gizo's hospital.

'Don't you have one in Bougainville?' I asked innocently.

'Ya, aidu,' she replied bitterly, 'bifoa Niu Guini army man go burn hem down. Hem kill plenti wuman, pikinini. Hem no gut, no orait!' Suddenly the youngest, a burly, wide-faced man called Malagui, who had long ringlets, a ragged singlet and grubby shorts, leant across. 'As, BRA fightman,' he whispered, 'as here get gun.'

Amazed, as I'd never heard of the Bougainville Revolutionary Army, I invited them for lemon drinks in Gizo Women's Happy Hour, a shack serving cheap meals. Shortly, Malagui was telling me more. 'Bifoa, taosin-naen-handred-siksti-foa, Bougainville Copper Compani, bilong Australee waitman, find copper Panguna,' he explained. 'Quick, quick, plenti Australee fella, hem bagarup river, tree, hem no give-mi plenti. All-we make BRA, nao laek as bilong, laek hem go-go baek, stop hem use as!'

The following day, still ashamed of my ignorance of the barbarous civil war raging only 100 kilometres away – over 60,000 people had fled at this point – I hired Joshua, a local teenager, to take me round the island in his dugout. We glided across to Fishin, the village on stilts I'd seen from Restaurant PT 109, and coasted onto a sandy beach, where I was swamped by crowds of handsome, dark-skinned boys with astonishingly blond curly hair. I was shown around by William, a gentle, half-blind young man, who told me the boys' parents were settlers from Malaita.

Then we rowed past wooded atolls until, in a cove, Joshua pointed down to the *Tia Moru*, a Japanese freighter sunk in 1943 by American planes, which, lying only eleven metres deep, is one of the country's most famous dives. Soon we reached New Georgia Sound, where I could see long low islands smeared across the skyline, including Vella Lavella.

Here, when the Japanese withdrew in 1944, 300 troops hid in forests rather than face Allied capture. On hearing numerous reports of a small man raiding villagers' gardens, in 1965 the Japanese ambassador flew over the area dropping leaflets saying 'The war is over!' and encouraging him to surrender. He did, and returned home to receive the nation's highest honours; thirty years on, there continue to be sightings of long-bearded, elderly stragglers in loincloths, although cynics suggest these are ruses to lure Japanese tourists.

Two hours later, we were at the island's western tip. Leaving Joshua to go ahead, I waded ashore and, watched by friendly men repairing canoes, strolled along the water's edge to Saeraghi village. I played football with some boys in clearings ringed by thatched huts and later I trekked after them, still laughing uproariously, through lush trees to look for Joshua. He was asleep under bushes on one of the Pacific's most exquisite bays, where shallow, jade water lapped at a curving golden beach lined with gracefully leaning coconut trees.

Unable to resist, I stripped off and dived in, only to find, when I surfaced, a toothless, desiccated-looking man waiting patiently under the trees. He was Ezekiel, Saeraghi's chief, come to collect my 'landing' fees (a nominal amount paid as a courtesy). I apologized, before he told me how Japanese brutality during the war turned the islanders into America's

Canoe at Saeraghi Bay, Ghizo Island, the Solomons

invaluable ally.

'Japan ol man no gut,' he went on. 'Hem take basket, take kanu, burn haos, made as workim plenti, no giv money. As rimemba!'

Then, as if in a dream, escorted by leaping dolphins and shoals of silver flying fish, Joshua and I continued round the savage, palm-fringed coasts to Titiana, an idyllic, if scruffy, thatched village dominating a magnificent white beach protected by a lagoon. Waving to smiling villagers as they prepared meals in their huts, I ambled over to children furiously playing blackjack in the dust. Within seconds the group opened up like an anemone, and the most beautiful little girls I'd ever seen, with dusky skin, lily-white teeth, long eyelashes and laughing eyes, encircled me.

Later, I was sitting on logs when Harrison, a melancholy, thirty-year-old villager, joined me. He told me that everyone was originally from overpopulated Kiribati, formerly the Gilbert Islands in Micronesia, 1,000 kilometres away. But he quickly disabused me of the notion that Titiana was paradise. 'Malaria so no-gut, parent dead wen thirty-five,' he sighed,

327

pointing to the children, who were once again passionately playing cards. 'As, world most no-gut malaria problem, wan-fella every tu-fella get – no pill money.'

Shortly, it was time to leave, so, accompanied by the giggling girls, I returned to the beach and climbed reluctantly into the dugout.

'You no forget as?' Harrison shouted as we paddled away.

'No,' I replied, waving, 'I won't forget you.'

Marovo Lagoon and Head-hunting

Two days after I returned from Saeraghi I went to Gizo's airport to take a plane to New Georgia Island. There I wanted to explore the magnificent Marovo Lagoon on the island's south-east seaboard, as well as find out more about its once-notorious tradition of head-hunting. I checked in at a corrugated-iron shack, where all eighteen passengers were weighed on a set of scales. Soon our small, Honiara-bound plane took off from the 200-metre-long landing strip. Below, as we flew south, there were dozens of uninhabited coral atolls fringed with aquamarine lagoons and white beaches.

One of them was Kasolo Island, to which the young lieutenant J.F. Kennedy, who was a champion swimmer, had towed one of his wounded crew for two kilometres after the Japanese destroyer had sunk his patrol boat in 1943. His astonishing feat hadn't stopped there; afterwards he had swum to a nearby atoll to try to get help or supplies for his ten stranded men, before, on the return journey, he had been almost drowned by strong currents.

I leaned across to one of six burly, middle-aged American men on the other side of the aisle. They were wearing baseball caps on which was written 'US NAVY DEEP SEA DIVERS'; Western Province is as renowned for its wrecks of sunken Second World War ships and aircraft as it is for its stupendous marine life.

'Which is Kennedy Island?' I asked, using its more popular name.

'What're you talking about?'

'You know, the island where John F. Kennedy was marooned during the Second World War?'

'No idea,' he replied, 'we are only here for the diving.'

I was still reflecting on how little was known about Kennedy's heroism, even by his fellow citizens, as I looked at the view from the window. The indented west coast of ninety-kilometre-long New Georgia Island consisted of mangrove-fringed swamps. Ten minutes later, I could see Seghe below, where a row of thatched huts lined the coast and a grassy airstrip was carved out of the rainforest.

When the plane made a brief stop, I found that I was the only person getting off. Within minutes it roared off again, leaving me standing alone on the deserted runway. Outside a shack, a portly Melanesian man in his fifties and a teenage boy were waiting patiently on the grass verge. They were Deventa and his son, Michael, a serious-looking fourteen-year-old, who had been sent to pick me up by Vanua Rapita, the eco-lodge where I had arranged to stay. Before long we were chugging across the lagoon in its motor canoe.

The Marovo Lagoon is not only a World Heritage Site, but is also, according to James Michener, a present-day wonder of the world. It was very different from what I'd expected. Instead of being shallow and translucent like so many other Pacific lagoons, it is a seemingly infinite inland sea, cut off from the ocean only by a line of low-lying, forested atolls to the north-east. As far as the eye could see, it was almost uninhabited. To the right, in the middle of the wild interior of Vangunu Island, the flanks of a colossal volcano were covered with virgin rainforest. Far away, at its foot, I could make out a solitary hamlet and, just offshore, an islet with five brown dots.

'Michi village and the eco-lodge,' Michael announced, pre-empting my inquiry. He bent across until his face was close to mine. 'I'm on holiday from school in Seghe,' he confided to me earnestly.

'Are you?'

'Yes.' He looked at me with trusting, soulful eyes. 'I love reading and hearing stories. Will you tell me stories?'

'Yes,' I promised.

'I'd like that,' he added. 'We will have a good time together.'

Thirty minutes later we drew up on the islet where Robert, the lodge's Melanesian manager, was waiting to greet me. He was a portly, taciturn sixty-year-old with curly, greying hair and a beard. He led me to one of three leaf huts on stilts over the water. Inside, it was spartanly furnished, with wooden floorboards, twin beds, a mosquito net, a paraffin lamp and a window flap propped open by a pole. The immaculate white sheets had been neatly turned down and a red rose was lying on top of cleanly laundered towels. On the veranda, which looked across to the village, there were wicker rocking-chairs, a table, a tray containing tea bags, a Thermos flask, and a plate of freshly sliced lemon.

I was settling in when Guy and Peter, the young Peace Corps volunteers I had met on the *Iuminao*, popped their heads around the door. They had disembarked at Munda, the anchorage for the Marovo Lagoon, while I had continued to Ghizo Island.

'We've been here since we saw you two weeks ago,' Guy continued. 'It's a real neat place to hang out. We're the only ones here, and we spend hours on the balcony watching all sorts of fish. We've even seen stingrays, which sometimes drift right under us.'

They had also paddled a canoe a few hundred metres out into the lagoon.

'Weren't you afraid of crocodiles?' I said; Western Province is famed for its fresh- and seawater crocodiles.

'Oh, you don't have to worry about those!' Peter replied. 'They only live near mangrove swamps or river estuaries.' For a moment we fell silent as the sounds of a congregation singing, accompanied by basic guitar chords, drifted across from the village.

'What's that?' I asked.

'It's amazing!' Guy exclaimed. 'They're these Seventh-day Adventist women who are doing a tour of the lagoon. They took the evening service two nights ago and the village hasn't stopped singing since.' Suddenly I realized he was referring to a group I had seen get off the *Iuminao*, along with Guy and Peter, at Munda.

That afternoon Robert showed me round. It didn't take long, as the islet was only a hundred metres long. Opposite, on the other side of a clearing, were two huts housing the administration and the dining room. At the other end, tucked away in palm trees, were two sheds. One of these contained the shower, which was merely a goatskin bag full of water hanging from a pole. The other one housed the lavatory, a white porcelain toilet that, mounted on a block, looked like a throne.

'We don't have any electricity or running water,' Robert remarked apologetically, 'but we recycle everything.' He pointed to some rotting poles. 'This is where the original village was until it became too small and was moved opposite.'

At dusk, Guy, Peter and I ate by kerosene lamplight in the dining room over the water. In his congested office behind a partition, Robert was receiving messages on his crackling two-way radio. Two girls from the village prepared the carefully presented meal, and we tucked into delicious mango, coconut slices, home-baked bread, freshly caught seafood, local vegetables and fruit.

When supper was finished, the girls, along with Robert and Deventa, paddled across to Michi village, where they lived. I retired to my porch and sat gazing at the great, unbroken expanse of water. Above the looming volcano, orange clouds hurried into the sunset. Water slapped against coral rocks under the hut and schools of silver fish jumped out of the calm water. There was still the sound of singing, this time accompanied by ecstatic clapping and hilarious laughter.

The next day Robert, who spoke excellent English, told me about the lodge. He was a quiet, placid man, but his face lit up when he talked about eco-tourism.

'At first, it was difficult to find money to build Vanua Rapita,' he began. 'Our chief knew there was a lot to be made from selling logging rights. But, like everyone else here, he was totally opposed to it. We had all heard too many stories of companies who broke their promises. So we approached the Australian World Wildlife Fund. They hired a team of management consultants to draw up a plan for the lagoon.' He pulled out an impressive-looking report from a drawer. 'Look, here it is. The work, which was funded by the Japanese World Wildlife Fund, began in 1993 and was finished two years later.'

The villagers of Michi, who owned the lodge, had also built it. 'We were helped by craftsmen from Cheke, a village just down the lagoon,' Robert continued. 'Still, the lodge wasn't ready by the time the first guests arrived, so they helped us finish the huts! It was the first of the seven eco-lodges in the Marovo Lagoon, and when some of the villagers

Boys at Auki village, Malaita Island, the Solomons

sums for the hire of a canoe with an outboard motor. But they were much friendlier than expected, and dreamy Auki (population 4,000), which is located on a protected, half-enclosed bay overlooked by jungle-lined ridges, was no place for impatience. On the quay, in the shade of a blue-and-white steamer called *Sa Alia*, some of Malaita's remarkably blond-haired boys dangled fishing lines or splashed naked in the shallows. Yellow-and-red canoes drifted across to Ambu and Lilisiana, two thatched villages on stilts at opposite ends of the bay. In Auki Market, next to the jetty, ragged men with orange, betel nut-stained teeth lazed in shady stalls selling homemade cigarettes, and women squatted beside piles of taro, coconut and cassava. It was baking hot, and towering clouds mushroomed over the ocean, where Guadalcanal's wrinkled mountains lay faintly sketched on the horizon.

The next day I met Joseph and Marguerite, who were in the market looking for baskets. They were an unlikely looking couple. With sturdy thighs and a bulging head, he was a burly thirty-year-old from Auki who looked like Idi Amin, while she was a pale, podgy, Danish nursing assistant with glasses. They'd met in 1990 on a 'mission ship' that travelled round the Pacific spreading the gospel. Although they had been married in Malaita, where European women, far less men, are exceedingly rare, they'd been living in Jutland in north Denmark for nine years. Now, as she was temporarily unemployed, they'd returned to stay with his family for four months.

'I love coming home, but I'm so used to Western comforts I couldn't live here again,' he went on in almost-flawless English over a lime juice in Cynthia's Cafe, a neglected-looking shack next to the wharf. 'When I first went to Denmark I worked as a cleaner until Marguerite's father-in-law, who makes doors, offered me a job in his factory. I had no training but I worked hard and studied Danish at night class, so he made it full-time. Now I speak good Danish, and we have enough money, but I'm worried about Nazis in Denmark who want to get rid of foreigners.' He looked anxious. 'Anyway, my brother has a canoe with an outboard motor, which I'm sure he'll hire out cheaply. I know Laulasi well. Meet me on Thursday, and I'll take you there.'

That was three days away, but there was plenty to do in the meantime. Early every morning, when it was still cool, people ambled down the main street to the market to buy betel nuts or throng the jetty to watch *Sa Alia* arrive from Honiara, the capital, six hours away. By 11 a.m., after passengers had flooded onto the bustling jetty and sweating gangs of joking, muscular young men had unloaded countless rice sacks into waiting trucks, the brief flurry of activity subsided as everyone retreated under grubby parasols, away from the blistering heat.

By noon the town was empty and nothing moved. The clouds would grow increasingly heavy until there would be a mid-afternoon downpour. When it was over, the handful of dusty hardware stores reopened. Most were half-empty and stocked mainly tins of tuna and corned beef, but, watched by stony-faced Chinese owners, tattered figures pored over the cracked glass display cases, examining toothpaste tubes or bush knives at 'specially reduced prices'. By 6 p.m. it was dark, and only betel nut chewers huddled in the shadowy porches under flickering street lights.

One morning I decided to make a trip to a village ten kilometres away. I jumped onto one of the passenger trucks filling up with young women and babies with towels over their heads to protect against the sun. As soon as the market was over, we set off into the interior of the island. Within minutes the paved road, which was only the second one I'd seen in the Solomons, had deteriorated into a potholed track. We crossed a bridge over a curving, pebbly river and entered cool rainforest strewn with outsized palms and giant creepers.

Tired of the incessant jolting, and with the village nowhere in sight, I got off an hour later and started to walk back. I was sitting on a shady bank near a hamlet tucked away in a glade below, when a truck stopped. The only passenger in the half-empty hold was a man called Norman, who introduced himself as a businessman taking taro sacks to Auki. He wore a baseball cap embroidered with the words 'Golden Oldies' and studded with fake sapphires. He was very chatty, and spoke confident, if at times ungrammatical, English. Nonetheless, his eyes glazed at the mention of shark-calling.

'It the work of Satan,' he declared reproachfully. 'I been Laulasi, you know. Before, I work as co-ordinator of youth organizations and I invited there with South Seas Evangelical Church group. When we arrive, we say to them, "Let's see whose god the greatest. You tell sharks to come, and we pray our god to keep them away, and we see which one win." Of course, sharks not come, and everyone see our god strongest.'

Still, he seemed proud of the tradition. 'I live sixty kilometres up coast, near Mbita'ama Cave,' he continued. 'It well known for sharks that sleep there. A few years ago an American come. He stay long time and manage to learn priest's magic. Then he go to Hawaii, where he make lot of money calling sharks for tourists.' There was a resentful silence. 'He bad. He steal from us, and our sharks not come back.'

Hot and humid Malaita is a narrow, mountainous 120-kilometre-long island indented by crocodile-ridden creeks and mangrove swamps. It has a long history of exploitation. At first, during the early nineteenth century, shipwrecked sailors were regularly cooked and eaten by ferocious tribes who also conducted head-hunting raids against each other and neighbouring Isabel Islanders. By 1870, despite its reputation as one of the Pacific's most dangerous places, the island had become a centre for ruthless blackbirders, and 10,000 people were transported to sugar-cane plantations in Queensland alone. Thus began an increasingly vicious circle, with vengeful murders of missionaries and attacks on European ships leading in turn to brutal official retaliation. In 1927, when English district officer William Bell and thirteen police officers were massacred during a campaign to collect taxes, the British hanged the ringleaders, sprayed taro gardens with weedkiller, desecrated ancestral shrines and dispatched Australian cruiser HMAS *Adelaide* to shell the coast. Sixty villages were destroyed and 1,250 people killed.

By 1939 the increasingly unruly islanders were refusing to work on plantations where expatriate European owners used dogs and whips to maintain control. In 1942 the USA invaded Guadalcanal and three years later, after they encountered generous African-American troops who were dressed like white people and seemingly enjoyed equal rights, Malaitans founded the Marching Rule movement. Based on self-reliance, it was opposed to co-operation with the restored British authorities, which it hoped to swap for the Americans. The movement was brutally suppressed in 1949, when 2,000 of its members were arrested. Not surprisingly, these events left many islanders deeply distrustful of outsiders. Even after independence in 1978, the Kwaio, Malaita's most traditional tribe in the jungle-clad south-eastern mountains, refused to have any contact with Westerners at all.

Two days later, Joseph, who was always dressed, unlike the destitute-looking, barefoot locals, in a clean white shirt, neatly ironed shorts and flip-flops, glided up to the wharf in his brother's canoe and we set off for Laulasi. First, though, we stopped for petrol at Auki.

'My grandfather was chief here until it became too crowded,' Joseph began as his brother-in-law filled the spare tank. 'Of course, in those days everyone believed in shark worship. The sharks were fast, faster even than this canoe, which is twenty-five horsepower. And they often came from far away, sometimes even Western Province. When I was a child, my grandfather told me a shark off Honiara attacked his fishing boat. He was sure it was sent by an enemy on Malaita, so he called on his shark for revenge, and next week his enemy and his fishing boat disappeared and were never seen again.'

Then we rounded a headland and were in the thirty-kilometre-long Langa Langa Lagoon. Formed by an almost continuous line of islands cutting off the ocean, it was full of circular islets covered with mangrove swamps and coconut palms. As the powerful canoe sped south, Joseph explained the origins of shark-calling. 'Malaitans always lived by the sea,' he shouted above the engine's roar. 'We needed gods which helped in times of trouble – for example, if our boats sank or there weren't enough fish in lagoon. So we started to worship sharks. We believed that our spirits entered them when we died, and that through priests' magic words we could speak to our ancestors.'

Halfway down the emerald lagoon we glided to the white beach of a deserted atoll, where a graceful wooden hull lay on stocks. 'Langa Langa was famous for building passenger boats like *Sa Alia*, but now we've no money to finish them,' Joseph lamented as we waded ashore through the crystal-clear water. He pointed to a break in the islands to the west, near which, on the other side of the half-submerged reef, the deep blue ocean began. 'Over there was one of the lagoon's man-made coral islands until it was destroyed by a cyclone in 1972. But there are still others, including Laulasi.'

Although some of those date back to the 1550s, most were built in the nineteenth century as a means of escaping the endemic tribal warfare plaguing Malaita. As all land

Laulasi coral islet in the Langa Langa Lagoon, Malaita Island, the Solomons

Wooden carving of man with shark on Laulasi islet, Malaita Island, the Solomons

was already owned there was no room for an expanding population, so new islands were established on sandbars a short distance offshore where the air was cool and mosquito-free. There coral from the reef was piled two or three metres above sea level, and thatched houses of bamboo, palm and pandanus leaves were constructed on stilts to allow air and tidal surges to circulate. Finally, coconut trees were planted and protective coral walls built, giving the constructions the appearance of fortified islands.

Soon afterwards we reached Laulasi. It was a stunning coral island, not more than 100 metres long. The chief, a stunted man in his fifties with no front teeth, welcomed us as the canoe drew up. For a while we haggled with him over the initially outrageous landing fee. Once we had agreed a price, we accompanied him to the huts where an emaciated, confused-looking old man with matchsticks legs, gaunt cheeks and saliva dribbling from his toothless mouth was pottering about. The chief yelled harshly into his ear, before turning round. 'This the priest,' he told me. 'He almost deaf, and not speak, but you pay him another four dollars, he show you House of Skulls.'

I reluctantly paid again, and traipsed after them to the other side of the huts, near which ghoulish-looking skulls were laid out in undergrowth. 'House here until cyclone in 1988,' the chief went on morosely, pointing to rotting timber. 'Here, six generations of his ancestors. They all priests, as it pass from father to son. It his father who do last shark-calling ceremony in 1972. Now he the last in Langa Langa, though perhaps others in Lau Lagoon. When he die, part of our tradition gone for ever.'

'Why is it dying out?'

'When our priests see everyone become Christian, they not pass on magic words. People still believe, but only as way of keep tradition alive.'

A few metres away was the island's thick, two-metre-high coral wall. 'Ceremony held here,' the chief observed. 'I remember well. His father call out name of young shark, which swim to a boy called William. He stand on that rock there and feed it pork and . . . '

'Why pork?' I broke in.

'Long ago we believed that shark ancestor promise if we give it pork, sharks not attack us and they make sure we have enough fish.' The chief pointed to a narrow channel through the reef. 'See that? Before, sharks drive many fish through there into lagoon. So red or black clothes taboo on Laulasi: red because sharks perhaps think it blood, and black because it the colour of pigs.'

'And what happened if they weren't given sacrifices?'

'They come and kill children. Anyway, during ceremony, boy feed several sharks until the oldest and largest finish eating. Then he climb on its back and it carry him round lagoon until it return him to rock.' He shot a glance at me out the corner of his eye. 'Two brothers called John and Walter Fairfax from Australia make video,' he added quickly, as if to pre-empt disbelief. 'They live with us for six months, here and on yacht.' His face clouded over. 'They promised send money and copy of video, but they lie. They use us. We not forget, and that why we charge big landing fee.'

'What happened to the boy?'

'The brothers show video in Australia, and people so surprised that some years later boy invited over and challenged to swim off beach famous for sharks. It like circus. Radio and television there, people make bets, sirens sound to warn swimmers before safety nets taken away and fresh meat dropped into water. But though he surround by sharks, he swim for two hours and come out safe.'

'Where's he now?'

'In Auki, where he work on *Sa Alia*.'

Later we trooped back to a previously deserted hollow where, obviously for my benefit, old women with drooping, tattooed breasts had suddenly materialized and were sitting under a thatched roof making necklaces for sale. Nearby, children with grooved stones were busily planing and polishing two-metre-long strings of shells. On Malaita, which has almost no cash economy, isolated villages still use these as traditional currency on special occasions – for example buying wives, for whom the usual sum is ten strands, or land. With a fixed rate of exchange to the Solomon dollar, they vary in value according to colour and size: pink and the smallest shells are the most prized, followed by orange, brown, white and black.

I spent the afternoon chatting and watching boys hurl themselves playfully into the translucent water. Further away, where the tide had receded, girls combed the exposed reef for shells. At 4 p.m., as veils of rain advanced across the mist-shrouded ridges, it was time to leave. Drenched but exhilarated, I stood at the prow as we raced back up the lagoon, whose surface was splattered by drops the size of coins and resembled myriads of water lilies.

341

A few days later, instead of returning on *Ocean Express*, the antiquated hydrofoil on which I'd come, I boarded the by-now familiar Guadalcanal-bound *Sa Alia*, where I hoped to meet William, the boy at the 1972 shark-calling ceremony. To my intense disappointment, the crew explained he was off sick. As Auki receded, a lump came into my throat; in less than a week I had grown to love Malaita, and, strangely, the idea of shark-calling no longer appeared quite so preposterous.

SAMOA

At first I thought I would be the first person ever to dislike Samoa; rarely have my initial impressions been so wide of the mark.

Imagining it to be the highlight of my first three-month journey through the Pacific, I was disgusted as I wandered along the harbour embankments of Apia, its diminutive capital (population 35,000) on Upolu Island. Samoa had been a New Zealand colony until 1970, but many of the characterful wooden administrative buildings lining the bay were derelict ever since the government had moved across a busy dual carriageway to its new headquarters, a monstrous, Chinese-designed tower block surrounded by acres of tarmac. Elsewhere, luckily, Apia was still lazy and rambling, but I wondered for how long it would remain so.

Weary of wandering the clogged backstreets, I stopped for refreshments in the world-renowned Aggie Grey's Hotel on the waterfront. Founded by one of Apia's most prominent women, on whom James Michener supposedly based Bloody Mary in his *South Pacific Tales*, it had been a home for bored US servicemen during World War Two until it became a beacon for Pacific travellers in the late 1940s. Regrettably, the original wooden building had also been recently demolished and now, rebuilt in mock south-Pacific style, it was a four-star hotel, with its foyer awash with brochures for Western honeymooners, noticeboards for Mobil Oil delegates and expensively dressed Americans discussing the prices of yachts. Nor were its grounds any more appealing, with fake *fales* (traditional Polynesian thatched huts) named after Marlon Brando and William Holden, who stayed here in the 1950s, and sunbathers reading Jackie Collins by the pool.

That afternoon, I waited outside the covered market for a bus to Vailima, Robert Louis Stevenson's mansion. The market was full of old Samoan men sharing *kava* bowls with burly policemen wearing blue *lavalavas* and white bobby's helmets. When the bus came, it took me up winding roads to the 300-acre estate high on looming Mount Vaea. Used by the German, New Zealand and Samoan administrations as their official residence after his death, it had been destroyed by cyclones until, financed by wealthy American Mormons, it too had been rebuilt, emerging in 1994 as a lovingly restored, if sanitized, museum. Not that I was given long to see it; an obligatory guide, who was wearing a Royal Stuart skirt – the same tartan Stevenson instructed his servants to wear – rushed me through the dark, mahogany-lined rooms and, apart from fireplaces Stevenson had installed in 1891 to remind him of Scotland, not much was original.

Nonetheless, I lived only 200 metres from his home in Edinburgh's New Town, and nothing could destroy the thrill of being there and seeing his gaunt face staring seemingly straight at me from the photograph-lined walls. The climb through cool tropical forest up to his burial place, just below the summit, was atmospheric as well, while his sarcophagus, inscribed with the self-composed requiem: '*Home is the sailor, home from the sea / And the hunter home from the hill*', brought tears to my eyes. Not even the arrival of panting, overweight American joggers could break my reverie. Lost in a time warp, I looked down to the bay far below, in which a white, three-masted schooner rode peacefully at anchor – just as, I imagined, it might have done in the days of Tusitala (Teller of Tales), the name the adoring Samoan chiefs gave Stevenson.

A day later I decided to travel round wild, little-inhabited Savai'i, which, next to Hawaii, is Polynesia's biggest island. I boarded one of the pink or purple or yellow buses thronging the bus station behind the harbour embankment, and shortly we were passing through traditional villages lining Upolu's north coast. *Fales* were set in neat gardens overflowing with roses, and through banana groves I could see white churches and luxuriant, green hills. The bus, with its glassless window frames, low roof and creaking wooden superstructure, was crowded with soft, graceful women, while bull-necked, sumo-like men wearing traditional brown-and-white, floral-patterned *lavalava*s lovingly cradled infants on their muscular knees.

By midday the bus had reached Mulifanua Wharf at Upolu's western tip, from where ferries cross the twenty-two kilometres to Savai'i. More traditional than even Upolu, it has a population of only 50,000 living in villages clustered mainly along the south-east coast, while jungle-covered slopes rise to Mount Silisili, a spectacular-looking volcano dominating the mountainous, crater-dotted interior. It also has numerous archaeological sites, including fortifications, star mounds and ancient platforms; indeed, its inhabitants believe it to be the cradle of Polynesia's culture, and not Hawaii or French Polynesia's Raiatea, as James Michener's book *Hawaii* maintains.

Two hours later my ferry was in Saleologa, Savai'i's largest town. It seemed to consist only of shabby shacks dotted along a dirt track, so I hitched up the east coast to the hamlet of Lalomalava. There I booked into Safua Lodge, where I hoped to meet Warren, the knowledgeable resident guide, and Moelagi Jackson, the lodge's legendary owner. I was sitting in the dining room, when a thin, nervous, sixty-year-old New Zealander asked if I would like some tea. It was Warren, and although he had a sharp nose and a frosty, cerebral air, he was friendly. After a while he began telling me about how he had spent his life as a geologist in the Amazon, prior to settling in Savai'i fifteen years ago. He also liked to talk about people who had stayed in the lodge.

'I especially remember a famous travel writer who wanted to see the Taga Blowholes,' he said with a smile. 'If you're lucky, locals will throw coconuts into them, and the surf's so powerful these are often hurled thirty metres into the air. Indeed, legend maintains one even reached New Zealand. It's just fun, of course, but he was a humourless character and thought it all ridiculous.' Warren loyally refused to disclose his name, but I suspected it was Paul Theroux, researching his *The Happy Isles of Oceania*.

Later that evening, I was sitting at one of the long tables when an elderly, distinguished-looking woman introduced herself. She had a full figure and grey hair in a dignified bun, and wore an elegant purple dress. It was Moelagi, and it wasn't long before she was fulfilling her reputation as a vivacious raconteur. She told me, to my astonishment, how she'd married an Englishman who, until he'd died some years previously, had worked for the United Nations.

'We met in New Zealand,' she volunteered, 'but fourteen years ago I became so homesick I gave him an ultimatum, and he agreed to return here so that I could start a lodge. He was a real English gentleman and I adored him. But he was very traditional, and couldn't accept me as his equal, particularly when I became *matai*.'

'I thought only men could be chiefs,' I said, surprised.

She laughed reproachfully. 'Why do Western men always make such assumptions? You're such chauvinists!' Afterwards we adjourned to listen to staff that had spontaneously taken out drums and ukuleles. In next to no time achingly beautiful girls with long black hair and pearly teeth were serenading me with yearning Polynesian love songs. Moelagi, still a great dancer at sixty years of age, dragged me to the floor until at last we flopped into armchairs, where she told me how she had travelled the world, fighting for women's rights.

At sunrise the next morning, I hitched back down through Tafua Peninsula's rainforest reserve in south-east Savai'i, hoping to see the flying foxes that circle the extinct, forest-choked Tafua-tai Crater. Shortly, plagued by mosquitoes, I gave up, although I was convinced that the blunt-beaked birds I saw were *manume'as*, or Samoan tooth-billed pigeons – the dodo's closest living relative – soaring above their last remaining habitat.

When I returned to the coast road I hitched to Vailoa village, where I walked up through copra plantations to Olemoe Falls. This is Samoa's most spectacular waterfall, which plunges into an idyllic aquamarine pool. Then I continued up tracks, searching for nearby Pulemelei Mound.

The Pacific's largest ancient structure, this is a twenty-metre pyramid that, swallowed by jungle, is notoriously difficult to find. Nevertheless, after blundering around for hours, I miraculously stumbled across it. For a while I sat euphorically on the overgrown summit,

Olemoe Falls, Savai'i Island, Samoa

listening to echoing birdsong and admiring the views over tree-tops down to the distant ocean. It is not surprising that archaeologists believe Pulemelei, which is similar to Meso-American religious structures, was built for strategic purposes and not pigeon snaring as tradition implies.

The next morning, I caught a bus for the three-hour journey from Salelologa to Falealupo, Samoa's most attractive village at Savai'i's western tip until it was devastated by cyclones Ofa and Val in 1982. On the bus I met Sa, an intimidating-looking, beefy young man with dark sunglasses, shaven head and ear studs. But he had a soft voice and an easy laugh and he sat joking with friends in the back seats; it was only when I saw his white stick that I realized he was blind.

He had had to come from Asau, 200 kilometres away on the north-west coast, just to pay his electricity bill in the island's only bank. Soon he was explaining how he had lost his sight. 'In 1990 our neighbour's son asked me to go with him to forest plantations which our families had had a dispute about. I thought he wanted to talk, but, instead, he shot me in the face. When doctors told me I'd never see again, I lay at home, just wanting to die. A year later, after he was sentenced to six years in prison, the government offered to send me to New Zealand for a one-year blind-skills course. Then, three years ago, they sent me to Indonesia to train as a physiotherapist. It's fantastic, as now I can do everything for myself and help *other* people.'

I mused over the reasons for Samoa's violent undercurrent (it has the most traditional, rigid social structure in Polynesia) as I looked out at the stunning scenery. There are few cars on Savai'i and the empty road ran high above the south coast where black volcanic cliffs were studded with lava tubes and blowholes. Through leafy groves, the sun glinted on the azure ocean.

When Sa told me we had reached the turn-off for Falealupo, I struggled off the packed bus, and set off down a road through badly damaged rainforest. Hours later, hot and sweating, I passed Moso's Footprint, an ancient rock enclosure reputedly made by the mythological giant of the same name as he stepped from Fiji to Samoa. Soon I arrived in Falealupo, which consisted of *fales* scattered among tree stumps, a sandy rugby pitch between bamboo poles, and, surrounded by weeds, a ruined white church overlooking the ocean.

I asked a burly man swinging a machete about accommodation, and he led me along

My fale (traditional thatched hut) near Falealupo village, Savai'i Island, Samoa

Above: Sunset over Cape Mulinu'u, Savai'i Island, Samoa

tracks through wilderness until, just as I was growing uneasy, we reached gracefully leaning coconut trees. Underneath them, on a magnificent beach curving round a savage, spume-covered bay, were three *fales*. They were not much more than thatched roofs supported by poles, with coconut-frond blinds against the elements. The man told me they were owned by the *matai*, who he offered to fetch. Shortly, Joseph, the *matai*'s oldest, bearded, forty-year-old son, arrived with sleeping mats. I settled in and spent the rest of the afternoon in the shallow, turquoise sea, where I tracked neon tetras and angelfish as they drifted through the jagged coral reef. But the undertow was ferocious, and, although I thought initially of joining the four sons harpoon fishing for the evening meal, I quickly became so badly lacerated that I returned to the beach. There I watched admiringly as they swam so far out that they became merely black dots.

The sun was dipping into the ocean and its dying light bathing the deserted bay brilliant pink, when I heard conches blow all around me to announce *sa* (prayers) before the evening meal. Soon Joseph arrived to take me to the main *fale*. Like most others it had only a double bed, some tatty suitcases and a few floor mats. An elderly couple sat cross-legged on the floor, playing with their naked, giggling grandchildren. The man was lean, seventy-year-old Sisi, the *matai*, who, with his receding forehead, high cheekbones and silver hair, looked like a wise Sioux warrior. The woman was his wife, Nisi, a plump, homely-looking sixty-year-old with grey hair and a blue cotton dress.

Before long, their married sons and daughters, who lived in four surrounding *fales*,

347

The chief's son, Oli, showing his tattoos, Savai'i Island, Samoa

arrived. We all sat in a circle holding hands, singing traditional songs of thanks until the women fetched plates of stodgy sweet potato and bony fish from ovens glowing in the darkness.

After breakfast the next day, I watched the good-natured Oli, my favourite of the sons, tie his ankles together with twine and bound, monkey-like, up palm trees above my *fale* to cut coconuts with his machete. In the afternoon I went into Falealupo with the other, more reserved sons for the Saturday afternoon match against Falealupo's arch-rivals, Falealupo-Inti. There, sitting on banks opposite the ruined church, men covered with tattoos told me, in-between cheering crunching tackles in flurries of sand, how the centuries-old tradition of tattooing is performed. The excruciating, three-week process is performed using sharpened boars' tusks and apparently takes months to heal, but the tattoos identify their wearers as proud and courageous Samoans. The men also described how villagers escaped the apocalyptic cyclones only by crawling inside their concrete water tanks.

That night I stayed at Sisi's until 10 p.m., when I returned through pitch darkness to the beach. There, caressed by inky, warm waves, I was lying at the water's edge, listening to soft wind sighing in palm trees and gazing at the new moon, when I noticed unexplained, underwater beams of light. Alarmed, as I knew Samoans believe that spirits wander about at night at nearby Cape Mulinu'u, I scrambled to my feet before I realized they were torches of Nisi's sons, who were out night fishing. Sure enough, soon three dripping, Neptune-like shapes with harpoons emerged from the waves.

The following morning, wearing Joseph's *lavalava* to cover my legs, I accompanied the family to Falealupo's makeshift church, a simple London

View from Vaiavaava's garden onto outrigger on lagoon, Falealupo village, western Samoa

Missionary Society hall set in coconut groves, for Sunday service. It was a lovely scene. Downstairs, girls in white satin frocks and boys in miniature *lavalavas* wriggled in front of strict Sunday School teachers, winking at me surreptitiously. Upstairs, women in crisp white dresses and straw hats, and men in *lavalavas*, ties and jackets sat in pale blue pews.

The service had just finished and I was thanking the minister, who, to honour the rare *palangi* (foreigner), had conducted half the service in English, when I met Vaiavaava. She was a petite, sweet-natured, thirty-year-old woman, who showed me Rock House, a cave in the bush behind which legend says Falealupo's furious men left unfinished when defeated by the women in a house-building contest, and then invited me for tea that afternoon. So, a few hours later, I joined her in her *fale*, where she had baked fresh pancakes and cut coconut slices. 'I know it's not much,' she apologized humbly, looking round as we sat on the floor watching her one-year-old baby crawl about.

'It's great,' I remarked truthfully; her 'garden' consisted of a white beach on which outrigger canoes were drawn up, and the shimmering ocean.

Soon she was telling me about her brothers in New Zealand, who, like many others, had emigrated to earn unheard-of sums on construction sites. Still, she wasn't tempted to join them.

'Oh, Samoans there have cars and washing machines, but they spend all their time fighting, drinking and on drugs,' she said, smiling gently. 'We're poor in comparison, but the climate's wonderful, apart from the occasional cyclones. Everything grows in the forest, the sea's full of fish, there are coconuts everywhere and everyone knows each other. When I hear about other places I realize we're rich.'

KIRIBATI

From the moment I woke up on the plane 1,500 kilometres north of Fiji and pulled up my window blind against the dazzling sun, everything about Kiribati promised to surpass my wildest expectations. I had wanted to go to the diminutive island state ever since I had been to Ghizo Island in the Solomons. There, in a squalid refugee village, I had come across the most beautiful-looking people I had seen in my two voyages across the Pacific. When I enquired where they were from, one of them explained that they were Micronesians from the Republic of Kiribati who had been resettled abroad because of overcrowding. Like most people, I'd never heard of it, but when I discovered it was one of the Pacific's most isolated, unknown group of atolls, it only made me want to go there all the more.

Now a long, boomerang-shaped atoll floated below the plane on the shimmering water. On one side was a magnificent turquoise lagoon and on the other was the deep blue ocean. Soon we landed at Tarawa, Kiribati's main island, where children were crowded behind a barrier awaiting the arrival of the weekly plane. A minibus took me thirty kilometres down to Bairiki, the administrative centre on southern Tarawa, where I wanted to stay.

The island comprised of interconnecting atolls, which were so narrow that at times I could almost touch the water on both sides. At first sight, everywhere seemed to be a heady combination of attractive *fales*, superb white beaches and belts of coconut trees.

The next day, to my dismay, I found out that Tarawa was far from being what it seemed. Rabid-looking dogs copulated on the never-ending beaches, which were strewn with plastic bottles, tin cans, excrement and mounds of decomposing clothes. Burnt-out shells of cars and disused machinery lay abandoned by the roadside. Packed minibuses drove by, with pounding rap music blaring from their stereos. Youths wearing Bronx-style baseball caps and calf-length baggy shorts hung out the windows, chewing gum. Many of the seemingly pretty *fales*, which ran the entire length of the isthmus, were shacks held together by ragged palm-leaf blinds or dirty sacking. In-between, separated by tangled wire fences, were corrugated-iron sheds or half-completed bungalows made of breezeblocks. Tarawa, I quickly learned, is one of the most overcrowded places on earth, with 42,000 inhabitants crammed into only thirty-one square kilometres.

Betio, where I stayed in a dingy room in a flaking concrete block, consisted of a cement factory, oil tanks and an industrial-looking harbour. On the few undeveloped parts of the coast, rusty artillery, concrete bunkers and pillboxes faced out to sea. The Japanese invaded the island in 1942 and fortified it so heavily that their commander boasted that 'A million Americans couldn't take it in a hundred years.' In 1943, 18,000 US marines stormed ashore, and thousands of Americans and Japanese died in the fierce fighting that ensued.

Disillusioned, two days later I set off for my real destination, the island of Butaritari, three hundred kilometres to the north. There I was interested, amongst other things, in seeing where Robert Louis Stevenson and his wife stayed in 1889 while he was looking for a new life. At Tarawa's airstrip I wandered across the otherwise deserted tarmac to a cramped eighteen-seater plane. On board, no one examined my ticket or gave instructions about seat belts or emergency procedures. We took off without any warning and soared above

Boy in Tarawa, Kiribati, central Pacific

351

Abailung Island, a spectacular, ring-shaped atoll. Before long, we were high over the ocean. I crossed my fingers and hoped we had enough fuel as well as a good navigator; Butaritari, which is one of Kiribati's thirty-three coral atolls scattered across 3.5 million square kilometres of the central Pacific, occupies only thirteen square kilometres, and locating it must be like finding a grain of sand on a beach.

An hour later the plane's shadow swooped low over a shallow lagoon and landed on a cracked airstrip lined by encroaching bush. Watched by a handful of sleepy-looking children and adults, we taxied to the 'terminal'. It was an empty echoing shell, which previously had been the location of an unsuccessful effort to establish a *bêche-de-mer* factory. Inside, a big-boned, middle-aged woman with a broad face and a mouth crammed with broken teeth was waiting for a package. Like a few people in Kiribati, which was a British colony until it became independent in 1979, she spoke good English, which is still the official language although most speak a Micronesian dialect called i-Kiribati. As luck would have it, when I asked her if she knew of anywhere to stay, it transpired that she ran the island's only guesthouse. Her name was Kapopay and, after she collected her package, she told me to clamber on the back of her creaking moped. Then, as we puttered along a dirt track through luxuriant rainforest, my eyes opened wide in astonishment.

Gone were Tarawa's crowded, ramshackle *fales*, litter-strewn beaches, polluted lagoons and eroded coasts. Instead, Butaritari was the nearest to primordial paradise I had ever seen. Under a heavenly blue sky, the rainforest was a riot of banana, breadfruit, papaya, coconut and palm trees. Occasionally, clearings were dotted with neat *fales* made from pandanus trees, where men reclined lazily and women's heads were bent over cooking pots. The main village, Butaritari, was a hamlet of only 2,000 people. In the centre was an enormous *maneaba* (communal meeting place), whose sloping thatched roof almost came down to the ground. Inside, women dressed in lilac, orange and yellow sleeveless *lavalavas* sat in a circle, playing a game. For boards they had pieces of cardboard and for pieces they were using pebbles. Like most young women in Kiribati, they were ravishing to look at, with elegant, swept-back hair, long graceful necks and high cheekbones. Outside, groups of children played rounders on the earthen track with balls made of coconut fibre and tin cans for bases. As soon as they saw me, their faces creased into smiles and they rushed up, shouting joyfully, 'I-Matang, I-Matang [European]!'

Kapopay's compound was on the edge of the hamlet and looked directly onto the sparkling lagoon. Measuring thirty by fifteen square kilometres, the lagoon was huge. On the horizon, where a layer of jade met a band of duck-egg blue, the outlines of two atolls were sketched.

That evening I sat in a cane chair outside my *fale* listening to the gently lapping water just below my feet. From the other side of the island, which was only 350 metres away, the roar of the ocean could be heard. Shortly, I climbed down some slippery wooden steps and swam across to play with some boys who were splashing each other next to a moored canoe. Nearby, blue-and-white outriggers were drawn up on a sandy beach, where a young man was handing octopuses up steps to a woman in the family compound. By the time I swam back to my *fale*, coconut trees on Tanononobi Promontory to the west were silhouetted black against the spectacular red sunset. Above, armies of cotton-like pink clouds advanced across the ocean. As the tide receded, I could hear the crackle of drying shells and the sound of leaping fish stranded in shrinking pools. Later on, a full moon rose into the sky bathing everything in ghostly white.

The next day I borrowed Kapopay's moped and set out to travel round the island. Separating her compound from the hamlet was a minute bay, where I had a look at the remains of the Second World War bomber that lay in four metres of water. When I got to Butaritari, I went to the Roman Catholic church, the island's largest – and practically only – stone building. There I wanted to find the missionary who Kapopay had suggested might know where Stevenson had stayed when his schooner, the *Equator*, stopped at Butaritari. Stevenson spent six months in the Gilbert Islands, and much of the second half of his book *In the South Seas* is devoted to his observations and history of Butaritari. After a brief hunt, I found the missionary in his messy, book-lined study. He was an insignificant-looking, stern man in his thirties, with broad, flat features. On the wall was a handwritten chart of the Greek alphabet.

Girl on Butaritari Island, Kiribati, central Pacific

'What's that for?' I asked.

'Because I want to be able to read the Old Testament in Greek,' he replied brusquely. Soon he thawed and told me over a cup of tea about the five days he had just spent on a neighbouring atoll. 'Foreigners call it Big Arse, because that's how it sounds in Kiribati,' he added with a smile. When I told him about Stevenson, he led me to the mission's 'guest-house'. It was a run-down shack that looked over a stone wall to the lagoon. Inside, it was empty apart from some grimy mattresses strewn with clothes. 'I think this is the site of the store where he stayed, but I'm not sure as I've only been here three years,' he said uncertainly. He followed my eyes to bras and knickers drying outside on a line. 'Those belong to some visiting Sisters,' he added hastily.

After I left the church I headed north. Just outside the village I stopped to talk to a man repairing a beached outrigger. He told me that four generations of his family lay asleep inside his nearby *fale*. Not far beyond was the 3,000-metre-long airstrip, which had been built by the Americans during the Second World War. The track forked twelve kilometres later. To the right it ran through seemingly endless coconut groves to the south coast, where breakers thundered against the reef. To the left was the hamlet of Tanimaiaki, where men were rethatching the roof of a *fale*. Next to it was a school, where the English teacher proudly showed me the day's lesson. On the blackboard was written: 'Personal experience is something which happens to you – for example, making oil for hair, feeding pigs, weaving mats, planting, fishing, building canoes and sailing canoes.'

Once I was north of Tanimaiaki I decided to turn back. My map told me that it was possible to wade across from Butaritari to Makin Island, as the northern half of Butaritari was formerly called. But that was only if the tide was out – which it wasn't – and even then there was nothing except rainforest all the way to Kuma, the only hamlet at the north of the ten-kilometre-long reef. When I got back to Butaritari hamlet I set out for the island's southern tip. Here too there was only rainforest – the island has a population of only 4,000 – until the track reached a smattering of *fales* at Ukiangang. There, inside another *maneaba*, men were languidly playing cards and spellbound children watching a video. One of the men told me that it was the island's first, newly arrived television. 'We cannot get any channels yet, but we hope to soon,' he said.

The video was of I-Kiribati women practising the traditional *Te Buki* dance. They looked extraordinarily sensuous, with bare midriffs, swaying hips, knee-length grass skirts and ornate straw bras and headbands. It was little wonder that Stevenson wrote: 'Of all they call dance in the Pacific, the performance I saw on Butaritari was easily the best . . . Gilbertese dance appeals to the soul; it makes one thrill with emotion, it uplifts one, it conquers one; it has the essence of all great art.'

During the meal that evening, Kapopay told me about the myths and history of Kiribati. People there believe the islands were created at the time the earth and the sky were

Girl in traditional costume practising Te Buki dance, Butaritari, Kiribati

separated. They also believe that Kiribati and Samoa were originally clouds that were transformed into islands when they came into contact with the plant called Terenga that sprouted
from the earth's core. In 1788 Captain Gilbert came across the islands ('Kiribati' is the local
pronunciation of the word 'Gilbert'), and European traders established themselves on Butaritari in the 1850s. They exchanged manufactured goods for coconut oil and turtle shell
and in 1915, after being a dependency for fifteen years, the Gilbert and Ellis Islands were
officially declared a British colony.

She also described what happened on Butaritari during the Second World War. In 1941
the Japanese occupied Makin Island. A year later a party of US marines landed from two
submarines in an attempt to draw Japanese attention away from the planned American
invasion through the Solomon Islands. Instead, the raid merely alerted them to the strategic
importance of the island, which they promptly fortified. Kapopay said that the Japanese
behaved very badly before the Americans captured the island in 1943. 'My mother told me
that if you didn't obey them, they beat you, or . . . ' She drew an imaginary knife across her
throat. 'We still hate the older Japanese, but the young ones are different. And the Japanese
are good at giving gifts to show how sorry they are for what they did. For example, they
built the school here, as well as Tarawa's hospital.'

Although she had a son, Kapopay was sad she had never found a husband and now lived alone. Previously, her brother and his wife lived in the compound, but after running a high temperature he had been flown to the hospital in Tarawa and had never returned. When I questioned her about crime on the island, she claimed that there wasn't much, although she confided in me that sometimes she was scared of eating by herself.

'Why? What of?' I enquired.

'Naughty boys. Sometimes they come and steal things.'

'Such as?'

'Cups and knives and other important things.'

According to her, few young people from Butaritari who went to Tarawa wanted to come back. 'There they get used to Western ways, which are much easier than our traditional ones. And they're afraid of the hard work you have to do if you live here. For example, *fales* need a new thatched roof every few years. Metal roofs are much more expensive, but they're still good twenty years later.'

One evening Kapopay asked whether I wanted to join the outrigger that was leaving the following day for one of the two atolls that could be seen on the horizon. When I told her that I'd love to, and would possibly even spend the night there, she remarked, 'Well, be careful of Watara. Although he's an intelligent man, he's a snake and I wouldn't trust him. He's always looking for ways to make money.' Then she disappeared with a flourish to restock her miniature grocery store, which was one of only two in the hamlet.

I didn't have another opportunity to ask her who she was referring to or what she meant. The next morning I went down to the beach carrying only the absolute necessities and some spare provisions for unexpected eventualities in my saddlebags. There, two people were waiting in an outrigger canoe with a white hull, a pink keel and yellow yards. One of them was a handsome, well-built young man called Asimapaya, who had curly black hair and gleaming white teeth. The other was his wife, Kae Kae, a stunning beauty with hair in a waist-length pleat and a *lavalava* patterned with green, white and blue flowers. I clambered aboard, and Asimapaya pushed the canoe into the lagoon.

Sailing the long slim outrigger, which had identical prows at either end, was a slow, extremely hazardous operation. To make progress, Asimapaya had to tack. To do this he had to lift the heavy wooden mast that held the sail from its base and stagger with it, without overbalancing, from one prow to the other. After exchanging it for the rudder, every twenty minutes for the next three hours he had to repeat the same manoeuvre all over again, except in reverse. As if that wasn't enough, he had to bale water with a pump – a plunger in a plastic tube – as well as steer the outrigger. It took a lot of skill, as the boat sat so low in the water that oncoming waves threatened to swamp it if he wasn't careful.

I myself had to sit completely still, as sudden movements were equally perilous. Once I became accustomed to the canoe's delicate equilibrium, Asimapaya requested that I pump the plunger, or bale water with a bucket. The rest of the time I lay listening dreamily to the sound of water slapping the hull as we glided across the lagoon, or watching wispy clouds scud across the water. Occasionally, fish jumped and, further away, a solitary outrigger's sail cut like a shark's fin across the watery horizon.

Before long, Butaritari was behind us and we passed Kotabu Island, a barren, uninhabited atoll. Two hours later, as we approached Tikurere and the colour of the increasingly shallow lagoon changed from deep green to a light jade, I nearly had to rub my eyes to make sure I wasn't seeing a mirage. Tikurere was exquisite. A miniature atoll less than a kilometre in length, it was divided in the middle by a sandbar. The southern half was deserted and consisted of only bush and pebbly sands. The northern half consisted of a row of coconut trees and, underneath, some *fales* overlooking a pristine beach, where four little girls were playing. They had gleaming, waist-length black hair and they gazed at me open-mouthed as crests of breakers carried the gently swaying canoe towards the shore.

As I waded towards the beach, feeling like Robinson Crusoe, I could see a chubby man waiting to greet us. He was about fifty and had a bloated stomach, jet-black hair and glasses

Approaching Tikurere atoll on the outrigger, Kiribati, central Pacific

held on by an elastic band. His name was Watara and to my amazement he spoke excellent English. After I told him I wanted to spend the night on Tikurere, he showed me to the first of the *fales*. Like the other two nearby, it looked neglected and inside, which was empty, I could see the lagoon through gaps in its pandanus walls. Still, I agreed when he said he would charge me only a few dollars to stay the night there, as well as have something to eat in the evening. I left my bags there and accompanied him to some *fales*, where three men and three women in their mid-thirties were dozing in the midday heat. In a glade, fishing nets and coconuts lay drying on the earth.

While he sat weaving palm leaves for the *fale*'s roof, Watara told me about himself. For years, he had worked as a clerk for the colonial administration and taught in a Seventh-day Adventist school on Tarawa. 'That was before Kiribati became independent,' he said. 'The new government tried to transfer me to a school on an atoll in southern Kiribati. I refused to go, so I went back to Butaritari, where I set up a *bêche-de-mer* business with a Chinese partner. But it didn't work out, which was just as well, because I hate being inside. So I made up my mind to return to Tikurere, where I was brought up.'

When he too nodded off, I went swimming. The water was so shallow that, a kilometre out, it was still barely two metres deep. Then five-year-old Veronica, one of the little girls,

The children playing on Tikurere, Kiribati, central Pacific

took me to pay my respects to the Old Lady of Tikurere. This was a long-dead woman who, Watara had told me, had lived on the island and was believed to be responsible for whether the fish catches were good or not. Holding me by the hand, Veronica led me along a root-strewn path through mangroves to the tip of the atoll. There I laid tobacco sticks, the traditional gift her mother had given me to offer to the Old Lady, at a childish-looking shrine surrounded by seashells. When we returned to the *fales*, Veronica took me through coconut groves to the atoll's west coast. It was only a hundred metres away but, unlike the sheltered beach overlooking the lagoon, it was exposed to the open ocean and foaming rollers crashed down on rough rocks.

I spent the rest of the afternoon doing handstands and running races with the children. There were seven of them, four girls and three boys, all aged between three and eight. I've never seen children have such fun. Despite, or perhaps because of, having no toys to play with, they spent the whole time giggling, rolling in the sand, climbing on each other's backs, frolicking in the lagoon, making Jew's harps from leaves and playing football with coconut husks. When I tired of playing with them, Watara suggested that I help the adults, who spoke only i-Kiribati, prepare the evening meal. So I collected some wood for the fire and then tried to draw water from the well. That was easier said than done, as it was more than five metres deep and every time I pulled up the rope the bucket tipped over and the water spilled out. Embarrassed, in the end I had to get one of the five-year-old boys to help me. Watara was flabbergasted. 'Why can't you do such an easy task?' he said laughing. 'But don't worry. If you stay long enough, we'll make an I-Kiribati of you yet!'

The meal, which we all ate in his *fale*, consisted of freshly cooked fish, rice, papaya and breadfruit, which were followed by coconuts and countless cups of tea. It was astonishingly tasty food. Watara was delighted when I told him how much I liked fish. 'That's good,' he declared. 'Only a short time ago, I-Kiribati ate only fish, coconuts, pandanus fruit and chicken. Now they want Western food. It's not good for them and many are dying younger and younger.' As dusk fell, he lit a paraffin lamp and candles in jars. While he lay on the floor reading a dog-eared book entitled *Politics in Kiribati*, the children nestled drowsily in their mothers' laps. Behind, shadows danced on the *fale*'s thatched roof.

Later I walked along the beach. It was pitch dark as the full moon hadn't risen yet, but I could still see a myriad of little white crabs scuttling away from my approaching footsteps. When I reached the sandbar in the middle, I stretched out on my back and gazed at the panoply of stars littering the galaxy.

After I returned to my *fale*, I relaxed on a frayed pandanus mat under the mosquito net Watara had rigged up and reflected on my extraordinary day. I had stumbled across what I was looking for not in Butaritari, as I had anticipated – although that was already extraordinarily beautiful – but three hours away by outrigger on Tikurere. It was impossible to get much further away from Western civilization, and I resolved that, instead of returning to

Butaritari the following noon as planned, I would spend every second of my six remaining days on Tikurere.

Time passed astonishingly quickly. Every day the men pottered about, filing saws, repairing fishing nets or chopping wood. In the afternoons, Asimapaya, who turned out to be Watara's son, trawled the shallows with his harpoon for fish. When he returned, Kae Kae filleted the catch, surrounded by clouds of flies. Opposite her, the three other women prepared food in the 'kitchen'. This was a thatched roof supported by poles on the edge of the compound, where two pigs were tied up. Not far away, the mother of one of the men sat cross-legged, cutting papaya and repairing wicker baskets. She was a toothless, shrivelled old woman but she had elegant silver hair and a serene face.

Most mornings it was gloriously sunny, with a balmy breeze and a brilliantly blue sky. By late afternoon, menacing black clouds loomed across the lagoon's eastern horizon. Often there would be squally showers until the blue skies reasserted themselves. One evening, when the clouds hadn't dispersed, everyone was in Watara's *fale*, chatting idly or listening absent-mindedly to the crackling static of his beloved radio. Without warning there was a strong gust of wind. At first, no one paid any attention, but instead of dying down as it normally did it only grew more and more violent. For at least three minutes everyone just sat looking at each other as if they were paralysed. Then curtains of rain lashed down as a storm hit Tikurere.

Suddenly there was a burst of frenzied activity. The men sprang to their feet and with their torches checked the sturdy timber pillars that held the *fale*'s roof, while the women urgently woke up the sleeping children. Alarmed, I ran through the torrential downpour to my hut, where I hurled my meagre possessions into my bags and raced back with them to Watara's place. It was only then it dawned on me that it didn't offer any protection either, and in fact there was nowhere to flee to. For ten minutes we all cowered in Watara's swaying *fale*. The women crouched with their arms over the heads of the sobbing, frightened children. Outside, the gale whipped the leaning coconut trees and the air was full of flying palm fronds, fishing nets, blinding sand and coconut shells. Huge waves crashed upon the beach and surged almost up to the stilts of the *fales*.

For the first time in the Pacific, I felt icy fear grip my stomach. I didn't mind being isolated on one of the remote places on the earth; indeed, I loved it. I wouldn't even have been too bothered if the outrigger from Butaritari had capsized in the middle of the lagoon. At least I could have done something about it. But this was different. Rarely have I felt so exposed, vulnerable and powerless.

Fortunately, to everyone's intense relief, the storm dissipated as swiftly as it had arisen. Still, it was a taste of how terrifying tropical cyclones must be when they rage in across 3.5 million square kilometres of unbroken ocean, with nothing for protection on the exposed atolls except beaches only a metre above sea level, a few flimsy thatched huts and coconut trees. In 1979 Typhoon Tip, the most powerful typhoon ever recorded, hit the north-west Pacific; experts estimated that its winds, which reached 305 kilometres per hour, contained the power of a ten-megaton nuclear bomb.

I found Watara increasingly difficult to make out. I couldn't help suspecting that, as Kapopay had implied, behind the façade there was a shrewd, calculating mind. On the one hand, he seemed an educated man and he spoke quietly, articulately and with authority. He frequently listened to the radio when the reception wasn't too bad, although it irritated him that he could only rarely pick up the BBC World Service. In a corner of his *fale* there was a yellowing pile of old *Australian Weekly* magazines, which he frequently browsed through. He had even read Sir Arthur Grimble's magical book *A Pattern of Islands*, which recounts the experiences of a British colonial administrator who lived in the Gilbert Islands in 1911. On the other hand, he seemed surprisingly naïve.

'You know, the world's a strange place,' he observed one evening. 'When I went to New Zealand I saw a stuffed elephant in a museum. Of course, I had no idea what it was, so I ran away. Later on, while I was in the zoo, I tried to touch a tiger. The wardens told me not to, as it's really dangerous. But how could I have known? I mean, we don't have tigers in Kiribati!'

Four days after I arrived, I realized that Tikurere, like Tarawa, wasn't what it seemed. When I returned to the *fales* after basking in the warm pool left by the receding tide at the sandbar, I found, to my dismay, that all the adults and children had vanished, leaving only Watara and his family. 'Where's everyone gone?' I asked him.

'Back to Butaritari, of course.'

'But I thought they all lived here?'

'Oh no. They were only here for a few days. They still like coming over and using the *fales* their parents used to live in, but they live in Butaritari, where the children go to school.'

It was only then I learned that my initial impressions of Tikurere, like those of Tarawa, were hopelessly romantic. Watara told me that, far from it possessing the tiny, stable community I had fondly imagined, Tikurere had been abandoned forty years ago. It was then that his parents, the last inhabitants, had left for Butaritari. Now only he and his son lived on Tikurere, although he also had a *fale* on Butaritari that was only fifty metres from Kapopay's compound. When I asked him why he wanted to live on Tikurere, he answered without hesitation, 'Because I want to keep our traditions alive, of course! My father, who built our canoe years ago, taught me how to sail it while I was a boy, just as I have taught Asimapaya. Now he is an "ewenako". This means that he has become a man, as he knows how to fish, and handle the catch and the canoe by himself. Unfortunately, even on Butaritari, the craft of building and sailing outriggers is dying out. But I won't swap mine for a canoe with an outboard motor!'

A day later he suggested that I go fishing with them for eels. That afternoon, he, Asimapaya and I set off in the canoe. When we were four kilometres into the lagoon, they lowered wicker cages into the water, put on snorkels and goggles, and dived in with their harpoons. As I watched them, I had to remind myself that instead of snorkelling for pleasure, they were catching their daily food. After they surfaced for a break, Watara asked me why I hadn't gone into the water.

'Because in the Pacific I never go out further than the shallows.'

'Why not?'

'Because I'm afraid of sharks.'

'But there are no sharks here!' he said, laughing. 'They only come into the lagoon if they're hungry. That's quite rare, but even then they're usually no problem. You just have to know how to defend yourself.'

'How do you do that?'

'With your harpoon, of course! Look, I've got mine here. Don't worry, I'll stay close by and keep an eye on you.'

Ashamed, I borrowed the snorkel and face mask he had brought along for me and dived into the warm water. It was an extraordinary experience. Underneath the surface was a fantasy world. Shoals of brilliant yellow, fluorescent green, and lurid blue tropical fish flitted in and out of giant, mushroom-like sponges, red underwater grottoes and coral with dozens of interlocking, stag-like pointers. Everywhere there were bonito, cockles, clams, octopuses, starfish, swordfish and baby turtles. By the time I clambered clumsily back on board the rocking canoe, Watara and Asimapaya were returning with the cages. They were full of eels almost a metre in length and as thick as a man's arm. Apart from smelling like excrement, they also had a vicious bite, and Watara was extremely cautious as he teased them out of the cages and dropped them into smelly sacks.

I'd only been back on Tikurere for an hour and was idling on the beach outside my *fale* when, to my surprise, I saw an outrigger drift up and three raffish-looking men, the first I'd seen since I'd arrived on Butaritari, wade ashore. One of them was a scrawny old man with white hair and bandy legs. He looked at me quizzically as he passed my hut, but I didn't think any more of it and they left shortly afterwards.

Finally, after what seemed like weeks on Tikurere, it was time to leave. Although there were still forty-eight hours to go until I was due to fly back from Butaritari to Tarawa, I didn't want to risk being stranded by bad weather on the atoll. In spite of that, as I climbed into the outrigger with Watara and Asimapaya, I had grave doubts about the wisdom of leaving that day. To the east, accompanied by distant thunderclaps, a wall of ominous, black clouds advanced towards us across the lagoon. Watara must have noticed the look of concern on my face. 'Don't worry,' he reassured me, 'it's a good sign. It means the wind is changing from south-east to north-east.'

Rarely have I felt such a sense of regret on leaving a place as when we slowly glided away from Tikurere. But there was no time for nostalgia. While I worked the plunger, Watara kept a watchful eye on the horizon as the canoe plunged into deep troughs. He was an exceptionally skilful sailor, and it was remarkable how little water it shipped compared to when Asimapaya had taken me from Butaritari to Tikurere. For some time, as the outrigger wallowed along in the heavy swell, we were lost in our own thoughts. I was wondering what I'd do if the outrigger capsized. I told myself that – providing sharks didn't get me first – I could probably swim to the nearest atoll. In any case I had no choice but to trust his judgement and place my destiny in the lap of the gods; I had to be on that plane to Tarawa if I was to catch the weekly flight back to Fiji.

Eventually I asked him if he had ever been in real difficulty while sailing the outrigger.

'Once,' he replied, smiling mischievously, 'when I was caught by a thunderstorm in the middle of the lagoon.'

'What did you do?'

'What I always do – watch every wave and listen to the music the water makes. If it always makes the same sound as it slaps against the canoe, you'll be all right.'

'What'd happen if you lost your sail during a storm?'

'You can't,' he snapped. 'If you do, there's nothing to stop you being swept out into the open ocean.'

There was a brief squall and the lagoon remained choppy, but most of the bad weather passed to the south of Butaritari. Two hours later we drew up on the beach next to Kapopay's compound. It was then that the storm broke, although it wasn't the one I'd expected. I had paid Watara the money I owed him for my week in the *fale* on Tikurere, and had settled in at Kapopay's. I was in her store, buying some expensive milk powder and tobacco sticks as a present for Watara, when the scrawny, bandy-legged old man I'd seen on the outrigger in Tikurere abruptly barged in. He was almost apoplectic as he shouted at Kapopay. After a while she turned to me.

'I warned you to be careful of Watara!' she cried reproachfully. 'The old man here says that while he was on Tikurere he saw you sleeping in his *fale*. Watara, who's his brother-in-law, had no right to say you could do that, and any money you paid him for staying in the old man's *fale* should have gone to the old man. Now he says that, for using his *fale* without his permission, you must pay him for the seven days you spent there at the same rate as you paid me per day.'

'That's ridiculous!' I retorted. Even if what the old man maintained was true, I certainly wasn't going to meet his demand. I had paid Watara only half of what I paid Kapopay, who had provided two meals per day, bedding and a shower in a comfortable *fale*. Yet the only thing the old man had done was to discover I had slept in his empty, semi-derelict *fale*. 'Right!' I proclaimed, 'Let's see what Watara's got to say about this.' We all trooped over to confront him. When we did, Watara, who had obviously hoped the old man wouldn't notice my bags in his *fale* during his brief, unexpected stop on Tikurere, had the sense to know he had been caught out. Even so, he had an excuse ready.

'But I was going to give him your money the moment I saw him!' he mumbled feebly. 'I wanted it to be a surprise!'

For five minutes they shouted angrily at each other. While the argument raged, I thought quickly. The easiest thing to do was for Watara to hand the money I had given him to his brother-in-law, and for me to persuade the old man to accept it. But this would mean that Watara, who had fed me for a week and given me one of the best experiences of my life, would get nothing. That didn't seem fair. Suddenly the solution hit me.

'Listen, here's what we'll do,' I announced, trying to avoid appearing like a district commissioner dispensing colonial justice. 'Watara will keep the money I gave him. As a gesture to the old man, I'll give him the same as I gave Watara, along with the milk powder and tobacco. It was expensive, so it'll go a long way towards meeting the difference between what I paid Watara and what I pay Kapopay per night.'

They had a good deal and, judging by the way they thanked me profusely, they knew it. I felt sad that such haggling should briefly threaten to taint my memory of Tikurere. Still, the dispute had been resolved amicably and, anyway, I shouldn't have been surprised. There's always been a serpent in the Garden of Eden.

EASTER ISLAND

The moment I arrived in Easter Island, I knew how Gauguin felt when he landed in Tahiti in the late nineteenth century. Expecting to find paradise, he discovered instead that the island's Polynesian culture had already been hopelessly compromised by Europeans, and lamented he was 'a hundred years too late'. I knew, naturally, that I would hardly be the first Westerner to set foot on Easter Island, which is also Polynesian, and claims to be the most far-flung place on earth. Chile, to whom Easter Island has belonged since 1888, is the nearest land mass 3,700 kilometres to the east, and Pitcairn Island, of HMS *Bounty* fame, is 1,800 kilometres to the west.

What I didn't anticipate, though, were the jumbo jets disgorging hordes of tourists twice a week during the summer, or that the main street of Hanga Roa, the island's sole, tiny village, would be dotted with souvenir shops and jeep- and motorbike-rental agencies. Nor did I expect that my shabby room in a dark, damp bungalow up the hill behind the church would cost $60 a night; owing to its isolation, Easter Island, I ruefully discovered, is one of the most expensive places in the world as there are only four cargo ships a year and most

Moai *with top-knot at Ahu Tongaraki, Easter Island, south-east Pacific*

goods have to be flown in.

Still, although it was spread out, Hanga Roa was pleasant enough. Overlooked by barren hills, which had previously covered with tropical forests before the Rapanui, the indigenous inhabitants, cut them down 300 years ago, it had the usual, red-roofed south Pacific bungalows and a laidback, leisurely feel. Occasionally, wild-looking, long-haired men trotted along the main street on unkempt horses. Offshore, tattooed, muscular teenagers flitted like gnats on surfboards, waiting for towering green breakers; few people know it, but surfing originated in the Pacific centuries ago. The indoor market was also atmospheric, with overweight women chatting behind piles of pineapples and exotic fruit, and it was a handy place in which to shelter from the frequent tropical downpours. The Rapanui people are very good-looking, and why Thor Heyerdahl tried to prove in his *Kon-Tiki* expedition that they came from South America, when they are so obviously Polynesian – they even speak a dialect related to the Cook Islanders' Maori – remains inexplicable.

The tourist groups, too, tucked away in hotels outside Hanga Roa, were easy to escape. The next morning, glad to get away from the nocturnal procession of cockroaches coming under my door, I hired a jeep and set off for Ahu Tongaraki, the site of the island's largest *moai* (statues of Rapanui gods). An empty paved road wound along the jagged, black, volcanic coast, past herds of grazing undomesticated horses. Twenty kilometres later, down in a bay, there was a row of fifteen massive statues silhouetted against the ocean. To my delight I was the only person there, and although the *moai* are so famous they are almost a cliché, I couldn't help being impressed by their strange heads, elongated ears, and prominent noses and chins.

Not far away, up a rutted track, was Rano Raraku, an extinct volcano from where many of the *moai* were quarried. Many of them still lay at the foot of rocky cliffs, each with their own character: some were gigantic, some lay face down, some had upturned noses and some were buried almost to their necks. It was in order to transport the *moai* from here that the island's two warring tribes, the 'corpulent people' and the 'thin people' cut down the forests, thus sealing their fate; with no wood left for boats to catch the fish upon which they depended, they almost died out.

The next afternoon I hired a scooter and set off for Orongo Ceremonial Village, reputedly one of Easter Island's most impressive sights. At the foot of the airstrip, which General Pinochet allowed the Americans to extend as an emergency landing-site for space shuttles, a red dirt track climbed to another extinct volcano, whose crater was filled by a reed-covered lake. From there a path meandered along the rim to the 'Village', which was a collection of low houses built from horizontally overlapping, thick stone slabs. Further along, there were birdman petroglyphs on the edge of plunging cliffs. Again, I was alone, and for a while I sat enjoying the solitude, the vastness of the ocean and the spectacular view down over the serrated cliffs of Bird Island, which lies immediately offshore, 300 metres below.

In the eighteenth and nineteenth centuries, this rocky clump was the focus of a bird cult dedicated to the gods Makemake and Haua. Each year, ritual ceremonies climaxed with a race in which the first young blood to descend the cliffs, swim to the island with the aid of a reed raft and obtain the first egg of the sooty terns breeding there was crowned birdman for the subsequent year, so winning the favour of the gods and elevated status in the community. The last ceremony was in 1866, just after the Peruvian blackbirding raid that decimated the remaining population still further by shipping off over 1,000 islanders to work at the guano deposits on Peru's Chincha Islands; legend has it that some of the slaves were so heartbroken they tried to swim the 3,700 kilometres home.

After a week of jolting up rutted tracks to see more yet *moai*, I began to tire of them, so one Sunday I took a taxi – there's no public transport – to Anakena, the island's largest beach on the north coast. The road passed through the sole remaining eucalyptus forest in the interior of the island, which is only twenty-four kilometres long and ten kilometres wide. The beach itself, part of a white, palm-fringed bay, was packed with locals from Hanga Roa, and I spent the day basking in the warm, emerald water, along with hordes of children riding gigantic breakers.

When he picked me up for the return journey, the taxi driver was very chatty. After I asked him how Easter Island fared under the murderous regime of General Pinochet, who visited the island in 1979, he replied, 'Actually, we didn't notice much difference. Remember that from 1888 until 1953 Easter Island was really just a sheep station run by a British shipping company, who leased it from Chile. Then the navy took over until the mid-1960s, and we weren't allowed to talk Rapanui. We had no vote, and we weren't even allowed to leave the island. But things have improved enormously under democracy, especially since tourists started arriving in the 1990s.'

The following Saturday I went to a local bar, where Topatangi, a catchy local band that played a fusion of contemporary and traditional south-Pacific music, wowed a wildly enthusiastic crowd at weekends. There I met Carmen, a forty-year-old Rapa Nui taxi driver who spoke excellent English. When she heard I lived in Scotland, she exclaimed, to my amazement, 'You must come and meet Mack, my boyfriend, who's Scottish!'

The next day I made my way to her shabby bungalow on cliffs just to the west of Hanga Roa. Mack was a young, thirty-something man from Fife, who had met Carmen when he first stopped off in Easter Island whilst backpacking round the world. She was obviously head over heels in love as she could hardly keep her hands off him. 'I fell for him the moment I saw him march into town in his kilt, playing the bagpipes!' she cried, before going inside to cook the meal. During her absence he confided that, although this was his third visit, it was probably his last.

'I really love her, though she's much older,' he went on. 'But I want children, and as she's got two already she doesn't want any more. Anyway, Easter Island's not the sort of place to spend the rest of your life in. Even if we both know our relationship won't be forever, we're determined to enjoy it while it lasts.' Suddenly he produced his bagpipes from a case and, silhouetted against the sun sinking into the ocean, played a slow, tragic lament. He played beautifully and, overcome by emotion, for a moment I was transported back to the Highlands, 24,000 kilometres away on the other side of the earth.

For the next few days I spent a lot of the time with Carmen and Mack, or down at Hanga Roa's harbour, where there was a miniature beach and two surf agencies. It was overlooked by a large *moai*, where local youths hung out with their horses. On my last day I hired a jeep and drove up an atrocious track to the summit of Maunga Terevaka, the island's highest hill. For a while I sat pondering the question that had been puzzling me for the last few days: apart from the *moai*, what was so appealing about Easter Island? As I gazed out over the vast, 360-degree view to gentle, grassy hills and the deep-blue expanse of water piled high against the horizon, the answer came to me: it was the infinite Pacific, and the indescribable feeling of being, geographically at least, in the most remote place on the planet.

View of the infinite ocean, Easter Island, south-east Pacific

III
JOURNEYING ON

When I tell people who don't know me well that I am a travel writer, they often exclaim jealously, 'How lucky you are! What a fabulous job, staying in those luxury hotels and being paid to go to all those incredible places!' They couldn't be more mistaken, as it hasn't been like that at all. Luxury hotels are the antithesis of everything I look for. I have rarely been paid to go on my mini-expeditions and I certainly haven't made my fortune writing about them. As for 'all the incredible places' that they mention, getting to many of these has been physically and mentally extremely hard. I have frequently been lonely and couldn't wait to go home. Still, I have always been attracted to exploring my physical limits and wouldn't have had it any other way. Even feeling forlorn in remote, desolate places has its advantages because it has enabled me to discover inner resources I wasn't aware I possessed.

For years I thought there was no connection between the events that have happened to me. Yet, when I look back, it feels sometimes as if there has been a pattern to them. Now I understand a little more why some sculptors maintain, after they have finished a piece of work, that it feels as though the sculpture was there the whole time, merely waiting to be uncovered. Every so often I sense, like Borges, that someone else has lived my life and I've just been a bystander. Occasionally, I also feel – although this may be an illusion – everything that has happened to me has been for a reason. Whatever, it has been my travels that have shaped me. They have made my life rich and varied. I have done what I wanted to do. I have been to most of the places I wanted to go to, many of which few others have seen. Moreover, I was lucky enough to complete many of my journeys when travellers were comparatively rare, and globalisation and cheap flights hadn't yet opened up the world.

In my travels I found myself increasingly passing through Buddhist countries, such as Burma, parts of China and India, Japan, Mongolia, Nepal and Tibet. For a while this too seemed to be accidental. Now it feels as if I was drawn to them unconsciously. Over the years I have steadily grown to distrust most '-isms' – for example, capitalism, socialism, Communism, Catholicism, Judaism, Marxism and Protestantism. Of course, Buddhism also contains an '-ism', but we need some moral code if we are not to live by the law of the jungle. It isn't necessary to accept Buddhism in its entirety to see that it provides a body of belief that isn't as steeped in blood as the other, to me, discredited religions and systems. Buddhism's emphasis on non-violence and the need to live modestly seems more and more relevant in these aggressive, rampantly consumerist times, when ever-greater industrialisation and exploitation of the earth's diminishing resources is leading humanity towards an increasingly uncertain future. Most useful, perhaps, is Buddhism's stress on the need for inner development. If we are not conscious of how we act, how can we expect politicians

Gabriella

and nations to act without the fear, hatred, prejudice and aggression that characterize so much of our world?

A major factor for me being able to travel is my partner and soulmate, Gabriella. She has provided me with a stable platform from which I can venture into the world and to which I can safely return. Over the years she has made me feel loved, valued and appreciated. We have also made some magical journeys together, especially to France, Spain, India and South America. Now the decades of doubt, searching and uncertainty about what to do with my life, and who to spend it with, are – hopefully – over. Naturally, sooner or later new challenges such as ill health or ageing will unavoidably beckon. The seemingly infinite possibilities of youth are no longer there. Most of the doors that seemed open to me have been closed. I have chosen to go, or perhaps have been led, through some and not others, but the ones through which I have passed have in the end made me happy, and new, unexpected ones continuously open in front of me. Many years have gone by and I feel a sense of completion. Only now do I realize that my real journey has been my life.

INDEX

Note: Illustrations are identified in **bold** type

ACKNOWLEDGEMENTS

With thanks above all to Jim Hutcheson, without whom I couldn't have done the book; Caroline Gorham, for her patient help in producing it; Tom Gorham, for the creative type-setting and layout; Jim Lewis, for beautifully implementing my ideas for the maps; Sarah Ream, for the editing; Anita Joseph, for her meticulous proof-reading; Dave Gardner, for stoically enduring my computer crises; Allan Laing of *The Herald*, who gave me so much space for my articles and photographs; my partner Gabriella Moericke, for her perceptive comments and advice; and all the countless, nameless people who have helped me on my journey.

To find out more about the author's journeys, go to www.reportsfrombeyond.com